THE AUTONOMY OF HISTORY

❧ THE ❧ AUTONOMY OF HISTORY

TRUTH AND METHOD FROM
ERASMUS TO GIBBON

Joseph M. Levine

THE UNIVERSITY OF CHICAGO PRESS
Chicago & London

Joseph M. Levine is Distinguished Professor of History at
Syracuse University and the author of five books, most
recently *Between the Ancients and the Moderns: Baroque
Culture in Restoration England.*

The University of Chicago Press, Chicago 60637
The University of Chicago Press, Ltd., London
© 1999 by The University of Chicago
All rights reserved. Published 1999
08 07 06 05 04 03 02 01 00 99   5 4 3 2 1

ISBN (cloth): 0-226-47541-7

Library of Congress Cataloging-in-Publication Data

Levine, Joseph M.
    The autonomy of history : truth and method from Erasmus to Gibbon
    / Joseph M. Levine.
        p.   cm.
    Includes bibliographical references and index.
    ISBN 0-226-47541-7 (alk. paper)
    1. History—Philosophy.   2. History—Methodology.   I. Title.
D16.8.L48   1999
901—dc21   99-30861
                                                              CIP

Contents

ᚲᚱ Preface ᚲᚹ

The essays that follow were written on different occasions over many years. I have thought to bring them together here because they share some common themes that may help to reinforce their individual arguments and because they are no longer so easy to retrieve. Several of them have not appeared in print before. My intention throughout has been to call attention to some neglected problems in the intellectual history of early modern Europe and to its theoretical underpinning, particularly to the way in which the Renaissance revival of antiquity continued to work on the European consciousness throughout the period, gradually transforming its notions about both the content and the method of history. My assumption has been that the alterations that the Renaissance introduced in reconceiving the past were among the great transforming ideas in Western consciousness whose consequences are still very much with us. I have elsewhere made some suggestions about that tangled subject; in these essays I have continued to explore the matter further in the hope of throwing some additional light both on the substance of those changes and how they might be investigated—in a word, both about the history of European history and the methods of intellectual history that might be employed to fathom it.

In particular, I have sought to describe what R. G. Collingwood once described as the "autonomy of history."[1] Autonomy is a relative term. It does not seem possible, nor even desirable, to write history in an intellectual vacuum apart from other concerns. What Collingwood was suggesting rather was that modern historiography, the actual practice of history, had

1. Collingwood, *Idea of History* (Oxford, 1946), pp. 201–3 (crediting Croce), 236–38, 261–63, 318–20.

developed over time in such a way as to declare its independence from every other form of knowledge. It was neither literature, theology, nor natural science; its logic was neither deductive nor inductive; its procedures were evidently its own. Historians, he believed, had become gradually aware of this, but the rest of the world, and especially the philosophers of his generation, had lagged behind. Collingwood thought that what was urgently required was a fresh philosophy adequate to comprehend and defend the claims to knowledge of modern historical practice. This he tried to provide in a series of essays that he began to write in the 1930s, in his *Autobiography* (1939), and in the *Idea of History* (published posthumously in 1946).

Collingwood died prematurely and left his own thought incomplete. Whatever we may make of it now, we may see it (as Collingwood himself tried to represent it) as an extension of a line of historical thinking that went back to Vico in the eighteenth century and that had descended to him through such nineteenth-century Germans as Schleiermacher and Dilthey, and more recently through the Italians, Croce, Gentile, and his good friend Guido de Ruggiero.[2] Unfortunately, this Continental pedigree did not generate much enthusiasm for his philosophical ideas at the time in either Britain or America, but his historiographical prescriptions were acclaimed anyway by many practicing historians, and his works have remained in print and influential since their first appearance. It may be that their time has finally come.[3]

Among Collingwood's ambitions was to write a history of historical thought and practice that would situate his own ideas in history and help to justify them. I do not think he succeeded very well, though the *Idea of History* remains helpful and endlessly stimulating. Perhaps the trouble was that, despite himself, Collingwood wrote too much as a philosopher and not enough as a historian. To be sure, the field was young and little labor had been expended by anyone yet on the history of historiography. For whatever reason, the *Idea* tends to scant the historians and the actual development of their techniques in order to concentrate on some larger underlying philosophical assumptions. As a result, among other omissions, Collingwood pretty much overlooked and certainly underestimated the

2. For tactical reasons, Collingwood did not always proclaim his debts; see my "Collingwood, Vico and the *Autobiography*," *Clio,* 9 (1980), pp. 379–92.

3. There is now a Collingwood Society and journal (*Collingwood Studies,* 1994–), a bibliography by Donald S. Taylor (New York, 1988), and a host of new books and commentaries, including a new edition of the *Idea of History,* ed. Jan van der Dussen (Oxford, 1993). I first wrote to explicate Collingwood in "The Autonomy of History: R. G. Collingwood and Agatha Christie," *Clio,* 7 (1978), pp. 253–64.

contributions of the historical writers of early modern Europe to the very development that he was tracing. He seems to ascribe the autonomy of history more to the speculation of writers about history than to the work of history itself. As a consequence, we learn more about Locke and Berkeley and Hume than we do about Robertson or Edward Gibbon, and almost nothing at all about the legions of forgotten scholars who once lined the shelves of the old libraries with their massive works of erudition. In the essays that follow, I have tried to remedy that situation a bit by calling attention to some of this more practical historiographical activity and its underlying assumptions. I mean to suggest that the development of historical method preceded or at least accompanied the modern idea of history and may help to account for it, rather than the reverse.

I have begun with three essays on the English Renaissance. In the first, I have looked again at Thomas More's *Utopia* to show how it reflects what I take to be a new Renaissance notion that fact and fiction could and should be separated. In the second, I have shown how More's great friend, Erasmus, helped to develop the Renaissance method of philology as the principal means of making good the distinction between history and fiction, both introducing and reinforcing this notion. And in the third, on Thomas Elyot, I have shown how the Renaissance idea of history was linked to humanist pedagogy and the primacy of rhetoric, and how this to some extent obscured and retarded the progress of a critical historiography. Taken together these essays are meant to illustrate the several different and sometimes contradictory ways in which Renaissance humanism broke with the Middle Ages and altered the means by which men conceived the past and tried to retrieve it. I have tried thus to defend the (admittedly problematical) idea that there was some sort of English Renaissance and to take its measure both for itself and in relation to the making of the modern historical consciousness.

In the second group of essays, I have skipped over more than a century to the eve of the Enlightenment to see how these Renaissance ideas worked out in time. In a previous collection of essays, I took some soundings in the intervening period to suggest some of the ways in which seventeenth-century historiography developed the techniques of source criticism and archaeology that prepared the path for the modern discipline—how Renaissance philology turned itself gradually into modern historiography;[4] and in a separate work I showed how the incipient clash between hu-

---

4. *Humanism and History: Origins of Modern English Historiography* (Ithaca, 1986). The full tale remains to be told and would require a crucial chapter on the Germans from Göttingen to Niebuhr, Ranke, et al., where the role of philology would have to be resuscitated.

manist critical method and humanist expository narrative—the one indebted to philology, the other to rhetoric—gradually developed into an
overt quarrel that drew finally to a climax in the famous contest that
Jonathan Swift called the Battle of the Books.[5]

Here I have pursued that dispute in two further essays. The first attempts
to situate the quarrel in the still larger (and seemingly eternal) intellectual
conflict between the two cultures of philosophy and literature, resumed in
our own time by F. R. Leavis and C. P. Snow. I have tried there to disentangle two different battle-sites in order to suggest again that the modern triumph was pretty much limited during the Enlightenment to the fields of
philosophy and science, while the ancients remained in command of the
arts and letters. And I have continued to insist that the practice of history
was also divided in its allegiance to the two cultures. Apparently, there was
to be no harmony, then or afterward, in the republic of letters.[6] In the second, I have looked more concretely into the long and noisy conflict over
Homer that stirred the period, especially about the Shield of Achilles that
is described in the *Iliad,* to illustrate in exact detail some of the issues that
continued to separate the ancients and the moderns over literature and
history in the eighteenth century, and to show how that both reflected and
helped to prepare the way for a new historical practice and a profoundly
new sense of change.

In the next two essays I have tried to show further how these concerns
formed the immediate intellectual context for eighteenth-century historiography. On the one hand, Englishmen, like Swift or, later, Hume, still accepted the ancients as their models and attempted to write a neoclassical
humanist narrative.[7] On the other hand, philologists and antiquaries continued to compile impressive topical and analytical works in happy disregard of conventional rhetoric. It was Edward Gibbon who understood
most clearly the merits of both sides of the argument and deliberately set
about combining the advantages of ancient rhetoric and modern philology. This precarious combination was unusual, hard to devise and even
harder to maintain, and Gibbon may be seen as perhaps the last, as he was
certainly the most successful historian, to attempt a rapprochement be-

5. *The Battle of the Books: History and Literature in the Augustan Age* (Ithaca, 1991). I have made
some corrections for the paperback edition (Ithaca, 1994).

6. I first set out this argument in my article "Ancients and Moderns Reconsidered," *Eighteenth-Century Studies,* 14 (1981), pp. 72–88.

7. For Swift, see *The Battle of the Books,* pp. 306–9; for Hume, see Philip Hicks, *Neoclassical
History and English Culture from Clarendon to Hume* (New York, 1996) and my forthcoming review in the *Journal of Modern History.*

tween the two antithetical traditions that had so long separated the historical writers of Western Europe.[8]

Meanwhile, far off in Naples, Giambattista Vico, who was also pondering
the quarrel, attempted to transcend the two rival positions in order to create nothing less than a "new science" of history. I have tried to show here
how the inspiration for his thinking seems to have developed out of a long
and careful consideration of the self-same arguments that were then in
progress between the ancients and the moderns. If this is right, the "historicism" that he invented—and much of what was to follow afterward in
European historical culture—may be seen as the result of a humanist dialectic between philology and rhetoric, anticipated by Vico but working its
way out over time, gradually reinforced by the steady accumulation of critical learning. No doubt it took a while for the Neapolitan's effort to be appreciated, for critical learning to catch up with his inspired intuitions, but
when it did, when history had in fact gradually won something of its autonomy, Vico came into his own, and with his teaching, the point of view that
Collingwood, among many others, found so congenial.[9]

My method throughout most of these essays has been to concentrate
attention on a specific document or argument conceived as an intellectual event, or sequence of events, in order to suggest some larger issues.
So, in my climactic example (Part Three), I have chosen to examine
closely the problem that arose in the early modern period over a single
text in the Bible: The Johannine comma, 1 John 5:7, "There are Three
that bear record in Heaven, the Father, the Word, and the Holy Ghost,
and these Three are One." Erasmus was the first to raise the question of
its historical authenticity, and it was debated thereafter more or less continuously for two centuries, until Gibbon resumed it and provoked a new
contest that pretty much decided the issue. It was not just the fate of Trinitarian conviction that seemed to rest on the resolution of this problem
but the very meaning and intention of the Scriptures and the place of history in Christian religion. When at length the problem of the comma was
finally resolved and all parties agreed to expunge it from the biblical
record, it was apparent that the conviction in the philological method of
history had come to outweigh all theological presuppositions. History,

8. See Levine, "Edward Gibbon and the Quarrel between the Ancients and the Moderns,"
in *Humanism and History*, pp. 178–189, and chap. 6 below; for a similar view of early modern
historigraphy, Arnaldo Momigliano, "Ancient History and the Antiquarian," *Studies in Historiography* (New York, 1966), pp. 1–39.

9. Collingwood's first work was a translation of Croce's *Philosophy of Giambattista Vico* (London, 1913).

that is to say, modern historiography, had declared and made good its autonomy.

In concentrating on these specific episodes, I have tried to situate each event in a precise setting in order to display some of the personal and intellectual conditions that moved each author to attempt a reconstruction of the past, and also to suggest its place in a larger story, to say something about how each may have contributed to the progress of the discipline—to that developing refinement of method to which we are all willy-nilly the heirs. The first task I take to be the basic intention of every ordinary history including the history of ideas—the indispensable precondition for all further reconstruction.[10] I assume that unless one can recover the original meaning of the documents (things as well as words) that provide us with access to the events of the past, historical knowledge is impossible. Now it appears that the only way that we can hope to retrieve the historical meaning of the documents and events of the past is to situate them in their original settings, in the context of other documents and events. This hermeneutical circle, as it has been called, was the crucial discovery of renaissance humanism, but it has taken centuries to work out its practical and theoretical implications, which—to judge by the spate of recent theory in the humanities—is still not entirely appreciated.[11] I shall say less about the second task of historiography, which is to integrate these findings into a whole, in this case the whole long story of the course of Western historical writing, a grand undertaking that must raise further questions about method and that deserves separate attention. I have been content here only to make a few tentative suggestions.

Nevertheless, in concentrating on certain incidents in the history of the subject, I hope that I have been able to throw some light on our own immediate situation, on the present relationship between historical truth and method. It was Collingwood who argued that doing history should al-

10. I introduce the term "ordinary history" with some misgivings, since I doubt that anyone will much enjoy the label. I mean simply to furnish a name for the common practice of academic historians who, whatever their differences of field and outlook, share a common craft, a craft has that developed over time and in concert, and that is learned largely by example and apprenticeship. Without such commonality it is hard to see how a miscellaneous group of historians could serve together on juries to evaluate students and peers, or join in an intelligible dialogue over historical subjects far removed from their own. For more on this admittedly controversial notion, see my essays cited below on Skinner and Novick.

11. For the hermeneutic circle in practice, I can offer several examples from my own work; for instance the essays on the Donation of Constantine and on the Stonesfield Pavement—the one dealing with a literary text, the other with an archaeological monument—in *Humanism and History*, pp. 54–72, 107–22; and at much greater length in *Dr. Woodward's Shield* (Berkeley, 1977). For the hermeneutic circle in theory, see David C. Hoy, *The Critical Circle* (Berkeley, 1982).

ways precede thinking about the nature of history and who insisted upon putting practice before theory. (In this he had the rare advantage of being both an accomplished historian and archaeologist as well as a professional philosopher.) The *Idea of History* begins with history and ends with theory, though the history, I repeat, is not always adequate for his purpose. Still Collingwood's preoccupation with method has always appealed more to ordinary historians like myself than to his more philosophical commentators, who have often missed this crucial point or bridled at it.[12] In any case, my principal claim in these essays has been to reaffirm the view that intellectual history is, or should be in the first place, a branch of history, that is, it should be subject to the same methods and procedures—and philosophical problems—that have governed its parent discipline. I hope that I have been able to show something about how this came to be and also (by example) how to do it.

For the historian this may be obvious enough, though for others it will still need some justification. In fact, most intellectual history has been written by people in other disciplines: by philosophers, political theorists, theologians, literary critics, and others, not usually or specifically trained in the historical craft or responsible to it.[13] Long ago in a brilliant essay Quentin Skinner anatomized some of the dangers or misunderstandings that this entailed for the discipline, and which have been exacerbated, if anything, by more recent notions drawn from the various postmodern criticisms.[14] For the ordinary historian, the "linguistic turn" has been a mixed blessing, introducing some new and helpful possibilities of interpretation, but (at least in its extreme formulations) denying any possibility of reference in the "prison-house of language," and thus of any history as it has been traditionally practiced. It has had the unfortunate effect of turning intellectual history away from the reconstruction of events and away from

12. Even H.-G. Gadamer, who deeply admired Collingwood, typically inverted the Collingwoodian order in his *Truth and Method* in a deliberate effort to remove his philosophical hermeneutics from the demands of practical historiography. Hans-Georg Gadamer, *Truth and Method*, ed. Garrett Barden and John Cumming (New York, 1975). See also the introduction to Gadamer's *Philosophical Hermeneutics*, trans. David E. Linge (Berkeley, 1976), pp. xi–xii. Collingwood has been recently and rightly associated with the hermeneutic tradition, though he would have despised the term, and I suppose I should admit my own allegiance to its general vantage point, though I too would rather do without the label, which (like all such) is more likely to stop thought than to advance it.

13. See Donald R. Kelley, "Horizons of Intellectual History: Retrospect, Circumspect, Prospect," *Journal of the History of Ideas,* 48 (1987), pp. 143–69; reprinted in *The History of Ideas: Canon and Variations,* ed. Donald Kelley (Rochester, 1990), pp. 312–38. For earlier views to the same effect by Lovejoy (1940) and Leonard Krieger (1973), see in the same volume, pp. 1–21, 108–25.

14. "Meaning and Understanding in the History of Ideas," *History and Theory,* 8 (1969), pp. 2–53.

authors and intentions—the traditional ends and means of ordinary historiography—to arrive at a vantage point that is sometimes skeptical or even
hostile to the traditional methods of the historical discipline. From one
perspective, it appears to be just another episode in the battle of the books
in which rhetoric has sought its revenge on philology.[15] But it is probably
more complicated than that. In Donald Kelley's words, "Attention has
shifted not only from thought to 'discourse,' but also, in a number of ways,
from the conscious to the unconscious, from creation to imitation, from
intention to meaning, from authorship to readership, from the history of
ideas to the 'social history of ideas,'" and so on.[16]

Now it is true that the ordinary historian does not much welcome theory
of any kind, and he or she may perhaps be forgiven for suspecting any theoretical view that denies or undermines a practice that has often been
found to work. (I hope that some of the essays in this book may prove to be
practical examples of that kind.)[17] For the ordinary historian, even Skinner may seem to be too purely linguistic and textual, too little concerned
with the possibilities of reconstructing past events in their concrete whole-
ness.[18] It is clear from Peter Novick's engaging history of the American historical profession that there is much confusion and some uncertainty even
among contemporary historians about the relations between theory and
practice, though perhaps less than he imagines.[19]

If there is any way out of this dilemma, it seems to me that it may best be by

15. It is perhaps enough to mention the works of Hayden White and Dominic LaCapra.

16. Kelley, "Horizons," p. 329. See Richard Rorty, ed. *The Linguistic Turn* (Oxford, 1967).
Kelley thinks we need to reconcile the "efforts of purely historical reconstruction" with the
current projects of philosophy, literature, criticism, and the human and natural sciences. As
long as the distinctions between them are not obliterated, I don't see that anyone will want to
object.

17. Of course they are open to criticism, but presumably of the same practical kind, that is,
employing the same kind of method—only better. Geoffrey Elton, who wrote a lot of influential history from the archives, put the typical complaints of the ordinary historian to most theory. "When I read discussions of how historians think, how they can claim to describe that
which no longer exists, or whether historical fact has an existence independent of the thinker
about facts, I marvel at the ingenuity of the writers, for usually they are men who have never
apparently themselves tried to do the work, to see the manifestly surviving evidence of past
fact and event, or to practice critical judgment on the materials of history rather than the
minds of historians." *The Practice of History* (New York, 1967), p. v.

18. See my rejoinder to Skinner, "Method in the History of Ideas: More, Machiavelli and
Quentin Skinner," *Annals of Scholarship*, 3 (1986), pp. 37–60. Skinner replied briefly in a work
that takes on many other critics, but it does not appear that he really understood my point.
Skinner is that rare anomaly, a philosophical historian—too philosophical perhaps and too
little historical, or so it seems to me, in his theoretical pronouncements.

19. See my review of Novick's *The Noble Dream: That "Objectivity" Question and the American
Historical Profession* (1988), "Objectivity in History: Peter Novick and R. G. Collingwood," *Clio*,
21 (1991), pp. 109–27.

recalling the traditional goal of ordinary intellectual history, which is simply to situate ideas in real-life predicaments and subject them to the normal methods of ordinary historiography in the hope of recreating the events of the past and furnishing them with narrative explanations. (So Novick, who welcomes the uncertainty of postmodern theory for its freedom, had necessarily to employ just those traditional methods in his own work whose theoretical presuppositions he calls into question.) It looks as though Collingwood was right. Before we can arrange historical ideas and put them to present use we need to learn what they once meant; if so, the first task of intellectual history must be to set them again in their original contexts and determine what were the original problems that they set out to solve.

Without further apology then, I offer these chips from a practical workshop where the ordinary methods of history have been applied to some still problematical subjects in the history of ideas. It seems clear that ordinary history and the history of ideas in particular could use a fresh apology in these troubled times, as they have throughout their long careers. They need a theory to justify a practice that has developed over many centuries in response to a host of practical and urgent questions about the past. I do not think that we have an adequate one yet. Such a theory would have to start, as I have indicated, with a description of what history, the history of ordinary historians, is—and how it came to be that way. It would have to estimate the success of ordinary history in retrieving the past and compare it to alternatives. And it would have to consider the claims of ordinary history to the establishment of truth, to address the epistemological status of its results. It would, in short, have to take on something of the same role as the philosophy of science, which has not usually tried to prescribe the rules that scientists employ or to dismantle their conclusions, but prefers to anlayse their assumptions and consider the consequences. Collingwood attempted to provide answers for all these things but died before he could fully develop the implications of his thought or reply to criticism. No one, as far as I can see, has been able to advance the discussion much further, except by raising some useful difficulties. These essays are meant to confirm the Collingwoodian project as far as I understand it, but are confined largely to the first question about the method and definition of ordinary history. What we could still use no doubt is a philosopher with sufficient knowledge of what historians actually do to undertake the larger task. In the meantime, I shall be content to think that the stories I have told here are substantially true, that is, in strict accord with the usual procedures of the ordinary historian, and that as a result they may throw some further light on both the methods and theories of the discipline that were first raised some centuries ago and continue to bother us.

ॐ　　Acknowledgments　　৪১

These essays have been brewing for a long time—too long, perhaps, to recall all my debts. Nevertheless, I well remember some of the occasions that
inspired them and some of the people who encouraged me along the way.
For example, I remember being asked many years ago by Francis Haskell
and Nicholas Penny to deliver an address to the British Art History Association which resulted in the chapter below on the shield of Achilles. And I
remember sharing mutual interests with Françoise Waquet at the Institute
of Advanced Study which resulted in an essay on the republic of letters. I
recall also the occasion at the Woodrow Wilson Center when I was asked by
the organizers, to talk about Thomas More. All along, I remember being
encouraged by many old friends: in particular by Donald Kelley (whose
help and criticism began long before this project when we were graduate
students together), and by Tony Grafton, Mark Phillips, Peter Burke, Paul
Hunter, Michael Harris, John Pocock, Roger Emerson, Bert Goldgar, and
Scott and Giles Mandelbrote.

Closer to home, I must not forget the assistance of my graduate students,
Jeff Anderson and Bob Brown, who helped me with many tedious chores.
Above all, I must thank my family for their unfailing patience and interest:
DeeDee, my wife and companion in all ventures; my philosophical son,
Peter; and my literary daughter, Caroline. I have been lucky to live among
my staunchest supporters and frankest critics.

Finally, I must not forget to thank the several hospitable institutions
that from time to time helped to sustain this episodic project: in particular my own Syracuse University, which supplied time and support; the Fol-
ger and British Libraries for fellowships; and the Center for Advanced
Study in the Visual Arts, Washington, D.C., and the Institute for Advanced Study, Princeton, where some of this work was begun. I am also

grateful to the following publishers and journals for permission to re-publish work which first appeared there:

The Journal of the History of Ideas for two essays: "Giambattista Vico and the Quarrel between the Ancients and the Moderns" (vol. 52, 1991: 55–79); and "Philology and History: Erasmus and the Johannine Comma" (vol. 58, 1997: 573–96).

Eighteenth-Century Life for "The Battle of the Books and the Shield of Achilles" (vol. 9, 1984: 33–61). © 1984, The Johns Hopkins University Press.

The Cambridge University Press and the Woodrow Wilson Center Press for the essay "Thomas More and the English Renaissance: History and Fiction in *Utopia,*" in *The Historical Imagination in Early Modern Europe,* ed. Donald Kelley and David Sacks (Cambridge, 1997), pp. 69–92.

APA, University Press Amsterdam / Maarsen, for "Strife in the Republic of Letters," in *Commercium Litterarium: Forms of Communication in the Republic of Letters 1700–1750,* ed. Hans Bots and Françoise Waquet (Amsterdam, 1994), pp. 301–19.

PART ONE

History and Fiction in the English Renaissance

CHAPTER ONE

Thomas More and the Idea of History

1

One of the more elusive questions in charting the history of the modern historical consciousness is to ask when and how history separated from fiction. Perhaps the trouble arises because the distinction is so fundamental and so problematical, so full of difficulty that there are some in our own contemporary culture who would deny it altogether. Indeed, for the modern skeptic there are many arguments to collapse the discrepancy between knowing and inventing the past, between discovering what actually happened and making it up, and it has recently become harder somehow to defend the traditional distinctions between objective and subjective description, fact and value, truth and poetry. Doubt has spread even among historians.[1] The one thing that seems reasonably clear is that there was once a time during the Middle Ages when no one seemed much concerned about the problem, and that it was only later, beginning with the Renaissance, that it began to arise. I have written elsewhere about the peculiar role that humanism seems to have played in the discovery of the modern conceptions of history and fiction; here I should like to return to the subject by having another look at that most fascinating of all texts in the early English Renaissance: Thomas More's *Utopia*.[2] Whatever else More may have meant to do in that controversial work, he was certainly preoccupied there with the relationship between the real and the ideal in human

1. See my essay, "Objectivity in History: Peter Novick and R. J. Collingwood," *Clio*, 21 (1991), pp. 109–27.
2. See Joseph M. Levine, "Caxton's Histories: Fact and Fiction at the Close of the Middle Ages," *Humanism and History: Origins of Modern English Historiography* (Ithaca, 1987), pp. 19–53. The one general book on the subject remains the suggestive little volume by William Nelson, *Fact or Fiction: The Dilemma of the Renaissance Storyteller* (Cambridge, Mass., 1973).

life, and thus inescapably, with the distinction between history and fiction. In reexamining his work, I hope therefore to throw some more light on the general problem of the early modern historical consciousness, as well perhaps as on that equally intractable problem of how to read Thomas More. And I would like to suggest further that such a reading may be useful in putting some life back into the old idea that there really was some sort of "renaissance" in England, and that it began in More's generation.

Perhaps one should tread carefully when even the joint editors of the Yale *Utopia* cannot agree about how to interpret it.[3] Yet despite the immense controversy that has always beset this troublesome text, it seems to me that the chief interpretative question can be reduced to a single problematical point. The quarrel, I think, has never really been about what *Utopia* says, but rather about what it means. More's description of the ideal state is plain enough; but its purpose remains obscure. Whether we view it as medieval or modern, Christian or secular, communist or bourgeois, serious or frivolous, it seems to me that much will depend on what we think were Thomas More's intentions in writing his work. And so we must make some effort to recover More's situation in order to infer his aim in writing and publishing the *Utopia*. Can we discover what he meant his readers to get out of his work?

The difficulty arises of course in the relatively neglected first book, the so-called "dialogue on council." It will not do to dismiss this introduction too casually, or treat it separately on the ground that it was composed after the main body of the text. More chose to publish his finished work as a whole and with deliberate calculation by posing a problem. He sets *Utopia* in a quarrel, ambiguously, but one must suppose intentionally. If it is true that ambiguity "does not enhance the value of social comment," we must not therefore beg the question.[4] To assume that *Utopia* is the kind of social comment where clarity prevails is to assume the author's intention and not to prove it. Of two things only may we be reasonably sure: More's work *is* ambiguous in the form we have it (as the quarrels of the critics have shown) and *Utopia* is purposefully composed. Why may not More have intended ambiguity?

To what end? Before we attempt an answer we should be as clear as we can about the nature of the ambiguity. Insofar as it is formal, it results from More's choice of dialogue, a dialogue in which he sets himself (and his

3. *Utopia*, ed. Edward Surtz and J. H. Hexter in the *Complete Works of Thomas More*, 4 (New Haven, 1965). Page references in the text will be to this edition, but I shall quote occasionally from the sixteenth-century translation by Ralph Robynson.

4. See Hexter, *More's Utopia: The Biography of an Idea* (Princeton, 1952), p. 11, and "The Composition of Utopia," in *Utopia*, pp. xv–xxiii.

friend Peter Giles) in a realistic setting, at odds against his own chief spokesman, the obviously fictional Raphael Hythloday.[5] Insofar as it is substantive, it results from the unresolved dispute within the dialogue over the value of social comment. In the first instance, More has chosen an old literary device by which he can present two different viewpoints, but he has deliberately concealed his own opinion. The Hythloday of the dialogue is clearly as much More's invention and mouthpiece as the More and Giles of the dialogue. That the one is a complete fiction and the other two are founded on historical reality might well incline us to the latter. But Hythloday so dominates the dialogue—not to say the rest of the book—that we are left uncertain. How can we be sure that the More in the dialogue is identical with the More who has composed the dialogue? Hythloday has the fullest say; More has the last word. The very form of the invention leaves us puzzled.

But the argument between More and Hythloday is even more puzzling. It begins when Giles and More urge Hythloday to go into public service. They have been moved by the obvious wisdom of this extraordinary traveler who has seen so much of the new world and whose head is stocked with the examples of so many foreign peoples. His wisdom is the wisdom of political experience as it was usually attributed to the student of history[6]— but all Hythloday's knowledge is of the contemporary world. Hythloday declines public service, at first on the ground that there is nothing in it for him who is already satisfied with his lot; then (in answer to their argument that he owes it to the public) that his knowledge would be unwelcome. Here Hythloday interpolates a long reminiscence in which he recalls an argument at the table of Cardinal Morton about crimes and punishments in order to show that advisors are typically sycophantic and self-serving.[7] That done, he resumes his objections to service by offering two hypothetical examples to show how unwelcome his advice would be. In the first, he suggests how he would try to persuade a prince not to go to war to enlarge his kingdom; in the second how he would try to persuade him not to raise

5. This formal ambiguity is reinforced by More's style, particularly his insistent use of litotes, the rhetorical figure in which something is affirmed by using a double negative, and which has often been overlooked by his translators; see Elizabeth McCutcheon, "Denying the Contrary: More's Use of Litotes in the *Utopia*," in *Essential Articles for the Study of Thomas More*, ed. Richard Sylvester and G. P. Marc'hadour (Hamden, 1977), pp. 263–74.

6. *Utopia*, pp. 52–54. Typically, Thomas Elyot praises history as a fund of worldly experience (echoing Cicero's popular *De Officiis*) in *The Boke Named the Governour* (1531), ed. H. H. S. Croft, 2 vols. (London, 1883), 1, chaps. 10–11, esp. pp. 82, 90–91. Besides Cicero, a *locus classicus* was Diodorus Siculus in the preface to the *Historical Library;* see the contemporary translation by John Skelton, ed. F. M. Salter and H. L. R. Edwards, Early English Text Society, no. 233 (London, 1956), pp. 5–12.

7. Hythloday explains the reason for telling his tale at its conclusion, *Utopia*, p. 85.

taxes to enhance his own wealth and glory, but sacrifice his own interest for the general good. Significantly, More does not dissent from any of this but agrees that such advice would indeed be unwelcome and ineffectual. Apparently, Hythloday and his new friends share exactly the same perception of reality; they have no illusions about princes or their advisors, and their pessimistic views about this might have come right out of Machiavelli.

The difference between them occurs when More insists on Hythloday's serving the government anyway. The kind of advice that Hythloday has been suggesting is of no use; one needs something more subtle and indirect, something more devious, a practical not an academic philosophy. More agrees with Hythloday, "School philosophy is not unpleasant among friends in familiar communication; but in the counsels of kings, where great matters be debated and reasoned with great authority, these things have no place."[8] Fortunately, there is another philosophy, "more civil," which suits the occasion. Politics is like a play and requires that words be spoken appropriate to the situation. A realistic councillor must play his part accordingly, "with comeliness, uttering nothing out of dew order and fashion." The successful politician requires rhetoric, not philosophy. There is no point intruding into the drama, "other stuffe that nothing pertaineth to the matter . . . though the stuff you bring be much better"—you will only spoil the play. If you would succeed, therefore, in giving counsel and influencing events, you must renounce your haughty principles, and "with a crafty wile and a subtle train study and endeavor yourself, as much as in you lieth, to handle the matter wittily and handsomely for the purpose." Not that this will bring perfection; the best that one may hope for is to modify things slightly, or to put off the worst, "For it is not possible for all things to be well, unless all men were good, which I think will not be possible this good many years!" Still one does not desert a ship in a storm simply because one cannot tame the winds.

Hythloday is unmoved. To follow More's prescription is to compromise and endanger one's ideals. Plato was right to see that philosophers want to avoid meddling in politics. What good can it do to wink at naughty counsels and pestilent decrees! Is this not what the church has been doing in making Christ's teaching acceptable to the people![9] This time More listens silently and does not respond; neither side is allowed to win the argument.

8. I here follow Ralph Robynson's English translation (1551; 2d ed., 1556), modernized from the version given by J. H. Lupton (Oxford, 1895), pp. 97–104; cf. *Utopia*, pp. 98–102.

9. "But preachers, sly and wily men, following your counsel (as I suppose), because they saw evil men willing to frame their manners to Christ's rule, they have wrested and wried his doctrine, and like a rule of lead have applied it to men's manners, that by some means at the least way they might agree together. Whereby I cannot see what good they have done, but that men may more sickerly be evil." *Utopia* (Lupton), p. 102; *Utopia*, 4, pp. 100–101.

The first book closes when Hythloday offers the specific advice he would wish to give a king: that private property be eliminated. Earlier, he had paved the way for that radical remedy by recounting his argument in Morton's household. There he had inveighed against the injustices in English economic and social life, against punishing criminals unfairly and imprudently for crimes that they were (in some cases) being forced to commit because of the rapacity of the landowners. Hythloday's picture of the sharp practices of the wealthy—of rackrenting, enclosing, and so on—and of the evils of war and its economic dislocation, is justly famous for its realistic description. There is no ambiguity here, despite the fact that it occurs in a fictional dialogue. Hythloday proposes several possible remedies drawn from his observations abroad. One might simply alter or enforce the existing laws that restrain the wealthy; or one might make the punishments more equitable to suit the crime and reimburse the victim. When even these half-measures are rejected by the company, it is clear that a more radical solution, indeed any true solution to the problem, would have been out of place.[10]

Eventually, however, at the end of the first book, Hythloday offers what must be read as his own "school philosophy" (that is, still a conversation among friends.) He claims to have been to a country where crime and all basic social problems have been completely eliminated by drastically removing all the possible motives for them. In Utopia there is no private property, hence no reason to steal, nor any possibility of greed, ostentation, and the rest. Nor is there any need to change human nature, which presumably remains constant. The result is a kind of perfection, although one that has somehow been imposed and continues by restraint. Utopia has been constructed carefully to show just how the elimination of private property—and hence every sinful occasion—can be accomplished, right down to the smallest detail. Hythloday tries to meet every practical objection, but he does not fool anyone, least of all, the Thomas More in the dialogue who has been patiently listening.

More remains unconvinced there. Even before Hythloday begins to describe his utopia, he registers a doubt. Hythloday's notion, he argues, could not possibly work, because there would be no incentive to produce anything without the rewards of private property.[11] Hythloday's answer is to describe the utopia he has actually seen: the ideal society that by its very

10. Laws might lighten and mitigate the evils, "but that they may be perfectly cured and brought to a good and upright state, it is not to be hoped for, whiles every man is master of his own to himself." *Utopia* (Lupton, p. 109); cf. *Utopia,* p. 104–6.

11. Cicero had vigorously objected to the elimination of private property; for some anticipations of More's argument in scholastic philosophy, see *Utopia,* p. 382n.

name means "nowhere"! He attempts to meet every practical objection. But when Hythloday has finished his description at the end of book two, More repeats, though only to himself, some doubts about the utopian solution. Once again his skepticism is entirely practical. Utopia will not work because no one will want it to; the common opinion, he is sure, is that all those things that are denied in Hythloday's ideal state—wealth, glory, power, ostentation, etc.—are truly desirable and should not be eliminated.[12] We are back to where we started: the perfect solution to social and political problems, however we imagine it, is not possible in this life, since men are sinful and will not allow it. The only possibility is to retreat and save one's own soul (as Hythloday), or engage for very small, though perhaps still worthy, gains (as More in the dialogue). In short, both sides—and thus the author—agree about what the realistic *and* the idealistic alternatives are; we are left only with the problem of which to choose. It is not surprising to discover that just at this time the author was himself considering the real possibility of entering royal service.[13]

Now it seems to me that More's originality of thought lies just in this radical disjunction between the real life that he perceived and his political ideals—more perhaps than it does in his actual description of Utopia. In this he has at least one contemporary parallel: the Italian, Machiavelli. It is interesting to see in this regard that both men refer contemptuously to the many works of political advice that had already been offered by others, all of which are futile because they propose idealistic remedies to corrupt princes.[14] Both agree on the wickedness of their situations and the essen-

---

12. Common property, More reflects, means the end of all nobility, magnificence, splendor, and majesty (*nobilitas, magnificentia, splendor,* and *maiestas*), "which are in the estimation of the common people, the true glories and ornaments of the commonwealth" (*vera ut publica est opinio decora atque ornamenta Republicae*); *Utopia,* 4, p. 244. Quentin Skinner sees correctly that "common opinion" is not necessarily the opinion of the common people, but more aptly "public opinion," including many of the humanists; see "Sir Thomas More's *Utopia* and the Language of Renaissance Humanism," in *The Languages of Political Theory in Early Modern Europe,* ed. Anthony Pagden (Cambridge, 1987), p. 153n.

13. Hexter imagines More thinking to himself, "Should a man like me, Thomas More, enter the council of my King, Henry VIII of England?" "Thomas More and the Problem of Council," *Quincentennial Essays on St. Thomas More,* ed. Michael Moore (Boone, N.C., 1978), p. 61. Hexter has meticulously reconstituted More's situation on the eve of *Utopia* first in his *More's Utopia: The Biography of an Idea* (New York, 1952) and again in his introduction to the Yale edition. For More's actual involvement in politics and law, see Geoffrey Elton, "Thomas More, Councillor," and "Sir Thomas More and the Opposition to Henry VIII," in *Studies in Tudor and Stuart Politics and Government* (Cambridge, 1974), I, pp. 129–72; and his more recent essays in ibid, III (1983), pp. 344–72, 444–60; Margaret Hastings, "Sir Thomas More: Maker of English Law?" in *Essential Articles,* pp. 104–18; J. A. Guy, *The Public Career of Thomas More* (Brighton, 1980).

14. Philosophers had already given much counsel to kings in published books, Hythloday remarks, but kings had not been willing to take their advice; *Works,* 4, p. 87. More has Plato in

tial depravity of human nature; and both see the hopelessness of simply prescribing morality. But More, unlike Machiavelli, was still unwilling to submit and give in to the practical requirements of the moment. He was still too good a Christian, too much an idealist for that.[15]

The principal ingredients in More's recipe for perfection, he insists, lie easily accessible in reason and Scripture, more particularly in the classical philosophers, especially Plato, and in the Gospels. The utopians have both: reason at first unaided, but then bolstered by the appearance of Greek books fresh from the Venetian presses; then the Bible which they also receive from their European visitors, who bring news of Christ along with the classical authors. Both are swiftly and easily assimilated to their own utopian culture.

More's Christian humanism is thus easily established. And it is just in these years that he began to defend the new learning, the Greeks against the modern "Trojans," in a series of public and private letters where he vigorously defended the utility of classical learning.[16] Yet it is characteristic that even on this point he allows at least one ambiguity. In Utopia there are two orders of friars who are particularly virtuous and voluntarily do the dirty work of society. However, one lives according to ascetic rules and refuses to marry or eat meat, while the other participates freely in utopian life. The first, we are told, is considered the more holy by the people, the second the wiser. Utopian wisdom, we have learned earlier, is the wisdom of Greek moral philosophy, where happiness is the object and pleasure the instrument.[17] But More refuses here to choose between the two utopian al-

---

mind and his bad experience with King Dionysius, but he may also have been thinking of Erasmus's *Institution of a Christian Prince*, which was published (with two other classical precedents by Isocrates and Plutarch) just before *Utopia* in 1516. For Machiavelli's disparagement of previously imagined polities and his own desire to write about things as they really exist, see the *Prince*, chap. 15. For the traditional literature, see A. H. Gilbert, *Machiavelli's Prince and Its Forerunners* (Durham, 1938); Felix Gilbert, "The Humanist Conception of the Prince and *The Prince* of Machiavelli," *Journal of Modern History*, 11 (1939), pp. 449–83.

15. Though "parts of *Utopia* read like a commentary on parts of the *Prince*," the *Prince* had not yet been published; R. W. Chambers, *Thomas More* (New York, 1935), p. 132. For Machiavelli's pagan posture against modern attempts to rehabilitate him, see Mark Hulliung, *Citizen Machiavelli* (Princeton, 1983).

16. See the letters to Dorp (1515), to Oxford (1518), to Lee (1519), and to a monk (1519), all collected in *Works*, 15, with a useful introduction by Daniel Kinney. In general, see Paul O. Kristeller, "Thomas More as a Renaissance Humanist," *Moreana*, 65–66 (1980), pp. 5–22.

17. "This is their view of virtue and pleasure. They believe that human reason can attain to no truer view, *unless a heaven-sent religion inspire man with something more holy*. Whether in this stand they are right or wrong, time does not permit me to examine—nor is it necessary," *Works*, 4, p. 178. In *A Treatise on the Passion*, More seems to echo this passage; and he specifically allows the pagans to win salvation by natural reason; *Works*, 13, pp. 37, 43. Utopian philosophy, according to his Yale editors, is a modified form of Epicureanism. But see also George M. Logan, *The Meaning of Utopia* (Princeton, 1983), pp. 145–78.

ternatives, and his biographers tell us that he himself vacillated between
them throughout his own life, drawn almost equally to the monastic life
and the life of public employment.[18] The fit between medieval Christianity
and Renaissance humanism, like the fit between More's own active and
contemplative allegiances, was not, apparently, quite perfect.[19] The
Utopia, it seems, is first of all a dialogue of the author with himself, self-conscious to a supreme degree, but not always completely resolved.[20]

Among the ancients, it is Plato who most obviously inspired More; the
Republic is evidently his literary and philosophical model. It too is a dialogue that turns into a monologue; it too begins with the problem of justice
and becomes an effort to describe the ideal state. It too considers the elimination of private property, though only for the guardian class. And it too
ends somewhat ambiguously about the prospect of realizing true justice in
this life. (The Republic, admittedly, is to be found "nowhere on earth.")[21]
More read Plato with attention but did not forget that the ancient Greek
had failed in his own attempt to bring philosophy to a real king.[22] For More
who had read Plato and (better still) the Bible, and who had the benefit of

18. The young lawyer chose to live "religiously" in the Charterhouse without taking vows;
the lord chancellor never gave up wearing a hair-shirt and other austerities; see William
Roper, *The Lyfe of Sir Thomas Moore Knighte,* ed. Elsie Vaughan Hitchcock, Early English Text
Society, orig. ser., 197 (Oxford, 1935), pp. 6, 48–49; Nicholas Harpsfield, *The Life and Death of
Sir Thomas Moore, Knighte,* ed. Elsie Vaughan Hitchcock, Early English Text Society, orig. ser.,
186 (London, 1932), pp. 17, 64–66. According to Roper, More's hardest moment was to close
the garden gate behind him, leaving his family for his fate; *Lyfe,* p. 73.

19. According to Germain Marc'hadour, "this startling passage has not received enough at-
tention." However, Father Mac'hadour does not notice much tension here, in "*Utopia* and
Martyrdom," *Interpreting Thomas More's Utopia,* ed. John C. Olin (New York, 1989), pp. 63–65.
Among other things, More also leaves the sacrament of ordination an open question in
Utopia; according to Hythloday, the utopians, when last seen, were still disputing the matter;
Works, 4, p. 218. See Father Surtz's puzzlement, *The Praise of Wisdom* (Chicago, 1957), pp. 151–
52. For other discrepancies between utopian reason and Christian religion, see Logan, pp.
219–20.

20. "A dialogue of More's mind with itself," David Bevington, "The Dialogue in Utopia,"
Studies in Philology, 58 (1961), pp. 496–509; cf. Robert C. Elliott, "The Shape of *Utopia,*" *English Literary History,* 30, (1963), pp. 317–44. For More's choice of the active over the contemplative life, see Harpsfield, *Life,* p. 18.

21. *Republic,* IX 592B. This passage may have been the inspiration for More's title; see Logan, p. 131n. The prevailing contemporary view was that Plato's republic was impractical; see
the passages from Erasmus and Thomas Starkey's *Dialogue* collected by Surtz in *Utopia,*
p. 375n.

22. More reminds Hythloday that his "favorite author," Plato, had said that there would
never be a perfect commonwealth unless philosophers became kings, or kings philosophers.
Hythloday replies, "But, doubtless, Plato was right in foreseeing that if kings themselves did
not turn to philosophy, they would never approve of real philosophers . . . [as] he found from
his own experience with Dionysius." *Utopia,* p. 87. The story is told in Plato's own epistles, esp.
7 and 8, as well as elsewhere, and the Platonic advice was endlessly quoted; see Surtz, *Utopia,*
pp. 349n.

both reason and revelation, the problem was not so much how to define justice, as to see whether it could be realized in the state. Perhaps that is what the quatrain in the Utopian tongue means at the beginning of the book, when it announces that, "Alone of all lands, without the aid of abstract philosophy, I have represented for mortals the philosophical city." And what the humanist, Beatus Rhenanus, had in mind when he wrote that "the Utopia contains principles of such a sort as it is not possible to find in Plato. . . . Its lessons are less philosophical . . . but more Christian."[23] To More the problem seems less of knowing than of doing the good; he was, we know, as much attracted to St. Augustine as he was to Plato.[24] But if More faltered for a moment between the choice of an ascetic life or a worldly one, he did not doubt for a moment that the good life was measured by the deeds done in it. (Both kinds of friars, and all the citizens of Utopia, find justification in good works.)[25] In this admittedly ambiguous preference for the life of action over the life of contemplation, public service over philosophical retreat, More remained at one with most of his fellow humanists.

2

It is More's realism, along with his humanism, that is new in England. His allegiance to Greece and Rome he shared with his friends Erasmus, Colet, and the rest. His realism was more his own, a result perhaps of his actual experience in public life, as well as the new political setting.[26] Hexter puts it well, "More achieves a clarity of vision about the world he lives in unsurpassed by any contemporary but Machiavelli and perhaps Guicciardini."[27] More had been trained as a lawyer, unlike most of his friends, who were in the church or the university. It is true that his political career had been

23. Rhenanus to Willibald Pirckheimer, Feb. 23, 1518; More, *Utopia,* p. 253.
24. More lectured on the *City of God* as a young man; see Roper, *Lyfe,* p. 6; Harpsfield, *Life,* pp. 13–14.
25. See the passage (with the marginal gloss, *vita activa*), *Works,* 4, p. 224. Later, More's biographer seems to have felt it necessary to apologize for More's choice of the active life, Harpsfield, *Life,* p. 18.
26. I shall restrict the term largely to the ethical and political domain. Ethical realism, Johan Huizinga says, "springs from a need to see and depict life, man and the world as they really are, and no better, stripped of all trappings of an ideal or conventional form, without illusions." However, Huizinga specifically denies the association of realism with the Renaissance or any other period. Nor was he much interested in drawing the distinction between history and fiction that I am trying to make. See his cautionary essay, "Renaissance and Realism," in *Men and Ideas,* trans. James S. Holmes and Hans van Marle (New York, 1959), pp. 288–309.
27. Hexter in *Utopia,* 4, p. ci. For a further comparison, see Hexter's *Vision of Politics on the Eve of the Reformation: More, Machiavelli, Seysell* (New York, 1973), esp. pp. 179–203.

barely launched, but he had served the city of London in various positions, and was destined for royal favor. He was neither a cleric nor an aristocrat, and so quite outside the dominant culture of his time: the culture of chivalry and the church. The *Utopia* is expressly critical of each, and overtly hostile to the pretensions of both the church and the aristocracy to rule. There is some truth to the charge that *Utopia* is a bourgeois book, though More's attention was on the past, not the future.[28] Its originality derives first of all from the social and intellectual setting it portrays, to which it was unreservedly opposed.

I shall not dwell here on the failing culture of chivalry, except to say that by More's day it had lost almost all real connection with practical life.[29] When More was young he could have read in the only English books of his time, the publications of England's first printer, William Caxton, a complete description and hearty endorsement of the traditional culture of the aristocracy. It is true that Caxton, who was as thorough a bourgeois as More, laments the decline of chivalry in his day, but he can think of no alternative and urges its revival on the king as though it were still perfectly usable.[30] He seems to feel no discrepancy between the military ideals of a class in disarray and the actual situation of his readers. The "veil of illusion," to use Burckhardt's old phrase, was still in place. However, the tension between the real world of politics—the world of "bastard feudalism"—[31] and the idealized fictions of the later Middle Ages was now

28. For an exaggerated view, see Russell Ames, *Citizen Thomas More and His Utopia* (Princeton, 1949). Hexter is justly hard on Ames but understates the undeniably bourgeois elements in More's personal background: the city of London, its commerce and legal profession. More may not have been their spokesman in *Utopia*; nevertheless he was their employee in real life. See Hexter in *Utopia*, pp. liv–lvii. More's most recent biographer, Richard Marius, emphasizes More's city connections, *Thomas More: A Biography* (New York, 1985). For More's legal and political career, see Margaret Hastings, "Sir Thomas More: Maker of English Law?" in *Essential Articles*, pp. 104–18; J. A. Guy, *The Public Career of Sir Thomas More* (Brighton, 1980). For the restriction of the power of priests in Utopia, see Edward L. Surtz, *The Praise of Wisdom* (Chicago, 1957), p. 160.

29. See Arthur B. Ferguson, *The Indian Summer of English Chivalry: Studies in the Decline and Transformation of Chivalric Idealism* (Durham, 1960). I prefer this view and the older literature to the recent effort by Maurice Keen to rescue chivalry for politics, since even he recognizes that changes in the technology of warfare and the practical functions of knighthood had altered profoundly by the end of the fifteenth century. See his article, "Huizinga, Kilgour and the Decline of Chivalry," *Medievalia et Humanistica*, n.s. 8 (1977), pp. 1–20; and his *Chivalry* (New Haven, 1984).

30. See Caxton's translation of Raymon Lull's *The Book of the Ordre of Chyvalry*, ed. Alfred T. P. Byles, Early English Text Society, orig. ser., 168 (London, 1926), epilogue, pp. 121–25; Levine, *Humanism and History*, pp. 47–49.

31. For Burckhardt and the "veil" see below; for Huizinga, see his *The Waning of the Middle Ages*, trans. F. Hopman (London, 1924), chaps. 4–7; for "Bastard Feudalism," see K. B. McFarlane, *Bulletin of the Institute of Historical Research*, 20 (1945), pp. 161–80.

becoming acute, and the humanists who first spotted it suddenly found an English audience in their growing awareness of that discrepancy. In Italy the humanists had long ago discovered an alternative to chivalry in the political culture of antiquity and sold it to their Italian masters. They had ventured a new style and a new training for political life in which the rhetoric of antiquity was given preeminence as a practical preparation for life. They saw in classical culture a new set of political ideals to be imitated, and they found the ancients more contemporary than their immediate forebears. In a word, they preferred the forum of Cicero to the court of King Arthur, the *De Officiis* to the *Morte d'Arthur*. And so they transformed their education and culture accordingly.

Of course, Englishmen had for a long time been in contact with Italy, but for the most part they were content to ignore all this. However, as the tension grew between the real conditions of practical life and the old ideal of aristocratic rule which had been invented in very different circumstances, Italian humanism came suddenly alive in Renaissance England.[32] It was More's generation that first perceived the value of this cultural alternative and began to propagate it successfully among the political classes in England. And it may have been More who understood its implications best, better even than the humanist friends with whom he shared so much. Of course, there was still too much continuity with the Middle Ages—in society and politics and culture—for this emancipation to be complete; even contemporary Italy was making an accommodation with the aristocratic court. More himself remained caught between two worlds, and something of the ambiguity in his work lies there. His supreme merit is in his self-consciousness about the alternatives.

More read Plato then, not as a philosopher, but as a humanist rhetorician. His wisdom derives from experience in the world, not retreat into contemplation. Hythloday is not Socrates, nor even Erasmus, although he takes a little from each. More's practical political skills were tied to his real experience and to his humanist eloquence, the need to persuade the wealthy and powerful of their political obligations. Just so was he to make his own career in parliament and the king's council.[33] *Utopia* is not, therefore, a philosophical tract, but a rhetorical one meant to persuade by its literary skill.

32. This is not to deny the anticipations sketched by Roberto Weiss, *Humanism in England during the Fifteenth Century*, 2d ed. (Oxford, 1957). But no fifteenth-century Englishman (except perhaps for one or two who remained abroad) assimilated classical culture and put it to use like the generation that came to maturity in the 1490s: Grocyn, Linacre, Colet, Erasmus, and More. See Denys Hay, "The Early Renaissance in England," and "England and the Humanities in the Fifteenth Century," in his *Renaissance Essays* (London, 1988), pp. 151–231.

33. See William Nelson, "Thomas More, Grammarian and Orator," *Essential Articles*, pp. 104–18.

For the humanist rhetorician, it was poetry and history along with oratory, that furnished the models for expression and the fund of examples
that constituted political wisdom.[34] Through poetry and history, the individual could come to extend his own limited personal experience of the
world. And this is just what Hythloday is purported to have done. He has
traveled to a new world and seen for himself how things work elsewhere; he
is ready on every occasion to support his arguments with an appropriate
example. The only difference is that, instead of finding his examples in the
classical books, he has made them all up!

Hythloday's examples, including the utopia itself, are therefore, like
himself, all deliberate fictions, although they are presented as histories.
More has gone out of his way to give the traveler's story all the trappings of
verisimilitude. Erasmus had already suggested that if an entirely fictional
narrative was to be used to make a point, "we must make it as much like the
real thing as possible."[35] So More provides a map of Utopia and an alphabet for the language. He furnishes introductory letters from friends to attest to its historicity. He supplies a detailed and realistic setting for the
scene of the dialogue and the description of Utopia. Nevertheless, the
whole discussion in the prefatory epistles and book one has alerted us to
the likelihood that this is a fiction, and many of the persons and places are
deliberately given names that declare their fictional character.[36] As far as I

34. Students, More writes in his contemporary letter to Oxford (1518), must learn prudence in human affairs, "and I doubt that any study contributes as readily to this practical skill
as the study of the poets, orators and historians," *Works,* 5, p. 139. This, of course, is the ancient
sophistic, so vigorously opposed by Socrates in the *Republic,* and dismissed by the rest of classical and medieval philosophy.

35. *De Copia,* ed. Craig R. Thompson, trans. Betty Knott and Brian McGregor, in *The Collected Works,* 24 (1978), p. 634. See Logan, *Meaning of Utopia,* pp. 29–30.

36. "We forgot to ask, and he forgot to say," writes More to Giles in the preface, "in what
part of the world Utopia lies. I am sorry that point was omitted . . ." *Utopia,* p. 42. See also
Walter R. Davis, "Thomas More's *Utopia* as Fiction," *Centennial Review,* 24 (1980), pp. 249–
68; Richard Sylvester, "*Si Hythlodaeus Credimus:* Vision and Revision in *Utopia,*" in *Essential Articles for the Study of Thomas More,* ed. Richard Sylvester and Germain Marc'hadour (Hamden,
Conn., 1977), pp. 290–301. As for the names, the old view of Sir James Mackintosh, that "All
the names which he invented for men and places were intimations of their being unreal," remains standard; see Mackintosh, quoted by R. J. Schoeck, "Levels of Word-Play and Figura-
tive Significations in More's *Utopia,*" *Notes and Queries,* n.s., I (1954), p. 512; J. D. Simmonds,
"More's Use of Names in Book II of *Utopia,*" *Der Neuren Sprachen,* N.F., 10 (1961), pp. 282–84;
More, *Works,* 4, p. cxlvii. Thus the Polylerites, whom Hythloday pretends to have visited, are,
"People of Much Nonsense; the Anchorians who live near Utopia are "without place, re-
gion, district," etc., ibid., pp. 343n., 358n. And of course More refers to his work as
Nusquama (nowhere) when he sends it to Erasmus in 1516 and in subsequent letters; see
Erasmus, *Opus epistolarum,* ed. P. S. Allen, 12 vols. (Oxford, 1906–58), 2, pp. 339, 346, 354,
359, 372.

can see, no reader was ever taken in, and More was both attacked and admired for the "fictions" he had invented.[37] It became customary to couple the *Utopia* with Plato's *Republic,* and sometimes with Cicero's *De Oratore,* Xenophon's *Cyropaedia,* and Castiglione's *Courtier,* as fictional ideals, all "faire shadows in the aire," "too good to be true."[38] When Thomas Smith, a generation later, elected to describe the English commonwealth as he believed it was, he deliberately set himself apart from the fictional commonwealths of More and Plato, "such as never were nor shall ever be, vaine imaginations, phantasies of philosophers to occupie their time and to exercise their wittes." Even More's biographer, Nicholas Harpsfield, described *Utopia* as "an inventive drift of Sir Thomas Mores owne imagination and head," rather than "a very sure knowen story."[39]

In 1517, a second edition of *Utopia* appeared at Paris under the aegis of the young English humanist Thomas Lupset. Among its variations, the most important was a new letter from More to Peter Giles, appended to the text. In it, More carries his game further. He pretends to answer a critic, who had objected that if the work was true it was absurd; if a fiction, then it was lacking in judgment. More replies that if he had dared to introduce any fiction, it would only have been as embellishment, and he would anyway have tipped off the learned reader to his design by using fictional names, suggesting (for example) that the island was nowhere, the city a phantom, the river without water, and the ruler without a people.[40] If after that, anyone still wanted to doubt the history, More adds, let them seek out the others who were present at the conversation, or indeed Hythloday himself, who

37. So Tyndale accused More of "feigning" matters in *Utopia;* see *An Answer to Sir Thomas More's Dialogue* (1530), ed. Henry Walter, Parker Society, 44 (Cambridge, 1850), p. 193; while Thomas Wilson praised him for his "feined Narrations and wittie invented matters (as though they were true in deede)," *Arte of Rhetorique* (1553), quoted with many other examples in Jackson Campbell Boswell, *Sir Thomas More in the English Renaissance: An Annotated Catalogue,* Medieval and Renaissance Texts and Studies, 83 (Binghamton, 1992), pp. 336–37, and passim. More's early Italian readers had no trouble discerning the fiction and (among the friends of Machiavelli anyway) complaining about its impracticality; see Francesco Vettori, *Sommario della istoria d'Italia* (1527), in *Scritti storici e politici,* ed. Enrico Niccolini (Bari, 1972), p. 145; and (from a more sympathetic point of view) N. L. Tomeo to Pole (1524), in Edward L. Surtz, *The Praise of Wisdom* (Chicago, 1957), p. 6.

38. James Cleland, *Institution of a Young Nobleman* (1607); Samuel Purchas, *Purchas his Pilgrimage* (1613); Boswell, *More,* pp. 64–65, 252. For other examples, see Boswell, pp. 9, 86, 90, 103, 121, 158–59.

39. Sir Thomas Smith, *De Republica Anglorum,* ed. L. Alston (Cambridge, 1906), p. 142. Harpsfield, *Life,* p. 104.

40. See also Arthur E. Barker, "*Clavis Moreana:* The Yale Edition of Thomas More," in *Essential Articles,* p. 227; Peter R. Allen, "*Utopia* and European Humanism: The Function of the Prefatory Letters and Verses," *Studies in the Renaissance,* 10 (1963), pp. 100–101.

was still alive and well—now off somewhere in Portugal![41] They would soon find that More at least, had been a faithful historian in reporting his conversation with Hythloday, though whether Hythloday had been equally reliable in his account of Utopia was another matter. More could not vouch for that. "I am responsible for my own work alone and not also for the credit of another." The joke was a bit much, and it is not surprising that it was suppressed in the next edition (1518) and afterward. It was hardly necessary to make plain what every sophisticated reader surely knew already: that More had invented and labeled both his fictions: the conversation with Hythloday (nonsense) and the description of Utopia (nowhere).[42]

Now if there is anything unusual about all this, it is, I believe, in the self-consciousness of the author, which he willingly shares with his readers. Throughout the Middle Ages authors had invented fictions and passed them off as histories, or written histories into which they intruded fictions, almost without criticism.[43] The most notorious of these may have been that twelfth-century monk, Geoffrey of Monmouth, who seems to have invented (or borrowed) an entire fictional history for early Britain, culminating in the legendary Celtic King Arthur. His work was immediately employed by both poets and chroniclers, who embellished it vastly and took it for true, right down to Thomas More's day. Caxton received the story from Sir Thomas Malory and in one of his noblest works insisted on publishing it as genuine.[44] It would be nice to know what More thought about it; his father owned a copy and even recorded his birth in it. All we know is that he once made a joke about one of the sillier stories in the legend.[45] Perhaps his silence is suggestive. More's acquaintance, Polydore Vergil, was just then questioning its veracity, while More's friends and fellow humanists, Erasmus and Vives, were equally appalled by the immorality and improbability of the stories that were based on it. It was not long before English humanists were ready to discard the whole thing pretty

41. In an earlier prefatory epistle, Giles writes to Busleyden confirming More's recollection that they had forgotten to ask where Utopia was, and he repeats some speculation that Hythloday was either dead or that he had returned to Utopia; *Utopia*, p. 24.

42. On this point see the letter of Beatus Rhenanus (1518) in *Utopia*, p. 253 (quoted in Warren Wooden, "Anti-Scholastic Satire in Sir Thomas More's *Utopia*," *Sixteenth Century Journal*, 8 [1977], p. 44n.) For the name Hythloday, meaning "expert in trifles" or "well-learned in nonsense," see *Utopia*, p. 301; for Utopia as "nowhere," see above n. 36.

43. "Readers coming to medieval historians for the first time may be perplexed to find patent fictions presented as part of a true account; readers of medieval fictions may wonder why invented stories are offered as 'true.'" Ruth Morse, *Truth and Convention in the Middle Ages: Rhetoric, Representation, and Reality* (Cambridge, 1991), p. 4.

44. Levine, *Humanism and History*, pp. 40–45.

45. Richard Pace tells the story, *De fructu qui ex doctrina percipitur,* ed. and trans. Frank Manley and Richard Sylvester (New York, 1967), pp. 105–7.

completely on both grounds.[46] What Geoffrey thought he was doing is now beyond retrieval, but it is clear that no medieval author was willing to declare his purpose by making a bold distinction between fiction and history. When they told a fiction they pretended it was history; when they recounted a history, they included fiction; and neither authors nor audience seemed much to care.[47]

What was missing, apparently, was the early modern idea of history, in which it is thought that something like a true and literal description of the past could be winnowed out and distinguished from fiction. Medieval historiography worked largely by accretion, rarely ever by subtraction; a story once told gained authority by mere reiteration and the passage of time. In this context the humanist cry *ad fontes* was revolutionary. But equally important, there was lacking an idea of fiction independent of received tradition, fiction as something that could be deliberately and purposefully invented with a value all its own. What may have been required was a jolt of recognition, a shock to the English consciousness, perhaps like that delivered by Giangaliozzo Visconti to the Florentines at the beginning of the Italian Renaissance, which (according to Hans Baron) shook them from their medieval illusions about their own past and created a new critical history.[48] The English were not so lucky; and the Middle Ages receded only

46. Erasmus dismissed the Arthurian romances in the same year as *Utopia* in his *Institutio principis Christiani;* see *The Education of a Christian Prince,* trans. Lester K. Born (New York, 1968), p. 200. Polydore Vergil criticized the story in the *Anglica Historica,* which More may have seen; see Denys Hay, *Polydore Vergil* (Oxford, 1952), pp. 109–11. For more, see Robert P. Adams, "Bold Bawdy and Open Manslaughter: The English New Humanist Attack on Medieval Romance," *Huntington Library Quarterly,* 23 (1959), pp. 33–44; Nelson, *Fact and Fiction,* pp. 98–105; Levine, *Humanism and History,* pp. 48–49, 231.

47. C. S. Lewis, for one, doubted that any English author, including Chaucer, believed he was writing fiction; all proceeded as though they were composing histories; see his "The English Prose *Morte,*" in *Essays on Malory,* ed. J. A. W. Bennett (Oxford, 1963), p. 22. For other authorities, see "Caxton's Histories," p. 216 n. 3, and Ruth Morse, Truth and Convention (though one may now add on the other side Lee Patterson, *Chaucer and the Subject of History* [Madison, 1991]).

48. See Hans Baron, *The Crisis of the Early Italian Renaissance,* 2d ed. (Princeton, 1966); *In Search of Florentine Civic Humanism,* 2 vols. (Princeton, 1988), esp. 1, pp. 254–55; 2, pp. 6–12; 67, where Baron makes some suggestions about how his thesis might be applied to the English Renaissance. There are appreciations of Baron by Denis Hay and August Buck and a bibliography of his writings in *Renaissance Studies in Honor of Hans Baron* (Florence, 1971). The fullest effort to apply the civic argument to English culture remains Arthur B. Ferguson, *The Articulate Citizen of the English Renaissance* (Durham, 1965). Whether the Milanese wars were required to liberate Florentine civic humanism has been much debated and is unnecessary for our argument. What is required is an appropriate social-political context. See most recently Donald Kelley, *Renaissance Humanism* (Boston, 1991), pp. 14–28. And for civic humanism generally, the works of Eugenio Garin, especially *Italian Humanism: Philosophy and Civic Life in the Renaissance,* trans. Peter Munz (New York, 1965); and William J. Bouwsma, *Venice and the Defense of Republican Liberty* (Berkeley, 1968). It is worth emphasizing that Utopia is a republic.

imperceptibly before the gradual alteration of English political and social life. However, More was especially well-situated in his London setting to understand these changes, and they are wonderfully well-illustrated in Hythloday's description of the realities of English life in book one, where all chivalric considerations are banished and the aristocracy portrayed merely as rapacious landlords and courtly sycophants. It certainly looks as though More understood that there was a fundamental difference, and one that mattered, between the facts of life and their contemporary representation, between history and fiction. One has only to compare his account of chivalry with that of his contemporary, Stephen Hawes' in his *Pastime of Pleasure,* or any of Caxton's many publications.[49] But *Utopia* is very different from these works and Geoffrey of Monmouth in another way; unlike them, it was *meant* to be read and understood as a deliberate fiction. While there were many then who continued to believe in Geoffrey's "old Welsh book" (and a few who have not yet given up the search), it does not appear that anyone ever sought out Raphael Hythloday.

As often happens, theory followed afterward, and it was only later that another Englishman, Sir Philip Sidney, remembering (among other things) More's "feigned image of poetry," discovered a justification for poetic invention; his defense of poetry is apparently among the first to do so in England.[50] But by then, by the time of Queen Elizabeth, the distinction between history and fiction, which had been earlier elaborated on the Continent by such as Giraldo Cinthio and Ludovico Castelvetro, had become almost commonplace.[51] On the one side, the historians were busy defending their practices against the feigning of romance; on the other side, the poets were only too pleased to announce their freedom from the facts.[52]

49. Hawes "looked with regretful longing upon the Middle Ages," writes his modern editor, "upon the vanishing glory of chivalry, with its fantastic conception of honour and courtesy," and he hoped somehow to renew it. Stephen Hawes, *The Pastime of Pleasure,* ed. William Edward Mead, Early English Text Society, orig. ser., 173 (London, 1928), p. xli. (See chap. 3 below.) There were eventually four editions of the work, 1509, 1517, 1554, 1555.

50. *The Defense of Poesie,* ed. Albert Feuillerat, *The Prose Works of Sir Philip Sidney,* 4 vols. (Cambridge, 1963), 3, p. 15. "The defense of poetry . . . is a defense not of poetry as against prose but of fiction against fact. . . . What is in question is not man's right to sing but his right to feign, to 'make things up' . . . that debate, properly viewed, is simply the difficult process by which Europe became conscious of fiction as an activity different from history on the one hand and from lying on the other"; C. S. Lewis, quoted in Harry Berger, "The Renaissance Imagination: Second World and Green World," *Centennial Review,* 9 (1965), p. 39.

51. See Giraldo Cinthio, *On Romances,* trans. Henry L. Snuggs (Lexington, 1968), pp. 51, 167; Ludovico Castelvetro, *On the Art of Poetry,* trans. Andrew Bongiorno (Binghamton, 1984), pp. 3ff, 92ff. In general, see Baxter Hathaway, *The Age of Criticism: The Late Renaissance in Italy* (Ithaca, 1962), and the works cited in Levine, *Humanism and History,* p. 232, nn. 133–35.

52. For the *artes historiae,* see the collection in Johann Wolfius, *Artes historicae penus* (Basle, 1579), several of which were known in England. Thomas Blundeville's *True Order and Methode*

3

It was, therefore, out of a realization that there was a disjunction between the real features of English public life and the idealized versions of medieval fiction that I think the modern separation of history from fiction was first conceived.[53] Chivalry had been invented as a set of fictional ideals to meet the needs of medieval feudalism; Renaissance England badly required a new set of fictional ideals to replace the old ones that no longer seemed to matter. *Utopia* can be understood therefore, as an attempt to create one, but it differs fundamentally from chivalric romance by *openly pretending* that it is history: in other words by *displaying* its fictional character. The ancients had long ago defended the idea of poetry as suited to the purpose of teaching morality, and Aristotle (in the humanist *Poetics* that the Middle Ages generally ignored) had declared its superiority to history in that respect. When finally Philip Sidney came to reconsider the subject (in a work that was indebted both to Aristotle and to his humanistic predecessors), he argued vigorously for the superiority of poetry over history in exemplifying the highest ideals, precisely because the poet could shape his work freely and without the constraints of a recalcitrant reality. "If the poet do his part aright, he will show you . . . nothing that is not to be shunned. . . . Where [as] the historian, bound to tell things as things were, cannot be liberal, without he be poetical of a perfect pattern."[54] His contemporary, George Puttenham, also singling out the *Utopia,* made exactly the same point.[55]

---

of Wryting and Reading Hystories (1574) was adapted from the works of Patrizzi and Acontius; see the version in the *Huntington Library Quarterly,* ed. Hugh G. Dick, 3 (1940), pp. 149–70. In *Humanism and History* (p. 51 and note), I have quoted from Shakespeare, Marston, Dekker, Chapman, and Ben Jonson, to show the new confidence in the independence of fiction.

53. This could be extended to More's view of the religious life also, although that is a large matter that deserves separate treatment. More certainly shared with Erasmus a disdain for popular hagiography which, he complained, had interpolated many pious frauds into ecclesiastical history; see his defense of Lucian's *Philopseudes,* in the dedicatory letter to Ruthall which was prefixed to his translation; *Works,* 3, pp. 5–7. A contrast between the real lives of monks and friars and the idealized orders in Utopia is set up in the first book of *Utopia,* when at Morton's dinner table they are criticized for idleness, and again later when Hythloday points out how the church had deliberately corrupted Christ's teaching by making it agreeable to everyone.

54. Sidney, *Works,* 3, p. 16. Both poetry and history have the advantage over philosophy that they teach concretely by example, and thus move the reader to action.

55. The first poets were historians, he says, and did not worry about using "feined matter or altogether fabulous," because poetry could teach by invented examples at least as well as by true ones. "The poet hath the handling of them to fashion at his pleasure, but not so th'other which go according to their veritie and none otherwise without the writers great blame." The *Republic* and *Utopia* are his best illustrations. Both the authorship and the date of composition of this work remain problematical; see *The Arte of English Poesie,* ed. Gladys Willcock and Alice Walker (Cambridge, 1936), pp. 40–41.

I think that More must have understood this already. He saw that his fictional utopia could be more perfectly shaped to his ideal than any real polity in the past, not excluding Greece and Rome,[56] and so he drew up his ideal state in the shape of an imaginary example. The more acutely he observed the realities of contemporary life, without any of the illusions of late medieval chivalry, the freer he became to invent remedies.[57] It seems to have been his direct experience with contemporary affairs along with his Christian dissatisfaction with human nature that told him that history *could* not furnish him with a perfect example. And so he was perhaps the first writer in England to find himself suddenly emancipated from the necessity of concealing his views in a history. It is true, he pretends that his account is historical, and so doffs a satirical cap to an old convention, but he clearly wants everyone to know that it is a pretense.[58] Having separated the real and the ideal in his own mind, he was ready to separate fiction from history.

Still, it will not do to hurry this separation when the idea was yet so new and imperfect. More may well have grasped the idea that a writer was free to invent a fiction, and that fiction might even be preferable to history in the description of an ideal. But the corollary, still implicit, was that to describe reality, history might be preferable to fiction. It is not surprising therefore that More set to work on a history at this very time, and that its subject should be that wicked and realistic prince, Richard III, who (according to Shakespeare) "set the murderous Machiavel to school."[59] The

56. "It far surpasses and leaves a long way behind the many celebrated and much lauded commonwealths of the Spartans, Athenians and Romans," Jerome Busleyden to More, *Works*, 4, p. 34. More was widely read in classical history; see the poem of Robert Whittington to More (1519), *Huntington Library Quarterly*, 26 (1963), pp. 147–54; Erasmus to Bude, *Opus Epistolarum*, ed P. S. Allen, 12 vols. (Oxford, 1906–58), 4, p. 577; *Works*, 4, pp. lxxxi–xcv.

57. "The presentation of a defective contemporary world is meaningful only when seen against the contrasting ideal world. Vice-versa, the ideality of that realm finds its meaning only in its vis-à-vis position to reality. And that means its clear and distinct demarcation as irreality," Hubertus S. Herbruggen, "More's *Utopia* as Paradigm," from *Utopie und Anti-Utopie* (1960) in *Essential Articles*, p. 262. See also Kevin Corrigan, "The Function of the Ideal in Plato's *Republic* and Sir Thomas More's *Utopia*," *Moreana*, 27 (1990), p. 42. It seems to me that Thomas Nashe is saying something like this when he characterizes *Utopia*, in the *Unfortunate Traveller* (1594), quoted in Jackson Boswell, "The Reception of Eramus's *Moriae* in England through 1640," *Erasmus of Rotterdam Society Yearbook*, 7 (1987), p. 80.

58. Here too there was classical inspiration in the satires of Lucian which More and Erasmus had earlier read and translated; see T. S. Dorsch, "Sir Thomas More and Lucian: An Interpretation of *Utopia*," *Archiv für das studien der neuren sprachen und literaturen*, 203 (1967); *The Translations of Lucian*, ed. Craig R. Thompson, *Works*, 3 (1974).

59. *Henry VI, Part III*, act iii, sc. 2. More's immediate inspiration may well have been the newly retrieved portrait of Tiberius by Tacitus. The *Annales* were discovered in 1509 and printed in 1515. Some verbal similarities, the strong psychological interest, and especially the theme of tyranny and dissimulation, all suggest an immediate influence on More's choice of Richard III; see the Richard Sylvester's introduction to the Yale edition *Works*, 2, pp. lxxx–civ.

contrast between the ideally good rule of Utopia and the brutally bad rule of More's contemporary prince could hardly be more stark—and in its way instructive. But More's problem remained unresolved: it was more than ever difficult for him to see what the relationship was between the ideal of his imagination and the reality of life. And it was just here that More paused—he completed neither the English nor the Latin versions of his history. The sticking point may well have been his perception of the intractability of real politics. For if it was hard for him to see how the ideal of Utopia could be applied to real life, it must have been equally difficult for him to see how the grim realities of history could be made to serve the good life. Certainly, More had no illusions about an easy assimilation of the two. We have seen that in *Utopia* neither More nor Hythloday ever argues for the immediate application of high principle to real life; and both agree that the obstacle is human nature and desire. How far then could a realistic portrayal of the wicked life be helpful? "History," Sidney was to point out later, "being captivated to the truth of a foolish world, is many times a terror from well-doing, and an encouragement to unbridled wickedness." Not all tyrants got their due.[60] Of course, Richard did; but what about the successful, and unprincipled, Henry VII?[61] With something like that in mind, More may well have hesitated.

It is possible then that More's commitment to a realistic history was inhibited by his perception of political reality in much the same way that his idealism was hampered by his sense of what was practical. To be sure, there were some advantages to this dichotomy. *Utopia* gains in plausibility from its close attention to the details of ordinary life, even while we suspect its practicality. More's *Richard III* earns its moral stature, despite its close attention to the details of the king's wicked politics, by forecasting a just end. More's history is not impressive for its fidelity, but it is startlingly original in its lifelike descriptions, lengthy speeches, and splendid dialogues, few of which could have been authorized by the sources. In truth, the *History of Richard III* is almost as much fiction as it is history, though it is a fiction imagined as though it had happened that way.[62] Here again More

60. *Defense* in Sidney, *Works*, 3, p. 18. So too Sylvester in More, *Works*, 2, p. ciii.

61. More fell afoul of Henry VII toward the end of his reign and may well have hesitated before celebrating him as a moral agent. Roper tells the story of More's unpleasant encounter with the king, *Lyfe*, pp. 7–8. When Henry died, More wrote a Latin poem rejoicing at the end of slavery; see Richard Marius, *Thomas More: A Biography* (New York, 1985), pp. 51–52.

62. "It is questionable whether More regarded himself as writing history; his story is more like a drama . . . for which fidelity to historical fact is scarcely relevant." A. R. Myers, *History Today* 4 (1955), p. 515. See also A. F. Pollard, "The Making of Sir Thomas More's *Richard III*," in *Essential Articles*, pp. 421–35; L. F. Dean, "Literary Problems in More's *Richard III*," in idem, pp. 315–25; Alison Hanham, *Richard III and the Historians* (Oxford, 1975), pp. 163, 166–68.

was helped by classical precedent, for in ancient times historians had employed classical rhetoric for similar purposes and without embarrassment—thereby deliberately fudging the distinction between poetry and history.[63] Sidney repeats the received tradition when he points out that "a feigned example hath as much force to teach as a true example (for as to move, it is clear, since the feigned may be tuned to the highest key of passion.")[64]

Indeed, it looks as though More understood that the rumor and hearsay that he reports were not by eyewitnesses, and that the speeches and descriptions which fill his work were therefore not the literal truth.[65] But the moral value of his story, the dissuasive effect of a bad example, seems (for the moment, anyway) to have overcome whatever scruples he might have had, and his history is more like Hythloday's utopia than he dared to admit. Had he wished to use his history for a more practical purpose, as a guide to success in actual politics—as did Machiavelli, or his later English disciple, Francis Bacon—he must have written it differently, more realistically. More knew the world well enough and without illusions, but he had no desire to submit to it. If he did not finish writing his history, it may have been the result of immediate circumstances;[66] but he may also have found it unsatisfactory for his purpose. (He was eventually to disavow *Utopia* also, when it seemed unsuitable.) By 1516, the radical disjunction between his moral ideals and his perceptions of the real world had begun to oppress him, and he preferred to take flight in fancy, not history, knowing full well that it made a difference, and asking his readers to share that difference with him. As long as he remained in such a humor, realistic history with its emphasis on the wickedness of human behavior, could hardly be expected to provide much solace. In this respect at least, fiction clearly had all the advantage.

4

Burckhardt is no longer in fashion today and the "problem of the Renaissance" has largely been dismissed from the textbooks, having long ago out-

---

63. Critical historiography did not develop by imitating the ancients, but by recovering them through the invention of the methods of philology and archaeology. Here it is Erasmus who might have taught More. See chap. 2 below.

64. Sidney, *Works*, 3, p. 17; cf. Thomas Wilson, *The Arte of Rhetorique* (London, 1553), pp. 101v, 104.

65. See Alistair Fox, *Politics and Literature in the Reigns of Henry VII and Henry VIII* (Oxford, 1989), pp. 125–26.

66. *Richard III* ends in the English version with Morton encouraging Henry, duke of Buckingham, to rebellion against Richard III. In 1514, the son, Edward, duke of Buckingham, became Henry VIII's heir; by 1521, he was accused of treason and executed. The parallel may well have occurred to More and given him pause. See *Utopia*, 4, lxix; Hanham, *Richard III*, pp. 188–89.

lived its usefulness.[67] Among other things, aggrieved medievalists have properly restored the manifold achievements of the ten lost centuries after antiquity that Burckhardt seemed to deny, as well as the many anticipations of what had once seemed so original to the Renaissance.[68] It was, in any case, never easy to see how Burckhardt could have relevance to an English scene which was so thoroughly different in setting from Italy, so much further removed from antiquity, and so much more obviously continuous with everything medieval. Yet there is a sense in which Thomas More can be seen as a perfect Burckhardtian prototype, as startling and unprecedented in his setting as any in the great gallery of Italian Renaissance originals.

No part of Burckhardt's work has caused so much distress as that passage at the beginning of the second part of his book where he gives the fullest description of what he takes to be the essential character of the Renaissance. He has already described the new political situation in Italy which generated the mentality that (for the first time since antiquity) saw the state as a "work of art," that is, as an object of reflection and calculation. Now he says that during the Middle Ages, "both sides of the human consciousness—that which was turned within as that which was turned without—lay dreaming or half awake beneath a common veil." It was in Italy, during the Renaissance, that this veil was first lifted and "an *objective* treatment and consideration of the state and of all things in the world became possible," while at the same time a *subjective* understanding of the individual also developed.[69] The proposition is so ambitious and so general (so Hegelian despite Burckhardt's disclaimers) that it has even troubled some of his admirers.[70] Yet it makes sudden sense when applied to the Thomas More of *Utopia,* not only in the obvious way that his work displays an objective treatment of the state, but in the open subjectivity of the author who is accessible to us as no previous Englishman. More's dialogue with himself is as unprecedented in English literature as is his deliberate "self-fashioning."[71] And this is attested to by his son-in-law's remarkable biography, the

67. But see William Kerrigan and Gordon Braden, *The Idea of the Renaissance* (Baltimore, 1989), pp. 11–13.

68. The result is a long Middle Ages that purports to last at least until 1789; see Jacques Le Goff, *Time, Work, and Culture in the Middle Ages,* trans. Arthur Goldhammer (Chicago, 1977), pp. ix–xi.

69. Jacob Burckhardt, *The Civilization of the Renaissance in Italy,* trans. S. G. C. Middlemore (London, 1955), part 2, paragraph 2, p. 81.

70. See Sir Ernst Gombrich, "In Search of Cultural History," *Ideals and Idols* (Oxford, 1979), p. 43; Hans Baron, "The Limits of the Notion of Renaissance Individualism: Burckhardt after a Century," *Search,* II, pp. 155–81.

71. I refer of course to Stephen Greenblatt, *Renaissance Self-Fashioning from More to Shakespeare* (Chicago, 1980). Greenblatt defines the term as "an increased self-consciousness about the fashioning of human identity as a manipulable, artful process," p. 2; he indicates his own debt to Burckhardt on his first page and again, pp. 161–62. Greenblatt see More's *Utopia* as

portraits by Holbein, and by other contemporary sources, which manage
somehow to describe and display the interiority of More's life as though under the influence of his public introspection.[72] His self-deprecating sense
of humor may be unique in its time and has lost nothing through the passage of the centuries. Next to him, his predecessors and most of his contemporaries, remain two-dimensional.

What I am suggesting then is that More's originality, his modernity, rests
on his self-consciousness; and that his self-consciousness allowed him to
separate himself from his contemporary world and view it objectively, even
while he remained self-absorbed within his own soul. He was probably the
first person in England to explore the tension between the real and the
ideal, and thus between history and fiction, in a way that is still interesting
to us. He is, in Burckhardt's terms, the first English Renaissance individual.
But as the first of his kind he lived apart from other men, cut off from his
contemporaries and thoroughly uncomfortable in his time. We can read
him as a harbinger of things to come but we should not exaggerate his
modernity. It is only when the social and cultural scene shifts sufficiently to
turn everything medieval into anachronism that More's precocious self-
consciousness will become general and everyone will think of keeping a diary and writing an autobiography. But by then, paradoxically, *Utopia* will
have turned itself into a classic and appear to have values that are timeless,
even though its own argument can probably best be understood and
appreciated by retrieving the peculiar circumstances of its original composition.

"the perfect expression of his self-conscious role-playing and an intense meditation upon its
limits," p. 33. So far, at least, we agree, though I doubt that Greenblatt or any of the "new his-
toricists" would be very comfortable with my distinction between history and fiction.

72. Even Utopian music reflects this new inwardness. According to E. E. Lowinsky, "one of
the basic tenets of the Renaissance [was] that the true function of music is to express in tones
the inner world of man. And while this ideal originated in vocal music, it was an Englishman
who, at the beginning of the century, foresaw its application to instrumental music." "English
Organ Music of the Renaissance," *Musical Quarterly,* 39 (1953), p. 542; More, *Utopia,* pp. 236
and note. Huizinga had already noticed this example in "Realism," p. 300. For More's meticulous observation of living things, see Erasmus's portrait in his letter to Ulrich von Hutten,
July 23, 1519, *Opus Ep.,* 4, pp. 12–23. For Holbein's remarkable portraits of More and his family, see David Piper, "Hans Holbein the Younger in England," *Journal of the Royal Society of Arts,*
111 (1963), pp. 736–55; Stanley Morison, *The Likenesses of Thomas More* (London, 1963).

CHAPTER TWO

Erasmus and the Problem
of the Johannine Comma

1

When Edward Gibbon decided to banish primary causes from the *Decline and Fall* and integrate secular and ecclesiastical history, he was completing a revolution that had begun unwittingly two centuries before.[1] To bring into his narrative of empire a consideration of the Johannine comma (the biblical phrase 1 John 5:7) was not perhaps either digressive or inevitable, but it would certainly have surprised and dismayed some of Gibbon's immediate predecessors, like the Catholic Frenchmen Bossuet and Tillemont, each of whom had written about his subject and exercised an important effect on him at different times in his life.[2] And it would have seemed even more incomprehensible to earlier generations. Something had happened in the two centuries between Erasmus and Gibbon to make this new vantage point possible and congenial.

It was, I think, nothing less than a victory for the idea of history. At the beginning of the sixteenth century, theology still ruled as queen of the sciences and the claims of religion were largely justified by an appeal to reason and authority, that is to Aristotelian logic and the dictates of the church. By the end of the eighteenth century, theology had become dependent on history, and religion was now justified by an appeal to "matter of fact."[3] Even

---

1. See Momigliano, *Studies in Historiography* (New York, 1966), p. 52; David Womersley, *The Transformation of the Decline and Fall* (Cambridge, 1988), pp. 125–26.

2. The biblical phrase (1 John 5:7) has now disappeared from most texts. In the King James version it reads: "For there are three that bear record in Heaven; the Father, the Word, and the Holy Ghost: and these Three are One." The best short discussion is Raymond E. Brown, *Epistles of John* (New York, 1982), app. 4, pp. 775–87.

3. I hope to publish an extended treatment of the subject, entitled provisionally *The Trial of the Witnesses: History and Religion from Ralegh to Gibbon.*

such mysteries as the doctrine of the Trinity, which had eluded the reason of St. Thomas and the schoolmen and had remained dependent on the dictates of church councils from Chalcedon to Trent, had come now to depend in some fashion on the evidence of Scripture considered as history. At the same time, the removal of final causes from the narrative of human events threatened to leave it—with every other Christian doctrine and event—to the arbitrament of ordinary scholarship. Gibbon brings us to the edge of religious modernity, and the history of the comma exactly spans the period of that development. It was Erasmus, however, as Gibbon himself suspected, who had first set some of the key problems, which he and his enlightened friends believed they had solved.

For Erasmus, the decision to edit the Greek New Testament was the result of an early commitment to Renaissance humanism, and a response in particular to several lively currents in the contemporary intellectual scene. On the one hand, Erasmus, encouraged perhaps by his new friend John Colet, began to think of the Bible principally as a record of history, rather than as an arsenal of theological texts, above all as the story of Christ on earth—Christ as the supreme exemplar to be followed and imitated. Apparently, he had been well prepared for this by his acquaintance with the Brothers of the Common Life, and by a characteristic humanist distaste for logic and metaphysics—and a preference for rhetoric and history—which he displayed in all his early writing.[4] It seems to have been Colet's Lectures on the New Testament that encouraged his view that Paul and the apostles, if not Christ himself, were best understood in their historical setting and that their message was primarily ethical.[5] In effect, the churchman Colet and the wandering monk Erasmus wanted to place Christian responsibility back in the hands of the laity, in the conscience and behavior of the Christian believer, rather than in what they took to be the mechanical observances of church ritual. And this required that the Bible be placed at the very center of worship, in the hands of every man (and woman), accessible and intelligible as the Vulgate was not, and read in the first place for its story. There were others on the Continent who

4. See Eugene F. Rice, Jr., "Erasmus and the Religious Tradition, 1495–99," *Renaissance Essays,* ed. Paul O. Kristeller and Philip P. Wiener (New York, 1968), pp. 162–86. Recently R. R. Post has tried to underplay the influence of the Brethren on Erasmus against the older interpretations; see *The Modern Devotion: Confrontation with Reformation and Humanism* (Leiden, 1968), pp. 1–12, 658–73.

5. This is essentially the view that was elaborated in the classical treatments of Seebohm, Lupton, and Allen, and by most students since. Recently, however, John Gleason has argued against the notion; preferring to give the credit to Erasmus as an influence on Colet; see his *John Colet* (Berkeley, 1989).

shared the same impulse—which, of course, the Protestant Reformation was also to endorse.[6]

Secondly, Erasmus was encouraged to his work by his accidental discovery of Lorenzo Valla's notes on the New Testament.[7] He had already pledged himself to the culture of Italian humanism, to its determination to recover the Greek and Latin texts of classical antiquity and put them to use by imitation. Valla was the master of humanist technique, the greatest philologist of his time. He understood better than any contemporary the historicity of language and the need to place it in a cultural context in order for it to be understood. Erasmus twice paraphrased and eventually published the *Elegantiae,* the great grammar in which Valla had examined the uses of classical Latin and discriminated the changing varieties of its expression.[8] And he knew Valla's treatise on the *Donation of Constantine* in which he had laid out the linguistic and historical anachronisms of that famous forgery. For Valla, grammar was the supreme science, or at least the indispensable preliminary that was required for understanding any writing, and hence any doctrine—including such technical terms as *persona* and *substantia* in the doctrine of the Trinity.[9] In these crucial matters, the philologist was above the theologian, who was necessarily dependent on him. It was not enough to accept the authority of tradition. Nevertheless, it took some daring to think of applying these lessons to that greatest of all the ancient texts, the Greek New Testament, and subject it to ordinary philological scrutiny.[10]

6. For Erasmus's reform views, see the *Enchiridion* (1503, and the second edition of 1518, with the letter to Paul Volz); and for the hope to put the Bible in every hand, the *Paraclesis* (1516). Both are conveniently available in *Christian Humanism and the Reformation,* trans. John C. Olin (New York, 1965), pp. 92–106, 107–33.

7. See Jacques Chomarat, "Les *Annotations* de Valla, celles d'Erasme et la Grammaire," *Histoire de l'exégèse au xvie siècle* (Geneva, 1978), pp. 202–28. Erasmus's discovery is described in a letter to Christopher Fisher, (c. March) 1505, *The Collected Works of Erasmus,* in progress at the University of Tornoto (hereafter abbreviated as *CWE*), 2: no. 182, pp. 89–97.

8. Erasmus first abridged the work before 1500 for his pupil, Christopher Fisher, and published it eventually in 1529. The revision of 1531 went through forty editions in the next twenty years; *Opus Epistolarum,* ed. P. S. Allen, 12 vols. (Oxford, 1906–58) (hereafter abbreviated as Allen), 1:108n. The text is given in the *Opera Omnia,* 1–4 (Amsterdam, 1973), pp. 191–351; the preface to the second edition (1531) by Allen, no. 2416, 9: pp. 98–99. See E. Garin, "Erasmo e l'Umanesimo italiano," *Giornale critico della Filologica italiano,* 50 (1971), pp. 1–13; A. Renaudet, *Erasme et l'Italie* (Geneva, 1954).

9. See Salvatore Camporeale, *Lorenzo Valla Umanesimo e teologia* (Florence, 1972), pp. 236–37, 277–43; Mario Fois, *Il pensiero cristiano di Lorenzo Valla nel quadro storico-culturale del suo ambiente* (Rome, 1969), pp. 535–46. For Valla on the *Donation,* see my article in *Humanism and History* (Ithaca, 1987), pp. 54–72.

10. See besides Camporeale, S. Garofalo, "Gli umanisti italiani del secolo xv e la Biblia," *La biblia e il concilio di Trento* (Rome, 1947), pp. 338–75. There are two versions of Valla's text:

For Valla, the aim then was to recover the original intention of the author by situating the work in a full context of history, culture, classical usage, and so on, by attending to its *doctrina* and *eloquentia,* as well as to its grammar and paleography. Erasmus understood this at once.[11] He was convinced, he wrote to Colet in 1504, that literary studies were impossible without Greek. "It is one thing to guess, another to judge; one thing to trust your own eyes, another to trust someone else's."[12] Like all the humanists and Christian reformers, he was obsessed by what he perceived to be the disparity between past and present. "In all my work," he wrote later, "my sole object has been to resuscitate the humanities, which lay almost dead and buried among my own people; secondly, to arouse a world . . . to a new zeal for the true religion of the Gospel; and finally to recall to its sources in Holy Scripture the academic theology of our universities."[13]

With Valla Erasmus saw that the restoration of antiquity, and the imitation of the past, depended on retrieving it exactly, and from Valla and the humanists he learned how to attempt this. It was first necessary to master the original languages, discover the early texts, collate them, and try to restore the originals. The work could be very tedious: examining the old manuscripts again and again, comparing, pondering, judging. "You waste your eyesight on decaying volumes covered with mould, torn and mangled, eaten into everywhere by worms and beetles, and often almost illegible." But only then could the true message of the past be recovered. Faith alone was not enough.[14] If Valla had pointed out the way for both the secu-

---

Erasmus's edition, the *Adnotationes,* which he brought out in 1505, and an earlier version, recently edited by Alessandro Perosa, *Collatio Novi Testamenti* (Florence, 1970). Valla had already commented suggestively on the text of Scripture in the *Elegantiae;* see Chomarat, "Annotations," pp. 203–8.

11. As early as 1500, in the *Adagia,* Erasmus disparaged those who presumed to discourse on theology without knowledge of the original languages, entering the temple with "unwashed feet." See also the important letter of Erasmus about the necessity of learning the languages for the study of Scripture, written apparently in the spring of 1501 to the Abbot of St. Bertin, *CWE,* no. 149, 2: 24–27.

12. Erasmus to Colet, (c. Dec.) 1504, *CWE,* no. 181, 1: 85–89.

13. Erasmus to Arkleb of Boskovice, *CWE,* no. 1183, 8: 149–53. How far the classical and Christian revivals could coincide was, and remains, a vexed question. Huizinga believed that the amalgamation of the two in Erasmus was not complete and that the Christian element always took precedence; *Erasmus of Rotterdam,* trans. Barbara Flower (1924, reprinted New York, 1952), pp. 102–3.

14. See the famous argument between Erasmus and Colet in 1499; Gleason, *John Colet* pp. 95–105; and John B. Tracy, "Humanists among the Scholastics: Erasmus, More, and Lefevre d'Etaples on the Humanity of Christ," *Erasmus of Rotterdam Yearbook,* 5 (1985), pp. 37–42. Erasmus complains about the Herculean labor required in collecting and editing, in the adage *Herculei labores* (1508); see *The Adages: A Study with Translations,* Margaret Mann Phillips (Cambridge, 1964), pp. 197–99.

lar and Christian classics, everything remained still to be done—not least for the New Testament and the early church.

Of course, the Middle Ages was not altogether indifferent to the problems and techniques of biblical criticism.[15] For example, at the monastery of Windesheim, the brothers prepared a Bible early in the fifteenth century in which (according to their chronicler), "they attempted to reduce all the original books of the Old and New Testaments to the text as translated by Jerome from Hebrew into Latin." They procured codices from various libraries—one all the way from Paris—and discovered the variants. One of these codices was a great Bible from the Knights of the Templars, which they believed had been "compiled from the library of Jerome" himself. They saw the value of old manuscripts over new (but not apparently the value of the Greek) and made many corrections; but once they had settled the text, they would allow no further changes. Their "mixture of scholarly sense and naivety" was typically medieval, and their motive was more to establish a uniform text for their chapter than to recover the original. In all this they can be compared usefully to Erasmus, who may even have known their work.[16]

It was inevitable that Erasmus should find a better precedent directly in St. Jerome.[17] The scholar saint appealed to Erasmus on many grounds, not least because of his great labor at making the Bible accessible to *his* generation by the translation of the Vulgate version that was still in use. He too had insisted on returning to the fountainhead, to the Greek and Hebrew originals, and he too had fearlessly corrected the Latin text against tradition.[18] Erasmus's preference for Jerome over St. Augustine, and his deliberate choice of that side of the ancient rivalry, was the natural result of his choice of grammar over theology, and this indeed was to be the same

15. See Beryl Smalley, *The Study of the Bible in the Middle Ages* (Notre Dame, 1964), and the first volume of the *Cambridge History of the Bible: From Jerome to the Renaissance,* ed. G. W. H. Lampe (Cambridge, 1963).

16. Post, *The Modern Devotion,* pp. 305–8. For the lack of an exact philology and historical sense during the Middle Ages, see P. C. Spicq, *Esquisse d'un Histoire de l'Exégèse Latine au Moyen Age* (Paris, 1944), p. 374.

17. Erasmus to the Abbot of St. Bertin, *CWE,* no. 149, 2: 24–27, ll. 72–73. In general, see John C. Olin, "Erasmus and St. Jerome: The Close Bond and Its Significance," *Erasmus of Rotterdam Society Yearbook,* 7 (1987), pp. 33–53.

18. See Bruce Metzger, "St. Jerome's Explicit References to Variant Readings in Manuscripts of the New Testament," in *Text and Interpretation,* ed. E. Best and R. Wilson (Cambridge, 1979), pp. 88–103; H. F. D. Sparks, "Jerome as Biblical Scholar," *Cambridge History of the Bible,* 1: 510–41; K. K. Hulley, "Principles of Textual Criticism Known to St. Jerome," *Harvard Studies in Classical Philology,* 55 (1944), pp. 87–109; Werner Schwarz, *Principles and Problems of Biblical Translation: Some Reformation Controversies and their Background* (Cambridge, 1955), pp. 27–36. Jerome even expressed a willingness to correct the apostles.

ground of the resistance to his labors, as it had been when Augustine objected to the work of Jerome. Erasmus had seen it coming when he published Valla's *Annotations*. The theologians, he wrote there, "will say that it is an intolerable insolence that the grammarian, having molested all the other disciplines, does not restrain his impudent pen from Sacred Scripture." But who else was competent to translate the Bible? In these matters, Jethro was clearly superior to Moses. The theologians might reply that exegesis depended entirely on the inspiration of the Holy Spirit, but how was one to explain the undoubted errors in the text that Jerome himself had had to correct?[19]

And so Erasmus persisted in his great work of making the Bible accessible in a correct modern version. He undertook to revise the Latin Vulgate, just as Jerome had once revised the Old Latin version, using the original Greek to help him.[20] He bolstered his edition of the New Testament with an edition of the works and letters of Jerome to help give it credibility. His great task in the latter was to separate the many spurious attributions from the genuine, to determine and as far as possible to eliminate the inconsistencies, implausibilities, and anachronisms that had accumulated over the centuries and obscured the original.[21] (Almost simultaneously, Erasmus was doing the same for the pagan Seneca.)[22] The life of Jerome that he af-

19. Erasmus to Christopher Fisher (c. March, 1505), *CWE*, no. 182, 2: 89–97. I quote from the translation in Heiko Obermann, *Forerunners of the Reformation* (New York, 1966), pp. 308–14. See, too, Erasmus's defense of Valla in his note to the Acts of the Apostles in his new Testament (in *Opera Omnia*, ed. Jean Le Clerc, 10 vols., Leiden, 1703–6, cited hereafter as LB; see LB 6: 519 D–E n. 11). In his reply to Poggio, Valla made the distinction between his corrections of the Vulgate, which was only a translation, and the original in Greek and Hebrew, for which he declared a proper reverence. Erasmus owned a copy of the *Antidotum in Poggium*. See Jacques Chomarat, "Les *Annotations* de Valla, Celles d'Erasme et la Grammaire," *Histoire de l'exégèse au xvie siècle* (Geneva, 1978), pp. 202–28; Jean-Claude Margolin, "The Epistle to the Romans (Chapter 11) According to the Versions and/or Commentaries of Valla, Colet, Levevre and Erasmus," in *The Bible in the Sixteenth Century*, ed. David Steinmetz (Durham, 1990), p. 151.

20. H. J. de Jonge has argued cogently that Eramus's first intention was simply an improved Vulgate, and that the idea of adding the Greek followed afterward. It is wrong therefore to think of it as simply or largely an edition of the Greek New Testament. Nevertheless, it is clear that Erasmus understood from the outset the necessity of employing the evidence of the Greek manuscripts for that purpose, and the need to collate the manuscripts in order to use them. See De Jonge, "*Novum Testamentum a Nobis Versum:* The Essence of Erasmus's Edition of the New Testament," *Journal of Theological Studies*, n.s. 35 (1984), pp. 394–413; "The Date and Purpose of Erasmus's *Castigatio novi Testamenti:* A Note on the Origins of the *Novum Testamentum*," in *Uses of Greek and Latin*, pp. 97–110.

21. Erasmus summarizes his efforts in letters to Cardinal Raffaele Riario and Domenico Grimani, 1515, *CWE*, no. 333–44, 2: 89, 96–98.

22. See the preface to Erasmus's edition of Seneca's *Lucubrationes* (Basle, 1515), in *CWE*, no. 325, 3: 63–68; and the letter of Robert Aldridge explaining how he went about making collations for a later edition of that work; Aldridge to Erasmus, c. Dec. 1526, Allen, no. 1766,

fixed to the letters was a brilliant recreation of the saint in his historical setting, rescued from medieval hagiography, and portrayed as a scholar in the
service of the church.[23]

It had taken a long time for Erasmus to learn Greek, but only a little while
for him to collect the New Testament manuscripts and edit them into shape.
By 1514, he could report that he had revised the whole Greek text from a collation of manuscripts and annotated over a thousand places, "with some
benefit," he hoped, to the theologians.[24] The printer Froeben may have
caught wind of a similar project in Spain, and the work was hurried into print
at Basle in 1516. It consisted of the Greek text and the Latin Vulgate in parallel, copious notes and commentary, and some extensive prefatory material (a *Paraclesis, Methodus,* and *Apologia*) explaining and justifying the
work.[25] But Erasmus was still not satisfied and almost immediately embarked on a second improved edition in which the annotations were to be
completely revised, a long essay offered to explain his method, and an improved Latin translation to replace the Vulgate.[26] The colophon dates the
completion of the work in March 1519. Eventually, Erasmus was to bring out
three further editions during his lifetime, each improved by further study.[27]

6: 433–36. For Erasmus as an editor, see L. D. Reynolds and N. G. Wilson, *Scribes and Scholars,*
2d ed. (Oxford, 1974), pp. 142–46, 240–41; Jacques Chomarat, *Grammaire et rhetorique chez
Erasmus,* 2 vols. (Paris, 1981).

23. See Eugene F. Rice, *St. Jerome in the Renaissance* (Baltimore, 1985), p. 124; Myron
Gilmore, "*Fides et Eruditio,* Erasmus and the Study of History," *Teachers of History,* ed. H. Stuart
Hughes (Ithaca, 1954), p. 25; John B. McGuire "Erasmus' Biographical Masterpiece: *Hi-
eronymi Stridonensis Vita,*" *Renaissance Quarterly,* 26 (1973), pp. 265–73. The text is given in
Erasmus, *Opuscula,* ed. Wallace Ferguson (The Hague, 1933), pp. 125–90.

24. Erasmus to Servatius Rogerus, July 8, 1514, *CWE,* no. 300, 2: 295–303, ll. 164–66. He
had also finished his Jerome, and "slain with daggers the spurious or interpolated passages,"
idem, ll. 162–63. For further collations and other delays, continued even while the work was
printing, see Jerry Bentley, *Humanists and Holy Writ: New Testament Scholarship in the Renaissance* (Princeton, 1983), pp. 117–21, who relies on letters to Colet and others.

25. *Novum Instrumentum* (Basel, 1516). There is a modern facsimile by Heinz Holeczek
(Stuttgart, 1986). The prefatory material was edited separately by Hajo Holborn, in Erasmus's
Ausgewahlte Werke (Munich, 1930); there is a facsimile edited by Robert Peters (Menston,
1970). The *Paraclesis* found an early English translation by Robert Wyer, *An Exhortacion to the
dylygent Study of Scripture* (1540). For the circumstances of the original publication—edited
Erasmus says, "swiftly but truly"—see Allen, headnote to no. 384, 2: 181–84. The reasons for
the title, which was changed to the traditional *Novum Testamentum* in later editions, are explained by Erasmus to Robert Aldridge in a letter of August 23, 1527, Allen, no. 1858, 7: 140.

26. According to Thomas More, William Latimer thought Erasmus had been too scrupulous (*religiosior*) in his revision of the Vulgate and wished he would alter the Latin more drastically. More encouraged him to supply suggestions; More to Erasmus, Oct. 31, 1516, *CWE,*
no. 481, 4: 114–17. Here was further reason for Erasmus to supply a completely new Latin version; but More warned him that others would be less enthusiastic.

27. 1522, 1527, 1535. The last is the one printed in Jean LeClerc's edition of the *Opera Omnia,* LB 6. It used to be thought that Erasmus's Latin translation had been prepared many

Erasmus dedicated his work to Pope Leo X. The greatest hope of restoring the Christian religion, he wrote to his patron, was to turn directly to the word of Christ in Scripture. "I perceived that the teaching which is our salvation was to be had in a much purer and more lively form if sought at the fountain-head and drawn from the actual sources than from pools and runnels." As a result, he told the pope, he had revised the whole New Testament with the aid of the Greek original, employing a number of old manuscripts in both languages. He had also turned to the fathers for their quotations and comments to help him correct the text. His annotations were intended to show the reader exactly what changes he had made and why, and to disentangle everything that was obscure or difficult.[28] In his introduction to the annotations, he explained again how he had tried for accuracy in returning to the fountainhead and collating the manuscripts (two of which he borrowed from John Colet). Wherever there was a difficulty or ambiguity, he had tried to restore the original reading, always presenting the evidence and leaving the final decision to the reader. If that meant struggling over minutiae, it was just those "thorny details" that had so often led the theologians astray. In themselves the philological facts might be rubble, but it was on rubble that the whole great edifice must stand. It was on the letter of Scripture, Erasmus maintained, on its historical sense, that all interpretation had to rest, exactly as Jerome had said.[29]

Erasmus used manuscripts from Britain, from Basle, and from the Low Countries, but he describes them only vaguely. In the *apologia,* he says he used four manuscripts for the first edition, and five for the second, and he referred to still others in his annotations.[30] The printing press, still so new to the world, afforded an opportunity to fix the text and make it available

---

years before this, but Andrew Brown has argued successfully that the manuscript version that survives was actually transcribed from the 1519 version rather than preceding it; "The Date of Erasmus' Latin Translation of the New Testament," *Cambridge Bibliographical Society Transactions,* 3 (1984), pp. 351–80.

28. Preface to the *Novum Instrumentum,* trans. in *CWE,* no. 384, 3: 216–24.

29. Preface to the Reader, trans. in *CWE,* no. 200, 3: 195–205. Erasmus did not deny the other (allegorical) senses, especially the tropological (moral), but he always emphasized the literal and tried to circumscribe the rest; *Methodus,* in Holborn, *Ausgewahlte Werke,* pp. 157–58. See Jerry H. Bentley, "Erasmus' *Annotationes in Novum Testamentum* and the Textual Tradition of the Gospels," *Archiv für Reformationsgeschichte,* 67 (1976), pp. 33–53. If there is movement in Erasmus's thought it is away from allegory (as in the early *Enchiridion*), and from the influence of Origen, toward the more plainly historical; Erasmus's fullest statement is in the *Ecclesiastes* (1535). See J. B. Payne, "The Hermeneutics of Erasmus," *Scrinium Erasmianum,* ed. J. Coppens (Leiden, 1969), 2: 13–49, esp. 25, 35–49; and Chomarat, 1: 568–85. Manfred Hoffmann tries to harmonize the relationship between Erasmian history and allegory in *Rhetoric and Theology: The Hermeneutic of Erasmus* (Toronto, 1994).

30. Holborn, *Ausgewahlte Werke,* p. 166; Bentley, *Humanists,* p. 125. Erasmus describes them only as *vetustissimus simul et emendatissimus.*

for collective scrutiny in a way impossible before, and Erasmus understood the opportunity better than most. Each medieval manuscript was unique and individual, whereas each printed copy was pretty much the same as any other. It was possible now to transform the manuscripts into printed texts and so furnish copies that could be worked upon in collaboration. Erasmus worked quickly (perhaps too quickly) here as elsewhere, on Jerome and the New Testament, and on many editions that followed of pagan classics and Christian fathers, content perhaps to think that they were bound to be improved in time. But he did not, could not yet, realize the full implications of a process that was to turn out to be vastly more complicated, laborious—and incomplete—than he imagined. It was after all only the beginning of modern philology.[31]

When Erasmus arrived in Basle, he was given several local manuscripts to use. He seems to have relied principally on one of these, which he corrected with a second, both of which are still extant and are now thought to be of the twelfth century or later. He inked his corrections directly onto the manuscript, which he sent directly to the printer.[32] Erasmus is usually accused of having chosen his text badly and overlooked the best codex in Basle, although this is not so clear and is anyway anachronistic, since it is hard to see just how he could have made a proper decision then.[33] None of his manuscripts contained the Book of Revelation, so he borrowed another from his friend Johann Reuchlin, who was then working on the Old Testament. Erasmus thought that it was so old that it must have been written in apostolic times, though it is now believed to come from the twelfth century.[34] On discovering that it lacked the final verses, Erasmus promptly supplied them by retranslating them from the Latin into Greek. (In 1527, to be sure, he restored the Greek from the Spanish Polyglot.) For the Vul-

31. See especially P. S. Allen, "Erasmus's Services to Learning," from the *Proceedings of the British Academy* (1925), reprinted in *Erasmus: Lectures and Wayfaring Sketches* (Oxford, 1934), pp. 30–59. There is a full list of Erasmus's editorial labors in Chomarat, 1: 452–79.

32. See the headnote to Allen, no. 373, 2: 164–66; and K. W. Clark, "Observations on the Erasmian Notes in Codex 2," *Texte und Untersuchungen zur Geschichte der altchristlichen Literatur,* 73 (1959), pp. 749–56; Bentley, *Humanists,* p. 127. Basil Hall, following Allen, assigns them to the fifteenth century, "Erasmus: Biblical Scholar and Reformer," in *Erasmus,* ed. T. A. Dorey (London, 1970), p. 96.

33. There is still no agreement about how Erasmus employed these manuscripts, or why he gave preference to one over the other. Needless to say, he did not yet know how to date or relate them. See Bentley's, "Erasmus' *Annotations,*" pp. 33–36, with citations to the literature.

34. See the note to Allen, no. 373, 2: 165. Erasmus's note was to Revelations 3:7, added in the 1527 ed., LB 6: 1097–98. When afterwards Erasmus was editing St. Augustine, he referred again to some manuscripts which he thought must have been written in Augustine's time but were undoubtedly much later; see the preface to *De Civitate Dei* (1522), Allen, no. 1309, 5: 119n; and *CWE,* no. 1309, 9: 170.

gate also, he used a variety of manuscripts, but as we have seen he preferred to print his own translation in 1519.

The point of the whole exercise was to recover the original as far as possible and to correct and explain the Vulgate so that Scripture could play its fundamental role in teaching true religion.[35] The problem was thus textual before it was exegetical, although it was not always possible to separate the two, and indeed Erasmus swiftly became aware of the "philological circle" (by which the part informs the whole and the whole the part). In the preface to the *Novum Instrumentum*, Erasmus points out that "those who narrate the sense are often forced to unfold the meaning of words: in the same way we are sometimes forced to lay open the full contents of the sentences while we busy ourselves with the unfolding of words."[36] In a larger sense, Erasmus assumed (with everyone else) that the meaning of Scripture must be essentially self-consistent even if the scriptural reporters were not always so, and he tried therefore to harmonize apparent anomalies.[37] This preconception made it difficult for him to arrive at a completely historical criticism, although his achievement was startling enough to his contemporaries. Revelation in Scripture might be self-consistent, but it was confined to matters of faith and salvation, although even there one could spot a development from the Old Testament to the New.

To some extent (like his master, Jerome) Erasmus was willing to humanize the text, that is, to see it as the result of fallible human efforts, even though the underlying message remained necessarily beyond history in the will and intentions of God. "All that is in Scripture," Erasmus wrote in one annotation, "is spiritual, because taught by the same spirit."[38] Yet it was not for us to dictate how the Holy Spirit used his disciples. "He was present in them so far as pertained to the business of the Gospel, but with this limitation, that in other respects he allowed them to be human none the less."[39] Thus Paul's language, like the language of Moses and the prophets, was adapted to the specific needs of the historical moment, and could only be understood so, though Paul's ultimate message was eternal and not his own.[40]

35. See the letter of Erasmus to Antonio Pucci, soliciting papal patronage for the revised edition of the New Testament, August 26, 1518, *CWE*, no. 860, 6: 96–98. The *methodus* of the first edition was enlarged as a *ratio* for the second, a "method" Erasmus explains in the title, *perveniendi ad veram theologiam;* see Holborn, *Ausgewahlte Werke*, p. 175.

36. See Schwarz, *Principles and Problems*, p. 152. Some helpful instances of Erasmus's exegesis, with a comparison of the various editions, are give by C. A. L. Jarrott, "Erasmus' Biblical Humanism," *Studies in the Renaissance*, 17 (1970), pp. 119–52.

37. In this respect Bainton finds Erasmus and Luther exactly alike; *Erasmus*, p. 191.

38. To Matthew 34: 23; LB 6: 125–C–D. See Chomarat, 1: 576.

39. Erasmus to Johann Eck, May 15, 1518, *CWE*, no. 844, 6: 844.

40. See the preface to Erasmus's *Paraphrasis ad Romanos* (1517), the first of his paraphrases on the Bible, *CWE*, no. 710, 5: 195–99. In his next paraphrase (to Corinthians, 1519), he com-

For the while, Erasmus followed Valla in thinking of the Greek as the basis for the Latin and the chief guide to its correct meaning. If anything, he was more interested than Valla in the Greek than the Latin, and his work extended far beyond that of his predecessor, who had provided only a few variant readings for that language and little explanation.[41] When, therefore, Erasmus discovered that the Johannine comma was nowhere to be found in his Greek manuscripts, and did not seem to be known to the early fathers, he left it out with a brief explanation.[42] What else could he do? Later, he was to try vainly to explain to his critics that it was not a case of omission but of non-addition. Indeed he could have restored the missing verse from the Latin just as he had the missing verses in Revelation.[43] But the presumption here was that the absent passage was missing because it had never been there, not because the single last leaf of a manuscript had evidently been lost. Erasmus was prepared to believe this because he thought he had discovered many other discrepancies between the Latin and Greek which made it look as though the Vulgate had been either inadvertently or deliberately altered. (Among other things, he raised questions about the authenticity of the last twelve verses in the Gospel of Mark as well as the whole story in John of the woman taken in adultery.)[44] He insisted that an accurate reconstruction of the text was required, even if the results should prove inconvenient for the theologian, and he began to suspect that many convenient readings in the Vulgate had been foisted on the text just for that very reason.[45]

---

pares his task of explication to the humanists' efforts to explain the intentions of the classical orators and poets, except that Paul is more difficult. It was thus necessary to restore Paul's situation fully and exactly; yet Erasmus never forgets that Paul is only the medium for intentions that transcend his own. See the preface to *Paraphrasis in duas epistolas Pauli ad Corinthios,* in *CWE,* no. 916, 5: 236–916.

41. Valla seems to have been more interested in evaluating the Vulgate than actually editing the Greek text; see Bentley, *Humanists,* pp. 39–41. Erasmus insisted that his own annotations had been systematic rather than selective and supported by argument and the evidence of the fathers; Erasmus to Dorp (1515), *CWE,* no. 338, 3: 336–37.

42. See the modern facsimile edition by Heinz Holeczek (Stuttgart, 1986). The note is on p. 618.

43. See Samuel P. Targelles, *An Account of the Printed Text of the Greek New Testament* (London, 1854), p. 22. There are other places where Erasmus used the Latin Vulgate to correct the Greek; see F. H. Scrivener, *A Plain Introduction to the Criticism of the New Testament,* pp. 382–83. Thus he thought (correctly) that the doxology at the end of the Lord's Prayer, Matthew 6:13 ("For thine is the Kingdom and the power and the glory, forever, Amen") was not in the original and had slipped into the text through the liturgy; see Bainton, *Erasmus,* p. 137.

44. Mark 16:9–20; John 7:53–8:11. But Erasmus was willing eventually to accept both passages because they did appear in some of the manuscripts and because they had been approved by "the consensus of the Church." LB 6: 473F–474F; 214E–215A. See Bentley, "Erasmus' *Annotations,*" pp. 49–50. For some further examples of Erasmian criticism, see Basil Hall, "Erasmus: Biblical Scholar," pp. 101–3.

45. Bentley gives many instances and points out how Erasmus extended Valla's method to do something new. *Humanists,* pp. 140–59, 186.

It is to Erasmus then that we owe the invention of the problem of the Johannine comma, if not the solution. The problem lay in the discrepancy of the texts, both Latin and Greek, and the only hope of solution lay in an even closer examination of the evidence than he was able to supply. It was no use to deny the difficulty or wish it away, as some of Erasmus's first critics tried to do. From now on, all eyes were fixed on the need for a reliable text: the only question was how to establish it.

2

Erasmus was attacked for his work even before it was published and often before it was read.[46] At one Cambridge college, Erasmus heard that it had been banned before it arrived. Did the philosophers there mean to say that no changes whatever were possible in the biblical text? What would they do then with those passages that were so obviously and unmistakably corrupt? They cried out in horror when someone dared to correct the Gospels, but Erasmus had no intention of undermining the text: he meant simply to restore it. In this respect he was doing just what the editors of the new Aristotle and the translators of Galen had accomplished. Nor was there any point in exempting Scripture from critical inquiry and relying on authority. Erasmus showed that the great commentators of the past had sometimes erred; now let others show (if they could) where it was that he had gone astray. "Knowledge of grammar," he repeats, "is not the making of a theologian, but much less is he made by ignorance of grammar; at the very least, skill in this subject is an aid to the understanding of theology and lack of skill is the reverse."[47]

Apparently, the first formal attack was by a young Louvain theologian named Martin Dorp. Dorp and his colleagues had already been offended by the satire directed against them in the *Praise of Folly*. Now they caught wind of the forthcoming edition of the New Testament. In a letter to Erasmus in 1514, Dorp defended the Vulgate against the Greek, questioning the whole enterprise that had begun with Valla and Lefevre d'Etaples. "If I can show that the Latin version contains no admixture of falsehood or mistake, will you not have to confess that the labors of all those who try to correct it are superfluous?" Was it reasonable that the whole church could have been wrong all these centuries? That the holy fathers and the

---

46. See Erasmus's amusing account of the Carmelite Egmond, who seems not to have been very bright but who recognized the danger of the new philology. *CWE*, no. 1196, 8: 179, 191–92.

47. Erasmus to Henry Bullock, August 1516, *CWE*, no. 456, 4: 43–54. The letter anticipates much of the argument of the *Apologia* in the *Novum Instrumentum* (1516). See also the letter to Pucci (n. 35 above), p. 97.

church councils—which everyone agreed could not err in matters of faith—were ill-advised to use the Vulgate? Was it likely that the Greek copies were better than the Latin ones? That they alone were correct? The Greeks, after all, were notorious for going astray in religious matters. If someone should insist anyway that the Latin varied from the Greek, then Dorp was ready to bid the Greeks goodbye. Did it matter if Erasmus merely meant to show that there were discrepancies between the Latin and Greek? Yes, indeed, "for a great many people will discuss the integrity of the Scriptures, and many will have doubts about it. Just so had Augustine written to Jerome, "If falsehoods were admitted in the Holy Scripture even to serve a useful purpose, what authority can they still retain?"[48]

It was not hard for Erasmus to reply, though it is doubtful that he believed he would quiet the theologians. Their ignorance was invincible. But he retained hopes for Dorp, who was a friend and had a smattering of the new learning. He defended the *Praise of Folly* and the New Testament, therefore, in a long letter that was often reprinted afterward.

> Why do Jerome and Augustine and Ambrose so often cite a different text from the one we use? Why does Jerome find fault with many things, and correct them explicitly, which corrections are still found in our text? What will you do when there is so much agreement, when the Greek copies are different and Jerome cites the same text as theirs, when the very oldest Latin copies concur, and the sense itself runs much better? Do you intend to overlook all this and follow your own copy, though it was perhaps corrupted by a scribe?

Which was more false, to see an error added or one removed?[49] Dorp had argued that the church councils all approved the Latin text. Where? Erasmus asked. "How could they approve a text whose author [as Jerome had shown] is unknown?" But even if some synod had approved it, was it forbidden to correct it by the Greek original? Were all the mistakes approved also? Even the Vulgate copies disagreed; were their discrepancies authorized by a council also? As for the danger in pointing out these things, it seemed hardly likely to Erasmus "that everybody will forthwith abandon Christ if the news happens to get out that some passage has been found in

---

48. Dorp to Erasmus, September 1514 (published the following year), *CWE*, no. 304, 3: 17–23. Augustine to Jerome, ep. 28.3.4. For Dorp and his relations with Erasmus, see Henry de Vocht, *Monumenta Humanistica Lovaniensia* (Louvain, 1934), pp. 63–348; and Jerry Bentley, "New Testament Scholarship at Louvain in the Early Sixteenth Century," *Studies in Renaissance and Medieval History*, n.s., 2, pp. 51–79.

49. Erasmus to Dorp, c. May, 1515, *CWE*, no. 337, 3: 111–39. He repeats the idea in the letter to Bullock (n. 47 above), *CWE*, 4: p. 45.

Scripture which an ignorant or sleepy scribe has miscopied or some unknown translator has rendered inadequately."[50]

For the moment, Dorp was not convinced, and despite the timely intervention of Thomas More and a brief reconciliation, the quarrel resumed in
1516, after the New Testament appeared. Dorp seems to have held to his
reservations about the role, or rule, of grammar over theology, until More
persuaded him finally to acquiesce.[51] For the Renaissance humanist, the
idea of a transmission of texts and ideas through time, necessarily imperfect but not beyond retrieval, was becoming commonplace; for the scholastic philosopher, the idea of a timeless truth, intelligible only to logic and
dialectic, seemed threatened, though it still prevailed. For Erasmus and
More, and for Dorp and his friends, the new humanist battleground was
theology, and the choice seemed full of consequence. John Colet, at least,
had no difficulty in siding with Erasmus in the impending battle.[52]

When the New Testament actually appeared, the clergy in several countries were stirred immediately into action. The German theologian, Johann von Eck (Luther's first opponent), wrote at once to Erasmus to put
his objections. Many were offended, he wrote, in particular by a note on
the second chapter of Matthew, where Erasmus had suggested that the
apostles had sometimes made mistakes in quoting from memory "like ordinary men." Eck drew the obvious conclusion. "If the authority of Holy
Scripture at this point is shaky, can any other passage be free from suspicion of error?"[53] Erasmus replied (to no avail) that if an evangelist mistakenly substituted one name for another, Isaiah, for example, for Jeremiah,
it would hardly imperil the whole of Scripture. (He insisted, however, that
he had left the question open, as had Jerome.) "We do not instantly form a

50. Erasmus to Dorp, *CWE*, no. 337, 3: 136. To describe the variants was important, Erasmus
explained to Cardinal Pucci, but nowhere was the variation great enough to imperil the orthodox faith, *CWE*, no. 860, p. 97. To be sure, Erasmus insisted again and again that his critical edition was meant for scholars who would know how to use it, rather than for the *plebecula*
for whom presumably a vernacular translation or paraphrase might be sufficient. See Erasmus's *Apologia*, quoted in C. A. Jarrott, "Erasmus' *In Principio Erat Sermo: A* Controversial
Translation," *Studies in Philology*, 61 (1964), p. 39. Needless to say, this was not altogether reas-
suring either to contemporaries or (as we shall find) to the divines in Gibbon's day.
    51. Dorp to Erasmus, August 27, 1515, *CWE*, no. 347, 3: 160. The whole incident is reviewed
in the introduction to *In Defense of Humanism*, vol. 15, in *The Complete Works of Thomas More*, ed.
Daniel Kinney (New Haven, 1986), pp. xix–xxviii. More's letter to Dorp is given there, pp. 1–
127; see pp. 13–15, for More's defense of "grammar."
    52. Colet to Erasmus, June 20, 1516, *CWE*, no. 423, 3, pp. 311–13. The New Testament, he
reported, was already selling like hotcakes.
    53. Eck to Erasmus, February 2, 1518, *CWE*, no. 769, 5: 287–93. Erasmus's note is at LB, 6:
12E–14D. For some other Erasmian reservations, see Hall, "Erasmus: Biblical Scholar,"
p. 102; and especially John Williams Aldridge, *The Hermeneutic of Erasmus* (Richmond, 1966),
pp. 63–69.

low opinion of the whole of Peter's life because Augustine and Ambrose affirm that he suffered a few lapses . . . nor does a book forthwith lose all credence if it contains some blemish." The Holy Spirit employed the apostles for his own purposes; the only thing one could say for sure is that he used them for the proper business of the Gospels, i.e. faith and morals, even while allowing them to be human.[54] The whole Erasmian hermeneutic depended (as he explained in his enlarged *Methodus*) on reading the biblical passages in their context, on gauging their moment and their milieu—the occasion, tone, intention, and order of each discourse for each speaker. Christ did not talk to the Samaritans as he did to the Jews.[55]

Further news from Germany brought further alarms, along with much good cheer. Apparently there was another theologian, still obscure, who was finding Erasmus's reading of Paul implausible. Martin Luther learned much from Erasmus's New Testament, and he was willing to use the new philology up to a point, but he too drew back from giving philology the rule.[56] In a conflict of biblical interpretations, the Spirit mattered more to him than the letter, while it is truer to say for Erasmus that understanding moved from the letter to the spirit.[57] Moreover, the humanists' "pyrrhonism," and an incipient notion that Christian dogma had developed over time, allowed him to leave open many questions that the more dogmatic Luther considered settled. For the later editions of the New Testament, Erasmus replied to his critics with a new preface, *Contra Morosos quosdam ac Indoctos*, proclaiming that he had not meant to depart even a hair's breadth from the authority of the church and that his annotations were offered merely as suggestions, not determinations—which left everyone free to choose as they wished.[58] Luther was more dogmatic; theology continued

54. Erasmus to Eck, May 15, 1518, *CWE*, no. 844, 6: 27–36. See also the notes in the New Testament which elaborate this idea, in Chomarat, 1: 501–2; and Rummel, *Annotations*, pp. 139, 144. Erasmus pointed out minor errors in the evangelists at Matthew 27:9 and Mark 1:2–3. But he later backed off a bit and in one case (in the *Apologia* of 1527) attributed the error at Matthew 2 to a careless scribe. See the text in Holborn *Ausgewahlte Werke*, pp. 168–69; and the note in Bentley, "Erasmus' *Annotations*," p. 47.

55. *Ratio ad verum theologium* in Holborn, *Ausgewahlte Werke*, p. 196; cf. p. 185. See Aldridge, *Hermeneutic*, pp. 63–64; Renaudet, *Etudes Erasmiennes*, p. 141; and Chomarat, 2: 579–84, who points out the influence of classical rhetoric.

56. Georgius Spalatinus to Erasmus, December 11, 1516, *CWE*, no. 501, 4: 165–69. Already, Luther objects to Erasmus underplaying original sin in his reading of St. Paul's Epistle to the Romans.

57. Albert Rabil, Jr., *Erasmus and the New Testament: The Mind of a Christian Humanist* (San Antonio, 1972), p. 122. The same contrast is drawn by Aldridge, *Hermeneutic*, who compares their different views on the canon, pp. 81–87, and their antithetical exegetical methods, pp. 120–26.

58. "Annotationes scribimus, non leges; et expendenda proponimus, non protinus habenda pro compertis," LB 6: sig. 3v.

to precede and govern grammar, though he tried not to dispute with its findings.[59] For Erasmus, grammar might be a humble attendant to theology, but it was always an indispensable preliminary. "I have shown," he wrote in answer to his critics, "that it is and always will be a pious undertaking to remove mistakes from the sacred books or to shed some light on them. . . . If anyone says I am no theologian, my answer is: I am playing the part of the grammarian. If they disdain the grammarian, let them take note that the emperor does not disdain the services of his barber or secretary."[60] Luther understood that their differences were reflected in their opposing preferences for Jerome and Augustine.[61]

Meanwhile the Louvain theologians refused to withdraw; Jacques Masson (Jacob Latomus) reiterated the authority of the Vulgate and the use of scholastic method, criticizing the view that Greek was necessary for understanding the New Testament. Erasmus, who was not named, nevertheless took up the defense of grammar once again with a new *Apologia* (1519). He repeated the idea that he had no desire to dispute with the church over matters that pertained to salvation; all that was required was belief in the articles of the Apostles' Creed.[62] Interestingly, Erasmus held to that minimal conviction, even though he was quite sure that the creed had not been composed in the time of the apostles but much later.[63] To be sure, all necessary truth lay plain in Scripture, but the rest could be—indeed had been—usefully elaborated over time, and some progress in Christian knowledge could be expected through a kind of developing Christian consensus. Clearly, Erasmus hoped he was making his own contribution to that development; in matters philological he never wavered.[64] In matters theological, however, it was conformity to the *philosophia Christi* as Erasmus un-

59. See A. Renaudet, "Le modernisme Erasmien," *Etudes Erasmiennes (1521–29)* (Paris, 1939), pp. 122–89, 169–71. Schwarz assembles some of Luther's strictures on Erasmus, *Principles*, chap. 6, pp. 166–211. For Luther, "Primum grammatica videamus, verum ea theologica," Aldridge, *Hermeneutic*, p. 126n.

60. Quoted from the *Capita contra morosos* by Erika Rummel, "God and Solecism: Erasmus as a Literary Critic of the Bible," *Erasmus of Rotterdam Yearbook*, 7 (1987), p. 72; cf. Marjorie O'Rourke Boyle, *Erasmus on Language and Method in Theology* (Toronto, 1977), p. 37.

61. Luther to Spalatin, October 19, 1516, quoted in Smith, *Erasmus*, p. 191.

62. *Apologia rejiciens quorundam . . . rumores natos ex Jacobo Latomo inscribitur*, March 19, 1519, LB 9: 88. See G. Chantraine, "*L'Apologia ad Latomum*: Deux Conceptions de la théologie," *Scrinium Erasmianum*, ed. J. Coppens (Leiden, 1969), 2: 51–75.

63. Erasmus expounded the Apostles' Creed both early and late; see the *Symbolum* (1533) (LB 5: 1133–96E). Following a tip by Valla, he thought that it was probably composed at the time of the Council of Nicaea; see Craig R. Thompson, ed., Erasmus, *Inquisitio de Fide*, 2d ed. (Hamden, 1975).

64. Thus Erasmus is still defending his procedures and explaining how he adds and subtracts from the text, in a letter to Johann Botzheim, August 5, 1531, Allen, no. 2516, 9: 309–12.

derstood it that was the best test of authenticity and the thing that mattered most.[65]

But the most irritating attack of all came from England, from another ambitious young prelate, Edward Lee. Pride, ambition, and personal pique all played a part in provoking a quarrel which absorbed Erasmus and filled his correspondence for several years, beginning in 1518. Suffice it to say that Lee began to draw up some of his own annotations in reply to Erasmus in that year, and after many threats and entreaties on both sides, published them in 1520. They included some 243 notes on the first edition of the New Testament, and 25 more on the second, an *apologia* addressed to the students at Louvain, and a long letter summing up the personal quarrel.[66] Erasmus replied immediately, and then twice more in the next several months. For a time peace was brought about through the intervention of friends, and several of the more moderate tracts by both men were brought together by Froeben in a fresh volume at Basle. The quarrel was later resumed when Lee threw in with the Spanish critics after 1525.[67]

In principle, Lee did not object to the Erasmian enterprise, and was indeed offended when Erasmus spurned his own attempt to help. He did not argue, like his fellow Englishman, Henry Standish, that any attempt to improve or translate the Bible meant the end of Christianity. Lee claimed later, with some justice apparently, that Erasmus had actually made use of some of his suggestions.[68] But he did object to many of the specific emendations and corrections that Erasmus had made in the text and explained in his annotations. He thought that he had found mistakes in Erasmus's use of the manuscripts and his citation of the fathers; he tried to defend the correctness and authority of the Vulgate; and he detected heresy behind many of Erasmus's judgments. In particular, he was offended by the omission of the Johannine comma.

Lee's comment appears toward the end of his *Annotations*. He was astonished that Erasmus should have discovered a manuscript where the passage was missing and publish it twice without (apparently) consulting any other manuscripts, although that passage was crucial to the orthodox

65. Typically, he thought that whether or not the Apocalypse belonged to the canon (and Erasmus doubted it), it should have no effect on Christian conviction; LB 6: 990E. For other questions that Erasmus raised about the canon, see Chomarat, 1: 503.

66. *CWE*, no. 1061, 7: 171–95. The *apologia* is printed in the *Opuscula*, pp. 225ff. See Robert Coogan, *Erasmus, Lee and the Correction of the Vulgate: The Shaking of the Foundations* (Geneva, 1992).

67. The quarrel can be followed in the correspondence of Erasmus; see the headnotes by Allen, 4: 108–11; and in *CWE*, 7: 226; and in Erika Rummel, *Erasmus and His Catholic Critics*, 2 vols. (Nieuwkoop, 1989), 1, chap. 5, pp. 95–120.

68. Rummel, *Erasmus*, 1: 101–3.

faith. It was impious to say the least! Valla's silence on the subject was proof that he must have seen the comma in his manuscripts.[69] Erasmus responded in the third of his replies to Lee. There he insisted that the passage had indeed been missing in all his manuscripts, which were more numerous than those Valla had employed. Anyway, Valla was human and might have overlooked the problem, although it was always possible that the phrase did appear in one of his manuscripts. Erasmus admitted seeing the passage once in an Antwerp codex but only as a marginal note. Had he found it correct in a single one, he most certainly would have reproduced it in both the Greek text and Latin translation. It was up to Lee to come forth with the evidence before he accused anyone of negligence or dissimulation.[70]

Erasmus continued to look at and use new manuscripts wherever he could obtain them. When he could not get to Rome, he asked a friend to inspect a famous old codex for him in the Vatican. In June 1521, he received a reply with a couple of the suspected passages duly transcribed from the Greek. The Johannine comma, it appears, was entirely lacking from the manuscript.[71] Yet it was in the very same month that Erasmus finally threw in the towel and actually reproduced the missing comma—in a separate edition by Froeben of his Latin translation. And a year or two later, Erasmus returned the comma to both the Latin and Greek of his third edition of the *Novum Testamentum* (1522), with an explanation. It seems that a Greek manuscript had in fact turned up in Britain with the passage intact and Erasmus felt obliged to print it, even though he thought that it too derived from the Vulgate. "From this manuscript," he explained, "I have substituted what was missing in the rest, lest I give any occasion for slandering me."[72]

---

69. *Annotationes Erasmi* (Paris, 1520), sig. Iiiv.

70. *Liber tertius quo respondet duabus invectivis Lei* (Antwerp, 1520), LB, 9: 227B. See Rummel, *Erasmus*, 1: 105; Holborn, *Ausgewahlte Werke*, p. 165; Aldridge, *Hermeneutic*, p. 103.

71. Paulo Bombace to Erasmus, June 18, 1521, *CWE*, no. 1213, 8: 245–48. This is the famous Vatican B, thought now to be the earliest surviving codex of the Greek New Testament. Erasmus acknowledged Bombace's help in his third edition of the New Testament (1523), LB, 6: 1080E. Jerry Bentley points out that Erasmus had doubts later about this manuscript also, believing that it might have been tampered with after the Golden Bull of 1435 when the emperor ordered the Greek manuscripts to be brought into line with the Vulgate; see "Erasmus's *Annotationes in Novum Testamentum* and the Textual History of the Gospels," *Archiv für Reformationsgeschichte*, 67 (1976), p. 48. The fact is that the Greek manuscripts were at least as corrupt as the Latin, but this was a discovery that could only be demonstrated in the fullness of time and after a great collective labor, and not by the intuitions of either Erasmus or his critics. For some other manuscripts consulted by Erasmus, see Preserved Smith, *Erasmus: A Study of his Life, Ideals and Place in History* (1923, reprinted New York, 1962), pp. 164–65.

72. LB 9: 275 B–C. See H. J. de Jonge, "Erasmus and the *Comma Johanneum*," *Ephemerides Theologicae Lovanienses*, 56 (1980), pp. 381–89.

So the comma was restored to the text, where it remained for the lifetime of Erasmus and beyond. It was just as Gibbon had said, a result of the prudence, not the conviction, of the editor. Erasmus's fear of calumny was justified; Lee had accused him directly of Arianism in this matter and elsewhere in his annotations. (The charge, needless to say, was dangerous.) It is true that Erasmus had pointed out more than once that the Fathers had stretched the meaning of a biblical text to give it a trinitarian meaning. His friend, Wolfgang Capito, had seen the danger already in 1516 and urged him to soft-pedal his arguments.[73] What Erasmus himself believed about the Trinity is still a little obscure. He was certainly soft on the Arians, whom he preferred to think of (with Jerome) as schismatic rather than heretical. He saw them in their historical setting, and made some effort to treat them dispassionately, even sympathetically.[74] On the other hand, he had no wish to see Arianism revived; as always, he abhorred division, and his own emphasis on the moral and practical purposes of Scripture and religion left him indifferent to metaphysical disputes. "Had I had any authority at those [ancient] synods where the peace of the world was at issue, I would have argued that it were better to profess ignorance of what the words *homoousion* or *homoiousion* portend with regard to the divine Persons, rather than either to maintain or attack them at the cost of such great tumult."[75] It was the "elaborate subtlety" of the Arians that had driven the orthodox to develop those deplorable terms and distinctions, which St. Hilary long ago had observed (in a work that Erasmus now took care to publish) were quite beyond our intelligence and understanding. Was one to be denied Heaven for being unable to disentangle what distinguishes the Father from the Son or the Holy Spirit from both? It was enough to believe that the three are of one nature, especially since no amount of argument could ever persuade the skeptic.[76]

Still the attacks would not cease. When an old foe, the Englishman Henry Standish, denounced him again at St. Paul's for having omitted the

73. Wolfgang Capito to Erasmus, September 2, 1516, *CWE*, no. 459, 4: 58–65.

74. What follows is largely from James D. Tracy, "Erasmus and the Arians: Remarks on the *Consensus Ecclesiae*," *The Catholic Historical Review*, 67 (1981), pp. 1–10.

75. Quoted in Tracy, p. 5. See also John B. Payne, *Erasmus: His Theology of the Sacraments* (Richmond, 1970), pp. 8–12, 56–59. Both Tracy and Payne agree to describe Erasmus's view of the Trinity as mildly subordinationist rather than Arian.

76. See the preface to Hilary, whose works were edited by Erasmus in 1523; Erasmus to Jean de Carondelet, January 5, 1523, no. 1334, *CWE*, pp. 250–51. This passage with several others was censured by the Sorbonne in 1516 and defended by Erasmus in LB 9: 920–21, 925–28 (esp. 925E.–F). See John C. Olin, "Erasmus and the Edition of St. Hilary," *Erasmus in English*, 9 (1978), pp. 8–11. Erasmus preferred to think that the Arians should have been persuaded by argument, rather than attacked as Satan or Anti-Christ, and he makes clear that he thinks this same charity should also be applied to modern schismatics and heretics.

word *datus* from John 7:39, he had to explain again that it was not in the Greek manuscripts because they were corrupt—excised, according to Standish, by the wicked Arians—but because it had never been there. If it had, Erasmus was certain that the orthodox fathers would have mentioned it. And if the Arians had excised it, the orthodox Christians would certainly not have kept silent about so impious an act. Nor was it clear to Erasmus just what the benefit would have been, since neither the addition nor the subtraction much affected the sense. Besides, Erasmus was only the translator of the Greek text; would Standish have him supply what was not in the manuscripts?[77] Standish did not forget; many years later in the reign of Queen Mary, he was still trying to keep the Bible out of the hands of the laity, convinced that the difficulties of scriptural understanding could only be surmounted by the authority of the church. Paradoxically, it was Erasmus (whom he quotes) who had taught him just what the difficulties in interpretation were and how they might be overcome by placing them in their textual context (i.e., what comes before and after), as well as "the time, the men, with other circumstances, as how, where, and when they were written." Unlike Erasmus, Standish believed there were many things *not* in Scripture that were necessary to salvation—among them the notion that "the iii persons in the Trinitie are of equall powers and of one essence." Was he implicitly accepting the absence of the Johannine comma?[78]

As the criticism grew, so did Erasmus's protestations. When he was denounced at Valladolid in 1527, he felt compelled to draw up an elaborate defense of himself in which he rehearsed all the orthodox comments that he had made, affirming the Trinity throughout his works—not omitting what he had said to elucidate the restored comma, especially in the fourth edition of the New Testament and the third reply to Lee.[79] He still reiterated the testimony of the Greeks, who did not speak of the heavenly wit-

77. The absence of the participle *datus* indicated to Standish that Erasmus mistook the Holy Spirit for a creature. Erasmus to Robert Aldridge, August 23, 1527, Allen, no. 1858, 7: 128–41. The first enmity of the two men is recounted in a note by Erasmus to his edition of Jerome (1516) when he already ridicules Standish's scholarship. *CWE* 61: 218–19.

78. Henry Standish, *A Discourse Wherein it is Debated Whether it is Expedient that the Scripture Should be in English for all Men to Reade that Will* (London, 1554), sig. Ciii, Eiv–v, fiv–v. For this quarrel with Erasmus, see Erasmus to Hermann Busch, July 31, 1520, and Erasmus to Thomas More, c. November 1520, *CWE*, 29, nos. 1126 and 1162, 8: pp. 7–17, 91–98; for Standish, (who became bishop of St. Asaph), see *Contemporaries of Erasmus* (Toronto, 1985), 3: 279–80.

79. *Apologia ad monachos quosdam Hispanos* (Basle, 1528), in answer to the first chapter of the Spanish attack, *Contra sacrosanctam Trinitatem.* See the preliminary draft in a letter to the Inquisitor-General, Alfonso Manrique, who was a friend and protector of Erasmus, c. September 2, 1527, Allen, no. 1877, 7: 170–79. Erasmus quotes the words he added to the later editions of the annotations, LB 6: 1080D–1081D. For the events at Valladolid, see Bataillon, *Erasme*, pp. 260–99.

nesses. And he recalled his argument that the church fathers, especially
Athanasius, were not likely to have overlooked the passage which would
have been so useful to their purposes. Nor did he see how the comma could
actually refute the Arians, who were satisfied with a single passage: *In principio erat verbum, et Deus erat verbum.* In such a matter, he repeated, it was better to submit to the authority of the church. From the bottom of his heart,
Erasmus pleaded, he detested the impiety of the Arians. In short, Erasmus
wanted to have it both ways: to continue to suspect the comma and at
the same time to affirm the orthodox view of the Trinity. Even under
the fiercest fire, he never retracted his belief in the evidence of the text, ir-
respective of all dogmatic convictions. And it is possible to argue that Erasmus's own theological (or antitheological) inclinations—his own
skepticism and indifference to such matters—were as much a *result* of his
biblical and patristic readings as the cause. The Archdeacon Travis, arguing against Gibbon, might well suspect Erasmus's orthodoxy and resume
the charge of Arianism, but it is hard to see how that was enough to have
dictated the Erasmian text.[80] The humanist rarely forgot his obligation to
philology, lead where it might.

3

Meanwhile, a coterie of Spanish scholars had been busy under the great
Cardinal Ximinez editing their own version of Scripture, the polyglot text
known as the Complutensian. The work was begun certainly by 1510 and
the New Testament volume was printed by January 10, 1514, two years before Erasmus. Publication was held up for want of a license, while the scholarly team continued to work on the Old Testament in Hebrew, Aramaic,
Greek, and Latin. Ximinez had mixed motives for his grand enterprise, but
he understood the importance of presenting a reliable edition of the biblical text in order to settle differences of interpretation. "Every theologian
should be able to drink . . . at the fountainhead itself. . . . To accomplish
this task we have been obliged to have recourse to the knowledge of the
most able philologists, and to make researches in every direction for the
best and most ancient Hebrew and Greek manuscripts. Our object is to revive the hitherto dormant study of Scripture."[81] The whole work in six

---

80. J.-B. Pineau shows how the debate over Erasmus's Arianism continued for a long time;
among other works he refers to Martin Lydius, *Apologie d'Erasme contre les calomnies de ceux qui
l'ont accuse d'arianisme* (1606), and to the criticisms of J.-L. de Burigny, *Vie d'Erasme* (Paris,
1757); see *Erasme: Sa Pensée Religieuse* (Paris, 1924), p. 267n. For Travis, see chap. 8 below.

81. See Ximinez's dedication to Leo X, quoted in James P. R. Lyell, *Cardinal Ximines* (London, 1917); cited in Bentley, *Humanists*, p. 74. For the story of the Complutensian version, see
Marcel Bataillon, *Erasme et l'Espagne*, ed. Charles Amiel, 3 vols. (Geneva, 1991), 1, i, pp. 1–75.

magnificent volumes was published at last in 1520, the fifth with the New Testament in Greek and Latin.

The Complutensian editors were not so concerned or self-conscious about philological problems as Erasmus. They say little about the manuscripts they employed, except to proclaim that they were so old and correct that it would be impious to doubt their authority. Apparently, several were borrowed from the papal library; another came from the island of Rhodes; but there are few clues to their identity, and the Rhodian codex has never come to light.[82] The marginal notes were spare, confined pretty much to pointing out matters of syntax and parallel passages. At only five places were there substantial comments. Inevitably, one of these was 1 John 5:7.

It is almost certain that the editors found the comma missing in their Greek manuscripts. On the other hand, they took the authority of Thomas Aquinas seriously, who argued that the passage was genuine but had been suppressed in many of the old manuscripts by the Arian heretics.[83] So they quoted Aquinas at length and (so it seems) translated the missing passage from the Vulgate back into Greek, interpolating it into the text at the appropriate point, but without saying so! This was consistent with their general view, reversing Lorenzo Valla, that it was more likely to be the Greek that was corrupt than the Latin. Their desire to preserve the Vulgate was thus, as Gibbon put it unkindly, due to the "honest bigotry" of the Complutensian editors.[84]

Apparently, Erasmus's New Testament arrived in Alcala toward the end of 1516 and at once provoked one of the Spanish team to action. Diego

82. See Jerry Bentley, "New Light on the Editing of the Complutensian New Testament," *Bibliothèque d'humanisme et Renaissance*, 42 (1980), pp. 145–56. Long ago P. S. Allen pointed out that it did not become the custom to mention the manuscripts used in an edition of the classics until the beginning of the seventeenth century; see "Erasmus' Services to Learning," *Lectures*, p. 35.

83. St. Thomas cites the comma in the *Summa Theologica*, I, q. 3, art. 4; and in I q. 30, art. 2; and in his commentary on Boethius, *De Trinitate*, q. 3, art. 4. Erasmus was not so kind to Aquinas, whose Biblical authority he challenges frequently in his annotations; see Hall, "Erasmus: Biblical Scholar," pp. 100–101. In the note to 1 Cor. 13:4 (LB 6: 725–26), Erasmus says frankly that St. Thomas should not have used the rubbish of unscholarly sources for his commentary; it was *indignus*. Elsewhere he writes that the saint would have done better had he lived in a happier intellectual time; see Erasmus to Hermannus Buschius, July 31, 1520, *CWE*, no. 1126, 8: 15.

84. Bataillon calls it "un religieux respect pour la version consacrée," *Erasme*, p. 44.; see also Bentley, whose conclusion is also very like Gibbon's, *Humanists*, p. 110. Bataillon compares the treatment by the editors of the passage, Matt. 6:13, which was removed from their version (against the Greek manuscripts), but this time with a marginal explanation quoting Chrysostom that nothing should be omitted that was in the old Latin manuscripts. Bataillon is sure they must have known that the comma did not have such support; see *Erasme*, p. 45n. It should be said that the Complutensian editors were to some extent right about the superiority of the Vulgate as a witness to the early text, but their reasons were more dogmatic than philological.

Lopez Zuniga (Stunica) was offended by Erasmus's criticism of the Vulgate and swiftly began to draw up some *Annotations* against it and against the work of Lefevre d'Etaples. Stunica claimed religious orthodoxy and a competent philological understanding of the ancient languages. He had spent many years, he boasted, carefully comparing the Hebrew and Greek with the oldest Latin manuscripts of the Bible and was thus perfectly equipped to judge the value of the Vulgate.[85] Ximinez refused to permit Stunica to publish his criticism, but soon after his death the *Annotations contra Erasmus* appeared in Alcala (1520). In the preface Stunica defends the Vulgate against the presumption of Erasmus. He would show just how shallow and faulty was the scholarship of the Dutchman and how dangerous his conclusions. He then offered 212 long notes criticizing in detail Erasmus's translation and annotations in order to defend the traditional Latin text. Unlike some other opponents, Stunica did not object to the use of philology; on the contrary, he employed it heartily himself. What disturbed him was Erasmus's attack on the authority of the church.[86] "Spain too," Erasmus was surprised to learn, "has a second Lee!"[87] When at last he received a copy of Stunica's polemic in September 1521, he immediately replied with a fresh *Apologia* taking up each of Stunica's objections in turn and disputing them all. In fact, he found Stunica a better scholar than Lee, and less spiteful, though full enough of spleen.[88] It was the beginning of a new pamphlet war which lasted for several years and produced a long series of polemical exchanges.

Once again the main thrust of Stunica's objections was to the heretical implications in Erasmus's annotations: first to their alleged Arianism, and in later works (with the help of Stunica's supporter, Sancho Carranza) to their alleged Lutheranism.[89] And Erasmus had to defend his readings, which tended to remove or underplay their trinitarian content, even while

85. *Annotationes contra Erasmum* (1520), pref.; in Erasmus, *Opera Omnia*, 9–2, ed. H. J. De Jonge (Amsterdam, 1983), p. 15. According to Bataillon, Antonio de Lebrixa, a better scholar and a biblical humanist, may have touched on the comma in his first (unpublished) *Quinquagena*. In any case, Bataillon does not doubt that in the ensuing debate Lebrixa sympathized with Erasmus; *Erasme*, pp. 45–46.

86. So Rummel, *Erasmus*, pp. 146–47; De Jonge, *Annotationes*, p. 34.

87. Erasmus to Johann Lang, August 2, 1520, *CWE*, no. 1128, 8: 23–24.

88. Erasmus to Pierre Barbier, June 26, 1521, *CWE*, no. 1216, 8: 250–52. The text of the *Apologia respondens ad ea quae Jacobus Lopis Stunica*, has been edited by De Jonge, in *Opera Omnia*, with a valuable introduction.

89. See Stunica to Juan Vergara, May 4, 1522, Allen, *Opus Epistolarum*, 4: app. 15, p. 630; and Vergara to Erasmus, April 24, 1522, *CWE*, no. 1277, 9: 69–73. Stunica tried vainly to publish a big book, *Erasmi Rotterodami blasphemiae et impietates* but only succeeded in getting part of it to press. See H. J. De Jonge, "Four Unpublished Letters from J. L. Stunica to Pople Leo X (1520)," *Colloque Erasmien de Liege* (Paris, 1987), pp. 147–60. For Carranza, see Allen, 5: 52n; Bataillon, *Erasme*, pp. 131–33.

maintaining his own orthodoxy. For example, he doubted almost every occasion where the name of God was attributed to Christ by the evangelists or the apostles. Stunica claimed to produce ten such places, as well as the authority of many of the fathers.[90] The charge was serious and is still open to debate; at one point, Erasmus actually removed an offending note from the third edition, although he insisted he was right, "so that there might be nothing in my words which would upset honest people." He wanted it known that he believed without qualification in Christ as both God and man.[91] Was it ordinary prudence again, or was it (more likely) the very real desire of Erasmus to preserve harmony in the church on a matter not worth fighting about?

Inevitably, Stunica objected to the absence of the comma. It is well known, he says, that the Greek manuscripts were often corrupt.[92] And in this case, Jerome's preface to the canonical epistles makes it clear that the comma was in the original. The old Latin manuscripts also confirm the passage, and there is no ambiguity or inconsistency between the comma and the rest of John's epistle, which corroborates the true Catholic faith in the Trinity.[93] Stunica had employed an ancient Rhodian manuscript throughout his work to rebut Erasmus. His opponent naturally suspected that it had been revised to accord with the Vulgate. But now Erasmus saw a better chance, for Stunica had failed to cite it—or any other Greek manuscript—as evidence for the comma. In any case, Erasmus added, he had not undertaken to emend the Greek texts, but simply to supply their evidence in good faith. He does not seem to have suspected that Jerome's preface was itself a supposititious work, probably added to the Vulgate only in the sixth century![94]

---

90. See Richard Homer Graham, "Erasmus and Stunica: A Chapter in the History of New Testament Scholarship," *Erasmus of Rotterdam Yearbook*, 10 (1990), pp. 9–60 (esp. pp. 19–20). Another hotly contested place was the note on Acts, 4:30, where Erasmus (citing Valla) preferred *servus* to *puer* for Christ; *NI*, p. 380. The question is still a lively one; Raymond Brown discusses the contemporary argument and opts for a position not unlike Erasmus's; "Does the New Testament Call Jesus God?" *Jesus God and Man* (Milwaukee, 1967), pp. 1–38. Carranza's *Opusculum in quasdam Erasmi annotationes* (1522) was answered by Erasmus in his *Apologia de tribus locis* (1522), LB, 9: 401–32; see Rummel, *Critics*, 2: 156–61. Allen supplies some useful correspondence between Stunica and Juan Vergara, who played the role of intermediary in the conflict, 4: app. 15, pp. 620–32.

91. See LB: 9, 413E; Bentley, *Humanists*, p. 210n; Graham, p. 23. Graham points out that Erasmus later, in his Paraphrases, accepted some of the readings he rejected in the New Testament p. 30.

92. "Sciendum est, Graecorum codices esse corruptos, nostros vero ipsam veritatem continere." See Samuel P. Targelles, *An Account of the Printed Text of the Greek New Testament* (London, 1854), p. 10.

93. Stunica, *Annotationes*, sig. Kii.

94. See Erasmus, *Apologia Respondens ad ea quae Jacobus Lopis Stunica, Opera Omnia*, 9–2, pp. 252–58. Erasmus could only imagine that Jerome must have seen it in a Greek codes un-

For Erasmus, it looked indeed like the Lee fracas all over again, although Stunica wrote independently and probably did not see Lee's annotations until the following year. Once again, Erasmus drew on the silence of the fathers to support his arguments, quoting especially, against the Arians, from the orthodox patriarch, Cyril of Alexandria, who would surely have found the text convenient to his purpose; and alluding also to its omission by St. Augustine.[95] Even the Venerable Bede could not find the comma in his copy of the Vulgate. Nor could Erasmus discover it in any of the old manuscripts of the Latin Bible that he consulted at Bruges. It is now that he cites for the first time the negative evidence of the famous old Vatican Greek manuscript that he had received from his friend in Rome. He was more than ever convinced that the lack of any early mention in the manuscripts and the fathers meant that the comma was a late and spurious addition to the text. But even if it turned out that the passage was genuine, it could not be used to refute the Arians, who would insist on reading *unum sunt* as meaning that the three are one in *testimony*, rather than in *substance*.[96] He concludes with the notion so common in all his works that too much "curiosity" in these speculative matters was a waste of time.[97]

In the last paragraph, however, almost as an afterthought, Erasmus noticed the new manuscript that had recently come to light in England. Here at last was the missing comma in Greek! And here, unhappily, was new ground for the calumnies that were being leveled against him. But Erasmus remained quite sure that the English manuscript had been deliberately adapted to the Vulgate, probably, he suggested now, at that time (in the fifteenth century) when a rapprochement was being projected between the churches of East and West and when concord seemed desirable.[98] Nevertheless, Erasmus was prepared to concede, as we have seen,

---

known to Cyril or Bede, another indication of the uncertainty of the text even in the fourth century. The preface is given in *Novum Testamentum Latine,* ed. I. Wordsworth, H. I. White, et al., 3 vols. (Oxford, 1913–41), 3: 230–31. Erasmus did not hesitate to assert the fallibility of the fathers, including Jerome and Augustine; see Erasmus's note to Matthew 2 in the 1519 edition, discussed by Erika Rummel, *Erasmus' Annotations on the New Testament: From Philologist to Theologian* (Toronto, 1986), pp. 57–8.

95. De Jonge points out that Erasmus explains his point more fully in the annotations to the New Testament (LB, 6: 1079D), which he appears to be abridging here. Augustine in his *Collatio cum Maximino II* explains the spirit, blood, and water of 1 John 5:8, without ever mentioning the comma. See *Opera Omnia,* 9–2, p. 257n.

96. Erasmus had already made this point against Lee; see Bainton, *Erasmus,* pp. 136–37. And he repeats it against the Protestant reformer, Guillaume Farel, in 1524; *CWE,* no. 1510, 10: 411.

97. For the *impia curiosita,* see Erasmus's note on 1 Tim. 1:6 (LB, 6: 926–28); and *Apologia ad Stunicae,* p. 259.

98. *Apologia,* ll. 542–44, p. 258. See H. J. de Jonge, "Erasmus and the *Comma Johanneum,*" pp. 387–88. On this ground, Erasmus later came to suspect even Vatican B; see Allen's headnote to the letter of Erasmus to J. G. Sepulveda, October 13, 1533, ep. 2873, 10: 306–7; eps. 2905, 2938, 2951; and Bentley, "Erasmus' *Annotations,*" p. 48.

and so entered the suspicious reading in his next edition of the New Testament—where alas it was to remain, despite many reservations, for a couple of centuries more.

4

The reappearance of the comma did not end the quarrel with Stunica or Lee, or with any of the others who now joined in. Erasmus had gone too far on too many controversial points to evade trouble, although we have seen that even as the annotations grew, and new criticisms as well, he softened his stance on a number of controversial matters. Nor did he hesitate to use the Complutensian Greek for help with his next (1527) edition.[99] But we may perhaps be permitted to leave the matter there. For the purposes of our discussion the ensuing quarrels shed little further light, and Erasmus left both the comma *and* his doubts to posterity. Stunica turned more and more to charges of heresy and did not resume the argument over the disputed passage. It looks as though Erasmus was right and that the Spaniard could not find the comma in his favorite Rhodian manuscript—or in any other; and Stunica may even have had some further thoughts about the matter.[100] Condemnations by the faculty of the Sorbonne and the monks of Valladolid, were succeeded by prohibitions of the Congregation of the Index. The unresolved issues still remained as to how far grammar should direct the theologian, and whether Erasmus had drifted into heresy.[101] The debate over Erasmus's Arianism continued without cease through the seventeenth century into Gibbon's day, where Gibbon could read about it

99. For Erasmus's increasing caution under the pressures of Catholic orthodoxy, see Aldridge, *Hermeneutic*, pp. 77–80. Thus the woman taken in adultery was restored to the text, in much the same way that the suspicious comma was returned to the epistles. Erasmus's increasing conservatism after 1522 is noted also by Huizinga, *Erasmus of Rotterdam*, pp. 197ff; and by Bainton, p. 305.

100. So Graham, pp. 49–50, who points out the fresh opportunities Stunica would have had in Rome, where he lived out the rest of his life. The absence of any discussion of the comma is particularly striking in Stunica's *Loca quae ex Stunicae annotationibus illius supresso nomine quos illi Erasmus Rotterodamus impegerat* (1524), where it might naturally appear. There is a full Stunican bibliography in *Opera Omnia*, 9–2, pp. 35–43.

101. For the quarrel with the Sorbonne, see Allen, 6: 65–67, and the ensuing correspondence with Noel Beda; James Farge, *Orthodoxy and Reform in Early Reformation France: The Faculty of Theology of Paris 1500–43* (Leiden, 1985); and Rummel, *Erasmus and His Catholic Critics*, 2: 29–59. In 1523, the Sorbonne denounced Erasmus's New Testament; in 1526, Beda published his *Annotations* against Erasmus and Lefevre; and in 1526–27 Erasmus replied with two long works. Erasmus calculated that Beda was guilty of 81 unfounded accusations or lies, 310 calumnies, 47 blasphemies, and numberless examples of stupidity and ignorance; his reply required 250 folio columns. See the *Elenchus in censuras Bedae*, in LB 9: 495–514, followed by the *Supputatio errorum in censuris Bedae*, col. 515–702.

in the biographies of the judicious Levèsque de Burigny and the even more congenial John Jortin.[102]

For Gibbon, it is fair to say, Erasmus was the best voice of the Reformation, infusing a spirit of freedom and moderation which had only been revived by the Arminians and Latitudinarians in more recent times. In this he thought he detected a "secret" as well as an orthodox reformation, silently working its way in the reformed churches in spite of Luther and Calvin and the rest, eradicating many weeds of superstition, and bringing about the liberty of conscience and practice of toleration that Erasmus had meant to teach.[103] Now, thank goodness, the old volumes of theological contention were overladen with dust, "and the forms of controversy, the articles of faith, are subscribed with a sigh or smile by the modern clergy." Yet even Gibbon noticed that alarm still ran through the ranks of the orthodox when they were forced to confront the boundless impulse of inquiry and skepticism. "The predictions of the Catholics are accomplished; the web of mystery is unravelled by the Arminians, Arians, and Socinians, whose numbers cannot be calculated from their separate congregations; and the pillars of Revelation are shaken." Gibbon was not altogether comfortable with the result, but he had undoubtedly played a role in it, even to reviving the old argument about the Johannine comma that Erasmus had begun. Late in life, he thought of writing a dialogue in which he would have had Lucian, Erasmus, and Voltaire mutually acknowledge "the danger of exposing an old superstition to the contempt of the blind and fanatic multitude."[104] Erasmus, might well have agreed to that, but he would almost certainly have had more serious doubts than Gibbon at the unexpected outcome of his philology.

102. See Jean Levèsque de Burigny, *Vie d'Erasme,* 2 vols. (Paris, 1757), and John Jortin, *The Life of Erasmus,* 2 vols. (London, 1758–60). Erasmus, according to the latter, had proclaimed his orthodoxy often; yet he had said enough to be suspected of Arianism "by violent and unreasonable men." See Jortin's *Life of Erasmus,* quoted in Bruce Mansfield, *Phoenix of His Age: Interpretations of Erasmus c. 1550–1750* (Toronto, 1979), p. 283n. For Erasmus's later reputation, see Mansfield, *Man on His Own: Interpretations of Erasmus: c. 1750–1920* (Toronto, 1992).
103. For what follows, see Gibbon, *Decline and Fall* (1912), 6: 133–34.
104. *Memoirs of My Life,* ed. Georges A. Bonnard (London, 1966), p. 195.

CHAPTER THREE

Thomas Elyot, Stephen Hawes, and the Education of Eloquence

1

To be sure, Thomas Elyot was an unlikely revolutionary. Nevertheless, it is true that when he sat down to pen the book he named the *Boke of the Governour* in 1531, he called for nothing less than the overthrow of the existing order. Elyot was himself a man of substantial stock and noble ambition, and he wanted more than anything else to become a devoted servant of the crown and help to serve the commonwealth. He addressed his new book to Henry VIII with the deliberate purpose of calling attention to his rhetorical skills and political acumen. And there is no reason to doubt that he would have been successful, except for the unlucky accident of the breech with Rome and the suspicion that fell upon his religion and his friendship with the traitor Sir Thomas More. Elyot was forced into a premature contemplative retirement.[1] But the *Boke of the Governour* which had been written earlier, is by no means a complacent tract; it is a call for change of the most fundamental kind. Elyot wanted nothing less than to persuade his king and his class to throw off their traditional medieval habits and replace them with the language, culture, and political institutions of ancient Rome.[2]

Of course, Elyot was not inventing the idea but merely transmitting to his audience what had become commonplace abroad and that had been re-

1. Elyot was deeply indebted to More and Erasmus and the circle known since Frederic Seebohm's account as the "Oxford reformers." He and his wife had both attended More's family school. However, when the chancellor was found guilty of treason, Elyot prudently tried to downplay the "amity" that had existed between them. See Elyot to Cromwell (1536), K. J. Wilson, "The Letters of Sir Thomas Elyot," *Studies in Philology,* 73 (1976), pp. 30–31.

2. I use the edition by H. H. S. Croft, *The Boke of the Governour,* 2 vols. (London, 1880). References are to book and chapter. The work appeared first in 1531.

cently advocated by the more advanced party of English humanists—including Thomas More.[3] Elyot was a practical visionary, somewhere between the utopian Thomas More and the politic Thomas Starkey, and in the *Boke of the Governour* he was intent on laying out a practical program of reform that could be enacted in the England of his time.[4] He believed that the new political order demanded a new manner of governing and that it could only be supported by an appropriate education and training.[5] In the first part of his work, therefore, he applied himself with particular relish to the details of such a preparation, setting out for the first time in England a full and close description of the new classical education of Renaissance humanism.

Unlike More's, Elyot's ideas about the form of government were perfectly conventional and he accepted the traditional order of the estates, grounded upon a "great chain of being," and fixed for all time—an order that affirms and underlies the entire order of nature and of man. Change was not natural to Elyot or welcome, but he recognized that great changes had in fact occurred through the centuries as the English and their European contemporaries had fallen away from the perfections of ancient Greece and Rome. Elyot did not waste time disparaging the Middle Ages, but he implicitly accepted the humanist denigration of everything that had happened in the past thousand years and the consequent division of all history into ancient and modern. Moreover, his silence was as eloquent in its own way as the more forthright denunciations of some of his contemporaries. The whole culture of the "middle age"—that is, the still prevailing culture of his own time—was almost entirely disregarded, as Elyot fixed his eye unwaveringly on antiquity. We hear almost nothing of scholasticism, chivalry, or Gothic art, and if a small dose of medieval thinking still survives in his work anyway, particularly in the long chapters on morality, where allegory and occasional medieval examples keep popping up, it seems somehow unwitting and perhaps inadvertent. Like the rest of his humanist friends, Elyot would have preferred to reverse the direction of

3. See Leslie C. Warren, *Humanistic Doctrines of the Prince from Petrarch to Thomas Elyot: A Study of the Principal Analogues and Sources of the Boke Named the Governour* (Chicago, 1939). Still useful for the continental background is W. H. Woodward, *Studies in Education during the Age of the Renaissance* (Cambridge, 1906).

4. For an unsympathetic account of Elyot's "humanist wish-fulfilment fantasy," and his frustrated political ambition, see Alistair Fox and John Guy, *Reassessing the Henrician Age* (Oxford, 1986), pp. 45–47, 52–73. Fox argues that Elyot was caught eventually in the same dilemma as Thomas More in *Utopia*, and was unable to resolve the tension between his Erasmian idealism and practical life. He does not pay much attention otherwise to Elyot's educational views or their influence.

5. See the preface to Henry VIII, Croft, 1: cxcii.

history and turn England back upon the past, to recover the ancient commonwealth and employ it directly as a model for the present, and so expunge whatever remained of the barbarousness of later times.

Elyot preferred a mixed monarchy to any other form of government, but it is not so much the form of government that interested him as the manner of governing. What Elyot imagines is a style of politics where calculation is employed rather than custom, where words (both written and spoken) matter as much as arms, where the governor is more a clerk than a soldier. In 1544, when Elyot looked back upon his own life, he portrayed himself as a knight defending his faith and his country against vice and error, "having thereto for his sword and speare his tung and his penne." He was remembering his own career as a lawyer, a clerk of Wolsey's council, an ambassador, a member of parliament, above all as a writer.[6] He was recalling Cicero and Augustus and thinking of the new men of state like his friends Thomas More and Thomas Cromwell; and he was thoroughly contemptuous of the armed and unlettered knights of medieval romance. For Elyot, the governor was always a counsellor, an ambassador, a magistrate, and these were the services most required by the new monarchy. No doubt the Tudor state was already turning in this direction, and the "modernizing" of English political culture was soon to be hastened by Thomas Cromwell's "Tudor revolution in government."[7] But it was still unclear just how the governors were to be equipped for their new responsibilities.

Fortunately, there was already at hand, clearly and conveniently formulated, a whole curriculum that could be adapted to the occasion. Elyot discovered it in classical Rome as mediated by the Italian humanists. It was in Quintilian particularly, and in his modern interpreters, especially Erasmus, that he found his inspiration. It was a lucky accident that had preserved the *Institutes of Oratory* after a millennium and allowed its rediscovery in a single manuscript at the beginning of the fifteenth century.[8] Yet

6. For Elyot's life and career, see, besides Croft's introduction, Stanford Lehmberg, *Sir Thomas Elyot* (Austin, 1960); John M. Major, *Sir Thomas Elyot and Renaissance Humanism* (Lincoln, Nebraska, 1964); and Pearl Hogrefe, *The Life and Times of Sir Thomas Elyot* (Ames, Iowa, 1967).

7. This was of course the argument of Geoffrey Elton, originating in his book with that title (1953), and who argued it persistently throughout his long career; see, for example, his review of David Starkey's dissenting *English Court from the Wars of the Roses to the Civil War* in the *Historical Journal*, 31 (1988), pp. 425–34. For Cromwell's interest in humanists and education, including that of his son, Gregory, see Elton's *Reform and Renewal: Thomas Cromwell and the Common Weal* (Cambridge, 1973), pp. 10–36.

8. For the discovery by Poggio Bracciolini of the complete text in 1416, see his letter to Guarino, in *Two Renaissance Book Hunters*, trans. Phyllis Gordan (New York, 1974), pp. 193–96, and the congratulations of Leonardo Bruni, ibid., pp. 191–92. For its immediate impact on Italian Renaissance education, see William H. Woodward, *Vittorino da Feltre and Other Human-*

one may may be allowed to conjecture that even in the absence of that crucial text, someone during the Italian Renaissance would have found a way to reinvent its pedagogy; for Quintilian had only meant to transmit the classical ideal of eloquence that had held sway in the ancient schools from Isocrates to Cicero and turn it into concrete and practical form, and it is likely that a reawakening of that goal would have led to the discovery of many of the same means. In any case, it was enormously useful to find it all worked out for immediate use, carrying the full authority of antiquity itself, and it is not too much to say that the history of education in early modern Europe is little more than a gloss on that remarkable text.

Nevertheless, to translate Quintilian into sixteenth-century English, to revive an educational program that had lapsed for a thousand years, required a bit of legerdemain. Elyot seems to have understood at least something of the problem. For one thing, he had to win over a recalcitrant governing class that was still rooted in medieval ways and reluctant to pay the costs of an ambitious education. In a chapter entitled "Why gentlemen in this present time be not equal in doctrine to the ancient noble men," Elyot regrets that it was still "a notable reproach to be well learned and to be called a great clerk." (1: xii) The culture of chivalry had little place for the learned nobleman. Typically, the best of the young gentry were snatched away from school by their parents with only a smattering of Latin, "and either brought to the courts and made lackayes or els are bounden as prentises." Their instruction was so superficial that a schoolboy had a hard time telling whether "Fato, whereby Eneas was brought in to Italie, were other a man, a horse, a shippe, or a wild goose!" "Lorde god how many good and clere wittes of children be nowe a dayes perished by ignorant schole maisters!" How different it was in ancient times when all the great rulers, Philip and Alexander, the Roman emperors, and every other important man, admired learning and sought it for their sons.

Elyot saw another serious difficulty in having to obtain tutors, "excellently learned in both Greek and Latin" and of a virtuous disposition—no easy matter at that time. And he found himself in the paradoxical situation of pleading for a purified Latin in a barbarous English, ill-equipped with even the right words for the lost Roman things that mattered so much to him. But there was no other way to reach his audience. In addition, the schoolboys of ancient Rome had begun life with the advantage of Latin and needed only to add Greek, whereas the English schoolboy had only Eng-

ist Educators (Cambridge, 1897), pp. 25–26; Paul Grendler, Schooling in Renaissance Italy (Baltimore, 1989), pp. 120–21. For the recovery of the classical authors generally, the old work of Remigio Sabbadini remains fundamental, Le scoperte dei codici latini e greci ne' secoli XIV e XV, ed. Eugenio Garin, 2 vols. (Florence, 1967).

lish. It seemed essential to Elyot to recover something of that ancient advantage, and so he advocates teaching the infant Latin from the cradle, although he has to admit the difficulty of finding nurses (or others) who could speak properly in the ancient language. Still it was only in that way that the child of seven could begin the education that Quintilian, and now Elyot, wished to set out for him (1: v).

And so, despite the daunting nature of the task and some misgivings, Elyot enthusiastically resumed the program of classical humanism. He does not dwell much on the alternative, the clerkly education of the schools which was already in place, but it is clear that he shared the same contempt for scholasticism as did his masters, More and Erasmus.[9] He could not see how an unlettered knight was likely to receive any benefit from the education of the clergy with its bad Latin and hopeless inattention to eloquence. When in the course of his book, Elyot touches upon the characteristic scholastic disciplines of medicine and law, he can only decry "the great fardelles and trusses of the most barbarouse autours, stuffed with innumerable glosses, whereby the moste necessary doctrines of law and physicke be mynced into fragmentes" (1: xiv). (In the event, he tried to rescue both subjects—law in the *Governour,* medicine in a work called the *Castle of Health*—by recovering the classical sources and ignoring contemporary learning altogether.)[10] As for theology, the queen of the scholastic sciences, Elyot seems to have found it altogether irrelevant for training the governor, and replaced it completely with the moral philosophy of the ancients. In short, Elyot was no less determined to replace the clerkly, as he was the knightly, culture of his own time in favor of the education of antiquity.

Since no time was to be lost, he begins with the infant, calling for support upon a little work by Plutarch, which he later translated.[11] The infant, he wrote, "is tender and facile to be wrought: and lernynge is beste instylled and brought in wittes, whiles they be soft and delycate." The object is, "by little and little to trayne and exercise them in spekyng of latyne" (1: v). At seven, the nurse gives way to the tutor, "excellently lerned both in greke and latine, and therewithall of sobre and vertuous disposition." Now be-

<hr/>

9. In a letter to Thomas Cromwell, prudently endorsing the reformation, Elyot wrote, "Sir, as ye knowe, I have ben ever desyrouse to reade many bookes specially concerning humanitie and morall philosophy . . . for in questionistes I never delyted, unsavory gloses and commentes I ever abhorred." "The Letters of Sir Thomas Elyot," pp. 26–30. Nowhere does he display any interest in scholastic philosophy or method.

10. *The Castel of Helth* appeared first in 1534 and in many editions thereafter. It is likely that Elyot was taught medicine by Thomas Linacre, one of the humanists in the More-Erasmus circle. See Croft, *The Governour,* 1: pp. xxxiv–xl.

11. *The Education or bringinge up of children* (1540).

gins the formal education of the child in reading and writing the two ancient tongues. The first books to be employed are the classical poets. A few rules are enough, since Elyot is anxious not to extinguish a natural desire for learning—to put out a small fire with a "great heape of small stickes" (1: x). His method here and throughout will be by imitation of models rather than by precept. His reading list is chosen to capture the interest of the child, to teach him the two languages while "inflaming" him to further knowledge and an appetite for the great world. Aesop's fables are followed by Lucian and Aristophanes, suitably expurgated, then Homer and Virgil. Greek and Latin are to be read together, Ovid, Horace, Silius, Lucan, and Hesiod, through the thirteenth year when the child's reason "waxeth ripe" and he is ready for more advanced learning. Elyot does not expect the pupil to understand everything; it is enough if he receives, along with the languages, a little "eloquence, civil policy, and exhortation to virtue."

The chief use of the poets is to learn grammar, the art of speaking and writing "correctly." When the student turned fourteen, Elyot thought it time for him to learn how to express himself "persuasively" (1: xi). The young man was ready now for rhetoric and the art of oratory, i.e. eloquence, and the pupil begins again with a few rules only, before taking on the classical orators: Isocrates, Demosthenes, and Cicero. "The utilitie that a noble man should have by redyng these orations," Elyot suggests, "is that, when he shall happe to reason in counsaile, or shall speke to a great audience, or to strange ambassadours of great princes, he shall not be so constrayned to speake wordes sodayne or disordered, but shal bestowe them aptly and in their places." He quotes Tacitus that the governor or orator "is he that can or may speke or raison in every question sufficiently elegantly, and to persuade properly." It is only by imitation of the ancients that Elyot can imagine creating a genuine modern eloquence.

Yet grammar and rhetoric were not of themselves sufficient. Elyot's goal, like Cicero's and Quintilian's before him, was the orator-statesman, and like them he wished to combine eloquence with wisdom. The governor needs to know what to say as well as how to say it; above all he must have moral and political instruction. "They be moche abused," Elyot remembers Cicero saying, "that suppose eloquence to be only in wordes or colours of Rhetoricke." The successful orator must have a broad knowledge of the arts; he needs the "encyclopedic" learning enjoined by Cicero. In fact, this meant for Elyot knowledge of history, moral philosophy, and law. And these, he thought, should occupy the student's remaining years, each taught as before by reading and imitating an exact list of classical authors (1: xi).

Elyot begins with history, which needs some geography and cosmology for preparation. Once again he introduces the subject with only a few rules and copious examples. "What incomparable delectation, utilitie, and commoditie," he exclaims, "shal happen to enperours, kings, princes, and all other gentil men by reading of histories!" He quotes Cicero's famous praise of the subject and agrees that nothing else is so important for the governor.[12] Quintilian guides his selection of authors: Livy first, then Xenophon and Curtius, Caesar and Sallust, and finally Tacitus. Each provides a model of style and a fund of wisdom. Livy describes the rise to power and greatness of ancient Rome and the nearly perfect form of a commonwealth in a sweet and flowing style. Xenophon and Curtius furnish examples of those incomparable rulers Cyrus and Alexander the Great. Caesar and Sallust offer military insight in a "compendius" manner, while Tacitus provides "counsayles very expedient to be had in memorie" in consultations and speeches of marvelous eloquence. Elyot would have the tutor "note and mark" for his student the order and elegancies in each work and also all those passages that throw light on the management of affairs in war and peace. In such a way, the student who hoped one day to govern might fill his mind and his notebooks with a store of learning to draw upon for his counsels, speeches, and actions. "Surely, if a noble man do thus seriously and diligently rede histories, I dare affirm there is no studie or science for him of equal commoditie and pleasure, havynge regarde to every tyme and age" (1: xi).

By now the student was seventeen. Elyot had equipped him with a correct and elegant style in both classical languages and a store of literary and historical learning. Now he furnishes the capstone of his education by adding moral philosophy, the last of the Ciceronian humanities, deliberately omitting the rest of the scholastic curriculum: logic, metaphysics, and natural science (1: xi). He accepts a few rules from Aristotle (read now in Greek rather than in the medieval Latin versions, which are "but a rude and grosse shadowe" of his teaching), and then turns to Cicero's *De Officiis* and Plato. "Lorde god, what incomparable swetenesse of wordes and mater shall he finde" in those works, "wherein is joyned gravitie with delectation,

12. "Historia vero testis temporum, lux veritatis, vita memoriae, magistra vitae, nuntia vetustatis," Cicero, *De Oratoria,* 2: 9; Croft, 1: xi, p. 82. "History," the Speaker of the House of Commons told James, in Ciceronian language that was by then entirely familiar, "is truly approved to be the Treasure of Times past, the Light of Truth, the Memory of Life, the Guide and Image of Mans present estate, Pattern of things to come, and the True Work-Mistress of Experience, the Mother of Knowledge; for therin as in a Chrystal, there is not only presented unto our Views the Virtues, but the Vices; the Reflections, but the Defects; the Good, but the Evil; the Lives, but the Death, of all Precedent Governors of Government, which held the Reins of the imperial Regiment." Sir Edward Philips to King James I, July 7, 1604, *Journals of the House of Commons,* I, p. 253.

excellent wysedome with divine eloquence." To this he adds also the Bible and Erasmus's *Education of a Christian Prince*.[13] At the age of twenty-one, the student's education is complete—or nearly so. Elyot recommends as a last fillip the study of English law, remodelled if possible on ancient Rome, rather than in its present barbarous form, "voyde of all eloquence." It was always Elyot's ambition, as it was the dream of all the Renaissance humanists, to see the whole of the ancient world restored. The reform of English education and culture meant to him nothing less than the re-creation of "a publike weale equivalent to the grekes or Romanes" (1: xiv). The best hope for modernity was, in a word, the revival of antiquity.

Elyot's reverence for antiquity and his contempt for the Middle Ages was thus complete. "There is fewe or none auncient werke," he added, "that yeldeth not some fruite or commoditie to the diligent reders." "No noble autour, specially of them that wrate in greke or latine before twelve hundred yeares passed, is not for any course to be omitted." On the other hand, one looks in vain through the *Governour* for mention of any later writer (after c. 330 A.D.), at least until the Renaissance and the classicizing works of Erasmus and Agricola had begun to make antiquity live again. Elyot's revolution meant a return full-circle to the sources of the Western tradition.

2

Elyot has a good deal more to say about education in the *Governour* and in the series of works that followed. He wanted his young students to become adept in a host of supplementary skills and exercises that were both practical and recreational: music and drawing, gymnastics, hunting and archery, and so on. And he had more to say about moral training, to which he devoted the last two books of the *Governour*, as well as several further tracts. But he never lost sight of his original goal: to prepare the young aristocrat for public service of a modern kind. The "knowledge which maketh a wise man" is the knowledge that is useful to the man of action, and even though Elyot was much taken by Plato he prefers the worldly virtues of prudence to any retreat into otherworldly contemplation.[14] For Elyot, it is experience that is the true foundation of wisdom and that is why he gives precedence to history. Knowledge divorced from experience, philosophy separated

13. "There was never boke written in latine that, in so lytle a portion, contayned of sentence, eloquence, and vertuous exhortation, a more compendious abundaunce," Croft, 1: xi, p. 95. The *Institutio Principis Christiani* appeared first in 1516, followed by seventeen editions and several translations during Erasmus's life; there is a translation with a useful introduction by Lester K. Born (New York, 1936).

14. In 1533, Elyot published a little book with that name. See the edition by E. J. Howard (Oxford, Ohio, 1946). It is a dialogue between Aristippus and Plato.

from life, looked to him "a thing vayne and scornefull and more like to a may game, than a mater serious or commendable." And although he was tempted by the thought, it was not enough for him to accept with Plato— and with Christian theology—that sufficient knowledge had been implanted by God in the soul and needed only be drawn out by philosophy. Plato had once suggested of his students that "he dyd put in theim no science, but rather brought further that which was already in them," like a midwife assisting at a birth. But Elyot believed that memory needed a basis in experience, and so he found that history—the full record of vicarious experience—was the indispensable ground for action. He returns to the subject in the third book of the *Governour* in order to point out that history was the recollection of the notable actions of men, "whereof profite or damage succedynge, we may (in knowynge or beholdinge it) be thereby instructed to apprehende the thing which to the publicke weale, or to our owne persones, may be commodious, and to exchue that thing, which . . . appereth noisome and vicious."[15] History comprehended actions and precepts, great events, and memorable speeches and counsels, in short, "all thynge that is necessary to be put in memorie" (3: xxv). It was thus the best foundation for prudence and politics.

Of course, Elyot knew that there were some who condemned histories, as they had poetry, for lying and feigning. Elyot defends both subjects in separate chapters of his work. The poets, he insisted, taught virtue by depicting human actions as the mirror of life, encouraging imitation of the good and disavowal of the wicked. If the ancient poets had occasionally slipped into bawdy, on the whole they had stood out for virtue and had supplied, as Horace himself had said, both the precepts and examples of the good life.

> If by redyng the sage counsayle of Nestor, the subtile persuasions of Ulisses, the compendious gravitie of Menelaus, the imperiall majestye of Agamemnon, the prowesse of Achilles, the valiant courage of Hector, we may apprehende any thinge whereby our wittes may be amended and our personages be more apte to serve our publicke weale and our prince; what forceth it us though Homer write leasinges? (3: xxv)

If anything, Elyot was even more insistent on the moral value of histories, for "in contemnyng histories they frustrate experience which (as the sayd Tulli sayeth) is the light of vertue" (3: xxv). In particular, he tried to defend the ancient historians against the charge of lying. Neither Scripture, the fathers, nor the church councils, he points out, had ever attacked them, and

15. "Of Experience whiche have preceded our tyme, with a defence of Histories," *Governour,* 3: xxv.

indeed had often used them in their own works. And if some of the deeds
that they described seemed incredible, so too could Scripture itself be criticized on the same ground. Reckless skepticism could only put everything
in doubt, for most of our knowledge of the external world depended upon
the reports of others, often of unlikely things. But even grant that histories
contained some fictions (that is to say, be "interlaced with leasinges"), like
poetry, Elyot believed that they still offered the indispensable guidance to
life. Apparently humanist rhetoric offered little incentive and no method
for discerning any real difference between historical truth and fiction, between Homer (say) and Herodotus, and it is not surprising that Elyot told,
and possibly invented, an elaborate history for the Roman emperor
Alexander Severus, which later generations, with a more critical historiography, were to decry as a fraud.[16]

In short, as a moral teacher, history was certainly no worse off, indeed
not very different, than poetry. (For Elyot and his contemporaries, the *Iliad* was obviously both.) Their parallel and complementary roles in the education of Renaissance humanism left the problem of distinguishing them
unresolved, just as it had in antiquity. Both furnished examples for emulation, and both depended for their effect not so much on literal accuracy as
moral rectitude and the eloquence by which they were expressed. And that
is why Elyot can think of no ancient writer, "whiche shall not bringe to the
redars some thinge commodious," especially when they "write maters his-
toriall." History like poetry was the "mirrour of mannes life," just as Cicero
and Isocrates had said.[17] Of course, this was not much of a reply to the
many philosophers and theologians who continued to think that dogmatic
truth might better be found elsewhere and in another manner. But for the
men of the world who required action, the philosophical objection, we
have seen, had never counted for much.

Elyot's educational program was thus intended for practical use, and he
must have taken great satisfaction in the popularity of his book and the
signs that the times were with him. The *Governour* was reprinted, quoted,
and mentioned often. And the ideas that it expressed began to be carried
out in the actual education of the world. Of course, Elyot had aimed high,
too high for perfect success. It was, as he feared, too much to expect that

16. Thomas Elyot, *The Image of Governance Compiled out of the Actes and Sentences notable of
the moste noble Emperour Alexander Severus* (1541). See Mary Lascelles, "Sir Thomas Elyot and the
Legend of Alexander Severus," *Review of English Studies*, n.s. 2 (1951), pp. 305–18. It was the
philologists John Selden and, later on, William Wotton and Humphrey Hody, who first exploded Elyot's invention.

17. In 1534 Elyot brought out a translation of Isocrates' oration to Nicocles as *The Doctrinal
of Princes;* there is a facsimile version in Thomas Elyot, *Four Political treatises*, ed. Lillian Gottes-
man (Gainsville, 1967).

the English gentleman would be willing to devote so many years with such single-minded devotion to the study of the classical languages. The revival of antiquity was thwarted from the first by the inability of humanism to re-place the vernacular; in the end it had to settle for small Latin, not very much Greek, and an English language increasingly imitative of the classi-cal virtues. But the goal of the governor, the orator-statesman who aimed at eloquence in the ancient manner, must have seemed nearer with ever pass-ing generation. And the reverence for an idealized antiquity certainly deepened with time and familiarity.

3

Needless to say, the Middle Ages did not give up and die with the appear-ance of Renaissance humanism. If we need a foil to Elyot's *ancienneté*, a sin-gle yardstick by which to measure the new learning and the continuity of medieval culture, we can probably do no better than to look at the work known as the *Pastime of Pleasure* by Elyot's contemporary, Stephen Hawes.[18] Unfortunately, we know little about the man, except that he was a groom of the chamber to Henry VII and that he wrote a number of poems. He may have been a student at Oxford and he may have received a rectory for his services to the crown about 1510. The *Pastime* appeared first in 1509 and was reprinted several times in the next few decades. For a while, its vogue was roughly coterminous with that of the *Governour*. In 1554 it was still being commended for its, "pleasant wytte and singular learnynge, wherein thou shalt finde at one tyme, wisdom and learnyng, with myrth and solace."[19]

The *Pastime* is a poem of 5,816 lines of irregular English verse with hardly a trace of classical influence and not much poetic merit. Like the *Governour*, the *Pastime* looks backward to portray an ideal, but it is to the later Middle Ages, not to antiquity, that the poet turns nostalgically. It is the world of chivalry that he extols, though without much practical point. The *Pastime* has no reform intention; the chivalric vision has become an aesthetic rather than a social ideal with even less substantiality than the Field of the Cloth of Gold on which Henry VIII met Francis I. The poem combines two traditional gen-res hitherto discrete, romance and allegory.[20] It is a tale of a knight in quest of love and it is an allegory on life, love, education, and death. It is long, pro-lix, and repetitive. Hawes chose for his model the poet John Lydgate (d. c.

18. I use the edition by William E. Mead, Early English Text Society, 173 (1928); citations are by line number.

19. Ibid., intro., p. xxxiii.

20. See John M. Berdan, *Early English Poetry 1485–1547* (New York, 1920), p. 91.

1451), who is praised again and again as "the monk of Bury, flower of Eloquence" (e.g., ll. 48, 1163, 1338, 1373–75, 1385–93, 5812).

The poem opens with the figure of Grand Amour walking in a meadow and enjoying a vision. Two paths open before him: the straight way of contemplation and the other way of worldly dignity. The first is hard and dangerous but very precious; the second is fair and pleasant and leads to the beautiful lady La Bel Pucell. After some deliberation, Grand Amour chooses the "actyfe way." Although there is an intimation that the knight should play some sort of social role, we are a long way from the world of Cicero and Thomas Elyot. It is true that the knight must protect the commonwealth against enemies, but his chief duties are to gird himself with chastity, give arms with largesse, restore widows, uphold the wealth of maidens, and above all "be ready true and eke obedient/In stable love first and not variant" (ll. 3376–87). Hawes admires some of the same virtues as Elyot (fidelity, justice, and sapience), but his real attention is fixed on the exploits of Grand Amour against the many-headed giants who obstruct the course of love.

However, before he can grapple with the enemy, the knight must be prepared. The first half of the *Pastime* is a treatise on the education and training of the knight, a fit counterpart to Elyot's first book of the *Governour,* in two thousand long and prosaic lines. Hawes hoped to combine the advantages of both the clerk and the knight, and so he furnishes his hero with the seven traditional arts of the *trivium* and *quadrivium,* along with the usual military skills, all served up in allegorical fashion. The tradition of the arts was a very old one, but Hawes could find it often enough in recent English and continental poetry.[21] That they were invariably taught as handmaidens to theology does not seem to have bothered this Oxford clerk, although the knightly reader might well have wondered how he was to make use of them.

Hawes may have known the English poem known as the *Court of Sapience* that put the matter most succinctly:

> Ther was Gramor, grounds of Sciencis all,
> And Dyalectyk, full of pure knowying,
> Anf Rhethoryk, science imperiall,
> Dame Arsemetryke was in proporcionying,
> Geometry, that measureth every thyng,
> The lady Musyk and Astronomy,
> These ladyes seven serveth Theology.[22]

21. Mead suggests the *Margarita philosophica* by Gregorius Reich as the immediate source, a popular work that appeared in many editions between 1496 and 1535, and that provided three woodcuts for the *Pastime,* intro., pp. lxiv–lxx.

22. *The Court of Sapience,* ed. Robert Spindler, *Beitrage zur Englischen Philologie,* 6 (1927), ll. 1541–47. See Curt F. Buhler, "The Sources of the *Court of Sapience,*" in ibid., 32 (1932), and Whitney Wells, "Stephen Hawes and *The Court of Sapience,*" *Review of English Studies,* 6 (1930), pp. 284–94.

In the *Pastime,* Hawes personifies the arts and meets them one by one in a tower. He is introduced first to grammar and asks her cunning (ll. 519–609). She replies by claiming to be the foundation of all the rest. Her function is to teach true Latin, to demonstrate good order in speaking and correct orthography in writing. She laments the decline of learning and takes on the willing Grand Amour. She teaches him first his "donet," then his accidence, then the eight parts of speech. She relies on the rules alone without any literary examples. But Amour is confident afterward that he may now know both the literal sense and the moralization of all his reading. It is clear that Hawes's grammar, unlike the new Renaissance variety, is not concerned to find its way back to antiquity but is content with its own medieval usage. As a result, Virgil is typically turned into a medieval courtly lover, rudely and comically described in misadventure (ll. 3692–3724).[23] And the great heroes of antiquity and the Old Testament from Joshua to Julius Caesar, as those of later times, from the legendary Arthur to the crusader Godfrey of Bouillon, are all homogenized as armored knights in a seamless chivalric past (ll. 5523ff.).[24] Hawes values the lessons of the distant times but has no sense of anachronism—no sense of history, one is tempted to say—to match the fundamental intuition of Renaissance humanism about the discrepancy between the ancients and the moderns. Hawes does not know he is in the Middle Ages.[25]

Now Amour climbs higher to meet the lady Logic and begins to learn how to distinguish the true from the false by dialectic (ll. 610–51). Were Hawes training a theologian, he might have dwelt here longer, but he is a poet—as is our fledgling knight—and so the next step is rhetoric (ll. 652–

23. For the long story of how Virgil was transformed during the Middle Ages, see Domenico Comparetti, *Virgil in the Middle Ages,* trans. E. F. M. Beneche (London, 1895); and John Webster Spargo, *Virgil the Necromancer* (Cambridge, 1934). For the story of how he was gradually returned to history, see Duane S. Reed, "Biographical Criticism of Virgil Since the Renaissance," *Studies in Philology,* 19 (1922), pp. 1–30. Hawes's immediate source was probably John Gower's *Confessio Amanti.*

24. For more on the "nine worthies" by Hawes's contemporaries, see my essay, "Caxton's Histories, Fact and Fiction at the Close of the Middle Ages," *Humanism and History* (Ithaca, 1987), pp. 25–26.

25. Hawes welcomes the memory of the deeds of pagan noblemen such as Hercules as an inspiration to the present, "which shall profit be/To the commonwealthe and their heirs in fee" (ll. 250–52). But he does not see the ancients as examples to be emulated in *contrast* to his time, rather as mirrors of the present. "Thus Plato is a 'cunning and famous clerk'; Joshua is a 'duke'; the centaur-king Melizius is the founder of medieval chivalry and knows St. Paul's Epistles; Minerva and Pallas are spoken of as distinct . . . Virgil too is the magician." W. Morrison in the *Cambridge History of English Literature,* 2 (1908), p. 231. For the discovery, or invention, of a "Middle Age," as a "process of self-realization," see Theodore Mommsen, "Petrarch's Conception of the 'Dark Ages,'" *Medieval and Renaissance Studies,* ed. Eugene Rice (Ithaca, 1959), pp. 106–29, and Erwin Panofsky, *Renaissance and Renascences in Western Art* (New York, 1969), pp. 8–21, 108–13 (with many references).

1293). Once again the contrast with Elyot is remarkable. The chivalric world offered little use for classical eloquence, and in the absence of the senate, forum, and the law courts of ancient Rome, rhetoric was confined largely to preaching and letter-writing—and poetry.

For Hawes the purpose of rhetoric is to order words and purify speech. He accepts the classical view that there were five parts to the subject and organizes his own account accordingly. His ultimate source was the ancient Latin rule-books, Cicero's *De Inventione* or perhaps the *Rhetorica ad Herennium,* which the Middle Ages also assigned (erroneously) to the great Roman. As with grammar, Hawes neglects both the ancient examples—orations, letters, and so on—and their philosophical justifications (the *De Oratore,* for example), with the predictable result that we are far removed from the classical world.

The poet begins with invention and immediately attaches "a commendacyon of poetes" (ll. 776–811). Here the defence of poetry finds its chief value in its allegorical meaning, its truth hidden in its "cloudy figures." Some there were who criticized the poets for lying, but they did not know how to "moralize a similitude." Of course, Hawes's master, Lydgate, did, and the poets of "old antiquity." After invention, which governed the choice of subject, comes elocution which determines style. Hawes's recipe for eloquence is to select words that are "expedient" in Latin or English so as to cloak the moral sense in "full subtlety" (ll. 911–50). He prefers a "misty cloud of covert likeness" to a real resemblance, and for once he gives some examples. The poets feigned that Atlas should bear the world upon his shoulders. They meant that his cunning in astronomy did surpass all others, especially in his knowledge of the planets. In the "Chronicles of Spain" Hawes finds the story of Hercules and the Hydra. Apart from getting the classical story wrong and euhemerizing it, he discovers a meaning to go with each of the seven decapitated heads of the hydra. He that "list their science to learn . . . ," the poet is confident, "their obscure figures, he shall well discern." (ll. 1049–50). But even C. S. Lewis was unable to unravel the meaning of much of Hawes's allegory.[26]

Still there is disposition, pronunciation, and memory to complete the parts of rhetoric, not to mention the several arts of the *quadrivium.* But it will be clear by now that there is nothing classical either in intention or result about Hawes's ideas of poetry, eloquence, or education, even though some bare skeleton of antique theory remains encapsulated in his scheme. Although Hawes sometimes echoes the classical precepts, he never follows classical practice, and it is unlikely that he knew any of the ancient authors

26. C. S. Lewis, *The Allegory of Love* (Oxford, 1936), p. 280.

directly. The education of the knight has no place at all for either oratory or history, which is not surprising for a knight who is never imagined to have any contact with practical life. Thus Hawes's view of antiquity remains, like Caxton's, thoroughly anachronistic, with all the ancient poets and heroes modernized into medieval characters. And as we turn the pages of the *Pastime of Pleasure,* we find ourselves in a world removed equally from the real world of antiquity and modernity, from the old Rome of Cicero and the new England of Thomas Elyot. And so we can begin to understand both the revolutionary significance and the popular appeal of humanist culture.

4

For Thomas Elyot the idea of history was a literal borrowing from his classical sources, taken from the rhetorical precepts of Cicero and Quintilian and the rhetorical practices of Livy and Tacitus. For Elyot and his humanist contemporaries, it was thought presumptuous to imagine rewriting ancient history in competition with the classics; it was enough to put the ancient works into modern English so that they could be read more easily and adapted to modern life. It was different for the national history, which had never received a proper form. Even as Elyot was writing, an Italian humanist visitor, Polydore Vergil, was attempting to recast English history in the form of a Latin narrative after the fashion of Livy, while Thomas More (we have seen) was writing up a recent piece of the past in a rhetorical Tacitean form. It even looks as though Elyot himself seriously contemplated writing, and may actually have completed, a history which he called *De rebus memorabilibus Angliae.* We can only guess that he would have attempted to improve on his chronicle sources by putting them into some sort of classicizing narrative.[27] Yet assimilation was slow; humanism was only gradually absorbed into English life against the stubborn resistance of the Middle Ages. Elyot's revolutionary program was inhibited by social and political considerations that were helpful but not entirely congenial. As a result it took a long time before England could become truly neoclassical and achieve a narrative history worthy of antiquity.

So Elyot's revolution was pretty much restricted to the court and to the schools of Elizabethan England, which universally adopted the new curriculum and made it standard until fairly recent times. For a while Hawes's chivalric notions lingered in tournaments and pageantry, and in the poetry of the court, though they soon began that long descent to the chap-

---

27. According to Roger Ascham the book was actually in the press in 1544; if so, its publication was cut short by Elyot's death. See Croft, *The Governour,* intro., 1: pp. clxxii–clxxv.

books of the lower classes, which continued for centuries to recollect them with nostalgia. At first the medieval culture of chivalry combined with Renaissance humanism to create a peculiar compound, as in the great chapel that Henry VIII built for his parents at Westminster Abbey—with a tomb from the Renaissance set in a Gothic frame—or in the more intricate and complicated poetry of Spenser's *Fairy Queen*. The great palaces and houses of Elizabethan England set their classical adornments into a still Gothic perpendicular style, and it was not until Inigo Jones appeared at the beginning of the new century that one could proclaim a truly neoclassical architecture. For the moment, Queen Elizabeth turned increasingly to the bureaucrats who were trained at humanist Cambridge by the students of Erasmus for her political servants, and there are hints at a Ciceronian rhetoric beginning to infect political discourse. But it will not do to hurry the victory of neoclassicism, which took nearly two centuries and the triumph of parliamentary politics to accomplish. To the extent that Elyot succeeded it was by helping to implant a new cultural aspiration in England, a desire to emulate the great cultural achievements of antiquity, as far as they were known and understood in the Renaissance. From the first it won powerful patronage from the great, who believed with Elyot in the practical applications of literary humanism for society and politics and shared his dream of restoring ancient Rome.[28]

In the meanwhile it was in the schools that the greatest advance was made, for it was there that Elyot's prescriptions were taken for granted and the aspiring governor was fed with an unrelieved dose of the classics. This was the natural result of an agreement between educators and patrons that the assimilation of the classics was essential for the aspiring governor-to-be. When a drunken nobleman confronted the humanist Richard Pace at a banquet, he swore that he would rather see his son hanged than be a student. "Sons of the nobility ought to blow the horn properly, hunt like experts, and train and carry a hawk gracefully." Studies should be left to country boys. Pace replied that when a foreign ambassador appeared before the king and needed an answer, it would not be from the nobleman's son, who could only blow his horn, but just from among those learned country rustics.[29] The message was not lost on the

28. For Elyot's influence on later generations, see D. T. Starnes, "Notes on Elyot's the *Governour* (1531), *Review of English Studies*, 3 (1927), pp. 37–46; "Shakespeare and Elyot's *Governour*," *University of Texas Studies in English*, 7 (1927), pp. 112–32; "Sir Thomas Elyot Redivivus," ibid., 36 (1957), pp. 28–40; Hogrefe, app. 2, pp. 357–60.

29. Richard Pace, *De Fructu qui ex Doctrina Percipitur* (1517), trans. Frank Manley and Richard Sylvester (New York, 1967), p. 23. The anecdote is still being told by William Camden in his *Remains Concerning Britain* (1607) (London, 1870), p. 298.

crown, and each of the Tudor rulers made sure that their own children received a thorough humanist education while they welcomed the newly educated to their service.[30] And it was not long before the curricula, statutes, and timetables of the schools were revised accordingly, while even the universities began to open their medieval doors to the *litterae humaniores*.[31] Elyot was read continuously for several decades until he was supplanted by newer advocates like Roger Ascham, who taught Elizabeth, and whose educational works were still influential in the eighteenth century.[32] The result was to create a small but influential group of professional humanist advocates who were able to promote at the very least that "small Latine and less Greeke," that Ben Jonson (who had himself done much better) scorned in his rival poet.

In this slowly developing revival of classical literature, the ancient histories grew ever more popular, in the originals and translation, and continued to furnish the essential textbooks and the further reading of the upper classes, for whom they were invariably prescribed in the gentlemen's manuals and advices for courtly culture that were written and read throughout Europe.[33] And ancient history finally took its place in the for-

30. "The technical requirements for public service had altered. The demand for military expertise had slackened and the demand for intellectual and organizational talents had increased. As the state bureaucracy grew and as modern diplomacy took shape, the highest public offices went to those who had been trained to think clearly, could analyze a situation, draft a minute, know the technicalities of the law, and speak a foreign language." The result, Lawrence Stone continues, was an "explosion" of education in the later sixteenth century, and a triumph for Elyot's humanistic views; *Crisis of the Aristocracy 1558–1641* (Oxford, 1965), pp. 673–77. See too Fritz Caspari for the similarity (up to a point) between the functions of the old Roman and new English aristocracies, *Humanism and the Social Order in Tudor England* (Chicago, 1954), p. 6.

31. The fullest account, complete with many documents, remains T. W. Baldwin's *William Shakespere's Small Latine and Lesse Greeke*, 2 vols. (Urbana, 1944). See also Kenneth Charlton, *Education in Renaissance England* (London, 1965); Joan Simon, *Education and Society in Tudor England* (Cambridge, 1966); Nicholas Orme, *English Schools in the Middle Ages* (London, 1973), and the still valuable older works of A. Monroe Stowe, *English Grammar Schools in the Age of Elizabeth* (New York, 1908), and especially Arthur F. Leach, *English Schools at the Reformation* (Westminster, 1896), *The Schools of Medieval England* (London, 1915), and his many articles in the *Victoria County Histories*. The new curriculum should be compared with the old, as in H. R. Mead, "Fifteenth-Century Schoolbooks," *Huntington Library Quarterly*, 3 (1939–40), pp. 37–42; Clara McMahon, *Education in Fifteenth-Century England* (Johns Hopkins Studies in Education, 38, 1947).

32. For Elyot's influence on Ascham, see Lawrence V. Ryan *Roger Ascham* (Stanford, 1963), pp. 62–64.

33. See Louis B. Wright, "The Utility of History," *Middle Class Culture in Elizabethan England* (1935; reprinted, Ithaca, 1958), chap. 9. An excellent example by a prominent civil servant of the assimilation of the Ciceronian view of history that seems to echo the *Governour* is in Francis Walsingham's advice to his nephew; see Conyers Read, *Mr. Secretary Walsingham and the Policy of Queen Elizabeth*, 3 vols. (Oxford 1925), 1: pp. 18–20.

mal curriculum at Oxford and Cambridge. It is true that the medieval chronicle lingered (like the medieval romance) and continued to be written well into the seventeenth century, but it was increasingly despised. Although it took a very long time to accomplish, English history was eventually written to the new standard; and no one would have been more pleased than Thomas Elyot.[34]

Yet curiously that other characteristic humanist activity, philology, was strangely ignored. Elyot admired Erasmus, but he preferred the rhetorician, the author of the *De Copia* and the *Institution of a Christian Prince*, to the grammarian, the editor and commentator on the ancient authors, whose works he never mentions. Elyot wanted to employ the ancient writers, but he does not seem to have been bothered much by the difficulties that were entailed by that ambition. Imitation depended on recovering the texts exactly and determining their meaning, and that meant a collaborative labor of learned men. Elyot was willing to compile an ambitious new Latin-English dictionary and to do some translation, but he does not seem to have understood the scholarship that was required for such an enterprise and was unwilling to commit himself to the task.[35] The distinction between the oridinary pedagogue who taught correct usage to students and the *grammaticus*, the philologist who needed an elaborate scholarship to interpret literature, was not yet clear.[36] Elyot argued against the common saying that "the greatest clerkses are not the wisest men"[37] and went on to list a host of learned politicians, from Moses and Cicero to Charlemagne and Henry VII to prove his point, but he left out Lorenzo Valla and Erasmus. He was impatient to put his learning to practical use, to serve the im-

---

34. I have covered much of this ground in the second part of the *Battle of the Books*.

35. Elyot boasted of including a thousand words more than any previous Latin-English dictionary, "whiche knowlege to the reders not only of histories and orations of Tullie, but also of holy scripture, and the bokes of auncient phisitians shall be found pleasant and also commodiouse." He did hope that it would be useful for scholars as well as children. The work appeared first in 1539, enlarged in 1545, and further enlarged after his death by Thomas Cooper (1557–87). See Croft, *The Governour*, intro., 1: pp. cxxxviii, cxlii; Lehmberg, *Elyot*, pp. 170–74; D. T. Starnes, *Renaissance Dictionaries* (Austin, 1954), pp. 45–67.

36. By 1625, the two functions are distinguished. "Among the Ancients he was called Grammaticus, who did not onely teach how to speake a tongue well, but also did examine, and discusse all the difficulties in the Poets, Historians, Orators, Philosophers, etc. Hee that taught the Elements of Words, letters, was called Grammatista. Grammaticus with them was as much as Literatus, a learned Scholar or Criticke, whom we now call a Philologer: a Grammatista as much as Literator, an Elementarie Pedant." Thomas Wise, *Animadversions upon Lillies Grammar, or Lilly Scanned* (London, 1625), pp. 1–2. A note in the margin lists Vives, Scaliger, and Casaubon among the philologists.

37. Pace disputes the saying also, which may be found in Chaucer's Reeves Tale; *De Fructu*, p. 15.

mediate needs of the men of the world.[38] He anticipates the paradoxical burden that scholarship, which was developing to facilitate the correct imitation of the ancients, was beginning to place on usage. Grammar, he pointed out in the *Governour* is

> but an introduction to the understanding of autors; if it be made to[o] longe or exquisite to the lerner, hit in a maner mortifieth his corage: And by that time that he cometh to the most swete and pleasant redinge of olde autours, the sparkes of fervent desire of lernynge is extincte with the burdone of grammer, lyke as a lyttle fyre is quenched with a great heape of small sticks: so that it can never come to the principall logges where it shuld longe bourne in a great pleasaunt fire. (1: xi, p. 54)

The Augustan wits could not have put it better. The wonder is that humanist scholarship developed at all under these circumstances, but there is no doubt that it too began to make its way, even in a relatively laggard England. The fact is that once the problem of interpretation was understood to require the new method of historical interpretation, there was no going back. By the beginning of the new century, Tacitus has become burdened with explanatory notes, Chrysostom has gained a massive Greek edition and commentary, and Vives' commentary on St. Augustine's *City of God* has also found its way into English. Even more than with rhetoric, the triumph of philology still lay in the future, but its implications were becoming clear.

Indeed, the rhetoricians could not remain forever in ignorance of this unanticipated challenge from within. Elyot only hints at the difficulty. When however both rhetoric and philology have had a chance to ripen, the tension between them will become clear. In England, the moment of self-consciousness, we shall find, is in the Battle of the Books.

---

38. "Learning is the augmentation of knowlege, which the more that it is the more maye be perceived what shalbe necessary in thinges which happen in consultation, and the more that it is perceyved, the better and more aptly may it be ministered and executed." Elyot, *The Image of Governance* (1540), pref.

PART TWO

Ancients and Moderns

CHAPTER FOUR

The Battle of the Books and the Shield of Achilles

The conventional notion that the beginning of modern times was ushered in by the "revival of antiquity" contains an evident paradox. How was it that the Renaissance humanists, who had deliberately tried to imitate and restore the culture of the distant past, could make so decisive a step into the future? The answer, I suppose, is that they did so inadvertently and despite themselves. They had merely meant to revive the classical ideal of eloquence and make that ideal live again through imitation. What they soon discovered, however, was that to accomplish that task it was necessary first to locate, compare, and decipher ancient manuscripts, to recover forgotten languages, to elucidate the meaning of obscure passages and so on—in a word, to invent the techniques of modern scholarship, or what they preferred to call "philology." Along the way they also discovered the value of ancient objects and so invented modern archaeology, or what they liked to call "antiquities." But just as they were successful in this grand new enterprise and began to reconstitute the shape of antique culture more fully and exactly than had ever been done before, they turned up an unexpected difficulty: the more they learned about the classical authors and their surroundings, the more distant and exotic, and thus the less immediately relevant to the modern world, some of them appeared to be. Pliny the Younger might seem the perfect English country gentleman and Quintilian the familiar grammar school headmaster; but what, for example, was one to do with the Homer of the *Iliad*, whose values and heroic manners were so unlike—perhaps even antithetical to—those of modern Christian Europe?

Needless to say, this difficulty appeared only gradually with the slow and steady advancement of learning. One obvious touchstone was the famous "quarrel between the ancients and the moderns," which began in the Renaissance and came to a climax at the end of the seventeenth century in the celebrated French *querelle* and in the English "battle of the books." The outlines of that long story are undoubtedly familiar: how the humanists, who began the fracas by upholding everything classical against everything modern, were forced to relinquish bit by bit each of the various fields of science and art until the proponents of progress and modernity were left alone and triumphant. But the quarrel was complex, embracing the whole map of learning, and many of its details and even some of its leading themes remain obscure.[1] What is sometimes forgotten is how stubbornly and successfully the "ancients" resisted modernity, particularly in the arts and literature, long after they had given up on science and philosophy. What is even more frequently overlooked is how the classicists themselves divided over the quarrel, some of them continuing to defend the authority and precedence of the ancients as models for imitation, others discovering in the new classical scholarship fresh arguments for freedom and for the competence and invention of the moderns. Indeed, when the quarrel resumed in England in the 1690s, it shifted almost at once from a general comparison of the whole of ancient and modern culture to a single overriding question. Once the redoubtable Richard Bentley joined forces with William Wotton in defense of the moderns by showing the full powers of modern scholarship in 1697, all attention turned to the claims of philology and antiquities. For two generations and more this became the nub of the contest.

Bentley had tried to expose the ancient Greek *Epistles of Phalaris* as fraudulent despite (or rather because) Sir William Temple, in urging the cause of the ancients, had pronounced extravagantly on the merit and authenticity of the letters. Bentley was right, of course, yet he was answered at once by a formidable combination of Oxford wits. Temple, with his young secretary, Jonathan Swift, and most of the polite world, preferred to believe that judgment in such matters belonged more appropriately to a statesman like himself, who had read and written letters to kings, than to a scholar and pendant like Bentley, who knew nothing but the cloister. No matter that the "ancients" had forgotten most of their slender Greek and knew little or nothing of the textual criticism and philological learning that Bentley commanded better than anyone else in Europe and that permitted him to see at a glance the many anachronisms that undermined the

1. I have made some suggestions and tried to revise the older views of R. F. Jones and others in "Ancients, Moderns and History: The Continuity of English Historical Writing in the Later Seventeenth Century," *Studies in Change and Revolution: Aspects of English Intellectual History, 1640–1800*, ed. Paul J. Korshin (Menston: Scolar Press, 1972), pp. 43–75; "Ancients and Moderns Reconsidered," *Eighteenth-Century Studies*, 15 (1981–82): 72–89; and *Dr. Woodward's Shield: History, Science, and Satire in Augustan England* (Berkeley, 1977).

fraudulent letters. The *Epistles of Phalaris* continued to be upheld as genuine for over half a century.

The issues in the new quarrel were thus plain. Was critical judgment to be left to those like Temple, who wanted to employ the arts and literature directly in their lives through the imitation of classical models? Or was it to be turned over to those who did not need it and therefore could hardly be expected to appreciate it, to scholars like Bentley, whose style and manners were rude and unpolished and who were as willing to struggle over a trifle by Manilius as over the epics of Homer?[2] Were the philologists to be allowed to subordinate original texts beneath a mountain of critical commentary and controversial remarks, marginalia, footnotes, appendices, and indexes? And were they—worse yet, with their eternal corrections and emendations–to be left alone to undermine the authority and perfection of the ancient authors? How much, indeed, did it really matter whether the letters of Phalaris had been written by a Greek prince at the beginning of history or by a playful sophist long afterward?

The "battle of the books" raised these questions but did not settle them. It raised them in the squabble about Phalaris, and it raised them again as soon as hostilities resumed. It is sometimes thought that the quarrel ended with the decisive intervention of Jonathan Swift, whose wicked satires, *A Tale of a Tub* and *The Battle of the Books,* first appeared in 1704 and were revised in 1710. These two little works remain the most memorable, if not the most reliable, accounts of that affair even today. But Swift's works were too partisan to be helpful, and his relentless flogging of Wotton and Bentley failed to settle any issues, though he certainly called attention to the pivotal role of modern philology in the argument. It was left to Swift's young friend Alexander Pope to take up the problem and renew it for another generation. Pope had no special desire to enter the controversy, but in 1713, when he decided to publish a translation of Homer, he could hardly avoid it. His motives were more opportunistic than ideological; he accepted a publisher's contract and made a small fortune. But Homer was by all accounts the greatest of the ancients, the prince of poets; his claims to preeminence thus represented the true crux of the argument. If Homer's work could be discredited, then all the other classical authors stood at risk. From childhood Pope had thrown in his lot with the ancients and had

2. "If you prefer Aeschylus to Manilius," wrote A. E. Housman to Arthur Platt, "you are no true scholar; you must be deeply tainted with literature," *The Letters of A. E. Housman,* ed. Henry Maas (London, 1971), p. 144. Both Bentley and Housman edited Manilius. Housman thought Bentley "the greatest scholar that England or perhaps Europe ever bred," though he never developed a true appreciation of poetry; see Housman's *Selected Prose,* ed. John Carter (Cambridge, 1961), p. 12.

learned to write poetry by translating and imitating the classics. He had always admired Homer; in 1713 the time was ripe to defend his classical men-
tors and to make the old poet directly accessible once again.[3]

The time seemed ripe because the debate over Homer had reached a
fresh climax, if not in England then certainly in France, where the *querelle*
had been recently and bitterly renewed.[4] At the turn of the eighteenth century the English reading public was surprisingly well informed about literary matters across the Channel; translators and reviewers brought swift
acquaintance with the French quarrel even to those who could not or
would not read it in the original. In such a manner Temple had been provoked by Bernard de Fontenelle and Wotton influenced by Charles Perrault, and even Swift may have drawn his inspiration from the satire of
François de Callières.[5] From the outset the French had provoked controversy over Homer, first by invidious comparisons with Virgil, then with
their own recent epic poetry, and finally (and most outrageously) with
their own increasingly rational aesthetic standards.[6] The confidence of
French modernity far exceeded anything to be found in England, where

3. In "On False Criticks," an anonymous contribution to the *Guardian* (25 Mar. 1713), Pope
wrote, "Nature being still the same, it is impossible for any Modern Writer to paint her otherwise than the Ancients have done," in *Prose Works of Alexander Pope*, ed. Norman Ault (Oxford,
1936), 1:88–92, quote on p. 90. See also Pope's *Essay on Criticism* in the Twickenham edition
of *The Poems of Alexander Pope*, ed. John Butt, 10 vols. (London and New Haven, 1961–69), 3:ii,
476–78, hereafter cited as Pope, *Poems;* the preface to *The Works of Mr. Alexander Pope* (London, 1717); and in general, Austin Warren, *Alexander Pope as Critic and Humanist*, Princeton
Studies in English, no. 1 (Princeton, 1929); and George Sherburn, *The Early Career of Alexander Pope* (Oxford, 1934).

4. See Hipplyte Rigault, *Histoire de la querrelle des anciens et des modernes* (Paris, 1856); Hubert
Gillot, *La querrelle des anciens et des modernes en France* (Paris, 1914); and, especially, Noémi
Hepp, *Homère en France au xviie siècle* (Paris, 1968). There is a good selection of texts with useful introductions in Werner Krauss and Hans Kortun, eds., *Antike und Moderne in der Literatur-
disskussion des 18. Jahrhunderts* (Berlin, 1966), and a recent discussion in Bernard Magne, *Crise
de la littérature française sous Louis XIV: humanisme et nationalisme*, 2 vols. (Lille, 1976). For the
classical background, see Félix Buffière, *Les mythes d'Homère et la pensée grecque* (Paris, 1956),
pp. 9–31.

5. François de Callières, *Histoire poëtique de la guerre nouvellement declarée entre les anciens et les
modernes* (Paris, 1688), trans. into English in 1725. Wotton accused Swift of plagiarism in his
Defense of the Reflections upon Ancient and Modern Leraning (London, 1705), but Swift has been
defended by A. C. Guthkelch in "'The Tale of a Tub Revers'd' and 'Characters and Criticisms
upon the Ancient and Modern Orators, etc.'," *Library*, 3rd ser., 4 (1913), 281–84; and in his
edition of *A Tale of a Tub* (London, 1908), pp. xliv–xlv, liii–liv.

6. For the sixteenth-century background, see Noémi Hepp, "Homère en France au xvie siècle," *Atti dell'Accademia delle scienze di Torino*, 96 (1961–62): 389–508. The invidious comparison with Virgil begins with Julius Caesar Scaliger, *Poetices libri septem* (Lyons, 1561), and
continues through such works as René Rapin, *Comparaison des poëmes d'Homère et de Virgile*, 3rd
ed. (1664), trans. John Davies, *Observations on the Poems of Homer and Virgil* (London, 1672),
and Jean Regnauld de Segrais, *Traduction de l'Énéide*, 2 vols. (Paris, 1668–81). It was recalled in
England by Henry Felton, *A Dissertation on Reading the Classics and Forming a Just Style* (London,

neither Wotton nor Bentley had dared to deny the preeminence of Homer or of classical poetry in general, however much they prized the modern achievement in science and scholarship. The provocation from overseas was thus too much to overlook.

The time was ripe for Pope's Homer in another way. While the French moderns were upbraiding Homer for his faults, scholars throughout Europe were studying the historical and critical problems that still obscured the text. Who in fact was Homer? When had the *Iliad* and the *Odyssey* been written and the Trojan Wars been fought? How reliable were the manuscripts, and what was the meaning of their more obscure passages? Little by little philologists increased their learning, delved into the language and customs of early Greece, collated the texts and tried to fathom their meaning. Whole treatises were written to treat the finer points, the poems were edited and reedited and the commentary grew steadily more voluminous. Meanwhile, antiquaries added their efforts. Asia Minor was too remote to investigate directly, but a number of monuments came to light and were examined minutely: a bust and a sculptured apotheosis of Homer, as well as some early medals and inscriptions. Words were thus joined with objects in an effort to illuminate the ancient poems, and the interest and appetite for Homer continued to grow.

Thus Pope and his publishers chose the right moment to bring forth a new translation of the *Iliad*.[7] A large audience had been aroused, although its interests were diverse and its critical sensibilities divided. Unfortunately there is not space here to describe the whole of that large background: the many different episodes in the *querelle,* beginning with Charles Perrault's challenge to Homer in 1687 and continuing through two generations of thrust and counterthrust, or the swift development of Greek philology, from the early days of Joseph Scaliger and Isaac Casaubon through the innumerable compilations brought together by the Dutchman Jacob Gronovius, to the comprehensive antiquarian manuals of John Potter and Basil Kennett and the magnificent critical edition of the *Iliad* (1711) by Joshua Barnes on the eve of Pope's translation.[8] If the young poet did not

1713), pp. 20, 24; and Joseph Trapp, *The Aeneis of Virgil, Translated into Blank Verse,* 2 vols. (London, 1718–20).

7. Proposals were issued in the autumn of 1713. For this and what follows, see in addition to Sherburn, *Early Career of Pope,* the introductions to the *Iliad* in Pope, *Poems,* vols. 7 and 8; Reginald H. Griffith, *Alexander Pope: A Bibliography* (Austin, 1922); Hans-Joachim Zimmermann, *Alexander Popes Noten zu Homer: Eine Manuskript und Quellenstudie* (Heidelberg, 1966). Two other translations of the *Iliad* were begun about this time by Richard Fiddes and Thomas Tickell but were eclipsed by Pope's work.

8. The scope of Greek philological learning can best be gleaned from Johann Albert Fabricius, *Bibliotheca Graeca,* 3 vols. (Hamburg, 1705–7); the extent of Homeric learning, from Lu-

know all these works when he first embarked on his long labor, he discovered them soon enough and was forced to pick his way between the poles of controversy in the impossible effort to satisfy all his readers about both his taste and his learning.

Pope's translation cost him more effort and took much longer than he had expected; it appeared eventually in six volumes from 1715 to 1720. The poetry was difficult enough but the surprise was the prose, which turned out (as Addison had warned) to be as bulky and as formidable.[9] The work carried with it an air of learning, with its long introductory life of the poet, its voluble commentary and learned essays, its pictures and its maps. Modern editors have usually suppressed this paraphernalia in order to leave the poetry unadorned, understandably because Pope failed—not in the translation, which was immensely successful, but in his learning, which was not.[10] Yet the commentary is worth retrieving for a moment if only to see just how Pope tried to come to terms with the controversy that raged about him.

This is not easy to do: the labor of five years, scattered over six volumes, is difficult to assess. It may be helpful, therefore, to describe Pope's dilemma by concentrating on one short but pivotal passage in the eighteenth book of the *Iliad* in which Homer describes the shield of Achilles. Thetis, it will be remembered, had Vulcan forge new armor for Achilles, and Homer carries on at great length describing his hero's marvelous shield with its elaborately inlaid facade. To the French moderns this description was puzzling to say the least. Not only did the passage appear digressive and tedious, but the description seemed inadequate and implausible. When, therefore, Perrault addressed the French Academy in 1687, he seized upon the shield in particular to criticize Homer. He had already found the epic heroes of the *Iliad* cruel and capricious compared to the refined modern French, and he had not the slightest doubt that if Homer had had the good luck to be born in modern times he would have done a better job. It was incredible, Perrault maintained, that any artist should think of fitting onto a single object a picture of the whole universe, nor was such a depiction plausible.

dolf Kuster, *Historia Critica Homeri* (Frankfurt, 1696). For the French background to Pope, see Émile Audra, *L'Influence française dans l'oeuvre de Pope* (Paris, 1931).

9. George Sherburn, ed., *The Correspondence of Alexander Pope*, 5 vols. (Oxford, 1956), 1:196, hereafter cited as Pope, *Correspondence*. Samuel Johnson thought that the prose was needed to satisfy subscribers, who would otherwise have had to rest content with little pamphlets: Johnson, *Lives of the English Poets*, ed. George Birkbeck Hill (London, 1905), 3:115, 240, hereafter cited as Johnson, *Lives*.

10. Nevertheless, it is worth mentioning that of his fellow wits, Swift thought that the notes and essays were more successful than the translation, and Dr. Arbuthnot believed that it was Pope's scholarship that placed his work above its rivals: Pope, *Correspondence*, 1:301–2, 305.

"This famous Buckler in a nicer Age," Perrault concluded, "had juster been and less engraved."[11] Homer's allegorical excesses were here, as elsewhere, deplorable; Horace was too polite when he admitted that Homer had only sometimes nodded.

This was too much for the "ancients"—among them Boileau, Racine, and Bishop Huet—who denounced the brash modern and turned the meeting into a brawl.[12] Perrault returned the insults in 1692 with his fourth *Paralèlle* on ancient and modern learning, in which he tried to pick apart the *Iliad* for its deficient story, badly drawn characters, immoral gods, and inept similes. Despite traditional assertions, he also found Homer to be a bad astronomer, geometer, and naturalist. Only time, he insisted, could bring about *politesse* and good taste. One character in his dialogue even wondered which was the more miserable, the poet or his heroes![13] He promised to say more about the shield of Achilles at another time. Meanwhile, Boileau replied by unmasking Perrault's ignorance: Perrault's modernity was all prejudice since he knew not a scrap of Greek and had to rely entirely on a translation for his criticism. "'Tis as if a Man born Blind, shou'd run about the Streets crying, Gentlemen, I know the Sun that you see seems very Beautiful, but I, who never saw it, declare to you that 'tis very Ugly."[14] He, at least, saw no weakness anywhere in the *Iliad:* no flaws in its heroes, no coarseness in its expression. The antagonists were eventually reconciled, but kept to their separate opinions.

Perrault never got back to the shield, perhaps because of a new rebuff from yet another "ancient," André Dacier. According to Boileau, Dacier "was not only a Man of very great Learning, but also very Polite," a combination, he hastened to add, only rarely found together.[15] In fact, Richard Bentley was not much impressed with Dacier's Greek—and it is doubtful that he thought much better of Boileau's—but Dacier's erudition was

11. Perrault's poem, *Le siècle de Louis le Grand* (Paris, 1687) was translated by Martin Bladen in *Characters and Criticisms upon the Ancient and Modern Orators* (London, 1725), pp. 181–211; esp. see pp. 188–89.

12. See Charles Perrault, *Mémoires de ma vie: Voyage à Bordeaux (1669)*, ed. Paul Bonnefon (Paris, 1909), pp. 136ff. Antoine Furetière, *Receuil des factums*, ed. M. Charles Asselineau (Paris, 1858–59), 1:302–3; Paul Bonnefon, "Charles Perrault littérateur et académicien: l'opposition a Boileau," *Revue d'histoire littéraire de la France*, 12 (1905): 549–610. The incident has been reconsidered from a Marxist point of view by Hans Kortum, *Charles Perrault und Nicholas Boileau* (Berlin, 1966) and in the anthology, n. 4 above.

13. Perrault, *Parallèle des anciens et des modernes en ce qui regarde les arts et les sciences* (Amsterdam, 1693), p. 52, reprinted with a valuable introduction by Hans Robert Jauss (Munich, 1964).

14. *A Treatise of the Sublime from the Greek of Longinus with Critical Reflexions* (1693), in Nicolas Boileau-Despreaux, *Works*, trans. Pierre Desmaizeaux (London, 1712), 2:115.

15. Ibid., 2:8.

certainly superior to Perrault's.[16] In 1692 the young scholar published a translation and commentary on Aristotle's *Poetics* that made his reputation. In the course of this work, Dacier defended Homer, his learning (including his astronomy), and his indelicate language, which Dacier was sure could be excused by changed circumstances.[17] Bad translations had misled some readers but the many parallels to the Old Testament which he and others discovered should, he thought, persuade everyone else of Homer's virtues. There was left only the shield.

Dacier had no doubt that the eighteenth book, far from being digressive, was the very crown of the poem. For centuries it had inspired the admiration of both the polite and the learned. That some moderns had raised doubts about the sound and movement of the figures astonished him. It was as though to explain a painting by Raphael or Poussin one could avoid describing the animation or speech of the figures. The critics were confusing the shield itself with Homer's description of it. One had only to remember Pliny's commentary on ancient art to see how such expressions were normally employed. If Perrault complained that Homer described two cities speaking two different languages and two orators pleading simultaneously on the shield, the fault lay entirely with the translations, for there was nothing in the Greek to justify criticism. As for the shield's place in the poem's design, had Perrault but read the ancient commentators, the monumental Eustathius, for example, he would have found only praise for its composition. To have represented the whole universe in so small a compass with so few figures, and to have described all the works of war and peace with such brevity, proved the work to be not only great poetry but great philosophy as well. Finally, the age-old comparison with Virgil could only work to Homer's advantage. The Roman shield in the eighth book of the *Aeneid* that directly imitated Homer was a supreme acknowledgment of the genius of the original. It too was a wonderful work, with its vivid depiction of the descendants of Troy creating the majesty of ancient Rome. But if one were to set the two shields side by side there could be but one verdict. "L'un paraît l'ouvrage d'un Dieu, et l'autre l'ouvrage d'un homme."[18]

For a short time at the end of the seventeenth century there was a lull in the *querelle,* and the debate over Homer was allowed to simmer.[19] Then

---

16. James Henry Monk, *The Life of Richard Bentley,* 2d ed. (London, 1833), 1:311–12. Boileau thought that too much learning was a dangerous thing: *Works,* 2:106–7.

17. Dacier, *La poétique d'Aristote* (Paris, 1692), trans. as *Aristotle's Art of Poetry* (London, 1705).

18. Ibid., p. 497.

19. See the summary of the quarrel in the anonymous *Verdicts of the Learned concerning Virgil and Homer's Heroic Poems* (London, 1697), which leaned toward the moderns.

in 1711 a woman resumed the contest. The insults to Homer had rankled in her scholar's heart, and she had long nursed her reply. She understood that what was most needed to stifle the moderns was a fresh and accurate translation of Homer from the original with an apologetic commentary. Only in a modern language could the poet hope to triumph over the otherwise invincible ignorance of the critics; only with an exact text could they be answered in every point. Anne Le Fèvre, Madame Dacier, devoted wife of André, combined learning and spirit with the infinite patience that was required for the undertaking.[20] Although few embers seemed left from the original quarrel when her version of the *Iliad* appeared, Madame Dacier's translation stirred them instantly to life. "It has ever been my Ambition," she wrote, "to present our Age with such a Translation of Homer, as, by preserving the main Beauties of that Noble Poet, might recover the great Part of Mankind from the disadvantageous Prejudice infus'd into them by the monstrous Copies that have been made of him."[21] Pope read her work attentively in both French and English and used it for his own.

In evaluating Madame Dacier's work, some have preferred her long and provocative preface to the translation itself.[22] Madame Dacier understood fully the difficulties of her undertaking. She had listened patiently to the barrage of criticism leveled against her favorite and saw that some modern readers would have trouble accepting the heroic world of Homer, so she set out unflinchingly to defend it. Popular romance, she believed, had so dulled contemporary sensibilities as to leave the audience satisfied only with the frivolities of courtly love. "What Hope is there," she exclaimed, "that our Age can be brought to relish these austere Poems, which, under the Veil of an ingenious Fable, contain profitable Instructions, and which do not present our Curiosity with any of those Adventures, commonly reckon'd moving and engaging, for no other Reason, but because they turn upon Love?" (*Iliad,* 1:iii–iv). Madame Dacier was determined to understand Homer as the ancients had, as the highest source of wisdom and inspiration excepting only the Bible. If this meant that one had to penetrate the allegory, a certain hurdle for the modern reader, here at least was a solution to the philosophical problem of Homer's gods, so annoying to a

---

20. See Enrica Malcovati, *Madame Dacier: Una gentildonna filologa del gran secolo* (Florence, 1952); Arnaldo Pizzorusso, "Antichi e Moderni nella polemica di Madame Dacier," in Pizzorusso, ed., *Teorie letterarie in Francia* (Pisa, 1968), pp. 16–55; Fern Farnham, *Madame Dacier: Scholar and Humanist* (Monterey, Calif., 1976).

21. Madame Dacier, *L'Iliade d'Homère, traduite en françois, avec des remarques* (Paris, 1711), trans. John Ozell, *The Iliad of Homer,* 5 vols. (London, 1712), 1:i, hereafter cited as *Iliad.*

22. Malcovati, *Madame Dacier,* p. 61.

Christian sensibility. Madame Dacier supposed them, as had many of the ancients, to be entirely allegorical, and she believed (with a nod to the idea of a perennial wisdom) that they might be perfectly reconciled with sound divinity. Like the Englishman Joshua Barnes and others, she supposed, for example, that the teaching of the Phoenix could easily be reconciled with the wisdom of Solomon.[23] Her English translator thought this a particularly brilliant stroke.

In the same way, Madame Dacier defended the manners and mores of the Homeric heroes. If they gave offense to the moderns, it was simply because they were so manifestly superior to the present. "The Gilding, that defaces our Age, and which ought to be taken off, is its Luxury and Effeminacy, which most certainly beget a general Corruption in our Souls" (*Iliad*, 1:xxii). This modest lady, devoted wife and mother, was determined to shame her most bellicose contemporaries. The rest of Madame Dacier's preface is an essay on the difficulty of translation. "The more perfect an Original is in Grandeur and Sublimity, the more it loses in being copy'd." She would make no effort to recapture the style and diction of the original, which were inimitable and must be lost; she preferred the precision of prose. If the result was not exactly Homer "alive and animated" it was closer than any previous translation (*Iliad*, 2:xxiv, xxxi). Unfortunately, this gave away too much to the opposition, for the moderns were still being asked to accept on faith what they had decried out of ignorance: Homer's merit as a poet. There was still plenty of room for Pope.

Meanwhile Madame Dacier surrounded her translation with an introductory life of Homer and a copious commentary, just as Pope was to do afterward. The life tried to take account of the latest scholarship in order to solve the awkward problems of Homer's biography. Unfortunately, Madame Dacier was compelled to rely on a work long ascribed to Herodotus, despite an accumulation of modern doubts about its authorship. Like many scholars, she was unwilling to give up the only extensive source of information that existed, however suspicious, for fear of facing what would otherwise have been almost total ignorance. She was able to add a few details: from Huet, that Homer had studied in Egypt; from her scholarfather,[24] that he was an Aeolian; and on her own, a calculation that Homer

23. So, for example, James Duport, *Homeri poetarum omnium seculorum facile principis Gnomologia* (Cambridge, 1660), and Edmund Dickinson, *Delphi Phoenicizantes* (Oxford, 1655), where Moses and Joshua are described as Bacchus and Hercules. In general, for the compatibility of Homer with Christianity, see the long list of authors in Hepp, *Homère en France*, 319–33.

24. Tannegui Le Fèvre, professor of Greek and author of *Les Poètes grecs* (Saumur, 1664), with an interesting article on Homer. Le Fèvre had educated his daughter himself; he described his method in a small tract, Englished as *A Compendious Way of Teaching Ancient and Modern Languages*, trans. Jenkin Thomas Philipps (London, 1721).

1. The Apotheosis of Homer, engraved in Gisbertus Cuperus, *Apotheosis vel Consecratio Homeri* (1683).

had lived about 250 years after the fall of Troy (*Iliad,* 1:19). It was with some relief, therefore, that she turned to the archaeological evidence that proclaimed Homer's reputation in antiquity: some ancient medals, a *tabula iliaca* recently described by Raffaele Fabretti,[25] and most important, the *Apotheosis of Homer,* a marble relief discovered in the seventeenth century, now in the British Museum. She was especially pleased with the latter (fig. 1), which she had engraved as an illustration, though she left off Zeus and the muses. On the whole she was content to follow the recent explication of the *Apotheosis* by Gisbertus Cuperus, a Dutchman who had identified most of the figures, except that she questioned his reading of the two little animals at the base of Homer's Throne, which Cuperus thought must be the mice of the *Batrachomyomachia.*[26] Madame Dacier preferred to believe that they were really two rats gnawing away at Homer's reputation: "those vile Authors, who not being able to attain to any Reputation themselves, have endeavor'd to revenge that Contempt upon such Works as are in greatest Esteem; and who, whilst Time and the Whole Earth are crowning Homer, have made it their Business to cry him down" (*Iliad,* 1:29). Madame Dacier did not like to mince words; her life of Homer concluded with several more pages of invective against those who had presumed to challenge the verdict of the ages, the new Zoiluses of her own time.

Apart from this, Madame Dacier did not burden her readers with much erudition, and her notes deliberately avoided the usual classical commentary. She offered no textual criticism and few outside references; instead she concentrated everything on proving the moral and aesthetic excellence of Homer. Despite her considerable learning, she was thus closer in spirit to the "Ancients" such as Temple, Swift, and Boileau than to Joshua Barnes or Bentley, content to expound upon "the principal Beauties of this Poem" (*Iliad,* 5:136), so that her readers might come fully to appreciate them. Her learning, when it appeared, was genuine, but it was prejudiced and uncritical. In a curious way, Pope, who certainly lacked her Greek, understood her weakness.

What then did Madame Dacier make of the shield of Achilles? Inevitably, she found it nothing less than "the most beautiful Episode and the greatest

25. These were pictorial representations of the Trojan War probably devised in antiquity for the use of schoolboys. Raffael Fabretti's discussion appears as an appendix to his *De Columna Traiani Syntagma* (Rome, 1683), 315–84. See also Laurentius Begerus, *Bellum et Excidium Trojanum ex Antiquitatum Reliquiis, Tabula* (Berlin, 1699).

26. Cuperus, *Apotheosis vel Consecratio Homeri* (Amsterdam, 1683); cf. [Johann Carl] Schott, *Explication nouvelle de l'apotheose d'Homère, representation sur un marbre ancien* (Amsterdam: Jean Boom, 1714). For Cuperus, see Levine, *Dr. Woodward's Shield,* pp. 173ff.; for the apotheosis, see Roger Packman Hinks, *Myth and Allegory in Ancient Art,* Studies of the Warburg Institute, no. 6 (London, 1939); and Gisela M. A. Richter, *The Portraits of the Greeks* (London, 1965), 1:54.

Ornament that Poetry ever employ'd" (*Iliad*, 4:130). Those who criticized it were completely ignorant of the nature of epic poetry. Among the long roll call of authorities that she enlisted to substantiate her claim, she singled out one above all: Damo, daughter of Pythagoras, who had written a profound and copious commentary upon it, unfortunately lost. Closer at hand there was, of course, her husband, Monsieur Dacier; Madame Dacier was content to recommend his work and to scatter his arguments throughout her notes. Here, certainly, was fuel to renew the controversy.

There is space to note only the two most ambitious retorts of the moderns. The first was a rival translation of the *Iliad* (1714) by yet another academician, Antoine Houdar de La Motte, who boldly altered (or as he thought, "improved"), the original; which he abridged, rearranged, and versified—in a word, modernized.[27] He prefaced it with an ode in which the ghost of Homer urged upon him a new translation, humbly pleading that the *Iliad* be corrected and amended of its copious faults. La Motte followed this with a discourse in which he directly answered Madame Dacier by relating most of Perrault's arguments about the grossness of the gods and heroes, the *longueur* of the descriptions, the monotony of the battles, and so on.[28] La Motte defended his obligation to transform and correct the original, to embellish what he thought beautiful and to omit the rest. Ignorance of Greek did not embarrass him; his touchstone was "reason," by which he seems to have meant some combination of Cartesian philosophy and the commonsense convictions of his time. He thus attempted to rid the *Iliad* of its tedious passages, to divest the gods and heroes of their bad manners, to abridge or suppress the endless speeches, to minimize the repetitions and to cut out the marvelous and improbable. In this way, Homer's twenty-four books became twelve, and the *Iliad* was adjusted to contemporary taste. In the process, the poetry vanished.

Needless to say, La Motte no more approved the shield of Achilles than he did anything else in the poem, and he accorded it the same treatment.[29] He thought the shield defective in precisely the way that Perrault had indicated. There were too many scenes crowded upon it, and the figures were shown in a movement impossible in a work of art. Homer had exaggerated even the powers of a god. There was but one obvious solution: to reduce

27. For La Motte, see Abbé Trublet, *Mémoires pour servir à l'histoire de la vie et des ouvrages de M. de Fontenelle* (Amsterdam, 1759), pp. 330–414; Hepp, *Homère en France*, pp. 661–88; and Paul Dupont, *Un poète-philosophe au commencement du dix-huitième siècle: Houdar de La Motte* (Paris, 1898).

28. "Discours sur Homère," *Les paradoxes littéraires de La Motte; ou, Discours écrits par cet académicien sur les principaux genres des poëmes*, ed. B[ernard] Jullien (Paris, 1859), pp. 181–268.

29. Ibid., pp. 264–65.

the variety of scenes and substitute a few static tableaux. La Motte settled upon three scenes: the wedding of Thetis and Peleus, the judgment of Paris, and the abduction of Helen. For the "ancients," it was an audacious performance, exasperating beyond measure.[30]

Yet even La Motte could be outdone; the Abbé Jean Terrasson was willing to press the claims of reason against Homer even more fervently. Terrasson knew more about Greek but even less about poetry than La Motte. For him, the method of Descartes was everything, reason and geometry almost identical. "The Greeks knew how to speak," he wrote in a philosophical work, "the Latins knew how to think, but the French know how to reason."[31] Time had brought about improvement, but to insure progress in literature it was necessary to depose Aristotle.

In 1717 Terrasson brought out two volumes of polemic, nearly a thousand pages against the *Iliad*, most of which found its way into English translation as *Critical Dissertations on Homer's Iliad*.[32] The work was a vast summary of all that had been urged against Homer in the name of reason. Authority was banished, and with it, the Daciers' arguments about the applause of the ages and Homer's reputation in antiquity. For the abbé, it was the philosopher and not the historian who best knew how to read the past; it was the philosopher "who makes the true System of the Human Mind his principal Study and Application [and who] knows how to transport himself into the remotest and earliest Ages of the World." He saw that the defenders of Homer had erred in making the ancient virtues timeless and their qualities perfect, but he insisted as adamantly upon the reverse: that is to say, on applying his own modern values to the past, even more deliberately heedless of circumstance. Homer had, in effect, failed for Terrasson because he did not know Descartes; Homer had lived in a barbarous age of darkness and ignorance. Should he not be excused, then, since he had done the best that he could for his time? Terrasson would not allow it. Common sense, if not mathematical reasoning, was always available to the human mind, and Homer could have done much better, even within the limits of his own time. "I have observed several Particulars," Terrasson declared, "in which it had been easy for Homer to have corrected the false Taste of his Age, by the easiest and simplest Dictates of Common Sense, and natural Morality";

---

30. For some approving reviews, however, see Hepp, *Homère en France*, pp. 688–89.

31. Terrasson, *La philosophie applicable à tous les objets de l'esprit et de la raison* (Paris, 1754), p. 21.

32. Terrasson, *Dissertation critique sur l'Iliade d'Homère, ou . . . on cherche les regles d'une poëtique fondée sur la raison* (Paris, 1715; 2d ed. with adds., 1716), trans. F[rancis] Brerewood as *A Discourse of Ancient and Modern Learning* (London, 1716) and more completely in two volumes as *Critical Dissertations on Homer's Iliad* (London, 1745).

the poet had a "confus'd and irregular imagination, and in whatever Age
he had liv'd, the Fault would have appear'd more or less" (1:lxi).

Inevitably, a point of reference was Achilles' shield. Terrasson objected
to that "terrible Number and multitude of Objects, in so narrow and limited a Compass, whatever Dimensions are given the Buckler of Achilles"
(2:259–60). The shield was a fantastic, "Gothic" notion. The Daciers' interpretation of the shield as a representation of the entire universe in one
picture was contrary to the rules of both perspective and painting. Using
the rule of tangents, Terrasson showed that a spectator would have to be far
above the highest mountain to obtain the perspective required to encom-
pass the whole earth. Needless to say, the abbé was appalled by Homer's astronomy and astonished at the movement of the figures. His objection to
one of the scenes on the shield, "the extravagant Comparison of a circular
Dance with the Swiftness of a Potter's Wheel," shows his method: he would
not, he said, enlarge upon the bad effect that that felicity would have upon
the eyes of the spectators, nor of the physical error of Madame Dacier in re-
marking that the weight of the matter diminished with the velocity. He
wrote:

> I shall only observe it is absolutely impossible, that without a successive
> Motion of the Figures, the Dance shou'd sometimes turn round like a Pot-
> ter's Wheel, and sometimes open, to make so many Windings; for when-
> ever it opens, the circular Motion must of Necessity stop. Nor can it
> happen that one Part should continually turn round while the other
> opens.

The scene was impossible as described; it was easy to see that "Homer is destroy'd by Reason" (2:274–79).

Perhaps so; Terrasson's work sold well and raised a great clamor. But the
"ancients" would not be silenced, and the Daciers replied at once: Madame
against La Motte, Monsieur against Terrasson.[33] Others joined in on both
sides, and satire followed once more.[34] If a reconciliation of sorts was again
arranged, the issues remained unresolved. In England the *Free-Thinker*
thought that most of its readers would incline toward Madame Dacier's
view, but pronounced the battle a draw: both parties had shown themselves

33. André Dacier, *Le Manuel d'Epictète et les commentaire de Simplicius* (Paris, 1715), 2:preface;
Madame Dacier, *Des Causes de la corruption du goust* (Paris, 1714); Antoine Houdar de La
Motte, *Réflexions sur la critique* (Paris, 1715).

34. See, for example, Jean Hardouin, *Apologie d'Homère, ou l'on explique le veritable dessein de
sa Iliade, et sa theomythologie* (Paris, 1716), trans. into English in 1717 and answered by Madame
Dacier, *Homère défendu contre l'Apologie du R. P. Hardouin* (Paris, 1716). The satire is by Saint-Hy-
acinthe, *Le chef d'oeuvre d'un inconnu* (The Hague, 1714). See also Étienne Fourmont, *Examen
pacifique de la querelle de Madame Dacier et de Monsieur de la Motte, sur Homère* (Paris, 1716).

equally blind, the one to the defects, the other to the beauties, of Homer.[35] On the whole, Pope and the duke of Buckingham agreed with this when they exchanged opinions about the matter a year or two later.[36]

Amidst this debate, one small work appeared that might easily have been overlooked, except that it made an original contribution to the argument and came to the attention of Pope. The author was Jean Boivin le Cadet, librarian to the king of France and a member of the Academy of Inscriptions and Belles Lettres.[37] He had already made a small reputation as a defender of Homer in several papers delivered to the academy and could not sit by when La Motte's challenge appeared in 1714, even though he did not relish controversy. Boivin's work concentrated largely on the shield, which he defended with all the traditional arguments plus one of his own. He saw that critics might be answered if it could be shown exactly how Homer's design might fit on the shield, and so he sketched out just how this might have been done, using twelve compartments around a central boss (fig. 2).[38] He fit each scene into place and engaged the artist, Nicolas Vleughels, to engrave it for his frontispiece. The result, it is fair to say, looked very persuasive to his contemporaries, and Pope did not hesitate to appropriate it, with much else, for his own (fig. 3).

With all of this, then, we can perhaps understand just how and why it was that the young poet thought he had to embellish his translation of Homer with so much prose and why he believed he must take up a position in the *querelle* and come to grips with the criticism and the scholarship of the moderns. At first Pope thought he could avoid the controversy. "There are indeed," he wrote to Joseph Addison in 1714, "a sort of underlying auxiliars to the difficulty of work, call'd Commentators and Critics, who wou'd frighten many people by their number and bulk, and perplex our progress under pretense of fortifying their author." Not Pope, however: "I think there may be found a method of coming at the main works by a more speedy and gallant way than by mining under ground, that is, by using the

35. *Free-Thinker,* 1 (1722): 119–26.
36. Pope, *Correspondence,* 1:485–87.
37. See the *éloges* to Boivin and his brother in the *Histoire de l'Académie Royale des Inscriptions avec les Mémoires de Littérature,* 5 (1725): 433–42; 6 (1726): 376–85; Christophe Allard, "Deux Normands membres de l'Académie des Inscriptions aux xviiie siècle: Louis et Jean Boivin," *Précis analytique des Travaux de l'Académie de Rouen* (Rouen, 1890), pp. 219–58; and Hepp, *Homère en France,* pp. 568–72, 584–88. In 1707 Boivin delivered an account of the quarrel over Homer to the Royal Academy of Inscriptions, which was later printed in *Histoire de l'Académie Royale des Inscriptions,* 1 (1717): 176–79.
38. Boivin, *Apologie d'Homère, et Bouclier d'Achille* (Paris, 1715), esp. pp. 234–41. It is summarized and approved in Bernard de Montfaucon's authoritative *Antiquité expliquée,* trans. into English as *Antiquity Explained and Represented in Sculptures* (London, 1721–55); 4:28–30.

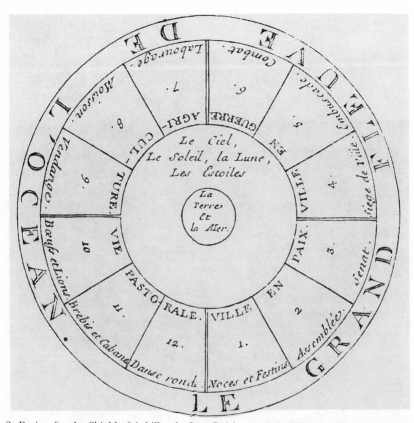

2. Design for the Shield of Achilles, by Jean Boivin, *Apologie d'Homère et Bouclier d'Achille* (1715).

Poetical Engines, Wings, and flying over their heads."[39] There seemed little other recourse for someone whose Greek was suspect and whose learning was deficient.[40] Eventually, however, Pope turned to friends for help. "You are a Generous Author," he wrote to Thomas Parnell, who was persuaded to contribute a life of Homer, "I a Hackney Scribler, You are a Grecian & bred at a University, I a poor Englishman of my own Educating." When his assistant suddenly vanished for Ireland, Pope's despair was genuine: "The Minute I lost you Eustathius with nine hundred pages, and nine thousand Contractions of the Greek Character Arose to my View—Spon-

39. Pope, *Correspondence*, 1:208–9.

40. For some opinions about Pope's Greek, see Johnson, *Lives*, 3:113; Pope, *Poems*, 6:lxxxiii; Douglas M. Knight, *Pope and the Heroic Tradition: A Critical Study of His Iliad*, Yale Studies in English, vol. 117 (New Haven, 1951), pp. 111–13.

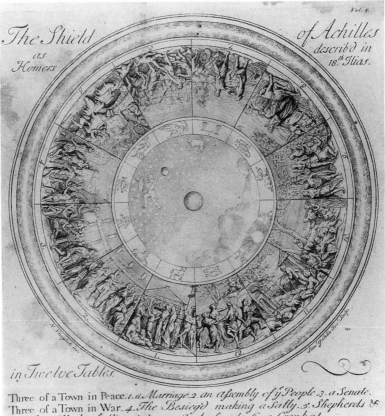

3. Design for the Shield of Achilles, by Jean Boivin, engraved by Nicolas Vleughels for Pope's *Iliad*, vol. 5 (1720).

danus. . . . Dacier's three Volumes, Barnes's two, Valterie's three, Cuperus half in Greek. . . . All these Rush'd upon my Soul at once & whelm'd me under a Fitt of the Head Ach, I curs'd them all Religiously, Damnd my best friends among the rest, & even blasphem'd Homer himself."[41]

Fortunately, there were others to help, such as William Broome, one of Madame Dacier's translators, who read Eustathius for Pope though he was

41. Ibid., 1:226, 225. Pope reviewed many of these works in a cancelled passage of his preface to the *Iliad*, BM Add. Ms. 4807, f.8ᵛ.

instructed to attend only to material about the beauties of Homer and to ignore anything about geography, history, or grammar.[42] Pope translated
swiftly: forty or fifty lines a day, using earlier translations and whatever
Greek he could muster, and enjoyed himself at it. But the prose was another matter. "I am wrapt up in dull Critical Learning," he complained to
Parnell, "& have the Headake every Evening." Even his dreams were troubled, and he worried that he would never finish.[43] The heavily scored manuscript of the preface, now in the British Library, still shows his labor as he
tried to assimilate the arguments of Madame Dacier, Perrault, La Motte,
and others.[44] On the whole, he followed Madame Dacier, though he tried
hard to dissociate himself from her inflexible defense of everything
Homeric. He was willing to allow the poet an occasional lapse and in a modest and surreptitious way to improve the work in his own translation, insisting all the while on the superiority of the original. In everything he tried to
steer a middle way between a "meer Modern Wit who can like nothing that
is not *Modern,* and a Pedant nothing that is not *Greek.*" His main task, he
thought, was to display the beauty of the poem, and he believed that his
own poetic talent was largely sufficient for the task, despite—or perhaps
because of—his scholarly ignorance.[45]

Yet there were many learned matters that proved impossible to avoid if
one were to understand Homer's meaning and correctly translate the text.
Pope was caught, like all the "ancients," on the horns of the modern
dilemma. He thoroughly disliked scholarly learning, yet he was compelled
to fall back upon it. It seemed necessary to him to know something about
the methods of plowing and harvesting in Homer's time, how the dead
were buried and what the ancients thought about the afterlife, the numbers of the contending forces, the forms of political life (did the Greeks
know absolute monarchy?), the ways that time and money were measured,
something about sacrifices and oracles, and more about their military affairs—their tactics, their fortifications, and, of course, their armor. Even
the aesthetic value of the poem seemed to depend on these details, for
Pope adopted the notion that Homer had written the poem long after the

42. Pope, *Correspondence,* 1:270–71; 2:40–41, 499–500.
> Pope came off clean with Homer; but they say
> Broome went before, and kindly swept the way.

Henley's distich appears in Johnson, *Lives,* 1:81.

43. Pope, *Correspondence,* 1:253; Joseph Spence, *Observations, Anecdotes, and Characters of
Books and Men, Collected from Conversation,* ed. James M. Osborn (Oxford, 1966), 1:83–85.

44. BM Add. Ms. 4807, ff. 2–15; reprinted in Pope, *Poems,* 10:409–44; see Douglas Knight,
"The Development of Pope's *Iliad* Preface: A Study of the Manuscript," *Modern Language
Quarterly,* 16 (1955): 237–47.

45. Pope, *Poems,* 7:23; 82n.

event, and (like every good poet) adapted his descriptions to the historical character of the actors and events that he described. If Homer's heroes were occasionally cruel or boorish, Homer was not necessarily endorsing them; he simply meant to portray them as they had been.[46] But who was this Homer: when had he written, and when had the Trojan War occurred?

Pope's notes and disquisitions were therefore full of philological and antiquarian matter, though he tried to fix his attention elsewhere. The biography prefixed to the work was drawn up largely by Parnell, and only the press of time seems to have prevented Pope from including essays on the theology, the morality, and the oratory of Homer.[47] He did include a long tract defending Homer's catalog of ships and another "On Homer's Battels," both replete with maps and accompanied by learned explication and antiquarian lore (fig. 4). Inevitably, the most ambitious piece of prose in the book was entitled "Observations on the Shield of Achilles."[48] Not surprisingly, Pope defended the piece as integral to the poem, believing with Boivin and the Daciers that the shield was—or at any rate could have been—genuine.

There is little point in repeating here Pope's summary of his French sources, which were almost literally translated; to their arguments he was eager to add only one of his own. The shield, Pope noticed, had been described by Homer both as sculpture and as painting. The outlines of the figures were engraved, but the rest was inlaid with various colored metals. Pope wished to show what everyone else had overlooked: that Homer's description was "in all respects conformable" to the pictorial art. He accepted Boivin's arguments for the shield's design, even appropriating Vleughel's engraving for his own, though the manuscript shows that he tried to work out the design for himself (fig. 5).[49] It remained only to demonstrate how the shield of Achilles had been exactly like a master painting.

Pope thought he could do this because he subscribed to the age-old doctrine of poetry as speaking picture.[50] Homer's descriptive powers,

46. Ibid., 7:13–14.

47. Spence, *Observations, Anecdotes, and Characters,* 1:83–84. A previous life that may have helped appeared in Basil Kennett, *The Lives and Characters of the Ancient Grecian Poets* (London, 1697), pp. 1–43.

48. Pope, *Poems,* 8:358–70. See Fern Farnham, "Achilles' Shield: Some Observations on Pope's *Iliad,*" *PMLA,* 84 (1969): 1571–81.

49. BM Add. Ms. 4808, f. 81ᵛ; Pope also drew a diagram to show how the buckler was fastened to the arm by three rings.

50. Pope, *Poems,* 8:32, 246; and the "poetical index" under "description of images," "painting, sculpture, etc.," 598–603, 614, 615. See Jean H. Hagstrum, *The Sister Arts: The Tradition of Literary Pictoralism and English Poetry from Dryden to Gray* (Chicago, 1958) pp. 229–33; Reuben Arthur Brower, *Alexander Pope: The Poetry of Allusion* (Oxford, 1959; reprinted London, 1968),

4. View of Troy in Pope's *Iliad*, vol. 2 (1716).

Pope insisted, must necessarily have been those of a great draftsman, a natural poet-painter. The shield of Achilles could thus be compared with
Raphael's cartoons and praised not only for its invention, composition,
and expression, but also for its characterization and contrast, for its "aerial
perspective," and for its observance of the classical unities of time, place,
and action. From this point of view the Abbé Terrasson's objections must
"fall to the ground." Pope had clearly benefited by learning to paint from
his friend Charles Jervas in 1713—the artist, incidentally, whose bust of

pp. 131–32; Rensselaer W. Lee, "*Ut Pictura Poesis:* The Humanistic Theory of Painting," *Art
Bulletin*, 22 (1940): 198–269.

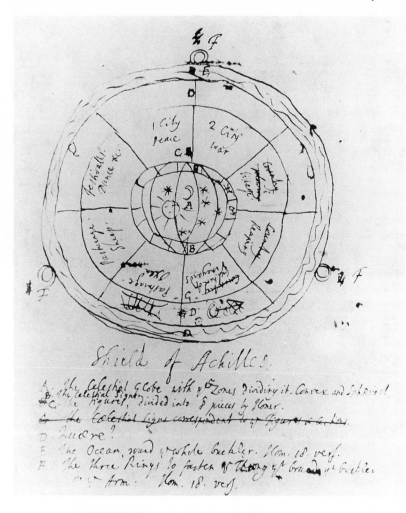

5. Design for the Shield of Achilles, by Alexander Pope, British Museum, Add. MS 4807. (By permission of the British Museum)

Homer adorned Pope's frontispiece (fig. 6).[51] Moreover, Pope assured his readers that he was careful to secure the advice of the best painters and connoisseurs of his time, particularly Sir Godfrey Kneller, who supported him enthusiastically.[52] Those who had raised the objection, on the authority of Pliny, that painting was still primitive in Homer's time were surely wrong; had not Homer described many statues, carvings, ornaments, and tapestries in a way that carried obvious conviction? Since Homer always con-

51. Pope, *Correspondence,* 1:376–77; Pope, *Poems,* 2:237n.
52. Pope, *Poems,* 6:212–23.

6. Bust of Homer, by Charles Jervas, in Pope's *Iliad*, vol. 1 (1715).

fined himself "to the Customs of the Times whereof he wrote," it was impossible to doubt that painting and sculpture must have been highly advanced then. If the argument was more than a little circular, the shaft
graves at Mycenae unearthed two centuries later seemed to bear Pope
out—or at least the Abbé Fraguier, from whom Pope borrowed this observation.[53]

53. A cancelled passage in Pope's manuscript gives a list of Homeric effigies still extant,
possibly drawn up by Pope himself: BM Add. Ms. 4807, f. 15. Fraguier's essay, "De l'ancienneté
de la peinture," appeared in the *Histoire de l'Académie Royale des Inscriptions*, 1 (1717): 75–89,
esp. 83–84.

Not everyone, needless to say, was pleased with Pope's performance, either the poetry or the prose. Once again there is not space to do more than hint at the proportions of the controversy. Even before Pope's work appeared detractors had begun their venomous work, casting aspersions on the enterprise from behind the safety of their pseudonyms: the High German Doctor, Aesop at the Bear Garden, the Grumbler, Nichedymus Ninnyhammer (author of *Homer in a Nut Shell*), and most wicked of all, Sir Iliad Doggrel and his *Homerides*.[54] Pope, they insinuated, had been won to Homer by greed; Pope was a papist; Pope knew no Greek; the *Iliad* was a fraud. They even threatened a new collaborative work: *Homer Defended: Being a Detection of the Many Errors Committed by Mr. Pope, in His Pretended Translation of Homer*.[55] But it was left to Pope's old enemy, John Dennis, to carry out the task. In *Remarks upon Mr. Pope's Translation of Homer* (1717), he proceeded to expose Pope's weakness in Greek, although he obscured his arguments with his invective; Pope had "undertaken to translate *Homer* from *Greek*, of which he does not know one word, into *English*, which he understands almost as little."[56] Pope and Parnell together replied with scorn and satire, perhaps most effectively by comparing their modern enemies with the ancient critic Zoilus, all moved by envy, rather than distinguished by love of truth or beauty.[57]

This was harder to do with some of the other complainants, such as Madame Dacier. She too was offended by Pope's translation when it was called to her attention.[58] Fortunately, she knew only the preface, which had just appeared in French; but even so, she objected strenuously both to Pope's equivocations about Homer and to his unacknowledged borrowing from her work. Pope replied that this was unfair; he was really on her side, although she had fallen into something of the same error as her opponents in overstating her case. Pope sided with the "ancients" but, unlike Madame Dacier, he believed that the world had mended its manners since the days

54. See J. V. Guerinot, *Pamphlet Attacks on Alexander Pope, 1711–1744: A Descriptive Bibliography* (New York, 1969); and Norman Ault, "Pope and Addison," *Review of English Studies*, 17 (1941): 428–51. For the conspirators behind the *Homerides*, see *The Letters of Thomas Burnet to George Duckett, 1712–1722*, ed. David Nichol Smith (Oxford, 1914). Pope drew up his own list in *The Dunciad, Variorum: Poems*, 5:207–12.

55. Sherburn, *The Early Career*, p. 174.

56. *The Critical Works of John Dennis*, ed. Edward N. Hooker (Baltimore, 1939–43), 2:115ff.; Hooker, "Pope and Dennis," *ELH*, 7 (1940): 188–98.

57. See Thomas Parnell, translator, *Homer's Battle of the Frogs and Mice. With the Remarks of Zoilus. To Which is Prefix'd the Life of Said Zoilus* (London, 1717); Pope, *Correspondence*, 1:333, 284–85, 291–93, 299, 395.

58. See the preface to Madame Dacier, *L'Odyssée d'Homère traduit en français* (Paris, 1719), 3:i–viii; this was translated as *Madame Dacier's Remarks upon Mr. Pope's Account of Homer Made English* (London, 1724).

of heroic simplicity in such things as "putting whole nations to the sword, condemning Kings and their families to perpetual slavery, and a few others."[59] Pope tried his best to be diplomatic, but Madame Dacier rightly saw that he had been tainted by the modern infection. What she would have replied we can only guess; she died before she could read Pope's words.

But Pope had even more to fear from the scholarship of the moderns than from the prejudices of either faction.[60] In the end, it was Richard Bentley and modern philology that seemed to threaten the most. There is a well-known story that tells how the two men once met at Dr. Mead's. Pope asked the formidable scholar what he thought of his translation. Bentley appeared not to hear, but was pressed for his judgment. "It is a pretty poem, Mr. Pope," he responded at last, "but you must not call it Homer."[61] When Pope struck back in later years, Bentley's nephew replied for him:

> You are grown very angry, it seems, at Dr. Bentley of late. Is it because he said (to your Face, I have been told) that your Homer was miserable stuff? That it might be called *Homer Modernized* or something to that effect; but that there were little or no Vestiges of all of the old Grecian? Dr. Bentley said right. Hundreds have said the same behind your back. For Homer translated, first in English, secondly in Rhyme, thirdly not from the Original, but fourthly from a French Translation and that in prose and by a Woman too, how the Devil should it be Homer? As for the Greek Language, everybody that knows it and has compared your Version with the Original, as I have done in many Places, must know that you know nothing of it. I my self am satisfied . . . that you can barely construe Latin.[62]

Bentley had had his own designs on Homer (a critical edition of the text), and his own ideas about Homer, each of which might well have redi-

59. Pope, *Poems*, 10:392–97, quotation on p. 394. Pope believed also that Madame Dacier had been too zealous in defending Homer's theology; 6:402, 112. For Pope's surreptitious modernizing of the text, see Pamela Poynter Schwandt, "Pope's Transformation of Homer's Similes," *Studies in Philology*, 76 (1979): 387–417. She has promised some further work along these lines.

60. When Spence raised the question of anachronisms in the translation—e.g., ship's crew, longitude, doubling the cope, architraves, colanders, etc.—Pope replied, "These are great faults; pray don't point 'em out but spare your servant," in S. W. Singer, "Pope's Revision of Spence's Essay on the Odyssey," *Notes and Queries*, n.s., (1850): 396.

61. Pope, *Poems*, 4:344. The story may be apocryphal; for some variant versions, see the *Gentleman's Magazine* (Oct. 1773): 499; and Joseph Warton, *Essay on the Genius and Writings of Pope*, 4th ed. (London, 1782), 2:234. Dr. Johnson believed that Pope's *Iliad* was "the greatest work of its kind that has ever been produced" but as he wrote elsewhere, "Pope's version of Homer is not Homerical. . . . it wants his awful simplicity, his artless grandeur, his unaffected majesty." In short, "Pope wrote for his own age and his own nation," Johnson, *Lives*, 3:238.

62. Bentley, *A Letter to Mr. Pope, Occasioned by Sober Advice from Horace, & c.* (London, 1735), p. 14. *Sober Advice, from Horace to the Young Gentlemen about Town* (1743) is printed in Pope, *Poems*, 4:71–89. Pope denied authorship and tried to escape from Bentley's censure; see Pope, *Correspondence*, 3:446, 451.

rected the controversy. He was dissatisfied with the state of the original text and wished to correct and amend it by consulting the rich manuscript tradition.[63] In a casual passage in one of his works, Bentley described Homer as a simple and careless rhapsodist, singing for a living in a primitive society long since passed.[64] Pope, on the contrary, imagined the ancient Greek as a learned poet like Virgil or Milton (or perhaps himself), deliberately composing an epic according to classical rules for a patron in a literate society substantially like his own.[65] Bentley neither developed his thoughts nor completed his edition, though he did make one astonishing contribution to the understanding of the poetry by retrieving the lost consonant known as the digamma, thus making sense of Homer's meter.[66] Pope inevitably missed the point and made fun of the digamma in the *Dunciad;* indeed, he spent a good part of his declining days satirizing his old enemy as though he could thus forestall the dangers of pedantic scholarship. Bentley was not an antiquary, and he never spoke about the shield, but Pope was obviously vulnerable. In his imagination Pope conceived of the shield as anachronistically as anything else in the *Iliad:* painted like a Raphael according to the laws of vanishing-point perspective, with all the compositional techniques of modern Europe. Pope believed that Homer had understood the art of painting perfectly and that he had represented in poetry exactly what the shield might have been in the days of ancient Troy.[67]

To carry our story further would require describing the whole evolution of modern Greek philology and archaeology through the eighteenth and nineteenth centuries to our own time, showing how Bentley's intuitions were largely confirmed and how they gradually undermined, though never quite completely, the faith of the "ancients" in Homer and the shield.[68]

63. *The Correspondence of Richard Bentley,* ed. C. Wordsworth (London,) 2:668–73; *Cambridge under Queen Anne,* ed. J. E. B. Mayor (Cambridge, 1911), p. 135–37.

64. Bentley, *Remarks upon a Discourse of Free-Thinking in a Letter to F. H. D. D.* (London, 1713), p. 18. Perrault had also hinted at something like this, borrowing from the yet unpublished speculations of the Abbé d'Aubignac, whose work appeared posthumously as *Conjectures académiques, ou dissertation sur l'Iliade* (Paris, 1715). Neither Frenchman, however, could boast Bentley's Greek; see H. L. Lorimer, "Homer and the Art of Writing: A Sketch of Opinion between 1713 and 1939," *American Journal of Archaeology,* 52 (1948): 12n.

65. Pope, *Poems,* 7:111, 236, 271, 389–90; 8:98, 118.

66. Monk, *Bentley,* 1:361–77; R. C. Jebb, *Richard Bentley* (London, 1882), pp. 145–54; J. L. Myres, *Homer and His Critics,* ed. Dorothea Gray (London, 1958), pp. 49–53. A visitor in 1735 reported Bentley as saying that Aristarchus, Demetrius, and all Bentley's predecessors "were all dunces who know nothing of the Digamma which he himself restored the use of, after it had been lost 2000 years," Samuel Blackwell to Roger Gale, 2 Oct. 1735, in William Stukeley, *The Family Memoirs . . . ,* Surtees Society (Durham, 1883), pp. 25–28.

67. The prevailing opinion was that Homer had been a faithful recorder; see for example Pope's friend Temple Stanyan, *The Grecian History* (London, 1707), 1:35.

68. Something of the story may be gleaned from Donald Madison Foerster, *Homer in En-*

Gotthold Ephraim Lessing delivered a famous blow when he tried to dissolve the venerable union of poetry and painting and expressly challenged the descriptions of Achilles' shield by Boivin and Pope. Poetry, he maintained in the *Laokoön* (1766), deals with action in time; sculpture and painting, with bodies in space. The descriptions of the one are therefore incompatible with the other. Homer had meant to concentrate attention on the forging of the shield, rather than on its depictions, and that is what gives us pleasure. It seemed to Lessing that the moderns had been right, therefore, to think Boivin's rendering inadequate. As for Pope, it was ridiculous to imagine Homer painting by the rules of eighteenth-century art; Lessing thought that the newfound antiquities at Herculaneum were proof enough that even after a thousand years the ancients had known nothing of modern perspective.[69]

And so, little by little, the anachronisms in Pope's version of the *Iliad* began to emerge, though it was only much later in the century, with the visit to Troy of Robert Wood, the discovery of the Venetian codex by Villoisin, and Wolf's invention of the "Homeric problem" that they became fully obvious. Richard Payne Knight, who was one of the first Englishmen to come to grips with the new Germanic scholarship, tried hard to steer a middle way. On the one hand, he continued to defend Homer as a "transcendent genius" and the prince of poets; on the other, he saw the necessity of rescuing the text from what he called "the varnishes of criticks, grammarians, and transcribers."[70] Knight tried his hand at a new edition of the *Iliad*, in which he systematically employed Bentley's digamma, and he was even willing to allow that the *Odyssey* was an inferior poem by a later poet. In the introduction to his *Analytical Essay on the Greek Alphabet* (1791), he drew the usual distinction between the two kinds of critics: those whose chief office was "pointing out the beauties, and detecting the faults of literary composition" and those who "undertake the more laborious task of washing away the rust and canker of time, and bringing back those forms and colours . . .

---

glish Criticism: The Historical Approach in the Eighteenth Century (New Haven, 1947); and Georg Finsler, *Homer in der Neuzeit von Dante bis Goethe* (Leipzig and Berlin, 1912). Less helpful is Kirsti Simonsuuri, *Homer's Original Genius: Eighteenth-Century Notices of the Early Greek Epic (1688–1798)* (Cambridge, 1979).

69. Lessing, *Sämtliche Schriften*, ed. Karl Lachmann, rev. ed. Franz Muncker (Stuttgart, 1886–1924). vol. 9; see Hugo Blümner, *Lessings Laokoön* (Berlin, 1880), pp. 1–140.

70. Knight, *Specimens of Antient Sculpture* (1809), 1: xii–xiii, quoted in Michael Clarke and Nicholas Penny, eds., *The Arrogant Connoisseur: Richard Payne Knight, 1751–1824* (Manchester, 1982), p. 8; Knight, *An Analytical Essay on the Greek Alphabet* (London, 1791), p. 23. For Knight, see Frank J. Messmann, *Richard Payne Knight: The Twilight of Virtuosity* (The Hague, 1974); M. L. Clarke, *Greek Studies in England, 1700–1830* (Cambridge, 1945), pp. 140–42.

to their original purity and brightness."[71] He placed himself unequivocally
with the latter, that is to say, with the "index-makers and antiquaries." Yet
even so he could not agree with the philologists Wolf and Heyne that the *Iliad* was patchwork, nor, as they insisted, that the description of the shield
of Achilles was the later interpolation of a Greek grammarian.[72]

Nevertheless, despite the efforts of Knight and others, modern philology marched on in the nineteenth century and shattered all confidence
both in the biography of the poet and in the integrity of the poem, while
further widening the distance between the poem and contemporary life.
When at last, with Heinrich Schliemann, the worm appeared to turn, and
the historical reality of the Homeric events seemed once more to be confirmed, the landscape had altered irretrievably. With the excavations at
Troy and Mycenae the remains of Homeric culture, including some tanta-
lizing bits of armor—though no shields—could be glimpsed directly for
the first time.[73] It now seemed possible to return to the poem and to try
again to determine just what the historical substratum was in this apparently cumulative work. A new effort to reconstruct the shield was thus begun.[74] But neither Homer, nor Troy, nor the *Iliad* itself would ever look
again quite the way they had to Alexander Pope and his friends.

Meanwhile, for generation after generation the shield continued to capture the imagination of scholars as well as poets and painters. A few years
after Pope, the Comte de Caylus, renowned collector and antiquary, resumed the traditional comparison between Homer and his rivals and
reprinted Boivin's design along with a reconstruction of imitations by Hesiod and Virgil (figs. 7, 8).[75] In England a new translation of the *Aeneid* respectfully proclaimed the superiority of the Roman shield over the Greek
and offered a fresh engraving to back it up (fig. 9).[76] With the new century,
the English artist Flaxman, who had already illustrated the *Iliad*, chose the

71. Knight, *Analytical Essay*, p. 2.
72. Porson treated Knight's views respectfully in the *Monthly Review*, reprinted in *Museum
Criticum; or, Cambridge Classical Researches* (Cambridge, 1826), 1:489–509. For the German
background, see the fine essay by Anthony Grafton, "Prolegomena to Friedrich August Wolf,"
Journal of the Warburg and Courtauld Institutes, 44 (1981): 101–29.
73. Carl Schuchhardt, *Schliemann's Excavations: An Archaeological and Historical Study*, trans.
Eugenie Sellers (London, 1891), pp. 229–32.
74. See, for example, A. J. Evans, "The Minoan and Mycenaean Element in Hellenic Life,"
Journal of Hellenic Studies, 32 (1912): 277–97; Walter Leaf and M. A. Bayfield, *The Iliad of Homer*
(London, 1888), 2:249–50; 2d ed. (1902), 2:app. I, 602–14. Also see John Linton Myres, *Who
Were the Greeks?* (Berkeley, 1930: rep. New York, 1967), pp. 517–25, fig. 21.
75. *Histoire de l'Académie Royale des Inscriptions*, 27 (1761): 21–33. For Caylus, see Samuel
Rocheblave, *Essai sur le Comte de Caylus: l'homme, l'artiste, l'antiquaire* (Paris: Hachette, 1889).
76. William Whitehead, "Observations on the Shield of Aeneas," *The Works of Virgil*, ed.
Joseph Warton (London, 1763), 3:457–92.

7 and 8. (*From top*) Shield of Hercules in Hesiod and Shield of Aeneas in Virgil, designed by the Comte de Caylus, *Histoire de l'Académie Royale des Inscriptions,* vol. 27 (1761).

9. Shield of Aeneas in *The Works of Virgil*, ed. Joseph Warton, vol. 3 (1763).

shield of Achilles as the subject of his masterpiece. And by 1854, William
Watkiss Lloyd, the dilettante historian, was ready to devote a whole book to
the subject, complete with foldout plan.[77] Gladstone, it is true, returned to
the design of Boivin in an essay in the *Contemporary Review* (1874), though
he criticized Pope's translation and offered one of his own.[78] But it was the
Germans who tried to reconstitute the shield in the light of the new archaeology, and the standard English works on Greek sculpture by A. S.

77. Lloyd, *On the Homeric Design of the Shield of Achilles* (London, 1854). For Flaxman, see
David Irwin, *John Flaxman, 1755–1826: Sculptor, Illustrator, Designer* (New York, 1979).
78. W. E. Gladstone, "The Shield of Achilles," *Contemporary Review*, 23 (1873–74): 329–44;
the translation is dated 1867. For Gladstone's view of Pope, see "The Reply of Achilles to the
Envoys of Agamemnon," ibid., p. 842. For Gladstone and Homer, see Frank M. Turner, *The
Greek Heritage in Victorian Britain* (New Haven, 1981), pp. 161ff.

Murray and E. A. Gardner reflect their efforts. Homer, Murray insisted, "could not have conceived the thought of a god executing a piece of imitative art, had no imitative art existed without his knowledge." He offered still another new design, this time worked up from some real objects of Homer's period (fig. 10).[79]

In the absence of the object itself a definitive solution to the problem was hardly possible, and it is not surprising that the doubts of Lessing and the moderns were heard again. "The shield of Achilles is a masterpiece," we have been told lately, "for which we must not expect to find material parallels in any age . . . the description is too poetical in character for it to be reliably related to any particular style or system of iconography. As well try to assign to its precise period the Grecian urn of Keats's ode."[80] And from another recent scholar: "Certainly the poet had in mind a typical contemporary shield with all its decorations set in. . . . But the choice of themes and composition of the whole are exclusively his achievement. Achilles' shield is a creation certainly conceived in Homer's imagination alone."[81]

Yet who can say for sure? In history the a priori imagination is not enough, or Pope and Lessing might have settled the issue long ago. It is not hard to conceive of new evidence: an inlaid Mycenaean shield, perhaps, that might bear on the historical question and even help to settle it.[82] But it is surely another matter with the aesthetic question, with our appreciation of the shield of Achilles as a work of art. Both the "ancients" and the moderns thought that its historical reality was important and did what they could to find out about it. Modern scholarship remains committed to the task as though it would make some difference to the poem, though most modern poetic theory would seem to doubt it. In history, issues are sometimes settled; in criticism, less obviously so. I suspect that the merit and the

79. A. S. Murray, *A History of Greek Sculpture* (London, 1897), pp. 69–72. Ernest Arthur Gardner, *A Handbook of Greek Sculpture* (London, 1897), pp. 69–72. Cf. Walter Copland Perry, *Greek and Roman Sculpture: A Popular Introduction to the History of Greek and Roman Sculpture* (London, 1882), pp. 36–39.

80. Frank H. Stubbings, "Arms and Armour," *A Companion to Homer,* ed. Alan J. B. Wace and Frank H. Stubbings (London, 1962), p. 512–13—a view that derives from Carl Robert, *Studien zur Ilias* (Berlin, 1901), pp. 14ff.

81. Johannes Th. Kakridis, *Homer Revisited* (Lund, 1971), p. 108. See also T. B. L. Webster, *From Mycenae to Homer,* 2d ed. (New York, 1964), p. 214.

82. Hilda Lockhart Lorimer, *Homer and the Monuments* (London, 1950), pp. 132–335; D. H. F. Gray, "Metal-Working in Homer," *Journal of Hellenic Studies,* 74 (1954): 1–15; Anthony M. Snodgrass, *Early Greek Armour and Weapons: From the End of the Bronze Age to 600 B.C.* (Edinburgh: Edinburgh University, 1964), p. 214. Some comparable objects from Homer's period have in fact turned up in recent times and are illustrated in works by Schadewaldt (1959 and Fittschen (1973); see Malcolm M. Willcock, *A Companion to the Iliad* (Chicago, 1976) pp. 209–14.

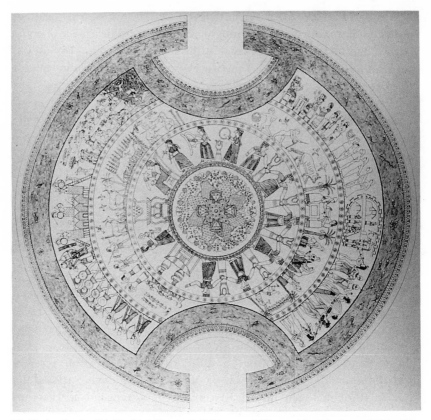

10. Design for the Shield of Achilles, by A. S. Murray, *A History of Greek Sculpture* (1880–83).

meaning of Homer's shield of Achilles will remain an issue whatever the progress of archaeology and scholarship. One thing alone is clear: Pope and the "ancients" were right to see that the *Iliad* could not survive the thrusts of modern scholarship as a contemporary poem, that is to say, a poem with a direct and immediate practical relevance. Today the distance between the "ancients" and the moderns has grown too great ever to read the *Iliad* the way Pope understood and translated it or to visualize the shield of Achilles with Boivin. "It is the unlikeness of the Greeks to ourselves," writes W. H. Auden, "the gulf between the kind of assumptions they made, the kind of questions they asked and our own that strikes us more than anything else."[83] The immediate value of the classics and their service as mod-

83. W. H. Auden, ed., *The Portable Greek Reader* (1948; rep. New York: Viking, 1955), p. 16. See Turner, *The Greek Heritage*, p. 8.

els to life have grown obscure. To that extent, we have, I am afraid, become the victims as well as the beneficiaries of contemporary historical scholarship and the modern sense of the past. And to that extent, the "ancients" in the "battle of the books" were undoubtedly right to fear and to distrust their learned contemporaries, however much we may regret their own anachronistic misunderstanding of the classics.

CHAPTER FIVE

Strife in the Republic of Letters

Republics were notorious for internecine strife; at least that is how they were often remembered in the early modern period. The "republic of letters" was no exception. Although it existed without laws or a constitution, it was generally believed to have a real existence and to be governed by long-standing conventions. It was first of all a community of scholars and writers who wanted to share their work. It thrived on communication and a shared sense of enterprise.[1] But there were many obstacles to communication, obstacles rooted in the cultural situation. There were religious differences; problems of language as the vernacular tongues began to replace the Latin; and there were, as always, bitter personal rivalries. Perhaps most obtrusively, there was a rift in the culture of the cultivated classes, a rift deep enough to separate the republic into two very different and hostile groups: the men (and occasionally the women) of letters and the scholars and savants. Between these two armed camps there was little communication and much contempt.

The division was profound, rooted in the ancient antipathy between the sophists and the philosophers of ancient Greece. The sophists espoused a paideia in which rhetoric and literature were supreme and which was skeptical of dogmatic truth; the philosophers proposed a paideia in which logic and dialectic were foremost and where the truths of nature and metaphysics were revealed.[2] The sophists declared a practical goal: the education of those who were to rule. The philosophers claimed a more

---

1. See Anne Hartman Goldgar, *Gentleman Scholars: Conduct and Community in the Republic of Letters, 1680–1750* (New Haven, 1998).

2. Jaeger finds the source of this antipathy, which "runs like a leit-motive throughout the history of ancient civilization," in the rivalry between the "humanist" Isocrates and the philosopher Plato; see Werner Jaeger, *Paideia: The Ideals of Greek Culture*, trans. Gilbert Highet,

contemplative end: the cultivation of the soul for the good life. There was not much communication between ancient science and philosophy on the one hand and ancient letters on the other, although there was some overlap. In ethics particularly, there were rival claims and sometimes overt hostilities. The rhetoricians, like Lucian or Quintilian, declared their contempt for what they took to be an unworldly philosophy; the philosophers, led by Plato, rebuked the rhetoricians and poets for their "sophistry."[3] Some, like Cicero, tried to bridge the gap, but the tendency of the Romans was to side with oratory and the practical arts.[4] All this was remembered when the ancients were restored during the Renaissance and classical rhetoric was once again installed in the schools of early modern Europe. The republic of letters was created in the throes of this division.

At the beginning of the "revival of letters," the rift that divided the world of learning was between the humanists and the scholastics. To that extent it was a recapitulation of the ancient quarrel. The scholastics dominated the universities, where they held forth particularly on theology, and on law and medicine, thus furnishing a foundation for theoretical knowledge and the only professional education of the day. Curiously, they advocated the use of Aristotelian logic and philosophy as the best means to their ends, thus restoring to some extent the scientific paideia of antiquity, but adapt-

---

3 vols. (New York, 1944), 3: pp. 46–70. See also, for the contrast between the Platonic idea of truth and the Isocratic reliance on speech, and for the "fundamental antinomy between scientific research and education," H. I. Marrou, *A History of Education in Antiquity*, trans. George Lamb (London, 1956), pp. 57, 81ff. This fundamental rivalry continues, according to Marrou, whenever the classical tradition persists or reappears (p. 210).

3. Plato, according to his French translator, André Dacier, perfected the art of reasoning, which treats the essence of things, "and leads us to distinguish that which is Eternal, from that which is but Temporal and Transitory; and this not by Reasonings founded in Opinion, but by Truths drawn from Science." According to Dacier, Isocrates preferred rhetoric to philosophy; in general, the orator chooses to move the passions rather than appeal to reason, and is unable to distinguish truth from falsehood. André Dacier, *The Works of Plato Abridg'd*, 2 vols. (London, 1701), 1: pp. 145, 149–50. See also Thomas Stanley, *The History of Philosophy* (London, 1655), p. 93. Isocrates replies, "It is much better to form probable opinions about useful things than to have an exact knowledge of useless things," *Helenae Encomium*, 5. For the skepticism of the sophists (still much disputed), see W. K. C. Guthrie, *A History of Greek Philosophy*, 3 (Cambridge, 1969), pp. 50, 176–225, 267. Although the later Plato (of the *Phaedrus*) and his pupil Aristotle eventually found a place for rhetoric in their philosophies, they continued to oppose the sophists and deny their pedagogical and epistemological claims; see, for example, John Burnet, *Aristotle on Education* (Cambridge, 1905), p. 136.

4. See Richard McKeon, "Introduction to the Philosophy of Cicero," in Cicero, *Brutus, On the Nature of the Gods, On Divination, On Duties*, trans. H. M. Poteat (Chicago, 1950), pp. 1–66; Alain Michel, *Rhétorique et philosophie chez Cicéron* (Paris, 1960), chaps. 2–3. On the whole, early modern Europe imagined a Cicero who never wasted his time in "idle speculations" but surpassed all the ancients in eloquence and the theory and practice of public life. See, for example, the translator of the *Five Books of Tusculan Disputations* (London, 1715), pp. x–xiii.

ing it to the practical needs of a Christian community.[5] Sophistry on the other hand, that is, the ancient culture of letters, was pretty much neglected, or left to flourish in the vernacular culture of the courts. It was the Italian humanists who rediscovered the special value of classical eloquence to the man of the world and who restored the classical paideia that had been invented by the Greeks for that purpose.[6] They soon took over the basic curriculum of the schools and the education of the upper classes and reinstituted the best of the classical authors (poets, orators, and historians) as the sole objects of study. In the great rivalry that ensued among the disciplines, it was, paradoxically, the advocates of antiquity who were the advanced party, against the medieval "moderns," who were generally content to neglect the ancient authors (except for a Latin Aristotle) and a "correct" Latin style, preferring their own language and purposes.[7] Still, for much of the early modern period, the scholastics (Protestant now as well as Catholic) continued to teach in the universities and supply the theological education that was thought necessary for aspiring clerics, often side by side in uneasy proximity with the newer humanistic disciplines.[8]

5. See Werner Jaeger, *Humanism and Theology* (Milwaukee, 1943).

6. For a useful summary and bibliography, see John Monfasani, "Humanism and Rhetoric," in *Renaissance Humanism*, ed. Albert Rabil (Philadelphia, 1988), pp. 171–235.

7. Petrarch fought with the Averroists; Valla is famous for his attack on dialectic; and there were many other outbreaks of hostility between the disciplines in the Renaissance and afterward; see, for example, Jerrold E. Siegel, *Rhetoric and Philosophy in Renaissance Humanism* (Princeton, 1968), pp. 137–69; N. W. Gilbert, "The Early Italian Humanists and Disputation," in *Renaissance Studies in Honor of Hans Baron*, ed. A. Molho and J. Tedeschi (Florence, 1970), pp. 201–26; Quirinus Breen, "Giovanni Pico della Mirandola on the Conflict between Philosophy and Rhetoric," *Journal of the History of Ideas*, 13 (1952), pp. 384–426, reprinted in his *Christianity and Humanism*, ed. N. P. Ross (Grand Rapids, 1968), pp. 3–38; *Juan Luis Vives against the Pseudodialecticians: A Humanist Attack on Medieval Logic*, ed. and trans. Rita Guerlac (Dordrecht, 1979); James H. Overfield, "Scholastic Opposition to Humanism in Pre-Reformation Germany," *Viator*, 7 (1976), pp. 391–420. For the origins of the quarrel, see August Buck, "Aus der Vorgeschichte der Querelle des Anciens et des Modernes in Mittelalter und Renaissance," *Bibliothèque d'Humanisme et Renaissance*, 20 (1958), pp. 527–41; Hans Baron, "The Querelle of the Ancients and Moderns as a Problem for Renaissance Scholarship," *Journal of the History of Ideas*, 20 (1959), pp. 3–22; Robert Black, "Ancients and Moderns in the Renaissance," *Journal of the History of Ideas*, 43 (1982), pp. 3–32.

8. See, for example, Charles Schmitt, "Towards a Reassessment of Renaissance Aristotelianism," *History of Science*, 11 (1973), pp. 159–93; *Aristotle and the Renaissance* (Cambridge, Mass., 1983); and *John Case and Aristotelianism in Renaissance England* (Kingston, 1983). Still useful is Charles Beard, "The Rise of Protestant Scholasticism," *The Reformation of the Sixteenth Century* (London, 1883), chap. 8; and for the continuing rivalry, William Costello, *The Scholastic Curriculum at Early Seventeenth Century Cambridge* (Cambridge, Mass., 1958). One of the best students of Renaissance thought, Paul Kristeller, would downplay the opposition between humanism and scholasticism, though he acknowledges that there were some "violent critics of medieval learning." He characterizes the humanists as "professional rhetoricians with a new ideal of classical culture," distinguishing them from the philosophers, and seems to hope

The same battle that was fought by Erasmus and More against the "Trojans" at Oxford at the beginning of the sixteenth century, when they tried to intrude Latin rhetoric and the Greek language on the old curriculum, was still being fought there some two hundred years later.[9] And some of the same satirical techniques that the humanists had employed against their enemies in the *Praise of Folly* and the *Letters of Obscure Men* were still remembered then.[10]

But the revival of the ancient authors required skills that were new, techniques of retrieval that were adequate to the task of recovering, understanding, and employing a literature that had been neglected for a thousand years and more. And so the first humanists, from Petrarch on, besides being advocates and imitators of the classical authors, were the inventors of modern philology and archaeology.[11] For a while, there was little conflict between the men of literature and the men of learning, who were dedicated to the same great task of reviving antiquity for its use in the present. And it was in this climate of scholarly and literary cooperation that we first hear the expression "republic of letters."[12] By the middle of the fifteenth century, it is true, the two tasks had begun to separate; neither

---

(like many then and now) that the fundamental difference in outlook can be comprised in a single harmonious whole; see Paul Oskar Kristeller, "Humanism and Scholasticism," *Renaissance Thought* (New York, 1961), pp. 99–102. On the other hand, Hans Baron and Eugenio Garin, believe that there was a real conflict of opinion that extended to philosophical issues; see Baron's *Crisis of the Early Italian Renaissance,* revised ed. (Princeton, 1966, and his essays now collected in *In Search of Florentine Humanism: Essays in the Transition from Medieval to Modern Thought* (Princeton, 1988); and among many of Garin's works, his *L'umanesimo italiano* (Bari, 1952).

9. For More and Erasmus, see More, *In Defense of Humanism,* the Yale edition of the *Complete Works of Thomas More,* ed. Daniel Kinney, 15 (New Haven, 1986); Jacques Chomarat, *Grammaire et rhétorique chez Erasme,* 2 vols. (Paris, 1981).

10. The *Praise of Folly* was freshly translated into English by White Kennett in 1683 and went through many eighteenth-century editions; and into French by Guedeville in 1714 with many Dutch and French editions. Erasmus was usually remembered during the eighteenth century as the first modern voice of Enlightenment. For the *Letters of Obscure Men* as a monument to the quarrel that "divided Europe into two hostile camps," see *Epistolae Obscurorum Virorum,* text and trans. Francis G. Stokes (London, 1925); Hajo Holborn, *Ulrich van Hutten and the German Reformation,* trans. Roland Bainton (1937; reprinted, New York, 1965). The *Letters* were republished in England in 1710, and again in 1742, by the Huguenot Michael Maittaire, who however, took the originals (like Steele in the *Tatler*), literally.

11. See, for example, Giuseppe Billanovich, "Petrarch and the Textual Tradition of Livy," *Journal of the Warburg and Courtauld Institutes,* 14 (1951), pp. 137–208; and in general Roberto Weiss, *The Renaissance Discovery of Classical Antiquity* (Oxford, 1969); L. D. Reynolds and N. G. Wilson, *Scribes and Scholars,* 2d ed. (Oxford, 1974), chap. 4.

12. I rely here on the essay by Marc Fumaroli, "The Republic of Letters," *Diogenes,* 142 (1988), pp. 129–52. Fumaroli finds the Latin expression in a letter of Rancesco Barbaro to Poggio in 1417.

Lorenzo Valla nor Flavio Biondo, the best philologist and the best archaeologist of the time, aspired much to poetry, although Valla at least wrote some history and cast his most famous critical work as an oration against the spurious Donation of Constantine.[13] But learning was still meant to serve the man of letters, and the great humanists, like Politian and Erasmus, could still contribute both to scholarship and to literature. The printing press made communication easier throughout Europe and it is no accident that it is the humanist-printer, Aldus Manutius, who seems to have brought the concept of a republic of letters into common parlance through the prefaces to his popular works.[14]

But it was not destined to last. The trouble was that while literature and the arts were imitative, learning was cumulative. In this respect classical scholarship was like the new experimental science that was later to take hold in the seventeenth century. Francis Bacon, in particular, became the great advocate of scientific cooperation and set out a scheme for institutionalizing it in the *New Atlantis,* the first of many such utopian projects and the inspiration for a real Royal Society. It was about the same time that a Society of Antiquaries was also established in England, which though it lapsed for a time was revived in the eighteenth century.[15] All over Europe, academies were being organized outside the universities, but the worlds of learning, science, and literature were not usually combined, and the encyclopedic ideal of the age, which produced some astonishing polymaths, did not usually include the poets and the orators, nor even the historians, who remained stubbornly indifferent to the accumulation of knowledge.[16] It did not help that the learning of the savants was written in a peculiar scholarly Latin for a very circumscribed public, and that each

13. For Valla, see Hanna Gray, "Renaissance Humanism: The Pursuit of Eloquence," *Journal of the History of Ideas,* 24 (1963), pp. 497–515; and my article, "Reginald Pecock and Lorenzo Valla on the *Donation of Constantine,*" *Studies in the Renaissance,* 20 (1973), pp. 118–43, reprinted in my *Humanism and History* (Ithaca, 1987), pp. 54–72.

14. Fumaroli, "The Republic of Letters," pp. 147–49; Martin Lowry, *The World of Aldus Manutius* (Ithaca, 1979).

15. See Joan Evans, *A History of the Society of Antiquaries* (Oxford, 1956).

16. According to one student, there were no less than 2,200 academies in Italy alone between the sixteenth and the nineteenth centuries, but Pevsner shows that the nice unity of purpose that had characterized the first Renaissance academies was torn asunder in the next centuries as the emphasis turned to every kind of special goal. There were, however, two rough categories: those devoted to philology and those to natural science; see Nikolaus Pevsner, *Academies of Art Past and Present* (1940; reprinted, New York, 1973), 1–24. For the continuing rift between historians and antiquaries, see Arnaldo Momigliano, "Ancient History and the Antiquarian," *Studies in Historiography* (New York, 1966), pp. 1–39; and Levine, *Battle of the Books,* pt. 2.

new work superseded the last—the fate of all scholarship and science—and thus immediately lost all interest, except perhaps for the history of learning.[17]

There were then, a number of divisions in the world of early modern letters. There was the old antipathy between philosophy and literature, resumed in the squabbles between humanists and scholastics, but prolonged now with the rise of the new science. Thus the "new" philosophers, Bacon, Descartes, and their followers throughout Europe, had little use for scholastic logic and metaphysics, which they publicly despised; but they had not much more patience for the humanities. Descartes found them generally worthless, and Bacon who certainly employed them in his own political career as an essayist and historian, nevertheless denigrated the works of the imagination, and some of his followers showed even less respect than he for rhetoric and the ancient authors.[18] Meanwhile, the Baconians, following their master, were able to turn the tables on both the humanists and the scholastics by arguing that it was the new science that was of the greatest practical use to society.[19] Yet curiously, the new science was often thrown back on classical rhetoric, whenever it was forced to defend its activities in public.[20] And it sometimes joined forces with the new

17. Mark Pattison, *Isaac Casaubon 1559–1614*, 2d ed. (Oxford, 1892), p. 434. Pattison wondered how long it would be before anyone would read again (as he had) through all of Casaubon's learned correspondence; Rudolf Pfeiffer thought Casaubon "the first pure type of a classical scholar destitute of sympathy for human and aesthetic values." "His enormous reading was not always in the service of the explanation of the text, but sometimes amounted merely to the accumulation of material for its own sake." *History of Classical Scholarship from 1300 to 1850* (Oxford, 1976), p. 122.

18. The Baconian, John Ray, typically dismissed oratory and poetry as frivolous because of their preoccupation with words rather than things; John Ray to Tancred Robinson, December 15, 1690, in *The Correspondence of John Ray*, ed. Edwin Lankester (London, 1848), p. 229. John Locke also downplayed the classical authors, though he was compelled to admit their usefulness to the young gentleman. "He affected to despise poetry, and he depreciated the ancients," according to Joseph Warton, which put him at odds with his pupil, the young earl of Shaftesbury; see Warton, *An Essay on the Genius and Writings of Pope*, 2d ed., 2 vols. (London, 1806), 2: pp. 271–72. John Locke, *Some Thoughts Concerning Education*, ed. John W. and Jean S. Yolton (Oxford, 1989), pp. 207ff.

19. And this allowed some, like John Evelyn, and even the defender of the English moderns, William Wotton, to embrace both, that is, both the new science and the old humanities. See my article, "Natural History and the New Philosophy: Bacon, Harvey, and the Two Cultures," *Humanism and History*, pp. 123–54.

20. Thus the Ciceronian Thomas Sprat was chosen, despite his lack of scientific competence, to uphold the Royal Society in his polemical *History of the Royal Society* (1667), to which the poet Abraham Cowley contributed some verses; see Michael Hunter, *Establishing the New Science* (Woodbridge, 1989), pp. 49–50. For the attacks in general, which frequently disrupted the English republic of letters, see Richard Foster Jones, *Ancients and Moderns*, 2d ed. (St. Louis, 1961).

scholarship in emphasizing the patient accumulation of evidence.[21] But now, as I have suggested, a further division opened up to complicate the intellectual scene in the ranks of the humanists themselves.

Perhaps it was inevitable. The first humanists had wanted simply to emulate the best of the ancients, but they needed to know more about the models that they so admired. As a result, they began to invent the instruments of modern scholarship. They insisted on learning more and more about the originals: on editing and reediting the texts from the manuscripts; on recovering the forgotten niceties of the ancient languages (now Greek and even Hebrew) down to the last detail; on retrieving the meanings of the ancient works by situating them again in their ancient settings, trying to resuscitate all the ancient manners and customs—even the contemporary lay of the land. And the more they looked, the more they found, accumulating mountains of facts, which they thought useful or necessary before a successful imitation could be accomplished.[22] But this created two problems. In the first place there was the problem of form: how to organize and present the findings of scholarship. And secondly there was the problem of content: how to handle an increasing understanding of the classical past, when the results turned out to be less useful and familiar than expected.

The first problem was attempted by a series of improvisations. The ancient texts could be surrounded by commentary—explaining variants, explicating meanings, and illustrating them by analogies with the rest of ancient literature—inventing or exploiting the footnote and excursus and appendix. Eventually, this information could be separated from the text and arranged topically in formal treatises on the particular customs and institutions of antiquity: on the religion, military means, social life, and political forms of the ancient world. These could then be collected into chapters in a single work, or indeed in a whole collection of works.[23] But

21. See Joseph M. Levine, "Natural History and the History of the Scientific Revolution," pp. 57–73.

22. The distance between Petrarch and the late sixteenth century can be traced by comparing the accounts of Roberto Weiss, *The Renaissance Discovery of Classical Antiquity* (Oxford, 1969), with Anthony Grafton, *Joseph Scaliger: A Study in the History of Classical Scholarship* (Oxford, 1983) and William McCuaig, *Carlo Sigonio: The Changing World of the Late Renaissance* (Princeton, 1989).

23. Momigliano finds the model in Varro, and the first modern reintegration in Rosinus, *Antiquitatum Romanorum corpus absolutissimum* (1583), "Ancient History and the Antiquarian," pp. 5–6. Petrarch was already transcribing antiquarian information in the margins of his Livy and Eusebius; see Roberto Weiss, "Petrarch the Antiquarian," in *Classical, Medieval and Renaissance Studies in Honor of B. L. Ullman*, ed. Charles Henderson (Rome, 1964), 2: pp. 199–209; Angelo Mazzocco, "The Antiquarianism of Francesco Petrarch," *Journal of Medieval and Renaissance Studies*, 7 (1977), pp. 203–24.

soon the accumulation of information began to outrun its original utility and take on a life of its own. The commentary began to overwhelm the text, as in those wonderful Dutch variorums, where only a tiny corner of the page was reserved for the original text, while most of the rest was devoted to a commentary in several different typefaces.[24] And the simple antiquarian handbook could eventually turn into the two dozen folio volumes of Graevius and Gronovius that seemed to be required by 1700 to describe the whole life of ancient Greece and Rome—not to mention the fifteen volumes of Montfaucon's *Antiquité expliquée* that were needed then just to enumerate and explain the ancient monuments.[25] In the face of this "advance of erudition at the expense of taste," what was the poor poet or orator, artist, or architect, to do, intent only on imitating the classical works?[26]

He could protest. Some time in the seventeenth century, if not before, the pedantic scholar became the butt of satire and, before the century was out, the object of outright attack. In England in the Battle of the Books, the "ancients" led by Sir William Temple and his secretary, Jonathan Swift, along with the wits of Christ Church, explicitly rejected the claims of philology and antiquities to any genuine use and preferred the plain unadorned text of the classics to the elaborate annotations of the learned.[27] The pursuit of philological facts looked to them no better than the pursuit of the facts of natural history—equally fruitless to the gentleman and man of the world. It seemed to them odd (and more than a little ridiculous) that the *Philosophical Transactions* of the Royal Society should give shelter to both scholars and men of letters. And indeed not all the naturalists were happy to be associated with the scholars.[28] In any case, the wits refused to

---

24. "Not to follow the Dutch commentators always, may be forgiven to a man who thinks them, in the general, heavy, dull-witted fellows," John Dryden, "Examen poeticum" (1693), in *Of Dramatic Poesy and Other Critical Essays*, ed. George Watson, 2 vols. (London, 1962), 2: p. 164. For more disparagement, see Joseph Addison in the *Spectator*, August 29, 1712.

25. J. G. Graevius, *Thesaurus antiquitatum romanorum* (1694–99); Jacob Gronovius, *Thesaurus graecorum antiquitatum* (1697–1702); to which were sometimes added still further volumes by Sallengre, Polenus, Pitiscus, and Gruter, until the collection filled some thirty-nine volumes in folio. Montfaucon's work appeared first in ten volumes in 1719, then with a five-volume supplement in 1724. It swiftly found an English translation.

26. The expression is Henry Hallam's, whose account of the progress of learning in this period is still among the best; see his *Introduction to the Literature of Europe in the Fifteenth, Sixteenth, and Seventeenth Centuries*, 2d ed., 3 vols. (London, 1843), 1: p. 474. For a more recent account, see Pfeiffer, *History of Classical Scholarship*.

27. "Comments are generally an Art of making Authors difficult with pretence of explaining them," writes Henry Felton in 1713. He had no use for the heaps of comments, "which are piled so high upon Authors, that it is difficult sometimes to clear the Text from the Rubbish, and draw it out of the Ruins." *A Dissertation on Reading the Classics and Forming a Just Style*, 2d ed. (London, 1715), pp. 48–50; Joseph M. Levine, *The Battle of the Books*, pp. 55–56.

28. Bacon had not much appreciated the advancement of classical scholarship; see the

join the game; the men of letters would have no truck with the republic of scholars. Learned men, complained the Sieur de Saint-Evremond, were "incapable of having nice sentiments and Thoughts. . . . They may succeed well enough in expounding Grammarians . . . but they never hit that of a polite, well bred man among the Antients, because that is diametrically opposed to it."[29] It did not help that a great philologist, Richard Bentley, took the trouble to show that the Greek epistles of Phalaris, which had long been revered by the men of letters as an example of correct style, and which had been newly commended by Temple and edited by the members of Christ Church, was but a late and inept forgery. Philology had unexpectedly become the enemy of good letters.[30] Who was better equipped to judge the value and authenticity of such a work, the wits demanded, a man who knew and practiced politics and letters, or an academic pedant? "He, Temple, had written to Kings and they to him, and this has qualified him to judge how Kings should write, much more than all Dr. Bentley's Correspondence with foreign professors."[31] So much for the republic of letters!

In France the situation was even worse; there the moderns were predisposed to reject learning altogether, this time in the name of Cartesian reason. Strangely enough, the rejection of scholarship was the one common ground between Perrault and Boileau, who disputed almost everything else.[32] And so the French Academy, though rent by faction, turned resolutely to the production of literature and away from pedantry, while the more learned academies of science and scholarship were left to go their

---

Novum Organum, in *Works,* ed. Spedding, (London, 1879), 2: p. 505, quoted by Grafton, *Defenders,* p. 2. But the seventeenth-century virtuoso managed often to combine both interests, and the antiquaries and the philologists found a home in the Royal Society and its *Transactions,* one of them, Sir Hans Sloane, even becoming its president. For a characteristic portrait of one of these virtuosi (Peiresc) by another (Gassendi), dedicated to a third (John Evelyn), see *The Mirrour of True Nobility and Gentility,* trans. W. Rand (London, 1657).

29. Letter to Crécqui (1665) in Saint-Evremond, *Works,* trans. Pierre Desmaizeaux, 3 vols. (London, 1728), 1: pp. 203–4.

30. Bentley's "Dissertation upon the Episles of Phalaris," appeared first as an appendix to William Wotton's *Reflections upon Ancient and Modern Learning,* 2d ed. (London, 1697); then more extensively in reply to his Christ Church critics in 1699. See the edition by Wilhelm Wagner (London, 1883). The story of the controversy is told amusingly by Thomas Babington Macaulay in his essay on Atterbury, in *Miscellaneous Writings* (London, 1860); and more completely in James Henry Monk, *The Life of Richard Bentley,* 2d ed., 2 vols. (London (1833); and Levine, *Battle of the Books.*

31. Charles Boyle (actually Francis Atterbury and his Christ Church friends), *Dr. Bentley's Dissertations on the Epistles of Phalaris Examin'd* (London, 1698), pp. 25, 92; Levine, *Battle of the Books,* p. 61.

32. See Paul Bonnefon, Charles Perrault littérateur et académicien: l'opposition à Boileau," *Revue d'histoire littéraire de la France,* 12 (1905), pp. 549–610; Hans Kortum, *Charles Perrault et Nicholas Boileau* (Berlin, 1966).

separate ways. The Academy of Inscriptions and Belles Lettres, which had once been a subcommittee of the forty, and was meant to further the two humanistic activities, increasingly delimited itself to philological and anti-quarian matters at the expense of letters.[33] In the face of this indifference or outright hostility, the outlook for classical learning was not very promis-ing on the eve of the Enlightenment.

As for content, the furious quarrel between ancients and moderns over Homer indicates something of what was at stake.[34] Homer was by general consensus taken to be the prince of poets, and his two epics were still be-lieved to be the greatest of all literary works. But like the rest of the classics, Homer required explication, particularly since the originals were in an ar-chaic Greek. As we have seen, much ingenuity was expended after the Re-naissance, editing and translating the texts and trying to restore their meaning through the culture and customs of early Greece. Nor did the paucity of information discourage the quest. When Alexander Pope de-cided to put the Homeric poems into modern English verse, he was much embarrassed by even the small accumulation of learning that modern scholarship had collected for the purpose but which was beyond his com-petence, and so he employed others more knowledgeable to help him through the more troublesome passages. (It is still not clear whether he knew any Greek at all.) He surrounded his translation with copious notes, pictures, maps, and apparent learning; but he could not fool the scholars like Bentley, who admired Pope's poem but doubted that it was Homer.[35] In France, Madame Dacier was better prepared to tackle the Greek and the learning, but when she turned the Greek into French prose she stumbled over the apparently awkward morality of the old poet, whose heroes res-olutely refused to behave themselves like the courtiers of Louis XIV. She had also to explain and justify the religion and manners of the primitive Greeks and their apparent ignorance of modern science, among the other discoveries of modern criticism.[36] Here for the while the moderns seemed to triumph, exulting in the disparity that they found between ancient Greece and modern France. They were not embarrassed to modernize the

33. See L. A. Maury, *L'Ancienne Académie des Inscriptions et Belles Lettres* (Paris, 1864).

34. See Noémi Hepp, *Homère en France au xviiie siècle* (Paris, 1968); and below, chap. 5.

35. For different versions of this possibly apochryphal story, see Levine, *Battle of the Books*, p. 222. Pope's *Iliad* appears in the Twickenham edition of his works, *The Poems of Alexander Pope*, ed. J. Butt et al., 10 vols. (New Haven, 1961–67), vols. 7–8. His scholarship is considered in the extensive prefaces there and in Hans-Joachim Zimmermann, *Alexander Popes noten zu Homer* (Heidelberg, 1966).

36. She attempts this in the prefaces and notes to her translation of the *Iliad* which ap-peared in three volumes (Paris, 1711), and the *Odyssey*, which appeared in three further vol-umes (Paris, 1716).

poems, boldly excising the inconvenient passages and setting them in a contemporary scene.[37] To be sure, Mme. Dacier was willing to allow something of the difference between the age of Homer and the age of Louis XIV, but she protested against the effiminacy of her contemporaries, who (she insisted) would do better to give up their modern ways and imitate the ancient models.[38]

But was imitation any longer possible? After two centuries, it still remained the most pressing problem for eighteenth-century criticism. The question had, of course, first turned up during the Renaissance, when the pedantic Ciceronians insisted on a rigid adherence to classical usage, only to be met by more liberal humanists like Erasmus, who argued that an adaptation to modernity was necessary. (For a long while no one was prepared to argue for an originality wholly unencumbered by the ancients.) The controversy was not forgotten, but the accumulation of scholarly knowledge about classical usage made the disparity between the ancients and moderns more obvious and the difficulty of imitation more complicated.[39] Should a modern hero, like Wolfe at Montreal, or for that matter Voltaire at Ferney, be portrayed in classical costume (or disrobed altogether like an ancient statue), or should they be pictured in contemporary dress?[40] The earl of Chatham might address the House of Commons like Cicero or Demosthenes and recite from the *Iliad* on his deathbed, but the politician who knew his Greek did not have much time for real scholarship and probably never read Richard Bentley, much less the assembled learning of Graevius-Gronovius. Neoclassicism triumphed for a time because the neoclassics had memorized the classical authors at school and knew enough about their ancient forebears to use them for contemporary pur-

37. See the version and its justification by Antoine Houdar de La Motte, "Discours sur l'Homère," *Les Paradoxes littéraires de La Motte* (Paris, 1859), pp. 181–268.

38. See Mme. Dacier, *Des causes de la corruption du goust* (Paris, 1714).

39. Erasmus's *Ciceronianus* has been edited by Pierre Mesnard, in the *Opera Omnia* 1: pt. 2 (Amsterdam, 1971), pp. 583–710. See also the useful edition and introduction by A. Gambaro (Brescia, 1965). There is an English translation with a helpful preface in Izora Scott, *Controversies Over the Imitation of Cicero* (New York, 1910). The *Ciceronianus* was reprinted in London in 1693; Gibbon is still recalling the controversy in *Miscellaneous Works,* ed. Earl of Sheffield, 5 vols. (London, 1814), 5: pp. 259, 262. For a bolder view of imitation, though still respectful of the ancients, see Edward Young, *Conjectures on Original Composition* (London, 1759).

40. See the first, Edgar Wind, "The Revolution in History Painting," and "Penny, West, and General Wolfe," in *Hume and the Heroic Portrait,* ed. Jaynie Anderson (Oxford, 1986) pp. 88–104; for the second, Dena Goodman, "Pigalle's *Voltaire nu:* The Republic of Letters Represents itself to the World," *Representations,* 16 (1986), pp. 86–109; and S. Rocheblave, *Jean-Baptiste Pigalle* (Paris, 1919), pp. 277–88; and for both, H. W. Janson, "Observations on Nudity in Neoclassical Art," *Stil und uberlieferung in der Kunst des Abendlandes* (Acts of the Twenty-first Congress in Art History, Bonn 1964), Bd. 1 (Berlin, 1967), pp. 198–207.

poses—but not too much to spoil the fun.[41] The enemy was learning, which despite the contempt of the worldly, continued to collect new knowledge for a steadily narrowing republic of letters from which most writers and artists were excluded by their carefully cultivated ignorance. Surreptitiously and without malice, the philologists kept worrying away at their specialized problems, still pretending to serve the ancient authors, and heedless of the consequences. But the men of letters sensed the danger and tried to mock it out of existence. It did not make for easy relations in the republic of letters.

In short, it was scholars like Richard Bentley and his good friend, the polymath William Wotton, who in taking up the cause of the moderns in England, came to be thought of as the enemies of literature. Bentley himself was deeply interested in poetry, not only the ancients but the moderns, and he even took the trouble to edit that modern classic, *Paradise Lost*, much as he had the perennial ancient favorite, Horace, in a text that was duly emended and surrounded by learned annotation. However, by tinkering with the text of each, he only succeeded in outraging the guardians of antiquity further, although he certainly believed he was serving both his authors.[42] Bentley also devoted much energy to theological matters, cheerfully bringing his knowledge of the latest advances in science and learning to the task, and further alarming his contemporaries. What would he have done to the text of the New Testament, had he ever completed his great enterprise?[43] Like Erasmus in the sixteenth century, he found the world still reluctant to apply the techniques of modern scholarship to the recovery of antiquity. Bentley's interest in the theological implications of modern science led him to expound the work of his friend Isaac Newton, whom he consulted in a remarkable exchange of letters.[44] All his life he defended the interests of the Anglican church which gave him employment,

41. I intend to treat this at length in my forthcoming book, *Why Neoclassicism? Culture and Politics in Eighteenth-Century England*.

42. See Joseph M. Levine, "Bentley's Milton: Philology and Criticism in Eighteenth Century England," *Journal of the History of Ideas*, 50 (1989), pp. 549–69; reprinted in the *Battle of the Books*, pp. 245–66.

43. Even in his earliest work, on the ancient Greek chronographer Malelas, Bentley had called attention to many "pious frauds" among the documents proporting to come from the early church; see Anthony Grafton, *Defenders of the Text*, pp. 14–17. His enemies at Christ Church hinted at the danger in their reply to Bentley's dissertation. Needless to say, his proposal to edit the Greek New Testament was greeted with alarm and fresh controversy; see Monk, *Bentley*, 2: pp. 126–46.

44. Isaac Newton, *Correspondence*, ed. H. W. Turnbull, 3 (Cambridge, 1961), pp. 233–60. Bentley's *Eight Sermons*, which incorporated the results, were delivered in 1692, and may be consulted in his *Works*, ed. Alexander Dyce, 3 (London, 1838).

but he did not endear himself much even to his fellow churchmen by his allegiance to modern learning, which could so easily cut both ways.

What then was Bentley's place in the republic of letters? His intellectual world and his natural audience included philosophers, scientists, theologians, and philologists, in England and abroad: a true republic of scholars, in which there was a common goal and continuous interchange.[45] But he spent most of his life in controversy with them, often personal, but just as often ideological. Bentley and Wotton believed that all the sciences, including philology and antiquities, had been steadily advancing since the Renaissance.[46] And they understood that advancement to be the result of the close collaboration of scientists and men of learning throughout Europe and over the generations. As a result, they extolled those institutions like the Royal Society and its foreign counterparts, which were meant to serve that end, and they kept up a lively correspondence with their friends abroad. They believed that a republic of letters was required for the advancement of learning, and they were pretty good citizens, except when they quarreled among themselves or when they insisted on writing in English about parochial concerns, when most foreigners could not then read the language. Fortunately, there were enough Huguenots throughout Europe to do the translations and make the exchanges which held the intellectual world together and made it possible to know what was going on throughout the far-flung European republic.[47] (It is Pierre Bayle, after all, who entitled his pioneering periodical the *Nouvelles de la République des Lettres*.) The still largely unpublished correspondence of these savants and journalists remains to testify to the real existence of this international community.[48]

But it is quite clear that the republic of scholars and the republic of letters, if I may now distinguish the two, had little in common but distrust.

45. See in particular the two volumes of his correspondence, ed. Christopher Wordsworth (London, 1842).

46. For the claims of philology, see especially, Wotton's *Reflections on Ancient and Modern Learning* (London, 1694), chap. 27, pp. 310–21; Temple replied in the *Miscellanea, The Third Part*, pp. 257–59.

47. So we find Jean Le Clerc complaining that the battle of the books had been conducted in English; he himself did his best to keep abreast of events through his correspondence with Wotton and others, and to transmit its substance to his Continental readers in the reviews of the *Nouvelles de la république des lettres* and the *Bibliothèque choisie*. See Annie Barnes, *Jean Le Clerc et la république des lettres* (Paris, 1938).

48. Goldgar supplies some valuable bibliography; see n. 1 above. See also Matin Ultee, "The Republic of Letters: Learned Correspondence 1680–1720," *The Seventeenth Century*, 2 (1987), pp. 95–112. Still useful is the first chapter in Joseph Texte, *Jean-Jacques Rousseau and the Cosmopolitan Spirit in Literature*, trans. J. W. Matthews (London, 1899), pp. 1–36.

The gentleman and the scientist might compose their differences after Newton had made the physical world intelligible and the popularizers done their work, but the gentleman turned *philosophe* and the *érudit* found it harder to make up their quarrel. For the most part, the poets and men of letters, and the politicians and men of the world, tried to ignore the learning of the learned world—although, needless to say, there were always exceptions. Even if one allowed some value to their findings, how was a busy practical man of the world to make the time to master a learning which was every day becoming more massive and specialized? All his life John Evelyn had made it his business to keep up with the progress of learning, even while carrying on his affairs as a landed gentleman and busying himself in politics and occasionally writing some bad poetry. But even he despaired in the end and called upon his young friend William Wotton to find a way to save him from having to read it all for himself. It was the philosopher Gottfired Wilhelm Leibniz, one of the best citizens and heartiest believers in the republic of letters, who cried out plaintively at the end of his life, "Would God that a way might be found to reconcile learning with the education of a gentleman!"[49]

Meanwhile, however, it was more characteristic of the men of letters to mock the labors of the learned. In England, from the anonymous *Transactioneer*, which poked fun at the *Transactions* of the Royal Society, to the *Three Hours after Marriage*, which ridiculed the learned naturalists, to Swift's *Tale of a Tub*, with its wonderful parody of philological learning, to Pope's *Dunciad*, with it speculiar amalgam of Grub Street writers and learned pedants, the refrain was apparently endless. Nor did the redoubtable Mme. Dacier escape the abuse of her French contemporaries; it was her critics, Houdar de la Motte and the abbé Terrasson, who undoubtedly had the best of it, cutting Homer and modern philology down to size.[50] It seemed necessary to the poet son of the learned German editor of the *Acta Eruditorum*, J. B. Mencke, to anatomize the problems of pedantic scholarship in two Latin dissertations, *De Charlateneria eruditorum* (1716).[51] At the beginning of the eighteenth century, it almost seemed that the great age of erudition had come to an end.

49. *Philosophical Letters and Papers*, ed. Leroy Loemker, 2d ed. (Dordrecht, 1969), p. 632. See chap. 4 above.

50. Jean Terrasson, *Dissertation critique sur l'Iliade d'Homère ou . . . on cherche les règles d'une poétique fondée sur la raison*, 2 vols. (Paris, 1715).

51. The work was swiftly turned into French by David Durand, *De la charlatanerie des savans* (The Hague, 1721). Johann Burchard Mencke (1674–1732), the son of Otto, was a poet who wrote under the name Philander von der Linde and presided over the *Deutschubende poetische Gesellschaft* in Leipzig; he was also editor of the antiquarian compilation, *Scriptores rerum Germanicarum* (1728).

Yet not everyone was prepared to admit that the division was irreconcilable. When young Edward Gibbon arrived in Paris in 1763 he was already deeply engaged in both worlds. As a child he had, like everyone else, encountered the literary classics, and he nurtured the idea that he might one day emulate them. Even then, he discovered the more arcane world of classical scholarship and took pleasure in working at the technical problems of philology and chronology, writing some short pieces in Latin which he submitted to the experts. A particular pleasure was the purchase for twenty pounds of the first twenty volumes of the *Memoirs* of the Academy of Inscriptions.[52] About the same time, he exchanged missives with Richard Hurd on the problem of imitation, then still very much current.[53] His reading in both cultures was prodigious. He was therefore alarmed to discover the basic antipathy that existed between them. In Paris he moved easily in both worlds, meeting the *philosophes* who, even more than the humanists, disparaged the minutiae of scholarship, and also the *érudits*, who taught him more about the many disciplines of modern scholarship: among them, paleography, numismatics, and epigraphy.[54] His first published work was written in French and addressed to the problem; he deplored the great rift in the republic of letters and hoped to reconcile both parties.

In the *Essai sur l'étude de la littérature*, Gibbon explained that he wrote to defend his own favorite pastime, the serious study of antiquity. "I wished to free an estimable science from the contempt under which it now languishes."[55] It is true, he allowed, that the ancients were still being read, but they were no longer regarded seriously, not at least the way Cicero or Bossuet had insisted they should be. There were plenty of men of taste, but few real students of the classics. The *philosophes* from the time of Fénelon had dismissed the discoveries of modern scholarship as a mere accumulation of useless facts, which they were happy to disregard. Erudition had received its deathblow when La Motte and Terrasson had attacked Homer, and his defenders could only reply with the minutiae of pedantic scholar-

52. Edward Gibbon, *Memoirs of my Life*, ed. Georges A. Bonnard (London, 1966), p. 97.

53. Richard Hurd, "Poetical Imitation," *Works*, 8 vols. (London, 1811), 2: pp. 107–241; Gibbon's manuscript reply is dated February 8, 1762; see *English Essays*, ed. Patricia Craddock (Oxford, 1972), pp. 27–53.

54. *Memoirs*, pp. 131.

55. The *Essai* was published in London, 1761; there was an English translation (from which I quote) printed in Dublin, 1777. In the autobiography, Gibbon recalled finding the Academy of Inscriptions degraded to the lowest rank of the royal societies in Paris, "the new appellation *Erudits* was contemptuously applied to the successors of Lipsius and Casaubon," and the *philosophe* D'Alembert allowed them only memory, without exercise of imagination or judgment; *Memoirs*, p. 99.

ship. Since then, "it has become a matter of astonishment to our philosophers, that men could spend a whole life in collecting facts and words, and in loading the memory instead of enlightening the mind." From La Motte to D'Alembert, *belles lettres* had been pitted against its former ally, classical erudition, to the detriment of both. Gibbon was intent on rescuing the work of the philologists and antiquaries, without losing the literary point of it all. He would have liked to put the republic of letters back into a whole in which writers, scholars, and philosophers could live happily together in fruitful communication. His editor, Matthew Maty, saw the problem more simply. "Can you believe that a man born to assist at the tumultuous meetings of parliament, or to destroy the foxes in his country, will be pardoned for discussing what was thought two thousand years ago about the divinities of Greece, and the early ages of Rome?" Gibbon's remarks were learned, but who would read them at the races in Newmarket or the coffeehouses in London?

The problem as always was to reconcile an appreciation of the classics, which even a Fontenelle or D'Alembert might still allow to have some use, and the learning that was required to succeed at it. Gibbon tries patiently to explain how it is impossible to read the ancient poets—the best that have ever been—without employing a close scholarship to recover the circumstances in which they wrote. He is willing to allow that many scholars had misunderstood their mission by assuming that the mere accumulation of detail was an end in itself, and he distinguishes those worthy *érudits* who combined learning with judgment (like Grotius, Casaubon, and others) with the mere pedants (like Gruter, Salmasius, et al.), for whom he shares a philosophical contempt. But it was undeniable that the beauties of ancient poetry were inaccessible without "a minute acquaintance with their times." He recalls the famous example of Perrault, who was shocked by Homer's description of the Greeks, forgetting (as Boileau pointed out) that Homer was describing the Greeks, not the French. Just so was it with Virgil. "It is impossible to understand the design, art, and details of Virgil without being thoroughly acquainted with the history, laws, and religion of the Romans, the geography of Italy, the character of Augustus, and the singular and unparalleled relation in which that prince stood to his people." The better the reader understood the circumstances of the work, the better would he appreciate the poet's invention and merit. The modern critic, Gibbon insisted, must employ philology to restore and correct the text and its language; rhetoric to discover its form and eloquence; and history to determine its subject matter. In this way, he believed, all branches of literature might be reunited and the rift in the republic of letters removed.

The essay is a youthful work, but Gibbon never gave up his hope, although its realization must have seemed more difficult year by year. The *Decline and Fall* is his practical solution to the problem of reconciling *belles lettres* with philosophy and erudition. In this great work Gibbon somehow was able to combine a rhetoric based on classical imitation with a careful critical reading of all the ancient sources, and a philosophical vantage point.[56] He was pretty much able to satisfy the gentlemen in the coffee-houses, the scholars bent over their massive folios, and the skeptical philosophers like David Hume who did not share Gibbon's scholarly patience. The trouble was that in just this respect, in this wonderfully successful synthetic enterprise, Gibbon's work turned out to be inimitable, the first but perhaps also the last of its kind.

Indeed, the course of historical and critical erudition was destined to diverge even further from traditional *belles lettres,* as every passing year brought a further accumulation of knowledge, until the original rift in the republic of letters began to seem almost unabridgeable. Perhaps this was most obvious in the new scholarly culture of the German universities, which eventually taught all Europe and America the value of philology and a rigorous technical training.[57] If the notion of a republic of letters continued in popular use, it was as likely now to be ironic as literal, and it could no longer be applied easily to anything on the intellectual scene. Sometime in the nineteenth century, the perilous amalgam of learning and letters that had been ushered in by the Italian Renaissance, and lingered for centuries through a continuously troubled existence, departed. In our own time, the furor that surrounded the quarrel between C. P. Snow and F. R. Leavis was a reminder of the ancient rivalry between science and letters, and it has by no means gone away.[58] Meanwhile, the attack on historical scholarship was also resumed by the "new critics" and their progeny, and prolonged by the deconstructionists and their disciples, none of whom have had much use for philology and the historical context. Thus the old divisions in the re-

56. The best guides here are Giuseppe Giarrizzo, *Edward Gibbon e la cultura Europea del settecento* (Naples, 1954) and Arnaldo Momigliano, "Gibbon's Contribution to Historical Method," *Studies,* pp. 40–55. See also Joseph M. Levine, "Edward Gibbon and the Quarrel between the Ancients and the Moderns," *The Eighteenth Century,* 26 (1985), pp. 47–62; reprinted in *Humanism and History,* chap. 7.

57. It was the new university at Göttingen that led the way; see Herbert Butterfield, "The Rise of the German Historical School," *Man on His Past* (Cambridge, 1955), pp. 32–61. Neibuhr and Ranke, both of whom set the fashion for the new academic historiography, the one a great orator, the other a great writer, were trained in classical philology, and taught their students, not rhetoric, but source criticism. The writing of history for the general public was left to others to accomplish, usually outside the academy.

58. C. P. Snow's "The Two Cultures" appeared first in the *New Statesman,* October 6, 1956, and was reprinted in *The Two Cultures and the Scientific Revolution* (New York, 1961). It was answered by F. R. Leavis in *Two Cultures? The Significance of C. P. Snow* (London, 1962).

public of letters have continued, perhaps deepened, and, with the continued accumulation of undigested information, show no early sign of diminishing. Perhaps it is wrong to exaggerate the conflicts that divided the world of letters from the world of learning, either then or now, but it will not do to paper over the very real enmities that troubled the republic of letters, then or now. For they were not—are not—built simply on envy. The fact is that the classical scholars who pretended to a disinterested investigation of the text were creating a monster they could not control, threatening the literature they loved—and most of us who are professionals are their undoubted heirs.

CHAPTER SIX

Giambattista Vico and the Quarrel between the Ancients and the Moderns

1

It was Benedetto Croce, one of Vico's best admirers, who remembered that when Nicola Capasso first opened the *Scienza nuova*, he "fancied he had lost his wits and . . . by a joke hurried off to his Doctor Cirillo, to have his pulse felt."[1] We may still sympathize a little. For us, the problem of understanding Vico and placing him correctly in Western thought, awkward enough in itself, is compounded by the difficulty in establishing a useful context. Over and over we have heard it said that Vico was ahead of his time and that he anticipated nearly everything in our own.[2] What we would seem to require, however, before anything else, is a contemporary setting rich enough so that we can see Vico addressing his own time and trying to solve his own problems before he anticipates any of ours. Even then, some obscurity will likely remain, because Vico was a truly original thinker who discovered his own originality only slowly and tortuously and perhaps never completely or clearly. Much has been done in recent years to set the Neapolitan scene, but I would like to call attention here to something that has been so far overlooked. I would like to suggest that, in creating a new science, Vico was responding directly and in large measure to many of the issues that had been raised in the famous Quarrel between the Ancients and the Moderns.[3]

1. *The Philosophy of Giambattista Vico*, trans. R. G. Collingwood (London, 1913), p. 259.
2. See, for example, Karl Lowith, *Meaning in History* (Chicago, 1949), p. 115, and the volume *Vico and Contemporary Thought*, ed. Giorgio Tagliacozzo, Michael Mooney, and Donald Varene (Atlantic Highlands, 1976).
3. For Vico's "originality," see Isaiah Berlin, *Vico and Herder* (New York, 1976), p. xviff. In the vast literature on Vico I have found most useful among the biographies, besides Croce, the

Unfortunately, the quarrel has not always received the attention that it deserves and it has often been read as anachronistically as Vico himself. The main trouble, I think, has been in considering it as a single great event with a definite and foregone conclusion in favor of the moderns. But it should be clear by now that the quarrel was much more a prolonged war with a great many skirmishes rather than a single battle; that it was fought out on a vast terrain over a myriad of issues; and that it ended, if at all, not with the victory of one side, but in something of a stalemate. Moreover, the quarrel was as ancient as antiquity itself, although it had been renewed and extended ever since the Italian Renaissance. When the humanists first proposed the ancients as models for imitation or emulation, they tipped the scales heavily in favor of the ancients, but there were soon challenges from one form of modernity or another and a growing uncertainty about the outcome. It took a long time before all this came to a head in the French *querelle* and the English Battle of the Books at the turn of the eighteenth century.[4]

It may be useful to begin by recalling that there were two different areas of conflict in the quarrel. In the first place, there was an argument over knowledge that involved, in particular, philosophy and natural science. Did the ancients *know* more than the moderns in these matters? In the second place, there was an argument over literature and the arts. Had the ancients *achieved* more than the moderns in these fields? For the first, the question involved accumulation; for the second, imitation. The issues in each of these traditional areas of culture were thus different, although related, and it may be helpful to take them separately.

With regard to the first, there were in Vico's youth at least two different forms of *ancienneté*. To begin with, there was the traditional scholasticism of the schools, still dependent on Aristotle as *the* philosopher and on his commentators as the best source of all scientific and philosophical wisdom. Vico received his first education from the Jesuits, reading along with

---

many studies of Croce's collaborator, Fausto Nicolini, especially *La giovinezza di Giambattista Vico* (Bari, 1932). See also Robert Flint, *Vico* (Edinburgh, 1884); Henry P. Adams, *The Life and Writings of Giambattista Vico* (London, 1935); Jules Chaix-Ruy, *La formation de la pensée philosophique de G.-B. Vico* (Paris, 1943); and Nicola Badaloni, *Introduzione a G. B. Vico* (Milan, 1961). For background, Gabriel Maugain, *Etude sur l'évolution intellectuelle de l'Italie de 1657 à 1750* (Paris, 1909); Nicolini, "Sulla vita civile, letteraria e religiosa Napoletana alla fine del seicento," *Atti della Reale Accademia di scienze morali e politiche di Napoli*, 51 (1928), pp. 175–255; Salvo Mastelloni, *Pensiero politico e vita culturale a Napoli nella secunda meta del Seicento* (Florence, 1965); Biagio de Giovanni, "La vita intelletuale a Napoli fra la meta del '600 e la restaurazione del regno," *Storia di Napoli* (Naples, 1970), 6, 1: 401–534; and Eugenio Garin, "Da Campanella a Vico," *Dal Rinascimento all'illuminismo* (Pisa, 1970), pp. 79–118.

4. I have set out my views on these matters in *Humanism and History* (Ithaca, 1987), pp. 155–77; and "Ancients and Moderns Reconsidered," *Eighteenth-Century Studies*, 15 (1981–82), pp. 72–89.

the classical authors some of the nominalist logicians and the Thomist Suarez. It is hard to know just what they meant to him, except that he later regretted the whole thing. In the second place, there was neoplatonism, which since its revival in the Renaissance had preferred Plato and his commentators to all the Aristotelians, and which had proposed a tradition of philosophical wisdom anterior even to the Greeks, a *prisca theologia* that hearkened backward through a succession of antique sages almost to the beginning of time. It was the quattrocentro Italians, Ficino and Pico della Mirandola, who had led the revival of this doctrine, and it was the later Neapolitans, Bruno and Campanella, who had done much to disseminate it across Europe.[5] In the 1690s, neoplatonic ideas became very popular in Naples, and at least one of Vico's friends, Paolo Mattia Doria, became a leading exponent of the *prisca theologia*.[6] Evidently, Vico felt the full attraction of these ideas, though with obvious circumspection he never mentions his heretical countrymen. Either way, Aristotelians and Platonists both looked back to an ancient philosophy that they thought superior to any that had been advanced in modern times.

For the several new philosophies of the seventeenth century, this reverence for antique authority looked like an obstacle that stood in the way and ought to be removed. It was Francis Bacon, for example, who complained that no progress in natural science, no advancement in learning of any kind, was possible when men accepted authority unquestioningly, and who pointed out that it was the moderns who were in fact the true ancients in terms of longevity and experience. The moderns might be pygmies but they had the advantage of standing on the shoulders of giants and seeing farther than any who had gone before.[7] Bacon's books were much admired in Naples in Vico's youth as the new science began to challenge the old, and the *De Augmentis* became one of the great books for Vico, who thrilled at its vision of progress and the possibilities of new knowledge.[8]

5. Vico could find the whole story of the ancient wisdom in the sixteenth-century writer Agostino Steuco, whose work he knew; see Vico, *Autobiography*, trans. Max H. Fisch and Thomas Bergin (Ithaca, 1962), p. 132. For background, see Charles Schmitt, "Perennial Philosophy: From Agostino Steuco to Leibniz," *Journal of the History of Ideas*, 27 (1966), pp. 505–32; Frances Yates, *Giordano Bruno and the Hermetic Tradition* (Chicago, 1964); and D. P. Walker, *The Ancient Theology* (Ithaca, 1972). There is a brief sketch in Emmanuele Riverso, "Vico and the Humanist Concept of the *Prisca Theologia*," *Vico Past and Present* (Atlantic Highlands, 1981), pp. 52–65.

6. *Autobiography*, p. 138. See Vincenzo Ferrone, "Seneca e Christo: La Respublica Christiana di Paolo Mattia Doria," *Rivista storica italiana*, 96 (1984), pp. 47–52.

7. For the long history of this notion, see Levine, "Ancients and Moderns Reconsidered," p. 76n.

8. *Autobiography*, pp. 139–40; seen Enrico De Mas, "Bacone e Vico," *Studi e ricerche di storia della filosofia*, 10 (1959), pp. 505–59.

Vico also admired some of the achievements of contemporary science, especially the works of Galileo, which were just then being read with renewed
enthusiasm, and whose dialogues on the two new sciences may have helped
him find the title to his own *magnum opus*. He seems even to have known
something about the experimental work of Robert Boyle and the English
Royal Society. In the end, Vico saw something to both sides in this quarrel,
to the idea of an ancient wisdom but also to the notion that the moderns
had discovered and invented many things unknown to antiquity—a view
that had first been popularized in Italy by Alessandro Tassoni many years
before.[9]

In any case, this conflict between the new and the old was undoubtedly
the most exciting intellectual event in the Naples of Vico's youth. It is true
that for a time Vico was not present, or only intermittently so. In 1686, he
left Naples for Vatolla to tutor the two young nephews of the bishop of Is-
chia. For the next nine years, he lived there in what he liked to recall (with
some exaggeration) as virtual isolation, even while the modernist challenge which had been long preparing reached a veritable crisis. According
to Vico, who disparaged it, and to his contemporary, Pietro Giannone, who
welcomed it, the battle developed in two stages.[10] It was the "Epicureans,"
the followers of Pierre Gassendi, who were the first to provoke the orthodox by trying to refurbish the ancient Greek atomists to meet the needs of
modern Christian philosophy. When Gassendi's works reached Naples,
they were swiftly acclaimed by the new generation who preferred them to
the Aristotle of the schools, especially for their apparent usefulness to the
new natural and experimental science. Traditional philosophy, says Giannone, had been "confined to the Cloysters, and reduced to logical and
metaphysical subtleties, or to some idle and useless Disputes."[11] Now
philosophical thought had been liberated by an improved method (observation and experiment) and a more correct understanding of nature (the
corpuscular theory of matter). But the Gassendists had to worry about two
alarming things in their philosophy: about the "atheism" of the ancient

9. Tassoni's *Pensieri diversi* appeared first in 1612 but without the tenth book on the ancients
and the moderns which accompanied the 1620 and later editions. His tract was eventually
translated into French and helped to stimulate the *querelle*. Galileo had been read all along, so
that it may be too much to speak of a rehabilitation; but see Vincenzo Ferrone, "Galileo, Newton e la *Libertas philosophandi* nella prima meta del xviii secolo in Italia," *Rivista storica italiana*,
93 (1981), pp. 143–85.

10. Compare Vico's *Autobiography*, p. 126ff., with Giannone's *Istoria civile del regno di Napoli*
(Naples, 1723), XI, 5, and with Paolo Mattia Doria's reminiscences in his *Difesa delle metaphys-
ica degli antichi* (Venice, 1732), p. 2.

11. Giannone, *The Civil History of the Kingdom of Naples*, trans. James Ogilvie, 2 vols. (London, 1729–31), 2: 840.

atomists, especially Lucretius, who was now read with renewed interest but much caution; and about the fate of Galileo, who had been forced to abjure his views about the motion of the earth. Vico admits reading Lucretius but denies that the Epicureans ever held any attraction for him.[12]

The second stage followed quickly upon the first, as the Cartesians, the French and Italian followers of René Descartes, began to be heard in Naples. But the Cartesians were loudly and defiantly modern in a way that the Gassendists (who had hedged their bets with an appeal to the ancient wisdom) were not. And, according to Vico and Giannone, they soon eclipsed their rivals. When Vico returned to Naples after his long absence, he found that the mechanical physics of Descartes had replaced all preceding systems, with Aristotle now a laughingstock; that the metaphysics of Descartes had superseded Vico's admired Platonism and obscured its wonderful insight; and that even ancient medicine and law had been upended from their once proud position. Vico, at least in retrospect, was not pleased.[13]

In fact, this collision between old and new seems to have come to a head in Naples at this time in two violent confrontations. The first was when the Inquisition, which had been concerned from the beginning with the theological implications of the new ideas, erupted against the atomists in a trial and sentence of 1692–93. Three of the victims were close friends of Vico's.[14] The list of their errors was long and improbable, though not without some vague plausibility. Nevertheless, some prominent Neapolitans, jealous always of their civic independence, rallied to the accused, including again some of Vico's friends and patrons, and the Inquisition was successfully resisted and eventually subdued. It was a victory for the moderns, but still, as Giannone warned (in 1723), it was always necessary to be on guard and keep "a watchful Eye upon the Clergy for fears of new Surprizes."[15]

The second episode was a propaganda battle over some of these same issues instigated by a Jesuit prefect, Giovan Battista de Benedictis, writing

12. *Autobiography*, p. 126. Fisch, Adams, and others find this unlikely. A translation by Alessandro Marchetti was already in circulation and was later placed on the Index; see Mario Saccenti, *Lucrezio in Toscana: Studio su Alexander Marchetti* (Florence, 1966).

13. *Autobiography*, pp. 128–32. Fisch agrees with Nicolini that Vico remained a Cartesian until about the age of forty; see ibid., pp. 36–37; Nicolini, *Giovinezza*, pp. 116–20. For the Cartesians, see Raffaele Ajello, "Cartesianismo e cultura oltremontano al tempo dell'*Istoria Civile*," in *Pietro Giannone e il suo tempo*, ed. Ajello, 2 vols. (Naples, 1980), pp. 3–181, and Claudio Manzoni, *I Cartesiani italiani (1660–1760)* (Udine, 1984).

14. Nicolini, *Giovinezza*, pp. 127–29; *Autobiography*, p. 25. See Luciano Osbat, *L'Inquisizione a Napoli: Il processo agli ateisti, 1688–97* (Rome, 1974), pp. 180–82.

15. Giannone, *Civil History*, XXXII, p. 577.

under the pseudonym of Benedetto Aletino. In 1694, he attacked the atomists and Cartesians with his *Lettere apologetiche,* singling out for criticism a modern, Lionardo di Capua, and provoking a volley of replies and counterreplies in which the double cause of freedom of inquiry and the merits of the new philosophy were argued.[16] Di Capua had been an early advocate of the Cartesian philosophy and, with his friend Tommaso Cornelio, had helped to introduce into Naples the teaching of Bacon and Galileo, Gassendi and Gilbert, Boyle and even Thomas Hobbes, all under the rubric of the *nuovo modo di ben filosofare.* His *Parere sull'incertezza della medicina* (1681–89) brought him a European reputation. For Di Capua, experience and reason were the only avenues to truth, never authority or antiquity, and he felt free to correct the errors of any of the ancients in the light of modern science. Thus Harvey's discovery of the circulation of the blood (which Di Capua thought had been anticipated by modern Italian science), "far exceeded the Invention of all Antiquity put together."[17] Aletino concentrated on the theological implications of Di Capua's teaching, dismissing Gassendi's attempt to Christianize Epicurus as whitewash and Cartesian mechanical philosophy as godless materialism. His mocking style and persistence were not easily dismissed and the battle went on for a full generation.[18]

Di Capua died in 1695 but he was ably defended by several younger men, including a number of Vico's friends.[19] Their task, among other things, was to find a theological defense of the new philosophy and to show its use to orthodox Catholicism, and they found in neoplatonism a particularly helpful source. What they tried to do was to combine Catholicism with atomism, Plato with Democritus, *ancienneté* with modernity, in several different combinations but all to the same effect: to try to liberate philo-

---

16. "La Novita delle opinioni a la Liberta dell'opinare," Mastelloni, *Pensiero politico,* p. 184. The *Lettere apologetiche in difesa della teologia scolastica e della filosofia peripatetica* (Naples, 1694) is discussed by Paolo Rossi, *Le sterminate antichita: Studi Vichiana* (Pisa, 1969), pp. 168–74, and Girolamo de Liguori, "Nota su Benedetto Aletino e la polemiche anticartesiane," *Rivista di storia della filosofia,* 40 (1985), pp. 271–83. I am grateful to Brendan Dooley for letting me see the relevant chapter of his manuscript, "Culture and Communication in Early Modern Italy."

17. From the English version of the first part, *The Uncertainty of the Art of Physick,* trans. John Lancaster (London, 1684), p. 91.

18. See the recollections of Aletino's implacable enemy, Costantino Grimaldi, *Memorie di un anticurialista del settecento,* ed. Vittor Ivo Comparato (Florence, 1964); and in general Nicola Badaloni, *Introduzione a Giambattista Vico* (Milan, 1961).

19. For a contemporary account, see the letter of Francesco D'Andrea to Magliabecchi, August 23, 1695, in *I Ricordi di un avvocato Napoletano del seicento: Frencesco D'Andrea,* ed. Nino Cortese (Naples, 1923), pp. 18–20. See also Fausto Nicolini, "Sulla vita civile," (n. 3 above), p. 201ff.; and the recent article by Antonio Borelli and Carmen di Ciampis, "I manuscritti filosofici Dandreani," *Bolletino del Centro di Studi Vichiani,* 16 (1986), pp. 375–96.

sophical reasoning from what they took to be the tyranny of orthodox Aristotelianism and the terrors of the Inquisition. To do this, some among them found that it was necessary to modify or even to give up on Descartes altogether, as did Vico's friend, Doria, and his patron, Giuseppe Valetta—and indeed Vico himself.[20] And it seemed necessary to reexamine the whole history of philosophy to discover just how far these various opinions were in fact either ancient or modern. Curiously, the more the moderns considered the subject, the more they came to believe (with the help of the neoplatonists) that modern atomism and true science had not only originated in antiquity, but that it had first been taught by Moses himself! According to Valetta, the new physics had been mistakenly named "modern," since it was in fact the most ancient. From Moses to Moschus the Phoenician, the corpuscular philosophy had descended to Pythagoras and ancient Italy (that is, Calabria or Magna Graecia), and from thence to Greece and the rest of the world.[21] As the argument developed, the discussion turned steadily away from natural philosophy toward problems of theology and human nature.

To all this Vico was witness, perhaps participant, though he later preferred to disclaim it. Was he afraid to admit his unorthodox opinions? Or did a genuine change of heart sometime afterward obscure his youthful views? In 1693 he wrote a "Lucretian" poem, and many years later he referred obliquely to certain "youthful errors" in a letter to a friend.[22] What is certain is that, on his return to Naples in 1695, Vico plunged into the intellectual life of the city, frequenting the salons of such wicked moderns as Valetta and Nicola Caravita and joining the new Palatine Academy of Medinacoeli. Here Cartesians like Gregorio Caloprese (whom Vico called *gran filosofo renatista*) could hold forth without embarassment.[23] It was at the

20. Doria's war with the Cartesians is described by a contemporary, Francesco Maria Spinelli, the prince of Scalea (and one of Vico's students) in his autobiography, *Raccolta d'opusculi scientifici e filologici,* 40 (Venice, 1753), pp. 498–99, 504, 508–8. See Rafaello Cotugno, *La sorte di Giovan Battista Vico e la polemiche scientifici e letterarie* (Bari, 1914), p. 78; Paola Zambelli, "Il rogo posthumo di Paolo Mattia Doria," *Ricerche sulla cultura dell'Italia moderna* (Rome-Bari, 1973); and Vittorio Conti, *Paolo Mattia Doria* (Florence, 1978), pp. 57–59.

21. *Lettere in difesa delle moderna filosofia* (1696–1700), in *Opere filosofiche,* ed. Michele Rak (Florence, 1975), pp. 83, 85–86; *Istoria filosofica* (1704), *Opere,* p. 282. Rak furnishes a useful chart of the transmission of the ancient wisdom as Valetta developed it in *La parte istorica* (Naples, 1971), pp. 32 n. 5. The idea was very common in northern Europe; see, for example, Danton B. Sailor, "Moses and Atomism," *Journal of the History of Ideas,* 25 (1964), pp. 3–16.

22. The poem *Gli affetti in disparato* may be found in Vico, *L'Autobiografia,* ed. Benedetto Croce (Bari, 1911), pp. 273–77; see Nicolini, *Giovinezza,* pp. 120–26; Maria Donzelli, *Natura e humanitas nel giovane Vico* (Naples, 1970), pp. 17–29. For the "debolezzi ed errori," see Vico to Padre Giacchi, October 12, 1720, in Vico, *L'Autobiografia,* pp. 142–43.

23. *Autobiography,* p. 136. Caravita and Valetta were coupled as leaders of the *ateisti* by

house of Caravita, Vico remembered, that he and Doria first began to discuss metaphysics. The new academy resumed the mantle of its famous predecessor, the Academy of the Investiganti, which had done so much under
the inspiration of Cornelio and Francesco D'Andrea to introduce modern
European ideas into Naples.[24] In three busy years (1698–1701), it met in
the royal palace twice a month to discuss natural science and history; and
among the 127 papers that survive in manuscript, there is one by Vico, "On
the sumptuous banquets of the Romans." More interesting perhaps are
those by Porzio ("the last Italian philosopher of the school of Galileo,"
Vico calls his old friend)[25] and the several *raggionamenti* by Valetta and
Giuseppe Lucina (also a friend) that attempt to trace the ancient wisdom
back through the Ionians and ancient Italians to the Assyrians.[26] It was in
this milieu that the new generation—Doria and Giannone as well as
Vico—began to think seriously about problems of the world and man.

Above all, it was Valetta who helped to bridge the generations and who
no doubt cast a spell over Vico as he did over so many of his friends. When
the Anglican Gilbert Burnet arrived in Naples in 1686, he found "an Assembly that is held in Joseph Valetta's library (where there is a vast collection of well chosen books) composed of men that have a right taste of true

---

Domenico Confuorto in his diary, *Giornale di Napoli dal 1679 al 1699,* ed. Nicola Nicolini
(Naples, 1930), 2: 199–200. It was Caravita who helped Vico get the chair of rhetoric. For
Caloprese and Cartesianism, see Enrico Nuzzo, *Verso la vita civile: Antropologia e politica nelle
lezione accademiche di Gregorio Caloprese e Paolo Mattia Doria* (Naples, 1984), pp. 65–103. For the
Academy, see Silvio Suppa, *L'Accademia di Medinacoeli* (Naples, 1971); Guiseppe Ricuperati,
L'Esperienza civile e religiosa di Pietro Giannone (Milan, 1971), chap. 1; "A proposito dell'Accade-
mia Medina Coeli," *Rivista storica italiana,* 84 (1972), pp. 56–79.

24. See Max Fisch, "The Academy of the Investigators," in *Science, Medicine and History: Essays in Honor of Charles Singer* (Oxford, 1953), 1: 521–63. For Andrea, see Salvo Mastellone,
Francesco d'Andrea politico e jurista (1648–98) (Florence, 1969). For Vico and Doria, see the *Autobiography,* p. 138; Harold Stone, "Vico and Doria: The Beginnings of a Friendship," *New Vico
Studies,* 2 (1984), pp. 83–91; and Vico's discourse to the Academy of the Oziosi in 1737, *Opere,*
ed. Fausto Nicolini, 8 vols. (Bari, 1914–41), 7: 36.

25. Vico remembers many discussions with Porzio on scientific matters, *Autobiography,*
pp. 152–53. Some of Porzio's pieces are collected in his *Lettere e discorsi accademici* (Naples,
1711). Vico's paper is in *Opere,* 6: 389–400, 440ff.

26. On Lucina, see Vico, *Autobiography,* p. 135; his two papers are discussed by Ricuperati,
L'Esperienza, pp. 10–16, and Suppa, *L'Accademia,* pp. 46ff. who provides a complete list of the
papers delivered in the Academy, app., pp. 313–19, many of interest for Vichian themes. The
manuscripts are described fully and the papers enumerated by Michele Rak, "La *lezioni* del-
l'Accademia di Medina Coeli," *Pietro Giannone e il suo tempo,* pp. 661–89. For another work
with a similar theme by Domenico Aulisio, where the Pythagorian philosophy is again considered as a synthesis of ancient thought, see Ricuperati, "La prima formazione di Pietro Giannone: L'Accademia Medina Coeli e Domenico Aulisio," *Saggi e ricerche sul settecento* (Naples,
1969), pp. 146–48.

learning and good sense."[27] Valetta's library, *sceltissima e copiossima*, was one of the wonders of Italy and won fame and visitors from all over Europe. At its sale in 1726, Vico was called in to evaluate its contents.[28] We have seen Valetta among the patrons of the Palatine Academy, leading the defense of the new ideas and the freedom to philosophize, but combining them with the old—Plato with the atomists—in a compound that was very appealing to the younger members. Valetta knew all about the famous *querelle* in France and thought that it might be possible to reconcile the views of the ancients and the moderns, of Pere Rapin and Charles Perrault.[29] He kept his library up to date with the latest news from all over Europe, especially through the many literary journals which were springing up everywhere.

Naples was thus no more isolated from European thought than Vico was from Naples. The young men of the new generation, Giannone, Doria, Vico, and the rest, were kept in intimate touch with the republic of letters. And in Naples, as elsewhere, the intellectual climate was galvanized above all by the clash between old and new ideas, by the quarrel between ancient and modern philosophy. It is not surprising therefore that Vico should give his first attention to issues raised in the quarrel, though, to be sure, it was only after long hard thought and some backing and filling that he was able to develop an answer that was truly his own.

2

Meanwhile, the quarrel had been heating up in another area, quite independent of philosophy. In literature as in science the new had come to rival and challenge the old; but now it was not so much over whether the ancients had known more, as whether they had spoken or written better. When the Renaissance humanists had insisted on classical imitation as the basis of all proper education, they did so in the confidence that the ancient Latin and Greek authors had perfected the humanities: the arts of grammar and rhetoric, poetry, history, and moral philosophy. Since there could

27. Burnet, *Some Letters Containing an Account of What Seemed Most Remarkable in Switzerland, Italy, etc.* (Rotterdam, 1686), pp. 195–96; see too Benedetto Croce, "Shaftesbury in Italia" (Bari, 1927), 1: 272–309.

28. See Vico to Padre de Vitry, January 20, 1726, *L'Autobiografia*, p. 192. For Valetta's place and influence, see the obituary in the *Giornale de' Letterati* in Valetta, *Opere*, p. 413; Vittor Ivo Comparato, *Giuseppe Valetta* (Naples, 1970), p. 80; M. Schipa, "Il Muratori e la cultura napoletana del suo tempo," *Archivio storico per la province Napoletane*, 26 (1901), p. 562; and in general, Biagio de Giovanni, "Cultura e vita civile in Giuseppe Valetta," *Saggi e ricerche sul Settecento* (Naples, 1968), pp. 1–47.

29. *Difesa* in *Opere*, pp. 172–74.

be no advance upon perfection, the best the moderns could hope to do was to equal their models. This was the dogma of the grammar schools throughout Western Europe in the early modern period, Catholic and Protestant alike, where a sample of the classical authors monopolized the curriculum and where "humanity" normally preceded philosophy. Vico does not tarry over his preliminary education in the *Autobiography*, but he early gained a love and admiration for the ancient poets, orators, and historians that he never lost and a conviction that the ancient Latin language and literature far surpassed the modern Italian. He accepted the classical goal of eloquence and after a time gained a vocation.

It was in an effort to escape this tyranny of the classics, to allow some measure of freedom for the modern vernacular writers and artists, that the literary quarrel first began. And although the moderns started up in the Italian Renaissance as anti-Ciceronians, it was in the France of Louis XIV that patriotism and the real accomplishments of French literature combined to bring the conflict to a boil. It was with a poem in praise of the achievements of Louis's reign, recited before the French Academy in 1687, that Charles Perrault began the climactic chapter in the *querelle*. The ancients, led by the redoubtable Boileau, replied, and the battle was on. Perrault was forced to draw up a series of parallels in which he paired the leading authors, ancient and modern, over the whole spectrum of human learning to depreciate the ancients and vindicate the moderns.[30] He was neither the first nor the last to make the attempt, Tassoni preceding him in Italy, William Wotton succeeding him in England.[31] And although he ranged far and wide across the whole field of the arts and sciences, it was his claims about modern literature that provoked the fiercest replies. For a decade or so, nearly every French intellectual and many other Europeans thought it necessary to enter the fray and declare themselves in favor of one side or the other.[32]

There were thus two separate areas of conflict between ancients and moderns—philosophy and literature—separate in origin, separate in the character of the issues that divided them, and separate as a result of that long continuing antipathy that had from ancient times divided the culture of the West into competing forms of paideia. And it was possible to be a

30. *Parallele des anciens et des modernes*, 4 vols. (Paris, 1688–97), facs. with intro. by Hans Robert Jauss (Munich, 1964). The poem, *Le siècle le Louis le Grand* is printed at 1: 165–71. See above, chap. 5.

31. For Wotton, see Levine, *Humanism and History*, pp. 156–62, 171–76. Wotton borrowed from Perrault but Vico probably did not know his work.

32. News carried fast; see the letter from Ruinart to Magliabecchi, *Correspondence inédite de Mabillon et Montfaucon avec d'Italie*, ed. M. Valery, 3 vols. (Paris, 1846), 3: 360–62.

modern with respect to one and an ancient with respect to the other. But Descartes and his followers showed an unqualified contempt for both— for the humanities in general and for the idea of an ancient wisdom—thus launching a double-barrelled blow against antiquity and provoking a crisis. Descartes doubted that the Greeks had known much about either mathematics or the mechanical philosophy, and he insisted upon the difference between the knowledge of science gained by reason and the casual knowledge of acquaintance (*connaissance*), which is acquired through language and history. Only a fool would wish to know everything; in the meantime, "it is no more the duty of an ordinary well-disposed man to know Greek or Latin than it is to know the languages of Switzerland or Britanny, or that the history of the Empire should be known any more than that of the smallest state of Europe."[33] Philology and philosophy were to be completely severed and the classical authors largely ignored.[34] But Vico's career and only livelihood was teaching classical rhetoric, and he wrote poetry and history and delivered orations throughout his life. It was hardly possible to stand by idly under this challenge, and his first published works were thus addressed to these issues.

Vico became Professor of Rhetoric at the University of Naples in 1698 and was required to deliver a series of inaugural speeches, the last of which he gave in 1708 and published in an enlarged version the following year. In keeping with the eclectic spirit of the moment, he wanted to call it "On reconciling the educational program [*ratio studiorum*] of antiquity with our own time," but feared being thought too pompous. Nevertheless, the discarded title aptly describes Vico's intention of mediating between the ancients and the moderns. He did not, he says, wish to make comparisons, as some had done, between the two sides in all the different fields of knowledge (an allusion perhaps to Perrault).[35] But he does attempt a broad balance in the introduction to his own modest work. In general, he accepts the division between the two cultures. He finds that the moderns have excelled in the sciences (in chemistry, pharmacology, anatomy, astronomy, geography, and mechanics), while the ancients remain superior in the humanities and fine arts (poetry, oratory, painting, and sculpture). Vico preferred ancient to modern medicine, but modern to ancient theology, with some-

---

33. *Recherche de la verité*, trans. Elizabeth S. Haldane and G. T. Ross, *Philosophical Works*, 2 vols. (1931, rep., New York, 1955), 1: 309. See also the *Discourse on Method*, ibid., 1: 85; *Rules for the Direction of the Mind*, ibid. pp. 5–6, 11–12.

34. So too the Cartesian, Pere Malebranche, well-known in Naples, *De la récherche de la verité*, ed. Genevieve Rodis-Lewis (Paris, 1965), 1: 147–51.

35. *De nostris temporis studiorum ratione*, in Vico, *Opere*, 1: 77–78. The work has been translated by Elio Gianturco, *On the Study Methods of Our Time* (Indianapolis, 1964).

thing from each side for jurisprudence. It seemed to him that both ancients and moderns knew some things and employed some techniques unknown to the other, and that each emphasized a different set of disciplines.
His chief intention here was simply to compare the study methods, the education, of both sides to see which was the better—or rather what was best
in each.

For Vico, modern education meant the method of Descartes. He begins,
therefore, with a contrast between the new philosophical criticism, which
starts with the certainty of clear and simple ideas and builds knowledge by
means of abstract reasoning, and the ancient tradition of rhetoric, which
preferred concrete sense perceptions and arrived at only a probable
knowledge of things by means of imagination and memory. But Vico does
not so much try to chose between the two rival forms of paideia as simply to
restore the claims of eloquence in the education of the young. This he does
on two grounds: first, because imagination naturally precedes reason in
the development of the mind of the child; second, because of the usefulness of rhetoric to civil life, the probable being the only possible knowledge in the world of prudence and experience. So far, Vico remained a
conventional humanist.[36] Yet Vico was no simple advocate of antiquity; he
wished to combine the advantages of eloquence and wisdom, antiquity and
modernity, rather than discarding the one or the other. And he believed
that the moderns might eventually equal the ancients in this, even, he says,
as they already excelled them in science.

Yet still Vico hesitated, for he saw that the humanist notion of imitation
had its own perils. On the one hand, he agreed that the ancients should be
read first in the curriculum, "since they are of proved reliability and authority," and that they should be used as standards by which to judge the
moderns. On the other hand, he saw that the greatest masters in the arts
had imitated nature directly, not models, and that it was impossible for imitators to surpass or even equal originals. "They must fall short of their
achievement." So modern sculpture remained beneath the Greek, though
modern painting (which had no surviving models to follow) had reached
perfection. "It would almost seem advisable, in order to have great artists,
to have the great masterpieces of art destroyed!"[37] Vico was not quite prepared to accept this modernist paradox, however, although he was seriously troubled by it and eager to find a way out. What was required, it began

36. *Study Methods*, pp. vii, 34–35, 42. The fullest treatment of Vico as a humanist is Michael
Mooney, *Vico in the Tradition of Rhetoric* (Princeton, 1985). In 1711 Vico wrote out a work on *The
Principles of Oratory* which Mooney describes, p. 69ff.

37. *Study Methods*, pp. xii, 70–72.

to seem, was a solution beyond any yet proposed by either the ancients or the moderns.

The following year Vico published another small Latin work, *On the Most Ancient Wisdom of the Italians,* which he dedicated to Doria.[38] In this, he argues even more vigorously than before against the pretensions of Cartesian method, and announces his famous *verum-factum* principle as a way of validating the knowledge of human life and institutions that Descartes had relegated to uncertainty.[39] Here again Vico takes a cue from Francis Bacon, this time from Bacon's work *On the Wisdom of the Ancients,* which he couples now with Plato's *Cratylus,* to urge that the ancient myths be deciphered in the light of modern philosophy.[40] Vico argues, echoing Valetta, Lucina, and the rest, that the Romans had derived their learning from their predecessors, this time Etruscans and Ionians, and that Latin etymologies (not only philosophical parallels) could be used to reveal their knowledge. Philology could thus be brought helpfully to the aid of the ancient wisdom. When Vico defended his work a year or two later, he lamented the fact that the study of language had declined, thanks to the influence of Descartes, "who says that to know Latin is to know no more than Cicero's servant-maid."[41] Nevertheless, the recovery of the *prisca theologia* was an enterprise which, like some other things in these early works, Vico was soon to abandon as misguided and anachronistic.

3

It was sometime in the next few years that Vico stumbled upon what he was later to call the "master key" to his new science. No one has yet given a satisfactory account of this discovery, least of all Vico himself, who attributed it in his *Autobiography* to reading Grotius on international law. Unfortunately, Vico's description of his own intellectual development, which may have been the first of its kind and was honestly intended, is too simple and schematic to tell all. (The *Autobiography* was meant, no doubt too polemically, as a kind of philosophical apologia and an answer to Descartes' auto-

38. *Opere,* 1: 127ff. There is a new translation by Lucia M. Palmer, *On the Most Ancient Wisdom of the Italians, Unearthed from Origins of the Latin Language* (Ithaca and London, 1988).

39. "The criterion and rule of the true is to have made it. Accordingly, our clear and distinct idea of the mind cannot be a criterion of the mind itself, still less of other truths. For while the mind perceives itself, it does not make itself," *De antiquissima,* chap. 1, Pompa trans., p. 55. See Croce, *Vico,* pp. 5, 23–24; Berlin, *Vico and Herder,* p. 27. Vico repeats the notion in the first *Scienza nuova* and the last.

40. *Autobiography,* p. 148. For Bacon's views, see Paolo Rossi, *Francis Bacon: From Magic to Science,* trans. Sacha Rabinovitch (London, 1968), p. 292.

41. See Vico's second reply to the review in the *Giornale de' letterati,* quoted by Croce, *Vico,* p. 292.

biographical *Discourse on Method*.)[42] Vico's master key, he says, was a literary
or linguistic discovery, that the origin of language and letters was a result of
the fact that the first men were natural poets who spoke in poetical characters—not philosophers concealing their wisdom in allegory.[43] This meant
breaking with the conventional view—still held by Vico himself and
Grotius—that there had been philosophers among the first men, and poets who shared their wisdom. It cost him, he remembered afterward,
twenty years of exasperating labor to find out how "to descend from these
human and refined manners of ours to those wild and savage natures
which we cannot at all imagine and can comprehend only with great effort."[44]

Now the sources for this novel insight were many and various and may
well have included (up to a point) Grotius and the natural-law theorists—
especially Hobbes—all of whom began with a primitive state of nature.[45]
No doubt they also included Lucretius, whose fifth book of the *De natura rerum* offers an elaborate picture of primitive man rising by degrees to a civ-
ilized state; and Tacitus, a favorite author whose portrait of the barbarous
early Germans made an unforgettable impression on him; not to say
his own children, growing up under foot as he tried to rough out his
thoughts.[46] However, it looks as though it must also have been develop-
ments in the *querelle,* which broke out with renewed virulence in the
decade 1710–20, that caught Vico's attention and played a crucial role in
his discovery; for it was not simply that the first men were primitive barbarians, but that they were "poets," and of their kind supremely good.[47]

42. For doubts about Vico's dependence on Grotius, see Dario Faucci, "Vico and Grotius:
Jurisconsults of Mankind," in *Giambattista Vico: An Intellectual Symposium,* ed. Giorgio Tagliacozzo and Hayden White (Baltimore, 1969), pp. 61–62; for doubts about the *Autobiography,*
see Fisch's introduction to it, pp. 6–7, 35–37; and Enrico de Mas, "Vico's Four Authors," ibid.,
pp. 4–5.

43. "Prima sapientia vulgaris fuit poetica," Vico wrote in the margin of his copy of Horace's
Ars poetica, 11. 391–401 (on Orpheus); he later credited Horace with the idea, though he
might have found it in other classical sources such as Cicero and Varro. See Mooney, *Vico in the
Tradition of Rhetoric,* p. 208n.

44. See the *Scienza nuova* (1744), *Opere,* 3: 338, repeating the *Scienze nuova* (1725), ibid., 4:
1–2. In the *Autobiography,* Vico seems to date the discovery to about 1719 when he drew up the
prospectus for a new work, the *Sinopsi del diritto universale;* see *Opere,* 2: 1–21.

45. See Vico's synopsis prefixed to the *Scienza nuova* (1725), *Opere,* 3: 5. For Hobbes in Italy,
see Eugenio Garin, "Per una storia della fortuna di Hobbes nel settecento Italiano," *Dal rinascimento* (note 3 above), pp. 153–74.

46. See Fausto Nicolini, "Giambattista Vico nella vita domestica," *Archivio storico per la
province Napoletane,* n.s., 11 (1925), pp. 227–98. Compare the bachelors, Descartes and
Hobbes.

47. Tacitus may have suggested the idea to Vico that history began in poetry, though there
were several other possibilities (see note 43 above); Vico quotes the relevant passage from the

It is true that Vico did not like to read in any modern language and it is unlikely that he knew very directly what was happening immediately in England and France. But the news from abroad was readily available in Neapolitan intellectual circles, if only through the journals that reported the *querelle* and that could be found in Valetta's library and elsewhere. As Giannone explained, "By means of the great Number of Journals which are published in these Countries, every Body may have an account of the Books that are printed in Europe, of the Matters they contain, and of the News of the Commonwealth of Learning."[48] Vico certainly knew the *Acta Eruditorum* and probably looked at some of the French reviews with which he later had business, not to mention the new *Giornale de' letterati D'Italia* that criticized his work in 1710 and caused him to reply.[49]

In the meantime, French books were becoming increasingly popular in Naples in the first decade of the new century;[50] and a patriotic rivalry (with ancient and modern overtones) between the Italian Marchese Orsi and the French critic Père Bouhours stirred the literary scene in 1703–6, and stimulated at least two of Vico's contemporaries, Ludovico Muratori and Gian Vincenzo Gravina, to write important works of literary criticism and to reconsider the *querelle*.[51] Vico rarely credits his contemporaries, but he does cite Muratori and he certainly came to know Gravina personally in Gravina's last years (1716–18).[52] And there is a distinct echo of the Orsi-Bouhours debate in *De nostris temporis*.[53] It does not require much imagination to see Vico among his friends discussing the latest news from the republic of letters, arguing about the conflicting claims of the ancients and

---

Germania in the *Scienza nuova* (1744), p. 470. In the edition that Vico knew, the editor, Justus Lipsius, already compares the ancient Germans to the modern American Indians; see Fausto Nicolini, *Commento storico alla seconda scienza nuova*, 2 vols. (Rome, 1949), p. 191.

48. Giannone, *History*, XI., chap. 5, p. 840.

49. *Opere*, 1: 195–294; *Autobiography*, pp. 153, 187–90.

50. See Maugain (note 3 above), pp. 354–62; Vico, *Autobiography*, p. 181.

51. Bouhours's work, *Manière de bien penser* (1687) was answered belatedly by Orsi in his *Considerazioni nella opere degli antichi* (1703) and *Quattro lettere alla Mad. Anne Dacier* (1706); see J. G. Robertson, *Studies in the Genesis of Romantic Theory in the Eighteenth Century* (1923; rep. New York, 1962), pp. 6–15; Gabriel Maugain, *Boileau et l'Italie* (Paris, 1912), pp. 87, 90–91. In the *Della perfetta poesia italiana* (1706) and again in the *Reflessioni sopra il buon gusto* (1708–15), Muratori tried to steer a middle way between the ancients and the moderns, defending and admiring modern science and philosophy but insisting on the need for authority in religion and the continuing role of the classics for the humanities. Selections from both works appear in *Dal Muratori al Cesarotti*, ed. Giorgio Falco (Milan, 1978).

52. For Vico and Muratori, see Croce, *Vico*, p. 228. For Vico and Gravina, see the *Autobiography*, p. 154. For the two, see Mario Fubini, "Muratori e Gravina," in *L. A. Muratori e la cultura contemporanea* (Florence, 1975). In each case the influence on Vico was by provoking contradiction; see Robertson, *Studies*, pp. 24–59.

53. *De nostris temporis*, *Opere*, 1: 90–96.

moderns, and thinking about the meaning and value of the ancient philosophy and poetry, and their relations—in short, addressing just those problems that seemed to require a master key for their solution.[54] And so, when the *querelle* suddenly resumed in France in 1715–16—specifically now about that other long-standing issue of moment, the place of Homer in Western culture—it too most likely caught his immediate attention.

How Homer got to be the nub of the quarrel is a story too long to tell.[55] Suffice it to say that any comparison of ancients and moderns was bound to begin with the "prince of poets" to whom the ancients themselves had given literary precedence, as well as philosophical wisdom.[56] And so, when Perrault first addressed the French Academy in defense of the moderns, as we have seen, he felt compelled to disparage the Greek poet to make his point. Homer might have been a great poet; he would have been greater still had he had the good luck to live in the modern age! As it was, there were many obvious flaws in the *Iliad*. In the *Parallele* that followed, Perrault took pains to show Homer's faults: his poor composition, weak plot, bad characterization, gross morals and boorish manners, and his awkward similes. Nor would he allow the poet any competence as a philosopher or scientist, all claims to the contrary. Only time, he insisted, could bring true knowledge and *politesse*.[57] Perrault did not fail to mention that there were some who denied the very existence of "Homer" and who claimed that the *Iliad* and the *Odyssey* were no more than many small pieces by different authors that had been strung together long after they had been composed; the abbé d'Aubignac, for one, was ready to publish a whole treatise on the subject.

Boileau led the rebuttal for the ancients; his strongest arguments were the absence of any plausible modern rival and Perrault's ignorance of the

54. Nicolini denied that Vico knew much about the quarrel, though he did admit the importance of the Cartesian atmosphere in setting the framework for Vico's thought; see the *Commento storico*, 2: 9–11, and Nicolini, "Sugli studi omerici di Giambattista Vico," *Atti della Accademia Nazionale dei Lincei, Memorie,* ser. 8, 5 (1954), p. 470. but his reservations were based on too restricted a notion of *quellenforschung*, as though influence can only be detected by explicit reference.

55. See Levine, "Battle of the Books," pp. 33–61; chap. 5 above; and at length in Noémi Hepp, *Homère en France au XVIIe siècle* (Paris, 1968).

56. Tassoni already asks in the *Pensieri diversi* "Si Omero nell'Iliade sia quel sorrano che i Greci si danno a credere," IX, quesito 9. And Muratori echoes Tassoni in the *Perfetta poesia,* 1: xi (*Dal Muratori,* pp. 81–84).

57. *Parallele,* 2: 108. The idea that Homer was a repository of knowledge was a familiar one; it can be found, for example, in Strabo and in the massive commentary of Eustathius. It was widely held in Vico's time, by both Gravina and Giannone among others. In 1732, Giannone is still calling Homer, "profondo filosofo ed esatto istorico"; see *Vita scritta da lui medisimo,* ed. Fausto Nicolini (Naples, 1905), *Saggi Vichiani* (Naples, 1955), p. 159; and Nicolini, "Sugli studi," app. 3, p. 501.

Greek language. Though much ink was spilled in the exercise, no victory was obtained, and the quarrel sputtered and died, until in 1711, it suddenly came to life with the appearance of a new translation and apology for Homer by Anne Lefevre, Madame Dacier. This time it was an "ancient" who was the aggressor and the modern who was forced to reply. Madame Dacier, and her husband, André (who had started the whole thing with a commentary on the *Poetics* of Aristotle), refused to give an inch; she praised Homer for his poetry and his learning, and defended the historical reality of both the poem and the poet. And she accepted the venerable tradition that Homer had found his philosophical wisdom in Egypt.[58]

It did not take the moderns long to reply. First in the field was another member of the Academy, Antoine Houdar de la Motte, a popular and pro- lific writer, who at once produced an alternative version of the *Iliad*, delib- erately improved and modernized, abridged, rearranged, and versified. An accompanying discourse resumed and embellished the now familiar arguments of Perrault and his ambivalent ally, François de Fénelon.[59] Ig- norance of Greek was no embarrassment to La Motte, who preferred "rea- son," by which he seems to have meant some combination of Cartesian philosophy and the good sense and taste of his own time. He thus at- tempted to rid the *Iliad* of its tedious passages, divest the gods and heroes of their bad manners, abridge or suppress the endless speeches, minimize the repetitions, and cut out the miraculous and impossible. In a word, he hoped to transform the ancient epic into an acceptable eighteenth- century poem.

There was worse to come. The abbé Jean Terrasson, we have seen, was even more eager than his predecessors to press the claims of reason and modernity against Homer. Terrasson knew more Greek, but less about po- etry, than La Motte. For him, philosophy was everything and Descartes the one true master, above all other sages ancient or modern. Now, to bring about progress in literature, as it had once been accomplished for science, it seemed necessary to dethrone Homer, just as once it had been necessary to remove Aristotle. In 1715, Terrasson published a massive two-volume work in which he criticized the *Iliad* and tried to found a science of criticism on reason alone. Few of his arguments were original, but the enterprise was carried out with a ruthlessness and detail that were impressive. Terrasson's

58. Levine, "Battle," pp. 38–41 and chap. 5 above. For Madame Dacier, see Enrica Malco- vati, *Madame Dacier: Una gentildonna filologia del gran secolo* (Florence, 1952); Fern Farnham, *Madame Dacier: Scholar and Humanist* (Monterey, 1962); and Arnaldo Pizzorusso, "Antichi e moderni nella polemica di Madame Dacier," *Teoria letteraria in Francia* (Pisa, 1968), pp. 16–55.

59. Levine, "Battle," pp. 38–41; Hepp, Homère, pp. 661–88; Paul Dupont, *Un poète- philosophe Houdar de la Motte 1672–1731* (Paris, 1898), pp. 257ff.

aim was, "to introduce the same Light of Reason and true Philosophy, by
Help and Assistance of which there has of late been such Great and Noble
Discoveries in the Study and Knowledge of Nature, into . . . Eloquence and
Poetry, Criticism and Philology, in a word . . . Belles Lettres."[60] For the
abbé it was evident that it was the philosopher, not the humanist, who knew
best how to read and understand the past, "who makes the true System of
the Human Mind his principal Study and Allocation [and who] knows
how best to transport himself into the remotest and earliest Ages of the
World."[61]

Terrasson saw at once that the defenders of Homer had erred in making
his virtues appear timeless and his qualities perfect; but (like all the moderns) he was equally ready to apply his own set of values to the past, even
more heedless of circumstance. Armed with modern reason—the one
"Crucible and Touchstone" of truth—Terrasson was ready to condemn
not only antiquity but all other cultures except his own. In effect, Homer
had failed because he did not know Descartes; he had lived in an age of
darkness and ignorance. Should he not be excused then, since he had
done the best that he could for his time? Terrasson would not allow it.
Common sense, if not Cartesian reasoning, had always been available to
the human mind. Homer could have done much better even within the
limits of his own age.

The battle was joined. Madame Dacier replied vigorously and many others joined the fray. D'Aubignac's tract was now retrieved and published
posthumously.[62] The satirists enjoyed deriding both sides. Echoes were
heard throughout Europe, in England especially, and in Italy.[63] But still it
was impossible to say who had won. In 1718, Antonio Conti, a young Pad-
uan nobleman of ample means and boundless curiosity returned to Paris
and drew up an account of the quarrel. On his return to Italy, he became a
patron of Vico's and one of his first admirers.[64] Conti's account of the

60. *Dissertation critique sur l'Iliade d'Homère, ou . . . on cherche les règles d'une poétique fondée sur
la raison,* 2 vols. (Paris 1715, 2d ed., enlarged, 1716). I quote from the English translation by
Francis Brerewood, *A Critical Dissertation upon Homer's Iliad,* 2 vols. (London, 1722–25), pref.,
p. xxxiii.

61. Ibid., p. lxi.

62. François Hédelin, Abbé D'Aubignac, *Conjectures académique, ou dissertation sur l'Iliade*
(Paris, 1715), pp. 82–87. The abbé's theories had been enunciated earlier in France but were
unlikely to have been known directly by Vico; see Nicolini, who treats the subject exhaustively,
"Divagazioni," pp. 55–278. He does notice, however, that D'Aubignac's tract was reviewed in
the *Mémoires de Trévoux* (1715) and the *Journal littéraire* (1717).

63. There were many reviews of works in the quarrel; see below. Pierre Bayle discusses it
fully in his famous *Dictionary,* art. "Achilles."

64. Eventually, Conti helped to promote Vico's *Scienza Nuova* which he thought might correct some of Newton's erroneous ideas about chronology. He gave a copy to Montesquieu.

querelle was drafted too soon and published too late to have been noticed by Vico, but it gives a convenient estimate of the issues and a firsthand report of the contest just about the time that Vico was casting about for his master key. Conti found Terrasson's arguments ridiculous and he defended Homer; the Frenchman had confused philosophy and poetry and ignored the continuing superiority of the Greek language and literature.[65]

Even though Vico did not read Conti's letter, he certainly had access to the French controversy in other ways. Whether he read French easily or not must still remain in doubt, although a translation exists in his hand of a review by Le Clerc of one of his books, from French into Italian.[66] He did know the journals, as we have seen, and many of them recounted the latest episodes in the quarrel. For example, in 1716, the Liepzig *Acta Eruditorum* reviewed Madame Dacier, Boivin, La Motte, and Terrasson, referring familiarly to the *celeberrima controversia*. The French journals, as might be expected, were full of the news: the *Mémoires de Trevoux*, the *Journal des scavans*, Le Clerc's *Bibliothèque choisie*, the *Journal littéraire*, etc. The *Giornale de' letterati*, on the occasion of Madame Dacier's death in 1718, reminded its readers, as though it were only too familiar, of the "civil war" that had lately preoccupied the literary republic.[67] It seems hardly possible that Vico could have missed the event altogether.

Just what he made of it is another matter. What is certain is that it was just about this time that he made his admirable discovery. And it was in 1721, at the very moment when Vico was tentatively developing his new science, that he determined to set down his first thoughts about Homer. The *De constantia philologiae* begins with a chapter entitled, "Nova scientia tentatur," and the *Notae*, a year later (1722), attend directly to the Homeric problem. "By certain canons of mythology," Vico says in the *Autobiography*, "which he had conceived, he gives these poems [the *Iliad* and the *Odyssey*] an aspect different from that they have hitherto borne, and shows how divinely the poet weaves into the treatment of his two subjects two groups of Greek stories, the one belonging to the obscure period and the other to the

---

Vico quotes two letters of Conti to him (1728) in the *Autobiography*, pp. 183–84, and refers to him as "a Venetian nobleman and a great metaphysician, rich in esoteric wisdom." For more on Conti, see the life by Guiseppe Toaldo in Conti's *Prose e poesie;* Giovanni Gronda, "Antonio Conti e l'Ingilterra," *English Miscellany* (Rome), 15 (1964), pp. 135–74, and Nicola Badaloni, *Antonio Conti: Un abbate libero pensatore tra Newton e Voltaire* (Milan, 1968).

65. Conti to Maffei, n.d., but probably 1719, in *Prose e poesie,* 2: cxx.

66. *Autobiography*, p. 164; the translation is in *L'Autobiografia*, pp. 89–97. See Maria Sina, *Vico e Le Clerc*, in *Studi Vichiani*, 12 (Naples, 1978), p. 10n.; and Gianfranco Cantelli, *Vico e Bayle: Permesso per un confronto*, in ibid., 4 (1971), pp. 31ff. Vico, remembering his early years, says he never cared to learn French (then?) and also abandoned Tuscan, *Autobiography*, p. 134.

67. *Giornale de' letterati*, 30 (1718), pp. 475–76.

heroic."[68] A little later (1725), Vico developed this idea further for the first edition of the *Scienza nuova*. "In this work he finally discovers in its full extent that principle which in his previous works he had as yet understood only in a confused and indistinct way . . . a new critical method for sifting the truth as to the founders of the nations from the popular traditions of the nations they founded."[69] In 1730, he was ready to devote a whole book of his revised work to the "Discovery of the True Homer." And still he was not done, adding, revising, and sharpening his thought. In seeking the master key for his new science in the origin of language and letters, Vico could not avoid the oldest and most famous work of antiquity—or the contest that surrounded it.[70]

Indeed, among all the works of antiquity, only the Roman Law of the Twelve Tables seemed to offer anything like an equal opportunity to retrieve the condition of early man—and even that ancient document was no longer extant and could be retrieved only indirectly. When Vico came to consider the matter more fully in the *Scienza nuova,* he decided that the Twelve Tables must itself have been no more than a kind of "poem" and all early Roman jurisprudence no more than a kind of "poetry."[71] In short, it looks as though the *Iliad* had somehow become paradigmatic in Vico's

68. *Autobiography,* p. 160. The work known as *Il diritto universale* appeared in three parts, 1720–22. The second is entitled *De constantia iurisprudentis* and is divided in turn into two parts, the one dealing with philosophy, the other with philology. See chap. 1 in part 2, *Opere giuridiche,* ed. Paolo Cristofolini (Florence, 1974), pp. 387–401; and chap. 12, "De linguae heroicae sive de poeseos origine," where Homer is discussed, pp. 451–71. The *Notae in duos libros* was added in 1722 and treats Homer, ibid., pp. 832–66.

69. *Autobiography,* pp. 166–67. The *Scienza nuova* (1725) treats Homer, 3: 18, 21–22. The relevant Homeric passages from these several works are conveniently collected by Nicolini, "Sugli studi omerici," apps. 2–4, pp. 501ff.

70. Vico's annotations to the *Scienza Nuova* (1730–40) were incorporated in the last edition of his work (1744); see the *Autobiography,* pp. 195–97. B. A. Haddock has some helpful things to say about Vico's Homer, but only briefly mentions the *querelle;* see "Vico's Discovery of the True Homer: A Case Study in Historical Reconstruction," *Journal of the History of Ideas,* 40 (1979), pp. 583–602.

71. See *Scienza Nuova* (1744), pp. 1036–37, 904. Max Fisch long ago pointed out the parallels between Vico's explication of the Homeric epics and the Twelve Tables; in each case it was in the *Diritto universale* (1721–22) that Vico began to see the anachronisms of the traditional interpretation. See Fisch, "Vico on Roman Law," *Essays in Political Theory presented to George Sabine,* ed. Milton Konvitz and Arthur Murphy (Ithaca, 1948), pp. 62–88. The importance of Roman law to Vico was properly stressed by Robert Flint (note 3 above) and has been shown in detail by Donald Kelley in a series of articles: "Vico's Road: From Philology to Jurisprudence and Back," in *Giambattiata Vico's Science of Humanity,* ed. Giorgio Tagliacozzo and Donald Verene (Baltimore, 1976), pp. 15–29; "Vico and Gaianism: Perceptions on a Paradigm," *Vico Past and Present,* pp. 66–71; "The Prehistory of Sociology: Montesquieu, Vico, and the Legal Tradition," *Journal of the History of the Behavioral Sciences,* 16 (1980), pp. 133–84. (As Kelley has suggested, there was also a quarrel between the ancients and the moderns in the inter-

thought, and that it was above all in attempting to unlock the meaning of that controversial poem that he had discovered the key to human history. The *querelle* had posed a host of problems of interpretation and evaluation, but none more urgent than this. It took some time for Vico to think it through, and he had obvious difficulty articulating his ideas; but it was not long before he was ready to offer his own solution to the old controversy and to try to reconcile the two sides.

4

What Vico learned from Grotius, he said, was the need to combine the methods of philosophy and philology, by which he seems to have meant the teaching of Christian Platonism and the history of language and culture.[72] The quarrel between the ancients and the moderns must have reinforced—perhaps even precipitated—this insight, since the conflict could only be resolved by recourse to both. (How else could one determine the nature of the antique achievement, except by philology; or evaluate it, except by philosophy?) Among other things, the argument over Homer required discovering whether the first of the poets was also a philosopher and whether the *Iliad* could still be made to serve as a model for present life and literature. Vico's training had from the first embraced the two rival cultures, and he had made an early effort to employ philology to recover the ancient Italian wisdom. The moderns, it appears, persuaded him of the futility of that, since early times were universally primitive. Now Vico was ready to forge the two disciplines into one new science to determine once and for all what was the true character of early human history.

Vico began with the suspicion that the ancient Greeks knew little of their own history, and that many of the ancient peoples had exaggerated their claims to antiquity. Varro, the most learned of the ancients, had suggested that of the three epochs of Roman history, the two earliest were obscure and fabulous; while Thucydides, the most reliable of the Greek historians,

---

pretation of Roman law, beginning in the Renaissance, a quarrel which Vico also came to know. For the antecedents, see Kelley, *Foundations of Modern Historical Scholarship* (New York, 1970).) But Isaiah Berlin probably exaggerates the role of Roman law in triggering Vico's discovery, neglecting the *querelle* and putting the cart before the horse; I prefer to believe with Michael Mooney that Vico's Homer was not so much a consequence as a cause of his discovery of the new science. See Berlin, *Vico and Herder,* pp. 123–42; Mooney, *Vico in the Tradition of Rhetoric,* p. 201.

72. Philology is defined in the *De constantia* to include the study of past words and things, "whence it appears that philologists study human governments, customs, laws and institutions, intellectual disciplines, and the mechanical arts," *Opere giuridiche,* p. 387; Kelley, "Vico's Road," p. 19.

had insisted that nothing could be securely known before his own time.[73] On the other hand, Chaldeans and Egyptians, Chinese and others, all claimed an antiquity extending back nearly to the Flood, though their chronologies were riddled with obvious inconsistencies. (Vico knew something of the massive literature that had been devoted to these problems.)[74] Vico believed that the trouble in every case resulted from the tendency of all human beings to judge the past by the present—and thus to think anachronistically. He believed that the "conceit of nations," as he later called these claims, as well as the "conceit of scholars," the similar boast of learned men for the antiquity of their own ideas, were both rooted in the same ahistorical mentality.[75] It seemed to Vico that modern philologists had erroneously accepted the fanciful testimony of late antiquity, while modern philosophers from Bacon to Vico himself in the *Antiquissima*, had mistakenly read their own opinions back into the distant past.[76] It was poets, not philosophers, who had written the first human history, using imagination, not reason. And the best proof of this must be Homer's *Iliad,* the oldest piece of antiquity that has come down to us.

It was from the "ancients" in the *querelle* that Vico learned that Homer was the first of the poets in language and imagination, but it was the moderns who taught him not to accept their claims to his wisdom and morality. Philosophy, Vico agreed, needed time to develop; and as it grew slowly to maturity in ancient Greece, it must only gradually have discarded the natural fancy of the poetry that preceded it. As philosophy (reasoning abstractly) advanced, poetry (imagining concretely) declined. How could Homer have taught modern physics when Thales, who wrote nearly three hundred years later, was the first Greek to offer even the simple hypothesis that water was the first principle of all things? From the moderns, therefore, Vico learned that Homer was a primitive poet living in primitive times, describing a culture whose manners and mores had largely passed away. The heroes of the *Iliad* were thus barbarians in exactly the same way that the heroes of that second barbarous age—Roland, Orlando, and the rest—had been described by the poets of the Middle Ages. It was, inciden-

73. *Scienza nuova* (1725), pp. 33–34.

74. Vico names many seventeenth-century works in the *Scienza nuova* (1730), and Nicolini supplies details in his admirable *Commento,* 1: 28–30, 34–36, 38–39. See also Paolo Rossi, "Il rifuto delle sterminate antichita," in *La sterminate antichita: Studi vichiani* (Pisa, 1969), pp. 133–64. Vico's notions might be usefully compared with Isaac Newton's (to whom he sent a copy, unacknowledged, of the first *Scienza nuova*). Newton's *Chronology* (1728), though idiosyncratic, is a much more conservative work; Newton continued to believe in the ancient wisdom long after Vico had abandoned it. See Manuel, *Newton Historian,* pp. 89–90.

75. *Scienza nuova* (1744), pp. 124–28.

76. *Scienza nuova* (1725), p. 24; ibid. (1744), p. 80.

tally, just about this time that the parallel between Dante and Homer—suggested perhaps by Gravina—began also to reinforce Vico's notion of *corso* and *recorso,* the idea that cultural cycles repeat themselves throughout gentile history.[77]

For Vico, Homer occupied a specially privileged position as a poet because he was nearest to that epoch when language was in its infancy, when sense reigned and reason hardly mattered. So Homer, or the rhapsodists who first sang the songs that he collected (a view that was held by Abbé D'Aubignac and by Richard Bentley, among others), needed correction and expurgation by the later Greeks, as well as allegorical interpretation to make his teaching acceptable.[78] Thus the indecorous behavior of the Homeric heroes that had so exercised the moderns seemed perfectly appropriate to Homeric times, though not to Vico's own. The moderns were right to see that Homeric morality was not the morality of the age of Louis XIV, but they were wrong to think that Homer had any choice in the matter. The ancients were right to see Homer as the prince of poets, but wrong to think of him as a suitable guide to modern life. Moreover, both parties were wrong to conceive of the *Iliad* and the *Odyssey* as deliberately composed. Poetic language was the first language of the world, and "Homer" was the collective expression of the entire Greek community describing the world in the only way it knew how. (So too, Zoroaster, Hermes, and Orpheus, among the ancient sages, were each dissolved into poetic characters of their respective peoples.)[79] Among other things, this explained why all the Greek cities had claimed Homer as their own and why the poet had drawn on all the Greek dialects of his time. The only question that remained for Vico was how to get back behind Homer to that mute, obscure time that had preceded the Homeric age, for which there was no direct contemporary evidence at all.

To see how Vico accomplished this, it would be necessary to turn to the *Scienza nuova* and follow Vico with his master key, unlocking the doors to the earliest human history, combining philosophical reasoning to determine what men *must* have been like in their bestial primitive condition with philological criticism of the ancient myths to divine what had *actually happened* in the evolution of human culture and institutions. Unfortunately,

---

77. See the *Discoverta del vero Dante* (written between 1728 and 1730) in *Opere,* 7: 79–82. In the *Scienza nuova* (1744), Dante has become "the Tuscan Homer," pp. 786, 564, 817.

78. Bentley's views were set out pseudonymously in *Remarks upon a late Discourse of Free-Thinking* (London, 1713), which Vico would not have known. However the review in the Leipzig *Acta eruditorum* for 1714, pp. 313–14, translated Bentley's comment into Latin where it is just possible that Vico might have come upon it.

79. *Scienza nuova* (1725), p. 27; ibid., (1744), pp. 59, 66, 79.

Vico's learning (i.e., his philology) was not in fact really up to the task of demonstration, and it was to take a century or more before proofs could be provided for his intuitions.[80] But it was the method that mattered, more perhaps than the conclusions, and the opportunity it seemed to furnish for recovering the obscure history of early man. Here indeed was a new science of history that suggested, perhaps for the first time, that human nature and values had not been fixed and unchanging from the beginning of things, but had varied essentially through time and circumstance. History was not to be explained by human nature, but human nature by history.

There is not space to describe all the ramifications of Vico's historicism (if I may use that awkward term).[81] What is clear is that Homer and the issues in the *querelle* seem to have mattered more and more to Vico as he drafted and redrafted his great work and developed his ideas. And his sense of exaltation grew as he came to feel the originality and superiority of his own thinking to any that had gone before. He thought he could show that everyone who had written about these matters before him had been wrong: the philosophers, from Plato and Aristotle to Patrizi, and the philologists and critics, including Scaliger and Castelvetro. (He tactfully spares his contemporaries.)[82] Beyond all his predecessors, he had revealed the paradox "that it was a *deficiency* of human power that gave rise to poetry so sublime that the philosophies that came afterward, the arts of poetry and criticism, have produced none equal or better, and have even prevented its production." In this the proponents of antiquity were right, though for the wrong reasons. "It is Homer's privilege to be, of all the sublime, that is, the heroic poets, the first in order of merit as well as in age." Bacon had said well that in the life of mankind it is we who are the elders, while it was the founders of nations who were like children.[83] But it was this very priority

80. See Arnaldo Momigliano, "Vico's *Scienza nuova:* Roman 'Bestione' and Roman 'Eroi'," *Essays in Ancient and Modern Historiography* (Middletown, 1977), p. 271. Vico seems to have known little of contemporary Homeric scholarship and even his Greek is suspect. He does not mention Kuster, Fabricius, Gronovius, etc. According to Nicolini, he probably read Homer in the Greek-Latin version of Lorenzo Valla; see *Giovinezza*, pp. 136–37. Vico sent his *Diritto universale* to the best Greek scholar in Italy, Anton Maria Salvini, who later translated the *Iliad* into Italian, but it does not appear whether Salvini read Vico or Vico Salvini; see *L'Autobiografia*, pp. 142–44.

81. Vico's historicism has been declared his most important and original achievement; see Erich Auerbach, "Vico and Aesthetic Historicism," *Scenes from the Drama of Human Literature* (New York, 1959), pp. 183–98; Friedrich Meinecke, *Historicism: The Rise of a New Historical Outlook*, trans. J. E. Anderson (London, 1972), pp. 37–51; Joseph M. Levine, "Eighteenth Century Historicism and the First Gothic Revival," *Humanism and History*, p. 192.

82. *Scienza nuova* (1725), p. 253; ibid., (1744), p. 384. Vico's reluctance to mention contemporaries does not, of course, prove that he never read them, though this has sometimes been alleged.

83. *Scienza nuova* (1725), p. 42; ibid., (1744), p. 384.

that gave them the advantage in just those things that are prior in human development, i.e., poetry and imagination. No wonder the Cartesians, like Capasso and his friend Dr. Cirillo, could only shake their heads.[84] In the second *Scienza nuova,* Vico was able to add to a whole long book on the poetic wisdom, a whole new book on Homer, in which all these ideas are worked out, and philosophy and philology, *ancienneté* and modernity, are combined in a new and unexpected fashion. Homer had become the crowning proof, as the quarrel over Homer had once been the inspiration, for Vico's new science—and its autonomy.

Thus Vico's originality—and his contemporaneity—can probably best be gauged by comparing him to those who fought the battle over Homer in the quarrel between the ancients and the moderns, or those who tried to take its measure immediately afterward, like Antonio Conti. For example, an illuminating contrast might be made with Abbé Du Bos, whose *Critical Reflections on Poetry and Painting* appeared in 1719 and was well known throughout Europe.[85] Du Bos had followed the whole *querelle* with attention and (like Vico) gradually emancipated himself from the Cartesians. He hoped to reinstate feeling and imagination to aesthetic judgment. And he wanted to separate the arts and literature from philosophy and science, where he was sure the moderns had the advantage. He saw that there was a fundamental difference between the learning that can accumulate and that depends on facts and experience, and that which requires feeling and imagination: i.e., poetry, history, oratory, and morality. Du Bos thought about matters for himself and sometimes sounds a little like Vico, as when he deplores the "prejudice" of men in favoring their own time and country, or when he writes that the early Greeks and Romans wrote their first history as poetry. He was willing to forgive Homer his faults and ready to assign them not to the poet but to the age. But he remains unwilling to surrender the values of his own (superior) time. One should certainly recognize

84. For these two friends of Giannone, see Giuseppe Ricuperati, "La Formazione," (note 26 above), pp. 122–26, 138; *Giannoniana,* ed. Sergio Bertelli (Florence, 1968), pp. 73–81; Paolo Zambelli, *La formazione filosofica di Antonio Genovese* (Naples, 1972), pp. 31–54, 800– 801; and the articles in the *Dizionario biografico degli italiani.* Giannone applauds them both in his *Civil History,* XL, pp. 842–43. Capasso's *Historiae philosophiae synopsis* (Naples, 1728), continues the views of Valetta and Aulisio on the identity of Moses-Moschus and the ancient wisdom; see Vittor Ivo Comparato, "Ragione e fide nelle discussioni istoriche, teleologiche e filosofiche di Costantino Grimaldi," *Saggi e ricerche sul settecento* (Naples, 1968), pp. 91–92.

85. The *Critical Reflections* was translated by Thomas Nugent, 3 vols. (London, 1748); see esp. chap. 32–38. It is just possible that Conti knew Du Bos's work, though Vico pretty surely did not. See A. Lombard, *La querelle des anciens et des modernes: L'Abbé Du Bos* (Neuchatel, 1908); and *L'Abbé Du Bos* (Paris, 1913). Frank Manuel sets off Vico's originality in a comparison with his contemporaries on the interpretation of myth in *The Eighteenth Century Confronts the Gods* (1959; rep. New York, 1967), pp. 149–68.

merit in Homer as an entertainer and reporter of contemporary life; but in
the end one could only pity him "for having had the misfortune of appearing in a time of rusticity and ignorance."[86] Compared to Vico, Du Bos still
hews to the conventional line, with a view of history and human nature that
is basically static and a critical judgment that remains deliberately anachronistic.

Du Bos's *Reflexions* were read for a long time, while Vico's *Scienza nuova*
slipped quietly into oblivion, until it was revived at a more hospitable moment. Voltaire was typical in admiring the one and ignoring the other.[87]
One can see why. Du Bos had tried to adjudicate the quarrel by choosing
the most sensible arguments on both sides and casting a balance, all the
while holding on resolutely to the values of contemporary good sense. In
this way the ancients could still be admired and even imitated though their
faults were acknowledged. Vico had plumbed the depths only to discover a
new world that imperiled the old. With the help of the moderns he had discovered among the ancients a preclassical substratum that was shockingly
different from the one he had learned as a schoolboy: different in essence,
different in the very qualities of mind and value that constituted their very
being. Thus for Vico, Homer was neither ancient nor modern in the terms
of contemporary parlance but a voice from a wholly different age that
could only be understood or retrieved with the aid of a wholly new science.
For Vico the gulf between Homer and Plato was as wide as the gulf between
poetry and philosophy, and as unbridgeable, wider indeed than the gulf
between Plato and Vico, who shared in the prosaic character of their minds
a common stage of culture, since Western civilization had repeated itself in
a new cycle from barbarism to philosophy.

And so Vico continued to believe in the study of antiquity, though now as
much for its use to philosophy and history as to literature. In the preface to
some poems of 1730, Vico explains that good poetry and oratory cannot be
found together; the one belongs to the heroic age, the other to the more
prosaic age of rational thought. To the extent that eloquence was still desirable, the ancients could still teach by example, though not in the undis-
criminating way of pedantic humanism.[88] For Vico there remained a real
commonality between the golden age of classical culture and his own time,
parallel stages in two cycles of history, which allowed the prosaic authors
among the ancients to speak directly to the modern world. But his sense of
cultural individuality was too strong for him to encourage literal imita-

86. *Critical reflections*, 2: 393–94.
87. *Le siècle de Louis XIV*, ed. Alfred Rebelliau and Marcel Marion (Paris, 1894), pp. 759–60.
88. *Opere*, 7: 39–41; and discourse to the Academy of the Oriosi (1737), ibid., pp. 33–37.

tions. When therefore, late in life, Vico once again addressed his students about education (1732), he once again urged them to combine the study of the ancients with an appreciation of the moderns, and pleaded with them, in the name of progress, to escape the tyranny of *ancienneté*.[89] All through his life Vico had flirted with modernity, even as he fought with some among the moderns; but Vico was himself a modern, more radical than any of the moderns in the quarrel, so modern indeed that he had found an altogether new way to appreciate the precedence of the ancient poets. His historicism set him apart from both sides and forebade him to advocate either the pedantic imitation of classical models, so dear to the defenders of antiquity, or the creative possibilities of the imagination, so tempting to some of the moderns, but which had now to give place (however regretfully) to reason. Vico was thus neither a rationalist nor a pre-Romantic, and so was bound to seem obscure to most of his contemporaries, who were either one or the other, however much he meant to resolve their problems. Progress was certainly real for Vico and had brought about much that was worthwhile—not least the *Scienza nuova*—but in the process it had undeniably lost something too. No one, Vico was sure, would ever write a heroic poem like Homer's again—not anyway unless the return of a new barbarism could make it possible, should *corso* become *ricorso* once again.

89. Vico assembles a full list of modern inventions and scientific discoveries; *De mente heroica dissertatio*, in *Opere*, 7: 3–20; trans. Elizabeth Sewell and Anthony C. Sirignano in *Vico and Contemporary Thought*, 2: 228–45.

PART THREE

The Autonomy of History:
Edward Gibbon and the Johannine Comma

CHAPTER SEVEN

Truth and Method in Gibbon's Historiography

1

The long story of the Johannine comma between Erasmus and Gibbon remains to be told. It is a story with two intersecting plots: a tale of how the Trinity came more and more to seem a problem as Unitarians and skeptics of different varieties raised questions about it; and a tale of how European scholarship developed in the meanwhile to more and more sophisticated levels of historical criticism and understanding. It is a story full of paradox, with some of the orthodox turning out to be the most incisive critics, and some of the heretics the most credulous believers. Above all, it is a story of the gradual triumph of historical method, as all parties began to turn to it to settle their disputes. I shall not attempt anything like a full recital here, but skip quickly from Erasmus to the climax with only an occasional retrospect. It was Edward Gibbon who awoke the controversy at the end of the eighteenth century and brought it to a head. In the quarrel that he provoked, all the ideological issues that had bedevilled the long dispute before his time were finally laid bare and resolved.

But before we do anything further to sort the matter out, we should make some effort to answer two preliminary questions. What brought Gibbon to address himself to this famous crux, and what sort of method did he think of employing on it?

2

The *Decline and Fall* is undoubtedly the most ambitious history of the eighteenth century. Its ambition lies in Gibbon's deliberate attempt to combine three current traditions of historical writing which were to some extent independent of each other and often antithetical.[1] In the first place there was narrative after the fashion of the ancients, and we know that Gibbon particularly admired Tacitus, whom he tried to emulate.[2] Then there was the reflective history of the *philosophes*, who took up the task of making the past intelligible to enlightened opinion, and which is exemplified by the works of Hume and Voltaire, whom Gibbon also admired, though he had some reservations.[3] And finally there was the historiography of erudition, the ponderous work of philologists and antiquaries who had been trying for three centuries to recover the lost world of antiquity by collecting and sifting evidence and assembling massive collections of facts and data. Perhaps because we still remember and continue to read the first two while we have nearly forgotten the last, we do not need to be reminded so much about Gibbon's debt to the classics and to philosophy, as to his relation to erudition. In trying to gauge Gibbon's method, we may begin by asking just how his allegiance to contemporary learning, in particular to the philology of early modern scholarship, affected his historiography; how far it helped him to realize his ambition to tell the historical truth, and to tell it well. In a brief space I shall limit myself to a few suggestions.

Already, in Gibbon's very first published essay on the study of literature, the young man took pains to defend learning against the contempt of the *philosophes* and men of the world. He was well aware of the great quarrel that had opened the century between the ancients and the moderns over

1. See my essay "Edward Gibbon and the Quarrel between the Ancients and the Moderns," in *Humanism and History: Origins of English Historical Thought* (Ithaca, 1987), pp. 178–99. I have found especially helpful in this regard the essays of Arnaldo Momigliano, "Ancient History and the Antiquarian" and "Gibbon's Contribution to Method," in *Studies in Historiography* (New York, 1966), pp. 1–55; and Giuseppe Giarizzo, *Edward Gibbon e la cultura Europea del settecento* (Naples, 1954). See also David P. Jordan, *Gibbon and the Roman Empire* (Urbana, 1971), chap. 2.

2. "Am I worthy of pursuing a walk of literature," Gibbon asked himself in 1761, "which Tacitus thought worthy of him, and of which Pliny doubted whether he was himself worthy?" "Hints on some Subjects for History," in Gibbon, *Miscellaneous Works*, ed. John Holroyd, Lord Sheffield, 5 vols. (London, 1814), p. 487. Suzanne Courchod was not the only contemporary who noticed Gibbon's dependence on Tacitus in the *Decline and Fall;* see her letter to Gibbon, Sept. 30, 1776, *Miscellaneous Works*, 2:177; and J. Whitaker to Gibbon, May 11, 1776, ibid., p. 151.

3. For Voltaire, see *The Autobiographies of Edward Gibbon*, ed. John Murray, 2d ed. (London, 1897), pp. 148–49; *The English Essays of Edward Gibbon*, ed. Patricia Craddock (Oxford, 1972), pp. 116–17; *Gibbon's Journal*, ed. D. M. Low (London, 1929), p. 129; *Le Journal de Gibbon à Lausanne*, ed. Georges Bonnard (Lausanne, 1945), pp. 238–40; Michel Baridon, *Edward Gibbon et le mythe de Rome* (Paris, 1977), pp. 691–93. For some reservations about Hume, see the *Decline and Fall*, 1: chap. 5, p. 112; 7: chap. 70, p. 298m. (I use the version by J. B. Bury, 7 vols. (London, 1897–1900).

the value of classical philology. He knew the attacks of Swift and Pope on Wotton and Bentley, and how the proponents of *ancienneté* in France as well as England had disparaged the new learning as irrelevant or dangerous to the precedence of the classics. They had firmly preferred rhetoric to philology and scrupulously avoided using the methods and apparatus of scholarship; they had only contempt for the footnote and the index, which they ridiculed with delicious wit. They wished only to hew to the narrow line of classical rhetoric and imitation. To some extent Gibbon agreed; he too believed that the first step for a writer was to imitate his predecessors.[4] But Gibbon also felt the attraction of classical philology; even as a child he had been fascinated by textual and chronological problems, and as a young man he dared to quarrel with the experts about dating and emending texts. Gibbon admired the proponents of modern learning, especially the great Bentley, who had embarrassed the ancients by exposing the epistles of Phalaris which they had extolled as a classic but which Bentley demonstrated to be a late and inept forgery.

Gibbon applauded philology first of all for its critical and destructive skills, but he did not ignore its claim to be able to recover the whole life and thought of the ancient (and by analogy) the modern world. Philology had been born of humanist grammar, but well before the eighteenth century it had enlarged its sphere to contain most of what we mean now by cultural history. So, for example, in the third edition of the *Encyclopaedia Britannica* (1797), philology was said to have developed from a narrow concern with words and language to a "more exalted signification." It now included, "the study of grammar, criticism, etymology, the interpretation of ancient authors, antiquities; and in a word, everything related to ancient manners, laws, religion, government, language, etc." It was a science that required enormous industry and multifarious erudition and was of the greatest utility—not least to history.[5]

It is clear that Gibbon agreed and that he owed a massive debt to philology both in its narrowest and broadest significations. Philology enlarged both his sense of what history was about and how it should be done. His autobiography and his letters and journals show us a young man trying diligently to learn the ancient languages and the arcane procedures of paleography, numismatics, and diplomatics, reading the treatises and visit-

---

4. "Nor may the artist hope to equal or surpass, till he has learned to imitate, the work of his predecessors," *Decline and Fall*, 6: chap. 61, p. 433; David Womersley, *The Transformation of the Decline and Fall of the Roman Empire* (Cambridge, 1988), p. 20.

5. *Encyclopaedia Britannica*, 3d ed. (Edinburgh, 1797), 14:485. The reader is referred to separate articles on Criticism, Etymology, Grammar, etc., and here given almost a hundred pages on the early languages.

ing the practitioners. He had no wish (he said) to become an antiquary, merely to employ the results of antiquarian science: to write a history that was still readable, as well as philosophical and learned.[6] How to do this was neither easy nor obvious. But his admirers were certain he had done the job. "The transcendent merit of Mr. Gibbon," wrote one, "was, that his mind always rose superior to his erudition, which often suppresses the mortal energies but invigorated his. . . . The stomach was so strong, that all food became salutary."[7]

3

With most of his contemporaries Gibbon accepted that the object of history was truth, and that fictions, however entertaining, should be clearly distinguished from history. Gibbon certainly enjoyed a good story—*Tom Jones* was a favorite—but he liked history better, and in no case were they to be confused. Poetry, Gibbon wrote in his journal, "is the history of barbarous ages." History depended upon facts that were properly averred, but poetry was willing to settle for "agreeable probabilities," and was helpless before "the harsh and sometimes unlikely truth."[8] That Gibbon held to a fundamental distinction between history and fiction, between the facts of the matter and the fancies of romance, is everywhere clear. Sometimes a history might resemble a fiction, as with the story of the Empress Eudocia, but still the historian must try always to distinguish the true account from the fanciful, what actually happened from what some have imagined.[9] The past was littered with frauds and forgeries, with hagiography and romance, and it was the first duty of the historian, borrowing his techniques from philology, to root out the fictions that disturbed it. It was Gibbon's aim, he said, in a characteristic passage, "to separate (if it be possible) a few authentic, as well as interesting, facts, from the undigested mass of fiction and error." On occasion, a single well-attested circumstance could undo a whole fabric of invention.

The "evidence of authentic facts" was therefore always his deliberate aim, although he was well aware that it was not always possible to achieve.[10]

---

6. He read Mabillon and Montfaucon on diplomatics; Spanheim on medals; a host of Roman antiquaries on archaeology and topography; and many other learned works that are recorded in his memoirs and journals, and were bought for his library. "I studied the theory," he remembered, "without attaining the practice of the art," *Memoirs*, p. 158; see Levine, "Edward Gibbon," pp. 178–89.

7. Pinkerton to Sheffield (1814), *Miscellaneous Works*, 3:579.

8. Gibbon, *Journal*, January 1, 1764, *Miscellaneous Works*, 4, p. 449; Bonnard, p. 138; "Index Expuragatorius," *English Essays*, pp. 121–22.

9. *Decline and Fall*, 3, chap. 32, pp. 387–90.

10. Ibid., 1, chap. 9, pp. 217–18; 2, chap. 16, pp. 72, 82.

Gibbon knew the vogue for historical pyrrhonism, but he despised the superficial efforts of its exponents, who did not have the patience to get beyond it. He followed with great interest the skeptical discussion of Livy's Roman history in the *Mémoires* of the French Academy of Inscriptions and the work of Louis de Beaufort. He decided that the pyrrhonism of the French critics was "useful but dangerous," since their scholarship was inadequate to their pretensions. Criticism was only a prelude to construction.[11] Whatever reservations we may have now about the naiveté of this eighteenth-century conviction, it is clear that Gibbon and his readers did not doubt that the distinction between historical truth and fiction could and should be made.[12]

What gave Gibbon confidence that he might root out the fabrications and discover the facts was a vantage point and a method that he believed could do the trick. From the rhetoricians, ancient and modern, he had learned about interest and passion and their influence in making, recounting, and distorting history. And from the *philosophes* and men of the world, he borrowed the ideal of objectivity, the notion that an historian could rise above party and partiality and review his subject with dispassion. It seemed clear to the enlightened, who could also rely here on the ancients, that the desire to tell the truth was a psychological precondition of genuine history and could be clearly distinguished from the desire to invent or distort the past (as Tacitus had put it) out of fear or favor.[13] They did not imagine that this was easily done, and they often had their own polemical intentions which they barely concealed, but they never stopped proclaiming that objectivity was in principle possible and desirable.

Gibbon shared this hope, but saw that it was not enough. What he wanted to do was to combine this lofty vantage point with the methods and insights of modern philology, particularly with its concern for documentary evidence and criticism.[14] "It is unfortunate," he noticed early, "that

11. See Gibbon's *Journal,* November 5, 1763, *Miscellaneous Works,* 4, pp. 406–9; *Essai sur l'Etude de la littérature* (1759), in ibid., 4, pp. 40–46. Gibbon actually met Beaufort, but he does not say what they talked about, *Memoirs,* pp. 110–11. The best contemporary answer to the pyrrhonists was from the antiquaries; later it would be Niebuhr. See Momigliano, "Ancient History and the Antiquarian," in *Studies* (n. 1, above), pp. 1–39.

12. The modern reader may object that "the signal that tells a reader that a narrative is historical rather than fictional (the title, the notes at the foot of the page, the insertion of the text into the context of other histories)," is *not* "sufficient to establish the authenticity or truth of the narrative or of the facts and events it relates," but Gibbon would have objected strenuously; precision was not for him just a "strategy" but the main goal of the historian who wants to know what actually happened. See Lionel Gossman, *The Empire Unpossessed: An Essay on Gibbon's Decline and Fall* (Cambridge, 1981), pp. 110–11.

13. See for example, Lucian's well-known tract on *How to Write History.*

14. "The criticism of Bayle joined to the erudition of Tillemont," as Baridon puts it succinctly, *Gibbon,* p. 688. When Tillemont's work runs out, Gibbon leaves him with regret, "that

the knowledge of facts, and the art of making use of them are so very seldom united."[15] He wanted therefore to borrow from the classical narrative
tradition the form of his work and its gift for analyzing motives, and from
the philosophes his basic posture towards his subject—dispassionate, he
liked to think, and above the battle—and combine them with the method
of the philologists and antiquaries who had taught him how to recover the
linguistic and material facts that could help him to expose the frauds and
forgeries, errors and misinterpretations, that cluttered the documents and
distorted the past. This led him to join to his grand narrative a set of analytical dissertations and an extended footnote commentary. In such a way,
he hoped to unite the insights and methods of all three prevailing forms of
contemporary historiography and achieve his goal of writing a reliable as
well as a readable history.

Needless to say, Gibbon was immediately attacked for his rhetoric, for his
partiality, and for his facts. Although his style and narrative won immediate
praise, it was also severely criticized. Even some of his supporters found his
writing mannered and artificial and his narrative deliberately digressive.
He was accused of abandoning the Roman Empire in the *Decline and Fall*
for whole chapters at a time to talk about other matters, far removed from
any direct connection with the subject.[16] His admirer Richard Porson was
reminded when reading Gibbon of that great man, Mr. Prig, the auction-
eer in Foote's play, "whose manner was so infinitely fine, that he had as
much to say on a ribbon as a Raphael."[17] Nevertheless, the *Decline and Fall*
was read and appreciated then and now, at least as much for its style and architecture as anything else.

As for Gibbon's pretended dispassion, it was generally believed, as one
critic wrote, that, "he who reads Mr. Gibbon with the least degree of attention, must see that he is strongly prejudiced against Christianity."[18] The
historian protested again and again, proclaiming his impartiality. In his
history, Gibbon tried to avoid all theological explanations to concentrate
on the purely secondary, that is, human, causes that he thought might explain the astonishing events of early Christian history. History, as history,

incomparable guide whose bigotry is overbalanced by the merits of erudition, diligence, veracity and scrupulous minuteness." *Decline and Fall*, 5: chap. 47, p. 132m.

15. He is here referring to Sir William Temple, "Index Expurgatorius," in *English Essays*,
pp. 112–13.

16. See especially John Whitaker, *Gibbon's History Reviewed* (London, 1791), pp. 18–20, 23–
24, 47–49, etc.

17. Richard Porson, *Letters to Mr. Archdeacon Travis* (London, 1790), pp. xxviii–xix. Gibbon
winced a little at this "pinch of salt."

18. Joseph Milner, *Gibbon's Account of Christianity Considered* (York, 1781), p. v.

had no way of discovering the divine intentions.[19] Thus Gibbon (perhaps following the example of Voltaire) wished to erase all distinctions between secular and ecclesiastical history. "We ought not," he admonished a clerical adversary, "to admit any thing as the immediate work of God, which can possibly be the work of man; and whatever is said to deviate from the ordinary course of nature, should be ascribed to accident, to fraud, or to fiction."[20] Only in such a way did he think it possible to concentrate attention on the historical facts and avoid the rancor and distraction that invariably attended the discussion and that, he believed, with his philosophical friends, must render it fruitless. He wished to set himself above the battles that had always disgraced his subject: neither orthodox nor heretic, believer nor unbeliever, merely the "philosophic" historian adjudicating among the fallacious dogmatisms of the past, just trying to get his story right. Others had let their passions and their prejudice intervene, and that was regrettable although all too human. Gibbon insisted that he had in the *Decline and Fall,* "without interposing his own sentiments, delivered a simple narrative of the authentic facts."[21] He pretended afterward to be surprised by the vehemence of the criticism that he received, but he was not really oblivious to the dangers—and temptations—of clerical orthodoxy.[22]

In short, Gibbon believed that he had a viewpoint and a method that could lead him through the labyrinths of past testimony and present opinion to a semblance of truth, to the facts of history. On the whole he accepted criticism with forebearance, until he was finally provoked by a young critic who had the temerity to accuse him of corrupting his story by

19. Gibbon may have found the same sentiments in Jacques Basnage; see Giarrizzo, *Gibbon* p. 316n.

20. Gibbon to Hurd (c. 1772), *Letters,* pp. 327–39. See also Momigliano, "Gibbon's Contribution to Historical Method," *Studies,* p. 52; and Womersley, *The Transformation,* p. 126.

21. Gibbon to Joseph Priestley, January 28, 1783, *The Letters of Edward Gibbon,* ed. J. E. Norton, 3 vols. (London, 1956), 2:320–21.

22. To Dorothea Gibbon, he wrote that his book had been well received by everyone, except the clergy "(I know not why)," March 26, 1776, *The Letters,* ed. Norton, 2, pp. 99–100; and to his friend George Deyverdun he expressed his indignation at the bishops, "who dared to attack the purity of my faith," May 7, 1776, ibid., pp. 104–8. He even expressed incomprehension to his translator, Septchenes, though he saw how the book might create a problem for the French censor, December 10, 1776, ibid., pp. 131–32. He told his friend Lord Sheffield that he had not had any intention of attacking Christianity in the two famous chapters, and he was still expressing surprise at the uproar late in life; see William Wilberforce to his son in Shelby T. McCloy, *Gibbon's Antagonism to Christianity* (London, 1933), p. 47n; and *The Memoirs of the Life of Edward Gibbon,* ed. George Birkbeck Hill (London, 1900), pp. 201–2. But Gibbon understood that he had provided an opportunity for clerical advancement and claimed to have made several bishops! For the contemporary reception of the *Decline and Fall,* see J. E. Norton, *A Bibliography of the Work of Edward Gibbon* (1940, reprinted New York, 1970), pp. 84–85.

misrepresenting his sources and plagiarizing his opinions. Gibbon could overlook a difference of opinion, even a slur on his style; he was not at all dismayed when Bishop Watson disagreed about the theological meaning of the *Decline and Fall*, and indeed the two respectful opponents eventually became friends.[23] But to be accused of fraud was another matter. When at last he was stung into action it was by the appearance of *An Examination of the Fifteenth and Sixteenth Chapters of Mr. Gibbon's History*, by one Henry Edwards Davis, with its vicious charges of "manifest falsification"—including "misrepresentation of Authors, Proofs of Inaccuracy, and Instances of Plagiarism."[24] Against that kind of criticism, Gibbon found it necessary to defend himself; and so he interrupted the progress of his great work to write a *Vindication*. His honor as a faithful historian had to be protected. Only once again was Gibbon tempted to defend himself publicly, and that too was due to an attack on his reliability.[25]

In other words, it was only the assault on the facts and on his erudition that really surprised Gibbon and that he particularly resented. From the philologists and antiquaries, Gibbon had learned the need to document his history, not casually or haphazardly, but exactly and in detail. From them he had learned also to share with his readers the grounds of his judgments as well as his conclusions. Now Davis had dared to question his scholarship; so Gibbon replied first of all by reexamining the footnotes in his two offending chapters. He calculated that he had provided some three hundred and eighty-three notes there with about eight hundred to a thousand references, each citation carefully distinguished into books, chapters, sections, and pages, "with a degree of accuracy and attention, which might claim some gratitude, as it has seldom been so regularly practised by historical writers."[26] Gibbon saw that a reliable history depended on its use

---

23. Gibbon to Watson, November 2, 1776, *Letters*, 2, p. 119; Watson to Gibbon, November 4, 1776; January 14, 1779; Gibbon's *Miscellaneous Works*, 2:181, 227.

24. For a good account of the controversy, see Norton, *A Bibliography*; and more fully, McCloy, *Gibbon's Antagonism*. Priscilla Craddock counts eighteen attacks before Davis, four of which extended to more than a hundred and fifty pages each, *Gibbon*, p. 122.

25. See Gibbon to John Douglas, May 9, 1782, showing concern for Bishop Newton's criticism that "my testimonies are not to be depended upon." Gibbon, *Letters*, 3:294–96. Otherwise, Gibbon seems rather to have enjoyed criticism, since it meant that he was not being forgotten; see Gibbon to his publisher, Francis Cadell, February 11, 1789, ibid., pp. 142–43.

26. *A Vindication of Some Passages in the Fifteenth and Sixteenth Chapters of the History of the Decline and Fall of the Roman Empire* (London, 1779), in *The English Essays of Edward Gibbon*, ed. Patricia Craddock (Oxford, 1972), pp. 236–37. It has been estimated that there are 3,000–4,000 citations to his authorities in the *Decline and Fall* and some 8,362 footnotes altogether. See I. W. J. Michin, "Gibbon's Debt to Contemporary Scholarship," *Review of English Studies*, 15 (1939), pp. 84–88. Gibbon's claim was true; the narrative historians had rarely attempted to combine the documentary scruples of the antiquaries with their rhetoric; see Momigliano,

of the sources, and he understood that that must be a collaborative undertaking, since no one scholar could master all the evidence by himself. He defended himself against Davis's frivolous charge of plagiarism by showing at some length just how he had depended on his predecessors—all duly acknowledged—just as they in turn had used the work of those who had preceded them. Scholarship was cumulative and it was progressive, just as the moderns had declared against their skeptical opponents in the Battle of the Books; if only for that reason, Gibbon could believe he had done better with his subject than anyone before in arriving at a just and accurate description of the past.[27]

Unfortunately, Gibbon never attempted to set out his views on these matters systematically, although I think he made a genuine effort to employ them systematically in his work. Still, in his *Vindication* he was compelled to defend his practice, and throughout his history Gibbon continued to scatter remarks that justify his method, so that it is not impossible to retrieve the historiographical principles that he thought were essential to writing history and judge just how far and in what way he thought he could retrieve the truth about the past. Let me try for a moment to set out some of his more insistent prescriptions.

To write a respectable history, Gibbon believed that it was necessary at a minimum to do the following:

1. *Discover all the original testimony and accept nothing at second hand,* except where the original was lost or could not be seen. Gibbon accepted with complete conviction the admonition of the Renaissance humanists to return to the sources, *ad fontes.* "Diligence and accuracy," Gibbon insisted, are the only merits which an historical writer may ascribe to himself." It was, he said at the outset of his work, the *one* indispensable duty. "I may therefore be allowed to say that I have carefully examined all the original materials that could illustrate the subject which I had undertaken to treat." And in the *Vindication,* he insisted again that this is what he had tried to do.[28] Nevertheless, Gibbon confined himself largely to the printed narratives and admitted his dependence on the great philologists who had preceded him for the rest. (This, he makes clear, was their principal value for

and Levine (n.1 above). He says of Raynal's work, "the total absence of quotation is the unpardonable blemish of his entertaining history," *Decline,* 2: chap. 20, p. 312m.

27. William Wotton, *Reflections upon Ancient and Modern Learning* (London, 1694), pp. 316–18; *A Defense of the Reflections* (London, 1705), pp. 23–26, 32–34. See Levine "Gibbon," pp. 183–84; and Levine, *Battle of the Books: History and Literature in the Augustan Age* (Ithaca, 1991), pp. 43–46.

28. Gibbon proclaimed his obligation in the "Advertisement to the Notes," which was placed at the end of the first volume (in the Bury edition, 1, p. xi), and reaffirmed it in the *Vindication,* p. 279.

him.) What else could he do? He understood the need to use the documents behind the histories, but he saw that it must be impossible for him to employ them all directly for so vast a subject. "I shall content myself," he wrote at the end of his great labor, "with renewing my serious protestation, that I have always endeavored to draw from the fountainhead; that my curiosity, as well as my sense of duty, has urged me always to study the originals; and if they have sometimes eluded my search, I have carefully marked the secondary evidence, on whose faith a passage or a fact was reduced to depend."[29] Thus the skeptical reader or critic could always check him out. Gibbon was eager to use the nonliterary evidence of antiquarian scholarship, coins and charters and inscriptions, but here he was a little handicapped by his own ignorance and the state of archaeology in his time.[30] No doubt, Gibbon seriously underestimated the importance of these materials, especially the manuscripts that were beyond his reach, but he certainly saw something of their value, and at the end of his life he gave his hearty endorsement to a plan to publish some of the more noteworthy of the medieval chronicles so that they might become accessible to historians.[31]

2. *Weigh each account for its veracity, bearing in mind such things as the relationship of the source to the event and particularly the motives for telling it—that is, the bias of each witness.*[32] Here Gibbon inherited a rich discussion that had developed particularly during two centuries of theological controversy about the reliability of biblical and Christian testimony and how to examine it.[33] In these things, he was as ready to deride the blind faith or simple credulity of the erudite as he was to reprove the ignorant[34]—and even on occasion to correct a *philosophe*. So, Voltaire "unsupported by either fact or probability," was taken to task for carelessly bestowing the Canary Islands

29. See the preface to the last volumes (1788), *Decline*, 1:xii.

30. Jordan briefly discusses Gibbon's use of numismatic and epigraphic evidence, pp. 61–62, 65. Needless to say, classical archaeology was still far in advance of medieval scholarship, but even its revolutionary consequences for the writing of ancient history still lay in the future. See my essay on "The Antiquarian Enterprise, 1500–1800," in *Humanism and History*, pp. 73–106.

31. Gibbon to John Pinkerton, July 25, 1793, *Letters*, 3:340–43; the plan is in the *Miscellaneous Works*, 3:578–90.

32. "Facts either moral or natural are related by men. The value of the evidence must be determined by the character of the witness." Gibbon is here criticizing Buffon, who was "too little acquainted with History or the laws of historical evidence"; "Index Expurgatorius," *English Works*, pp. 121–22.

33. I hope to describe this literature in a book to be entitled *The Trial of the Witnesses: History and Religion in Early Modern England*.

34. "The last century abounded with antiquaries of profound learning and easy faith, who, by the light of the legends and traditions, of conjectures and etymologies, conducted the grandchildren of Noah from the Tower of Babel to the extremities of the globe." *Decline and Fall*, 1: chap. 9, p. 217.

on the Roman Empire. And even Hume, who had himself found Voltaire undependable, was suspected by Gibbon.[35] It was the duty of the historian, Gibbon insisted, to consult every original source and "study with attention the words, the design, the spirit, the context, the situation," of each passage.[36] Only by such criticism could testimony be turned into evidence. He even hoped (in anticipation of Leopold van Ranke) that he might some day close his work with a critical account of the sources.[37] In the meanwhile, he used his footnote citations very fully for that purpose.

3. *Try to divine the interest of the men and women in his history and those who reported it, though their bias was often concealed, in order to understand their behavior.* "I like to notice," he wrote in an early essay, "how men's judgments take a tinge from their prepossessions."[38] So, typically in the *Decline and Fall,* Gibbon explains the conversion of Constantine on the assumption that "personal interest is often the standard of our belief, as well as our practice; and the same motives of temporal advantage which might influence the public conduct and professions of Constantine would insensibly dispose his mind to embrace a religion so propitious to his fame and fortunes."[39] It helped that for Gibbon and his contemporaries human nature was always the same, though each historical situation was unique.[40] Gibbon was usually, though not invariably, cynical about human motives. "It is the duty of an impartial judge," he explains in the *Vindication,* "to be counsel for the

35. For Gibbon on Voltaire, see *Decline,* 1: chap. 1, 26n. See also 2: chap. 19, 252n.; 5: chap. 50, 367n.; 6: chap. 55, 139n.; chap. 56, 188n. In his journal, Gibbon writes typically of Voltaire, "He follows some compilation, varnishes it over with the magic of his style, and produces a most agreeable, superficial, inaccurate performance." *Journal* (Low), p. 129. For Hume on Voltaire, "I know that Author [Voltaire] cannot be depended on with regard to Facts; but his general Views are sometimes sound, and always entertaining"; see *Letters of David Hume,* ed. J. Y. T. Greig (Oxford, 1932), 1:325–26. For Gibbon on Hume, see above, note 3.

36. *Vindication,* p. 279. "To decide judiciously between these opposite authorities," Gibbon wrote in his journal, "we must weigh the character of the witnesses, and consider the nature of the testimony," *Journal* in *Miscellaneous Works,* 5:370–71. As a practical example, see Gibbon's choice here of Polybius over Livy on Hannibal, ibid., pp. 371–77. See also Gibbon's remarks on the "laws of historical evidence" and the credibility of Buffon's witnesses in the "Index Expurgatorius," cited above, note 8.

37. "Advertisement to the Notes," *Decline and Fall* (1897), 1:ix; and Gibbon to his publisher, Cadell, November 17, 1790, proposing a seventh volume, which would include "a critical review of all the authors whom I have used and quoted." He thought it might take two years to complete; *Letters,* 3:209–10. Gibbon's editor, the post-Rankean J. B. Bury, tried to supply the deficit in an appendix to each volume.

38. Gibbon, *Essai,* translated in *The Miscellaneous Works* (London, 1837), p. 654.

39. *Decline and Fall,* 2: chap. 20, p. 206. This conclusion has been much contested.

40. This was the general view, espoused for example by Hume, to whom Gibbon defers on this matter in a note to chapter 15 (2: chap. 15, p. 42), and by Voltaire. See J. B. Black, *The Art of History* (London, 1926); Paul H. Meyer, "Voltaire and Hume as Historians," *Publications of the Modern Language Association,* 73 (1958), p. 53; and Womersley, *The Transformation,* chap. 2.

prisoner, who is incapable of making a defence for himself; and it is the first
office of a counsel to examine with distrust and *suspicion,* the interested evidence of the accuser." It was thus a "clear and fundamental principle of
historical Criticism," that whenever testimony was lacking for all the opposing sides, it was best to suspect the evidence where there was only one.[41]
However, to suspect was not to convict, and Gibbon rarely forgot to take
into account the peculiar circumstances and surprisingly divergent characters in his story, some of whom (even Christians!) had loftier motives
than narrow self-interest.[42]

    4. *Compare the testimonies and, where they disagreed, try to account for the dif-
ferences; compare the historians, and, where they disagreed, find the truth by seeing
that the opposing biases often canceled each other out.* "If we skilfully combine the
passions and prejudices, the hostile motives and intentions," of the several
witnesses, "we may frequently extract knowledge from credulity, moderation from zeal, and impartial truth from the most disingenuous controversy."[43]

    5. *Piece together the narrative so that the different witnesses, each of whom alone
might be partial or doubtful, come to support one another and the whole.* "The
Writer who aspires to the name of Historian, is obliged to consult a variety
of original testimonies, each of which taken separately, is perhaps imperfect and partial. By a judicious re-union and arrangement of these dis-
persed materials, he endeavours to form a consistent and interesting
narrative. Nothing ought to be asserted which is not proved by some of the
witnesses; but their evidence must be so intimately blended together, that

41. *The Vindication,* pp. 298–99. Davis had defended the integrity of Eusebius against his
enemies, whose testimony has not survived. "Under these circumstances, it is the duty of an
impartial judge to be counsel for the prisoner, who is incapable of making a defence for himself; and it is the first office of a counsel to examine with distrust and suspicion, the interested
evidence of the accuser. Reason justifies the suspicion, and it is confirmed by the constant experience of modern History, in almost every instance where we have the opportunity of comparing the mutual complaints and apologies of the religious factions, who have disturbed
each other's happiness in this world, for the sake of securing it in the next." Ibid., pp. 299–
300. "Abu Rafe was an eye-witness, but who will be witness for Abu Rafe?" *Decline and Fall,* 5:
chap. 51, p. 431n.
    42. Thus Gibbon can admire the Crusaders, and even Bernard of Clairvaux. "A philo-
sophic age has abolished, with too liberal and indiscriminate disdain, the honors of these spiritual heroes," *Decline,* 6: chap. 59, p. 332. And he can compare St. Athanasius, with his genuine
conviction in his theological cause, favorably to the pure politician, Constantine, although he
had only contempt for Athanasius's trinitarian beliefs (2: chap. 21, pp. 361–63). Nor does he
conceal the faults in his hero, Julian, as had Voltaire and Montesquieu; see Womersley, *The
Transformation,* pp. 162–63.
    43. *Vindication,* p. 277. See Gibbon's note on the celibacy of the clergy, where he uses the
testimony of Thomassin and Bingham. "By each of these learned but partial critics, one half
of the truth is produced, and the other is concealed." *Decline and Fall,* 2, chap. 20, n. 93, p. 318.

as it is unreasonable to expect that each of them should vouch for the whole, so it would be impossible to define the boundaries of their respective property."[44] Thus narrative method might come to the aid of historical truth, even as truthfulness was indispensable to narrative.

6. *Observe "the general law of partiality"; eliminate as far as possible one's own passion and bias.* Gibbon believed that the broad toleration and moderate skepticism that marked his own beliefs was the best, perhaps the only, useful vantage point from which to understand and evaluate the beliefs of others. The philosopher is always detached and expects his readers to join him in this. He hopes to be "a disinterested and rational spectator." Dogmatic convictions and partisanship can only blind the witness or the historian to the testimony of opponents and to the plain evidence of sense.[45] He can only think of a few historians who have met the test, and not a single divine among them.[46] Attacks from all sides seemed to him to demonstrate his own "honest neutrality."[47]

7. *Even so, allow that historical truth lies on a scale of probability from barely possible to almost certain.* Here again Gibbon had learned much from his prodigious reading in the theologians who had already elaborated on the probable, but sufficient, character of historical testimony.[48] Sometimes a guess may be the best that one can offer. At one awkward point, where the sources were particularly intractable, Gibbon describes his procedure, "Surrounded with imperfect fragments, always concise, always obscure, and sometimes contradictory, he is reduced to collect, to compare, and to conjecture; and though he ought never to place his conjectures in the rank of facts, yet the knowledge of human nature, and of the sure object of its fierce and unconstrained passions, might, on some occasions, supply the want of historical materials."[49] Nevertheless, the historian will sometimes

44. *Vindication*, p. 264.

45. "The philosopher, who with calm suspicion examines the dreams and omens, the miracles and prodigies, of profane or even of ecclesiastical history, will probably conclude that, if the eyes of the spectators have sometimes been deceived by fraud, the understanding of the readers has much more frequently been insulted by fiction." *Decline*, 2: chap. 20, p. 303. In general here, see Gossman, *The Empire Unpossessed*, pp. 75, 87–88, 90–91.

46. He suggests Ammianus Marcellinus, Fra Paolo (Sarpi), Thuanus, Hume, "and perhaps a few others," but certainly not Davis's model, the polemical Christian Eusebius; *Vindication*, p. 299. He had taken Eusebius to task for openly violating "one of the fundamental laws of history," suppressing inconvenient evidence, in 2, chap. 16, pp. 135–36.

47. Gibbon to Deyverdun, *Letters*, 2:104–8.

48. The aim of criticism, Gibbon had early seen, was not the kind of demonstration one obtained in geometry, "but to compare the weight of opposing probabilities." See the *Essai* in *The Miscellaneous Works* (1837), p. 646. As there were degrees of truth, so also there were degrees of fiction. *Vindication*, p. 298.

49. *Decline*, 1: chap. 10, p. 237. When Gibbon allows himself a conjecture, he labels it; see his

find plenty of testimony and thus be able to come closer to the truth. No doubt, language was a problem; how was a faithful representation of the past to be reported in words? But language provided a solution too; it offered an infinite gradation of possibility through which to report what happened.[50]

4

Needless to say, Gibbon's critics remained unconvinced. They naturally continued to prefer their own point of view, not detached but very much a part of the fray, believing that their religious convictions were true and privileged in a way that made them more reliable than Gibbon's pretended disinterest. They questioned the easy reconciliation of rhetoric and philology which (so they felt) allowed Gibbon to conceal his errors with his eloquence.[51] Thus it was easy enough for each side to detect the prejudice of the other, and doubtless a little naive of Gibbon to think that he could escape the charge.[52] Nevertheless, there was one thing anyway on which everyone appeared to agree: the historical account could only be settled by an appeal to evidence. "Matters of fact are stubborn," Davis complained, "and not easily made to bend even by the power of his rhetoric. . . . We now require proofs to authenticate assertions, and something more than the melody of a well-rounded period."[53] It was to justify his facts that Gibbon

---

account of the fall of the Britons, *Decline,* 3: chap. 31, p. 353m.; Womersley, *The Transformation,* p. 154.

50. The modern literary critic is inclined to emphasize the difficulty; Gibbon, I think, was more hopeful, and certainly less relativistic. See, for example, Leo Braudy, *Narrative Form in History and Fiction: Hume, Fielding and Gibbon* (Princeton, 1970), pp. 228–29; and Gossman, *The Empire Unpossessed,* pp. 110–11. J. W. Burrow supplies some examples of Gibbon's characteristic device of employing contradictory pairs of imputed motives, when he wished to leave the matter uncertain, e.g. "the credulity or the prudence of Gregory," "the avarice or humanity" of Philip Augustus, etc. *Gibbon* (Oxford, 1985), p. 91.

51. Davis quotes Burgh's *Inquiry into the Belief of Christians* (1778) to make the point. "Whatever occurs in the modern writers of history of a narrative nature, we find to be an inference from a system previously assumed, without any seeming view to the truths of the facts recorded." Misrepresentation was thus inevitable, as the examples of Hume and Gibbon plainly showed. How Burgh or Davis (or Gibbon for that matter) believed they could escape it does not easily appear. See Davis, *Reply,* pp. 9-10.

52. "Unfamiliar with modern discussions over the matter of historical bias," writes Owen Chadwick, "Gibbon occasionally sounds as though he supposed a perfect detachment from environment to be intellectually possible," "Gibbon and the Church Historians," in G. W. Bowersock et al., *Edward Gibbon and the Decline and Fall of the Roman Empire* (Cambridge, Mass., 1977), p. 223. For an example of Gibbon admitting his early pagan prejudice, which he contrasts with Burke's sentimental Christianity, see Gibbon to Sheffield, February 5, 1791, *Letters,* 3, p. 216.

53. Davis, *Reply,* p. 10.

replied in the *Vindication,* and here indeed it was Gibbon's superior historiography that gave him the advantage in the long run, even though his opponents remained obdurate.

For the larger audience that looked on, Gibbon got high marks both for his rhetoric *and* his erudition;[54] and his skeptical point of view may well have gotten some reinforcement from the persuasive character of the long narrative that he was erecting out of his astonishing command of the sources.[55] To be sure, there were always some readers who were willing to separate the two, that is, Gibbon's story and his judgments, his rhetoric and his philology.[56] But for the majority it was his scholarship, as much as his narrative style, that did the trick, and we should never underestimate the latter. David Hume certainly admired Gibbon's manner, but he also understood—and Gibbon's publisher immediately agreed—that the footnotes which had first appeared at the end of the book and that explained and justified each step in the historical argument, should be removed and placed at the bottom of each page where they could directly accompany the text.[57] Gibbon remained dubious, but he knew that it was only through his painstaking labor with the sources and the work of his predecessors that his story could prove decisive. It was only in this way that the truth of history could be avouched, and only so that history could be detached from theology—and from fiction.

And indeed, it was Gibbon's diligence and accuracy, even more than his style and his point of view, that impressed his fellow historian William Robertson, who immediately hailed him as the first of his kind in Europe and welcomed him (with Hume) into the new triumvirate. He praised Gib-

54. See for example the evaluations of the *Critical Review* and the *Monthly Review* (both in 1776), the one Tory and High Church, the other Whig and skeptical, quoted in Norton, *Gibbon's Bibliography,* pp. 64–66. There was in fact much more difference among the reviewers about Gibbon's style; see the opinions collected in ibid., pp. 68–69.

55. "You say," wrote a hostile Joseph Priestly, "that the two last chapters of Mr. Gibbon's History have made more unbelievers than anything that has been published of late years, and have greatly contributed to confirm many in their unbelief." *Letters to a Philosophical Unbeliever,* 2d ed. (Birmingham, 1787), p. 199.

56. "To his religious sentiments I avow myself inimical," wrote one correspondent to the *Gentleman's Magazine,* "for I think a more dangerous enemy to Christianity never appeared." Yet, he continued, "as a man of curiosity, and of fond attachment to literature, I acknowledge myself considerably indebted to Mr. Gibbon." See the supplement to vol. 55 (1785), pp. 1025–26.

57. Hume to Strahan, April 8, 1776, Gibbon, *Miscellaneous Works,* ed. John Holroyd, Lord Sheffield, 5 vols. (London, 1814), 2:161–62. Gibbon's friend George Lewis Scott had already pointed out to him, December 29, 1775, that "the notes and quotations will add not a little to the value of the work," ibid., 2:141–42. As early as 1776, Gibbon was pleased to find the footnotes squeezed comfortably onto the bottom of the page in the pirated Irish edition; see Gibbon to Deyverdun, September 5, 1776, *Letters,* 2, pp. 104–8.

bon's first volume when it appeared, and then the *Vindication*; and then, even more extravagantly, each of the succeeding volumes. "He possesses that industry of research," Robertson confided to Gibbon's publisher in 1776, "without which no man deserves the name of historian. . . . I have traced him in many of his quotations (for experience has taught me to suspect the accuracy of my fellow penman) and I find he refers to no passage but what he has seen with his own eyes." When he got the next two volumes in 1781, he found them to exceed expectations. "As soon as I have the leisure," he promised Gibbon, "I propose to trace you to your sources of information; and I have no doubt of finding you as exact there, as I have found you in other passages where I have made a scrutiny. It was always my idea that an historian should feel himself a witness giving evidence upon oath. I am glad to perceive by your minute scrupulosity, that your notions are the same." And when he got the last three volumes in 1788, he had to concede that where he had once prided himself on being the most industrious historian in Europe, he must now yield to Gibbon.[58]

Robertson's chief admiration was thus for Gibbon's careful research. Indeed, he was so taken by Gibbon's method of citation that he deliberately adopted it for his own *History of America* (1777). "The longer I reflect on the nature of historical composition," he wrote there, "the more I am convinced that this scrupulous accuracy is necessary. The historian has no title to claim assent, unless he produces the evidence of his assertions. Without this he may write an amusing tale, but cannot be said to have composed an authentic history."[59] For generations, English historians continued to admire Gibbon's industry and accuracy above all, even when they disagreed with his values.[60] J. B. Bury, who edited the *Decline and Fall* and had tilled the same field, and who represented the state of the art at the beginning of this century, still found Gibbon's accuracy "amazing." Perhaps it was only the Germans who had reservations, and that was because of the advance of the very same methods that Gibbon had employed: "a closer union of philology and history," as Bury puts it, "and ampler material."[61] More recently, G. M. Young had some serious reservations about Gibbon's method. He too attributed the advance of the discipline to the Germans of

58. See Robertson to Strahan, March 15, 1776; Robertson to Gibbon, May 12, 1781; July 30, 1788; *Miscellaneous Works*, 2:159–60, 249–51, 424–26.

59. *History of America* (1777), 1:xv–xvi; Patricia Craddock, *Edward Gibbon, Luminous Historian 1772–1794* (Baltimore, 1989); Craddock, *English Essays*, p. 382n. Gibbon reciprocated Robertson's admiration and sent him a copy of the *Vindication*; see the correspondence that passed between them, *Letters*, 2, pp. 152–54, 203–4.

60. So Mackintosh and Grote, Guizot and Milman; see McCloy, *Gibbon's Antagonism*, pp. 310–11, 318–19; *Memoirs*, pp. 335n; Norton, *Bibliography*, pp. 88–90.

61. *Decline and Fall*, 1:lxi–liii.

the nineteenth century, who were the first to apply the criticism of sources systematically—"which is simply the art of cross-examination applied to written evidence." But he too allowed that "Gibbon knew as well as anybody that the ultimate evidence for a fact in history is the testimony of a competent and disinterested contemporary: better still of several contemporaries: best of all the unconscious contemporary, the inscription or document." If Gibbon fell short, it was only in respect to the latter, and Young would probably have agreed that subsequent historiography was an improvement of methods that Gibbon was already employing and that Gibbon would have been the first to appreciate.[62] Even Horace Walpole (who had few pretensions of his own on that score) saw the point, and vigorously applauded Gibbon's victory over Davis.[63]

5

It would be a heroic undertaking, no less perhaps than Gibbon's own, to check him out thoroughly and evaluate the adequacy of his claims to truth and method. Yet the proof of any historiography must lie finally in the pudding, and so it is of continuing interest to dig in, at least here and there, and watch the historian at work trying to solve a problem. Gibbon faced innumerable questions in his vast canvas and did not pretend to solve them all, but he invariably gave it a try and reported his results in a way that enables us to see exactly what was involved and to estimate his success. If, as a result, we are compelled to examine our own assumptions about the nature and method of history, so much the better.

Inevitably, Gibbon's methods and assumptions continued to come under fire after the infamous fifteenth and sixteenth chapters, particularly since he was determined to continue his story of the early church and its internecine quarrels. No doubt, this was an awkward subject for a historian who insisted on reducing theological matters to human agency and who hoped to rise above bias to objectivity at a time when these issues were still very much alive and full of passion. But Gibbon saw no way to avoid the subject which arose naturally within his canvas of the dying empire and which indeed seemed to throw some light on its decline and fall, and he believed confidently that he had a method that could help sort out the issues and determine the facts. And so, despite criticism and controversy, Gibbon continued his history of "barbarism and religion," and, without flinch-

62. G. M. Young, *Gibbon* (London, 1932), pp. 72–74.
63. Walpole to Gibbon (n.d.), *Miscellaneous Works*, 2:156–58, 158–59. In his "Index Expurgatorius," Gibbon referred to Walpole as "that ingenious trifler," *English Essays*, pp. 122–23. See also his doubts about Walpole's *Historic Doubts* in *Miscellaneous Works*, 3:331–49.

ing, insisted on humanizing and secularizing his tale. Walpole, who had greeted the first volume as a masterpiece, was a little dismayed by the new subject matter which carried Gibbon to the East and once again into the thickets of religious strife. "Mr. Gibbon," he wrote, "I am sorry you should have pitched on so disgusting a subject as the Constantinopolitan History. There is so much of the Arians and Eunomians and semi-Pelagians; and there is such a strange contrast between Roman and Gothic manners . . . and though you have written the story as well as it could be written, I fear a few will have the patience to read it." For a moment, even Gibbon began to think he had delved a little too far into the Arian controversy; but the public remained amused and the work was a success.[64]

Indeed, popular interest was not altogether lacking. For a century and more, the English (and indeed much of Europe and America) had fought bitterly over the doctrine of the Trinity, and the quarrel was far from over. When Gibbon reached the reign of Constantine and the distractions of Christian heresy, he resumed just at the point where he had left off in chapter 15, retelling now with relish and detail the story of the new trinitarian controversies that had embroiled the early church—and that had been renewed in modern times. And once again, he assumed his Olympian vantage point of pretended detachment, unwilling to take sides in a theological problem which did not lend itself to rational investigation. According to Gibbon, even the great Athanasius had confessed his inability to comprehend the meaning of the doctrine that he had so warmly espoused.[65] In any case, whatever one might wish to make of that "high and mysterious argument," the temporal interests of the empire had been deeply engaged in its outcome. "The historian may therefore be permitted respectfully to withdraw the veil of the sanctuary; and to deduce the progress of reason and faith, of error and passion, from the school of Plato to the decline and fall of the empire."[66] In a dense essay, which Gibbon himself feared might be a bit digressive, he recounts the story. Though his learned predecessors (Cudworth, Basnage, LeClerc, and Brucker) had all offered different versions, it was still possible, he thought, to winnow the truth from uncertainty, to "derive instruction from their disputes, and certainty from their agreement."[67]

But it was imperative first to clear the way by removing some of the false or misunderstood documents that furnished the sources, to weed out the

64. *Memoirs of the Life of Edward Gibbon*, ed. George Birkbeck Hill (London, 1900), p. 201.

65. *Decline*, 1897, 4:340. The whole passage is worth repeating.

66. *Decline and Fall*, chap. 21 (1897, p. 335).

67. *Decline*, chap. 21, n. 12, p. 336.

many pious frauds and falsehoods that marred the traditional tale. And
that meant once again disturbing the tempers of the orthodox. Gibbon
had learned from the philologists how this might be done, how anachronisms of language and substance might give away the invalidity of a text and
betray the historical reality of an event. His first scholarly effort had been in
technical chronology, and his first scholarly works were exercises in the
emendation of classical texts.[68] He had read and studied the best critics
from the Renaissance to his own time, including that most influential and
exemplary work of its kind, the exposure by Richard Bentley of the false
epistles of the ancient Greek tyrant, Phalaris.[69] He was well acquainted
with the many "pious" frauds that had accumulated, for example under the
names of Orpheus, Hermes, and the Sibyls, until cast aside as spurious.[70]
He knew and applauded Laurenzo Valla's exposure of the *Donation of Constantine,* which like the false decretals and the sibylline oracles, had been
abandoned *despite* their use to the church. "Such is the silent and irre-
sistable progress of reason," Gibbon exulted, that the historian had persuaded the poets, the church, and even the popes of its falsity.[71] And he
had learned from Protestant critics—not least from Conyers Middleton—
who found the old humanist weapons only too convenient to apply to their
Catholic enemies, about the whole spurious hagiography of early Christian history. Middleton not only wrote against the miracles of the early
Christian centuries, but noticed "the many spurious books [that] were
forged and published by the Christians, under the name of Christ, and the
Apostles, and the Apostolic Writers . . . several of which are frequently . . .
applied to the defense of Christianity . . . as true and genuine pieces, and of
equal Authority with the Scriptures themselves."[72] In short, Gibbon had di-

---

68. His first essay, written while he was still at Oxford, was entitled "The Age of Sesostris,"
and was meant to correct the learned John Marsham's *Canon Chronicus;* in 1758, he wrote
some *Remarques critiques* on Newton's chronology. By that time he was ready for a learned correspondence on his emendations to Livy and some other Latin classics. See the *Memoirs,* p. 63;
and the *Miscellaneous Works,* where these essays appear. In the *Decline and Fall,* he tries a few
emendations on his sources, among others Lactantius and Ammianus Marcellinus.

69. In his "Index Expurgatorius" (c. 1768–69), Gibbon even tried to improve on Bentley,
English Essays, pp. 118–19. For his admiration of Bentley, see Levine, "Gibbon," p. 278, n. 40;
for Bentley's criticism of Phalaris and the storm it provoked, Levine, *The Battle of the Books,*
chap. 2.

70. "The adoption of fraud and sophistry in the defense of revelation, too often reminds us
of the injudicious conduct of those poets who load their *invulnerable* heroes with a useless
weight of cumbersome and brittle armour" (chap. 15, p. 69).

71. *Decline,* chap. 49, n. 72. Gibbon's "reason" is the progress of critical historiography. For
the exposure, see Joseph M. Levine, "Reginald Pecock and Lorenzo Valla on the *Donation of
Constantine,*" *Humanism and History,* pp. 54–72.

72. Middleton, *Free Inquiry* (1748), in *Works,* 1:liv. Middleton exempted only the Bible, p.
155. In chapter 15 Gibbon draws freely on the *Free Inquiry* (1749), which he calls "a very free

gested the accumulated criticism of the centuries about many of the frauds and forgeries, misunderstandings and misattributions—both sacred and secular—that had helped to generate the "pyrrhonism" of the period, and that seemed to cry out for correction. He found much philosophical amusement, so he wrote in his commonplace book, "in tracing the birth and progress of error."[73]

From that vantage point, it was perhaps inevitable that Gibbon should read even his Bible with a philological eye. That an alleged foe of everything Christian should be found reading the Bible at all may seem a little surprising, but Gibbon's personal religion—or irreligion—was never as transparent as his critics believed, and he certainly went through some dramatic changes. Not only did he convert to Catholicism as a young man and require a long and rigorous Protestant discipline to reclaim him, but he seems to have had afterthoughts late in life about his intervening skepticism, stimulated by the radical antireligion of the French Revolution, which he did not like.[74] In one of his memoirs, he recalled the period when he had returned to England as a young man and taken up serious reading. "I must not forget an occasional place of weekly study: the parish church where I frequented, commonly twice on every Sunday in conformity with the pious and decent custom of my family."[75] In the church pew, he remembered, he had placed the several octavo volumes of Grabe's edition of the Septuagint, along with the common Greek version, "and in the lessons, Gospels and Epistles of the morning and evening session, I accompanied the reader in the original text, or the most convenient version of the Bible." Gibbon assures us that this exercise was not confined to words, but

and ingenious inquiry," and recalls that "though it has met with the most favourable reception from the Public, [it] appears to have excited a general scandal among the divines of our own as well as the other Protestant churches of Europe" (p. 29). Middleton anticipated Gibbon's view about the constancy of human nature (pp. 186–87) and his contempt for the "stupid credulity and superstition of those primitive ages" (p. 188n.). Both Chelsum and Davis immediately tried to tar Gibbon with the same (scandalous) Middletonian brush. For more about Middleton, see Joseph M. Levine, "*Et tu Brute?* History and Forgery in Eighteenth-Century England," in *Fakes and Frauds,* ed. Robin Myers and Michael Harris (Winchester, 1989), pp. 71–97.

73. *Miscellaneous Works,* 5, p. 489.

74. "I said that the French Revolution had worked miracles for it had made Wyndham a Tory and Gibbon a Christian," Lord Glenerbie's diary (1793), quoted in Paul Turnbull, "The 'Supposed Infidelity' of Edward Gibbon," *Historical Journal,* 25 (1982), pp. 23–41, who remarks on the "rich diversity" of Gibbon's religious thought.

75. *The Autobiographies of Edward Gibbon,* ed. John Murray (London, 1897), (Murray), pp. 248–49. Gibbon's recollection is confirmed by various passages in his journal in 1762; Low *Gibbon's Journal,* pp. 98, 106–7, 110, 179. See David D. Smith, "Gibbon in Church," *Journal of Ecclesiastical History,* 35 (1984), pp. 452–63.

that he pondered the sense also, and that he tried to resolve the dubious passages by rushing home to consult the commentators and writing up the results. On one occasion he sent a short skeptical tract on the Old Testament Daniel to the critic Richard Hurd, who answered in a longer one.[76] Clearly, Gibbon's Bible appeared to him to be a historical text like any other which should be read, even in church, in the original language and with the tools of modern philology, to divine its meaning. Gibbon does not recall any consequence to his religious feelings; but he does say that he had thought long and hard about Grotius' effort to prove the truths of Christianity, with the only conclusion that "the most accurate philosophers and the most orthodox divines will perhaps agree that the belief in miracles and mysteries cannot be supported on the brittle basis, the distant report, of human testimony, and that faith as well as the virtue of a Christian must be fortified by the inspiration of Grace."[77]

With this in mind, it is perhaps easy to understand how Gibbon in his notorious chapter 16 had rudely deflated the number of Christian martyrs in the early church and suspected the extent of the early Christian miracles. And how, in chapter 15, he had dared to call into question (among other things) the biblical book of the Apocalypse against the convictions of both the Catholic church and Protestant divines. (Davis was particularly incensed by this assault on the biblical canon, although neither the specific criticism nor the general attack were new.)[78] The separation of history from religious conviction made it possible for Gibbon to keep up the pretence of being Christian, and it is still hard to know exactly what he believed about these things. Now in subsequent volumes Gibbon set about discrediting some other cherished ideas about the history of his religion. "Though the leaven of infidelity is more thinly diffused than in the former volume," lamented the *Gentleman's Magazine,* "and does not pervade whole chapters, yet enough remains to disgust the friends of Christianity."[79]

So, according to Gibbon, the whole foundation of the Trinitarian story was beset by fraud. The ancient Jewish historian Josephus had dared to say

---

76. Hurd to Gibbon, August 29, 1772, *Miscellaneous Works,* 2, pp. 83–94.
77. *Autobiography,* pp. 249–50.
78. See his *Reply to Mr. Gibbon's Vindication* (London, 1779), pp. 68–82.
79. Norton, *Bibliography of Gibbon* p. 67. Volumes 2–3 appeared together in March 1781. Once again, the work received a generally cordial reception; even the clergy, Gibbon wrote wryly to Dorothea, "(such is the advantage of the total loss of character) commend my decency and moderation," *Letters,* 2, pp. 265–66. Nevertheless, Gibbon showed some concern about how they might respond, in a letter to Suzanne Courchod, February 26, 1781, *Letters,* 2, pp. 262–64. Not all clergymen had been hostile; see Dr. George Campbell to Strahan, June 25, 1776, *Miscellaneous Works,* 2:168–69.

that Plato imbibed some part of his knowledge of it from the Jews, and the church fathers were pleased to repeat the story endlessly. "But this vain opinion cannot be reconciled with the obscure state and unsocial manners of a Jewish people, whose scriptures were not accessible to Greek curiosity till more than one hundred years after the death of Plato."[80] Plato's philosophy might have laid the philosophical groundwork for a belief in the Trinity, but if anything is clear, it is that Plato's ideas were not inspired by revealed religion; the naturalized Josephus had simply been ambitious to impress his Greek contemporaries with the wisdom of his countrymen.

A second prop of the story was the equally suspect *Wisdom of Solomon.* This too was a philosophical work, produced by the Jews of Alexandria about a century before Christ, a neoplatonic tract that had been received unanimously by the early church as the genuine work of Solomon. (The Protestants had rejected it, Gibbon tells us in a note, for want of a Greek original, but it was retained with the rest of the Vulgate by the Council of Trent.)[81] Later still, Philo and the Alexandrians confirmed the union of the Mosaic faith with Greek philosophy. Nevertheless, Gibbon concludes, "the eloquence of Plato, the name of Solomon, the authority of the school of Alexandria, and the consent of the Jews and Greeks"—all equally anachronistic and self-serving—"were insufficient to establish the truth of a mysterious doctrine which might please, but could not satisfy, a rational mind." A prophet or apostle could compel conviction only by faith, and this was conveniently supplied in the person of the last and most sublime of the evangelists, John.[82] It was left only for the church to develop the doctrine and dispute its meaning; and for the historian to analyze the bitter controversies that ensued among all Christian parties and tell the long story of their endless squabbling.

Of course, Gibbon did not forget to show how a metaphysical argument could become the cause or pretext of a political contest, and he lingers on the mutual intolerance and misunderstanding of all the combatants. He was rarely interested in religious history for its own sake. Nor was he any more sympathetic with the Arians or the Sabellians than with their orthodox enemies in the early church and more recent times.[83] His close analysis of the distinction between *homoousion* and *homoiousion,* and the fu-

---

80. *Decline,* 2, chap. 21, n. 11, p. 335.

81. Ibid., n. 16, p. 337.

82. Ibid., n. 16, p. 343. This argument parallels the one in chapter 15 where Gibbon points out the futility of ancient Greek and Jewish philosophy demonstrating the existence of an afterlife and requiring "the sanction of divine truth" in the timely appearance of Christ.

83. *Decline,* 2, chap. 21, p. 343. Arius, Gibbon reminds us, "reckoned among his most immediate followers two bishops of Egypt, seven presbyters, twelve deacons and (what may appear almost incredible) seven hundred virgins," not to say most of the Asian bishops and both

rious contests that were engendered by the disagreement over a single dipthong, is memorable both for Gibbon's close attention to detail and his deliberate incomprehension. He cannot help reminding his readers that the difference between the two "is almost invisible to the nicest theological eye."[84] For the "philosophical" historian and his audience, it was a distinction without a difference, and hardly worth the bloody battle that ensued. Gibbon concludes his long essay on these epochal but scarcely intelligible theological disputes with the triumph of the homoousian standard in the West—and then resumes his imperial narrative.

6

Still, there was no escaping from religion or from controversy—not for the historian who meant to traverse the whole complicated relationship between a falling empire and a rising faith. A little later in the narrative, toward the close of his third volume, Gibbon once again stumbled into trouble, this time in a long discussion of how the idea of the Trinity had continued to develop and divide the imperial world of Christendom. In a memorable paragraph, Gibbon maliciously renewed hostilities by daring yet again to meddle with a biblical text. It may be that he could have avoided the issue, but it would have been out of character for him to do so. Since he believed that the biblical passage 1 John 5:7 was actually a postbiblical interpolation that had been introduced for devious political purposes during the very years he was now describing, he felt bound to consider it at the proper point in his narrative, that is, at the point of its invention. And so, in a chapter which sets a complicated scene in North Africa (chap. 37), Gibbon once again resumes the story of strife and heresy, describing at length and with relish just how the doctrine of the Trinity received its final shape and how the Johannine comma came to contribute to it.

At the beginning of the fifth century, he writes, "*they* established, and *we* still embrace, the substantial, indissoluble, and everlasting union of a perfect God with a perfect man, of the second person of the trinity with a

---

Eusebiuses (chap. 21, p. 344). In two successive notes Gibbon discounts the testimony of Epiphanius and Philostorgius, because of their prejudice (chap. 21, nn. 42–43, p. 344). Gibbon remarks with characteristic impartiality about the learned Bishop Bull that the third part of his defense of the Nicene Creed, "some of his antagonists have called nonsense, and others heresy" (chap. 21, n. 60, p. 349). Yet the Nicene Creed was better adapted to a believing age than the cold rationalism of Arius, and that was why it had triumphed (chap. 27, 3:147–48).

84. *Decline,* chap. 22, n. 157, 2:387. It frequently happens, Gibbon remarks, that the sounds and characters nearest to each other accidentally represent opposite ideas; and so might it be the case here, "if it were possible to make any real and sensible distinction between the doctrine of the Semi-arians, as they were improperly called, and the Catholics themselves" (p. 352).

reasonable soul and human flesh." Just how this could be rationally accomplished was still beyond the philosophical Gibbon, who nevertheless
understood that it was the result of a deep theological split in the church
between "those who were most apprehensive of confounding, and those
who were most fearful of separating, the divinity and humanity of Christ."
From quarreling about a single dipthong, the Christian world had taken
now to arguing about a single particle. Was Christ formed *of* or *from* two natures, or did he exist (as the Roman party maintained) *in* two natures?—a
notion, Gibbon remarks, "which [only] the memory, rather than the understanding, must retain." At length, at the Council of Chalcedon, the issue was resolved in favor of *in* thanks to the intervention of the emperor,
"and the road to paradise, a bridge as sharp as a razor, was suspended over
the abyss by the master hand of a theological artist." In the ten centuries of
"blindness and servitude" that followed, the doctrine was confirmed, and
even the Protestant reformers who disclaimed the authority of the pope,
admitted it into their creeds. "The synod of Chalcedon still triumphs in the
protestant churches; but the ferment of controversy," Gibbon concluded
smugly, "has subsided, and the most pious Christians of the present day are
ignorant or careless of their own belief concerning the mystery of the in-
carnation."

Or so at least it seemed. But Chalcedon had not quite concluded the
trinitarian controversy in the ancient world; nor did Gibbon in the modern
world. He had to continue his story eventually into the fifth century, when
the Arians briefly got the upper hand with the barbarians in north Africa.
For a while, under the reign of Hunneric, it was the turn of the heretics to
persecute the orthodox. But once again, the superior force of the trinitarians prevailed, assisted by their numbers and by a more capable Latin and
Greek. They swiftly deployed all their learning—not least that formidable
weapon of controversy which they had so wilfully employed before, the *invention* of the evidence that they needed to support their troublesome doctrine. (It was about this time, Gibbon believed, that the creed attributed to
Athanasius—a hundred years too late—was composed.)[85] In short, the orthodox theologians were tempted by the ignorance of the barbarians and

85. Gibbon proposes this hypothetically, but argues certainly that St. Athanasius was not
the author of the Creed; that it does not appear to have existed within a century after his
death; and that it was originally composed in Latin, and therefore in the West. "Gennadius,"
he adds gratuitously, "patriarch of Constantinople, was so much amazed by this extraordinary
composition that he frankly pronounced it to be the work of a drunken man" (chap. 37, n.
116, 4:89). Gibbon refused to withdraw this story even under serious criticism in the *Gentleman's Magazine,* and to Richard Porson's regret; see below chap. 9.

by the assurance of impunity to compose new fictions in their favor, fictions which Gibbon was not too polite to label fraud and forgery.

Among these was the notorious biblical passage, 1 John 5:7, the so-called Johannine comma. By now Gibbon had learned a lot about forged texts and interpolated passages. He had himself just recently been taken to task for questioning still another suspicious passage in Josephus as a late interpolation.[86] But this was nothing to taking on the Bible itself. We have seen Gibbon's suspicions of the *Song of Solomon* and the book of the *Apocalypse*. Now he had the temerity to say directly that "even the [canonical] scriptures themselves had been profaned by rash and sacrilegious hands." To be sure, this was no longer a very startling notion; it was Dr. Johnson who complained that the apostles seemed to be charged once a week with the capital crime of forgery.[87] Nevertheless, the notion that the Bible had been open to deliberate manipulation still looked paradoxical and dangerous both to the devout and the professionally religious.

In the King James version, the dubious Johannine passage read thus, "For there are Three that bear record in Heaven; the Father, the Word, and the Holy Ghost: and these Three are One." In Gibbon's day this passage could be found in every vernacular Bible, including the Vulgate. As the most explicit of all biblical texts about the Trinity, it was naturally of immense utility to the orthodox of all persuasions. But Gibbon gives it short shrift. "The memorable text which asserts the unity of the THREE who bear witness in heaven is condemned by the universal silence of the orthodox fathers, ancient versions, and authentic manuscripts." He believes that it was first announced by the Catholic bishops whom Hunneric had summoned to the conference at Carthage, and that it was quoted soon afterwards in the African polemics of Vigilius and Fulgentius. Its original form, Gibbon thought, was likely a marginal gloss, an allegorical interpretation that had been incorporated into the Latin Bibles of the West, and recopied for many centuries afterward. (He points out that it was missing nonetheless from some twenty-five of the oldest and fairest of these.) "After the invention of printing, the editors of the Greek Testament yielded to their

---

86. This passage, which relates the prophecies, virtues, miracles, and resurrection of Jesus Christ, and which accepts him as the Messiah, Gibbon thought must have been inserted into the text between the time of Origen and that of Eusebius. (He canvases the usual authorities, but does not completely satisfy his editor, J. B. Bury; see chap. 16, n. 36, 2:86.) Gibbon defended the first interpolation of Josephus as a pious fraud against his first critic, James Chelsum, in the *Vindication*, p. 288.

87. Mark Pattison, "Tendencies of Religious Thought in England, 1688–1750," in *Essays*, ed. Henry Nettleship (1889; reprinted, New York, n.d.), 2, p. 49.

own prejudices, or those of the times; and the pious fraud, which was embraced with equal zeal at Rome and Geneva, has been infinitely multiplied
in every country and every language of Modern Europe."[88]

   It was these words which were to provoke the last, and perhaps the liveli-
est, of all the controversies that were produced by the *Decline and Fall.* Once
again, Gibbon seems to have been surprised at the response—or so he pretended.

   88. *Decline,* chap. 5, 1:96–97.

CHAPTER EIGHT

Travis versus Gibbon

1

For the layman who read Gibbon's remarks, at least the layman who shared Gibbon's enlightened outlook, the argument against the comma must have seemed persuasive enough, and indeed may have been familiar already. Gibbon makes clear that he had adopted it only after a close reading of the experts: in this case, the French oratorian, Père Simon; the Anglican, John Mill; and in particular, the Swiss Arminian, John James Wetstein. As usual, the philologists had not agreed, and theological prejudice had played a role; but as usual, Gibbon believed that it was possible to see through the prejudice to the facts; to adjust the differences and come up with the truth.[1] His chief contention was the argument from silence; the suspected passage was not to be found in any of the orthodox fathers, the ancient versions, or the authentic manuscripts. As a result, it could not have been in the original, but must have been interpolated later. Gibbon did not pretend to know this for himself; he relied instead on the accumulated scholarship of the centuries, about which he did know a great deal. The comma furnished a characteristic Gibbonian crux, and he solved it in

1. "In 1689, the papist Simon strove to be free; in 1707, the protestant Mill wished to be a slave; in 1751, the Arminian Wetstein used the liberty of his times, and of his sect" (*Decline*, chap. 37, n. 117, 4:89). It was Wetstein's Prolegomena to the New Testament (1751), the latest, and the most philosophically congenial, work of scholarship that Gibbon relied on more than any other. But Wetstein had used Simon and Mill, and Gibbon had read some other things also. For Wettstein (the correct but not the usual spelling), see C. L. Hulbert-Powell, *John James Wettstein 1693–1754*) (London, n.d.). For his contribution to biblical scholarship, see the tribute by Samuel Prideaux Tregelles, *An Account of the Printed Text of the Greek New Testament* (London, 1854), pp. 73–82. Wettstein had collated manuscripts for Bentley. He was accused of Socinianism and forced to go to Holland, although he protested his orthodoxy. His longest textual note is a history and rejection of the comma.

his usual fashion by referring to the original sources, each critically examined—though not in this case by himself.

He does this in just four sentences and six footnotes—not enough surely to prove his point, but just enough to set out his conclusions and indicate his sources. Thus the argument from silence (sentence one) is supported by a reference to the great scholars who had already canvassed the subject. Mill, Simon, and Wetstein had devoted their scholarly lives to the question, sorted out the evidence, and produced massive tomes for the purpose. It was clear to Gibbon, who read them through, that there was simply no manuscript support for the comma. Wetstein had searched for it in vain in the oldest codices that remained: the eighty or so that were over a thousand years old. In the few cases where someone had referred to manuscripts containing it, for example in the early printed versions of the sixteenth century, the manuscripts had somehow all mysteriously disappeared; while the only two that did have the passage, at Dublin and Berlin, were, he adds in a footnote, "unworthy to form an exception." They had long ago been challenged by Thomas Emlyn and dismissed more recently and persuasively by Cesar de Missy in four ingenious letters in the *Journal Britannique*.[2] Gibbon manages somehow to condense all this in to a single sentence and two footnotes.

How then did the comma get into the text? Gibbon offers his own conjecture in his next two sentences. "It was first alleged by the Catholic bishops whom Hunneric summoned to the Council of Carthage. An allegorical interpretation, in the form, perhaps, of a marginal note, invaded the text of the Latin Bibles, which were renewed and corrected in a dark period of ten centuries."[3] Gibbon concludes with a last sentence and another note suggesting that the early editors, who had all included the comma in their printed texts, did so either because of their own prejudices, or those of their times, and thus bequeathed the "pious fraud" to the Bibles of every country and language of modern Europe.

For the orthodox divines who read this paragraph, it was one more provocation, though not without opportunity. In the eighteenth century, the road to church preferment still lay very much through publication,

2. *Journal Britannique,* vols. 8–9 (1752). De Missy was a French chaplain at the English Court; he had gone to England in 1731 and died there in 1775. See John Nichols, *Anecdotes of Bowyer* (London, 1783), pp. 601–4. De Missy reviews all the manuscript evidence for the passage in a learned but satirical style, and finds it wanting.

3. Here a note points out that Wetstein was nevertheless unable to find it in the twenty-five Latin manuscripts that were the "oldest and fairest"—qualities, Gibbon cannot resist adding, that are "seldom united, except in manuscripts." For Hunneric, Gibbon cites Victor Vitensis, *De Persecutionis;* the comma, he adds, was then quoted afterward in the African polemics of Vigilius and Fulgentius.

and the occasion for controversy had already won some nice plums for the opponents of Gibbon.[4] The problem of the Johannine comma had been around for nearly two centuries, but to have the passage dismissed in so peremptory a fashion by so dubious a writer was like setting a flag before a bull. No sooner had the new volume appeared than another young clergyman saw his chance and began to answer it in a series of letters to the *Gentleman's Magazine*. These he swiftly collected and expanded in a sizable volume which appeared in 1784. As a result, the author, George Travis, was swiftly turned into an archdeacon and his book went on to two further editions. The old theological question had suddenly taken on new life.

That the question was an old one was perhaps the only thing about which the two sides could agree. As we have seen, it had been opened by the Dutch humanist Desiderius Erasmus, who was the first in modern times to edit and print the Greek New Testament. When he gave the world its first published version in 1516, it was without the comma because, as Erasmus briefly explained, he could not find it in any of the several manuscripts that he had used. His only alternative would have been to take the phrase from the Vulgate and retranslate it into Greek. A couple of years later he repeated his position in a second edition of the New Testament, but by then he had already come under attack, first for daring to question the text at all and meddle with its contents; next, for the specific alterations he had suggested, including most egregiously, his omission of the comma. When he was apprised of a Greek manuscript that suddenly turned up in England containing the suspicious passage, he resolved to print it after all in his next edition (1522) with a note explaining his decision and suggesting that the British manuscript had probably been altered from the Latin. He hoped thereby, so he said, to avoid the accusation of calumny. Nevertheless, although he continued to be censured and to defend himself, he never retracted this decision, leaving the text—and the problem—in his further editions and to posterity.[5]

The result was that it was no longer easy to accept the comma. In the next few years, the Protestant Reformation divided the world and all sides had to take a stand on the meaning and significance of the Trinity and its scriptural supports. The story of the comma can perhaps best be understood as

4. "My antagonists," Gibbon says proudly, "were rewarded in this World: poor Chelsum was indeed neglected, and I dare not boast making Dr. Watson a Bishop; but I enjoyed the pleasure of giving a Royal pension to Mr. Davis, and of collating Dr. Apthorpe to an Archiepiscopal living." *Autobiography,* p. 317.

5. See chap. 2 above. The best survey of the history of the comma remains the series of articles by A. Bludau in the *Biblische Zeitschrift,* 1 (1903), pp. 280–302, 378–407; 2, pp. 275–300; and *Der Katholik,* 84 (1904), 29–42, 114–42.

lying at the intersection of two related questions, each of which became swiftly complicated. On the one hand, there was the essentially philological problem of how to establish the text of Scripture, how to recover its original language and meaning. For Erasmus this was the province of humanist grammar, and the techniques he improvised—collecting and collating the manuscripts and employing all the devices of language and history to elucidate the text—were exactly analogous to what the humanists had been all along developing for the ancient pagan writings. In this he was anticipated and inspired by the Italian Lorenzo Valla, whose annotations on the New Testament he printed in 1505. Erasmus had hoped that his work could be divorced from theological prejudice and stand on its own, but he was immediately accused of Arianism and involved in theological controversy for undermining the authority of Scripture generally and the Trinity in particular.[6] Even today, his position on the matter remains a little obscure, while in his own time and for a long time afterward, he was both claimed and decried by all parties. On the whole, Gibbon, following Erasmus's eighteenth-century biographers, Levèsque de Burigny and John Jortin, was sympathetic.

The second matter was the meaning and significance of the doctrine of the Trinity. As Gibbon had meticulously shown, the early church was already deeply divided about the matter, and with the Reformation all the early divisions returned. Various kinds of antitrinitarian sentiments appeared among the radical reformers, and Arians were replaced by Socinians and worse.[7] Protestants as well as Roman Catholics were shocked and compelled to define a new orthodoxy in these matters. At first, Luther employed the Erasmian version of the New Testament for his own translation, as Tyndale did in England, and both left out or questioned the comma, even while they drew back in horror from the teaching of the Anabaptists. But Calvin burned Servetus, and by the end of the century the comma had returned to the German and English Bibles (including the King James version) in what seems to have been a deliberate effort to shore up the old doctrine of the Trinity against the new heretics. Meanwhile, the Roman Catholic Council of Trent proclaimed the authority of the Vulgate over the Greek, and by the end of the century had issued an authoritative new version, with the comma firmly in place, in an attempt to end the controversy.[8]

6. See Erika Rummel, *Erasmus and His Catholic Critics,* 2 vols. (Nieuwkoop, 1989).

7. See Earl Morse Wilbur, *A History of Unitarianism* (Cambridge, 1946); George H. Williams, *The Radical Reformation,* 3d ed. (Kirksville, 1992); Harry Loewen, *Luther and the Radicals* (Waterloo, 1974); Antonio Rotondo, *Calvin and the Anti-Trinitarians,* trans. John and Anne Tedeschi (St. Louis, 1968).

8. See H. J. Schroeder, *Canons and Decrees of the Council of Trent* (St. Louis, 1941), pp. 18–19, 297–98; for the Sixtine and Clementine Vulgates (1590, 1592), see Hugh Pope, *The Catholic*

Still the work of philology proceded, though under the continual inhibitions of clerical orthodoxy and intolerance. Already in Erasmus's day the Bible had been edited independently from the manuscripts by a team of Catholic scholars in Spain. The Complutensian version of the Old and New Testaments was published in the original languages in six impressive volumes in 1522.[9] This time the comma was retained, with a marginal note referring to St. Thomas Aquinas and the authority of tradition. (It was one of these Spanish scholars, Jacob Stunica, who we have seen became Erasmus's most severe and able critic.) But the next versions of the Greek text were by Protestants, by Robert Stephens who started out in France but wound up in Geneva, and by the staunch Calvinist Theodore Beza. Both preserved the comma, though under somewhat equivocal conditions, as we shall see. Both also claimed to use new manuscripts and make new collations, thereby enlarging the evidence that alone could settle the question. The direction of future inquiry was thus set.[10]

It was only in the later seventeenth century, however, that the philological enterprise really began to flourish. It was then that the work of editing Scripture from the manuscripts came back to life, especially in England, where the religious controversies among Protestants made the demand for a reliable Scripture seem imperative as a means of settling disputes. Needless to say, classical philology had continued to develop all the while, sharpening its tools and extending its province in a strenuous effort to recover and examine all the evidence of pagan—and Christian—antiquity.[11] One can describe a steady progression in ambition and achievement from the

Student's "Aids" to the Study of the Bible (London, 1926), pp. 223–32; Henri Quintin, Mémoire sur l'etablissement du texte de la Vulgate (Rome, 1922). The Englishman Thomas James was already pointing out the discrepancies between the two papal versions in his Bellum Papale, sive Concordia Discors Sixti V et Clementis VIII (London, 1600); see also his Treatise of the Corruption of Scriptures, Councils and Fathers by the Church of Rome (London, 1688), pt. 3, pp. 272–358.

9. See Marcel Bataillon, Erasme et l'Espagne, new ed., 3 vols. (Geneva, 1991), 1:1–75; Bentley, chap. 3.

10. For a convenient summary, see Frederick Henry Scrivener, A Plain Introduction to the Criticism of the New Testament (Cambridge, 1874), pp. 386–432; and the essays in the Cambridge History of the Bible: The West from the Reformation to the Present Day, ed. S. L. Greenslade (Cambridge, 1963). The Elzevir text of 1633, basically Erasmus as emended by Stephens-Beza, became the textus receptus of later centuries.

11. It is only necessary to recall the astonishing achievements of J. J. Scaliger (1540–1609) and Isaac Casaubon (1559–1614); for the first, see now Anthony Grafton, Joseph Scaliger, 2 vols. (Oxford, 1983–93); for the second, Mark Pattison, Isaac Casaubon, (London, 1875). Besides the general histories of classical scholarship by J. E. Sandys and Rudolf Pfeiffer, see E. J. Kenney, The Classical Text (Berkeley, 1974); Anthony Grafton, Defenders of the Text (Cambridge, 1991); and Sebastiano Timpanaro, Le genesi del metodo del Lachmann, 2d ed. (Padua, 1981), chaps. 1–2. There is a concise summary of post-Renaissance philology in L. D. Reynolds and N. G. Wilson, Scribes and Scholars, 2d ed. (Oxford, 1978).

polyglot text of Scripture edited by Brian Walton and his friends in six volumes (1654–57), through the new edition of Bishop Fell whose preface names a hundred manuscripts and versions (1675), to the magnificent work of John Mill, whose New Testament was published after a lifetime of labor in 1707.[12] Even Catholic France contributed reluctantly to this enterprise with a remarkable series of biblical commentaries by Richard Simon, who insisted on restoring the philological method of Erasmus and returning to the sources, though in the teeth of a formidable opposition led by Bishop Bossuet. (Simon had been inspired by Walton, and influenced Mill; most of his work was published outside France but was very well known in England.) Simon did not approve of the comma, wishing, as Gibbon put it, in contrast to Mill, "to be free."[13] Nor was it coincidence alone that it was just in these years that the trinitarian disputes in England came to a head, first in the struggle of orthodox Protestants to agree among themselves on the meaning of the doctrine, then, more bitterly still, between the orthodox and the radical antitrinitarians who began to go public about the same time.[14] The relative freedom of the period after the Glorious Revolution, a freedom that slowly expanded right down to Gibbon's day, made all these disputes possible and perhaps inevitable. It is almost unnecessary to say that in all of them the problem of the Johannine comma was rarely forgotten.

When, therefore, Travis decided to pick up the cudgels against Gibbon, he was resuming an ancient dispute in which the basic positions had long ago been worked out and developed. But the whole long argument had left the question of the Trinity and the meaning of Scripture uncertain. Perhaps its best accomplishment had been to put these theological questions to the arbitrament of history, to appeal to what Erasmus had called grammar and what the eighteenth century liked to call "matter of fact." Needless to say, it was still possible to hold to the idea of the Trinity on other grounds than the Johannine comma, and even some trinitarians were willing to give

12. For Mill and the background, see the fine work of Adam Fox, *John Mill and Richard Bentley: A Study of the Textual Criticism of the New Testament 1675–1729* (Oxford, 1954).

13. See especially Paul Auvray, *Richard Simon (1638–1712)* (Paris, 1974); and Jean Steinmann, *Richard Simon et les Origines de l'Exégèse Biblique* (Paris, 1959). Simon's *Critical History of the Text of the New Testament* appeared in London, 1689; *Critical Enquiries into the Various Editions of the Bible* in 1684. Among the many who were startled or alarmed by Simon's views was Thomas Smith, who responded with a vindication of the comma in his *Miscellanea* (London, 1690), pp. 123–50.

14. The controversy began with the appearance of *A Brief History of the Unitarians* (1687), which stirred William Sherlock to a *Vindication of the Doctrine of the Trinity* (1690), which in turn divided the orthodox and began a great battle that continued for a generation. See Hubert J. McLachlan, *Socinians in Seventeenth Century England* (Oxford, 1951); J. Hay Colligan, *The Arian Movement in England* (Manchester, 1913).

up the controversial phrase. But by the time Travis read Gibbon, the re-course to history had become almost reflexive, and it seemed more than ever important to ground one's religion on the evidence of the past, criti-cally examined. The old opponents of philology, who had hounded Eras-mus just for tinkering with the text, and who had assaulted Walton, Simon, and Mill, had begun their long retreat into obscurity.[15] All sides now re-mained hopeful that history would prove conclusive in their cause.

Travis began, therefore, by trying to rebut Gibbon's notion that all the first editors of the printed text had yielded to prejudice in embracing the pious fraud. "The three witnesses," Gibbon had explained in his note, "have been established in our Greek Testaments by the prudence of Eras-mus; the honest bigotry of the Complutensian editors; the typographical fraud, or error, of Robert Stephens in the placing of a crotchet; and the de-liberate falsehood, or strange misapprehension, of Theodore Beza." What did Gibbon mean by these peculiar allegations? Travis had first to explain before he could rebut, and so he offers a few words on each.[16]

Travis begins with Erasmus and fondly recalls the attacks that were made against him by the Englishman Edward Lee, and the Spaniard Stunica, and he finds Erasmus's decision to restore the comma welcome but reprehen-sible. Erasmus, he imagined, could only have restored the text on the au-thority of a single manuscript, either because he was unable to produce the other five manuscripts that he had originally claimed to consult, or be-cause he had evidence for it in them that he was unwilling to acknowledge. Travis thought it was more likely the latter—that Erasmus was suppressing evidence for the comma because he was secretly inclined toward Arianism and as a result strongly prejudiced against the passage. For this Travis was unwilling to forgive him. Whatever the case, Erasmus's "prudence" in rein-troducing the suspicious passage was only the desire to avoid persecu-tion.[17]

15. For the attacks on Erasmus by Dorp, Standish, and others, see Rummel et al.; for Owen against Walton, see Henry J. Todd, *Memoirs of the Life and Writings of the Rev. Brian Walton,* 2 vols. (London, 1821); for Whitby against Mill, see Adam Fox, *Mill and Bentley,* pp. 105–7; for Bossuet against Simon, see R. de la Broise, *Bossuet et la Bible* (Paris, 1890), pp. 335–70. These opponents all agreed that the dangers of criticism outweighed any possible advantage, and they would have called a halt to all investigation. "If in one point the Vulgate were in error," ar-gued one of Erasmus's critics, "the entire authority of Holy Scripture would collapse . . . the authority of theologians would be shaken, and indeed the Catholic Church would collapse from the foundations!" Pierre Cousturier (Suter); see Roland Bainton, *Erasmus of Christendom* (1969; reprinted, New York, 1982), p. 135.

16. *Gentleman's Magazine,* 52, February, 1782, pp. 65–68. This letter is reproduced as the first in the published book, with some alterations.

17. My quotations are from the book, which is almost identical with the letters in the *Gen-tleman's Magazine.* See Travis, *Letters to Edward Gibbon,* 2d ed. (London, 1785), pp. 8–10.

Travis next considers the "typographical error" in the Greek text of
Robert Stephens (1550). He assumes that Gibbon meant that Stephens
had preserved the verse only by accident. The argument that Gibbon was
referring to here was that the printer, instead of bracketing the whole passage to indicate that it was missing in his seven Greek manuscripts, mistakenly placed crochets around the last three words only, the Greek words for
"in Heaven." In this way, the comma was inadvertently shielded from suspicion. To Travis this notion appeared arbitrary and groundless, since
Stephens was a meticulous editor, and never acknowledged making such a
mistake in the errata that he added to his later editions.[18] As for Beza, who
followed Stephens with several further editions of the Greek text, it was
clear that he too accepted the comma only after deliberately considering
all the arguments against it. According to Travis, Beza's integrity alone, "as
a principal member of the reformed church, as a man famous for erudition and integrity," and as a careful and scrupulous scholar, was proof
against Gibbon's charge of "misapprehension."[19] Travis was astonished at
Gibbon's effrontery—his lack of literary candor and Christian charity—in
accusing such upright men of the deliberate crime of falsifying Scripture!

Finally, there was the famous Complutensian edition that had appeared
almost simultaneously with the version of Erasmus's. "It was the result of
the joint labours of many learned men, who were selected by the Cardinal
[Ximines] for that purpose, and furnished with all the Greek MSS, and
other aids, which his great political, as well as personal, influence could
procure."[20] To accuse the Spanish editors of bigotry seemed only bigotry
to Travis. It was clear to him (on their own testimony) that they had used
several Greek manuscripts from the Vatican and a very valuable one from
Rhodes, and faithfully printed the comma just as they had found it there.
After reminding Gibbon of the charges laid against *his* accuracy by his opponents, Travis concludes, "that if these editors had acted as you more
than seem to wish they had done, they would . . . have proved themselves
unworthy stewards of the oracles of God!"

For the moment, it seemed to Travis enough to suggest that it was Gibbon's prejudice, not the evidence or lack of it, that had led him and his
party to attack the Johannine comma. And here the brevity of Gibbon's
statement played into Travis's hands, though to be sure, a full rebuttal

18. Nor for that matter did Stephens' fellow citizen, Jean Crispin, in his edition at Geneva
(1553), who retained the same marks in the same place, Travis, *Letters,* pp. 10–11.

19. "He contrasted the Syriac version, etc., with his other authorities, and compared them
together so attentively, as even to note in which of them a single article, or epithet was wanting." Ibid., p. 12.

20. Ibid. pp. 13–16.

would have necessitated taking up the arguments of Mill, Simon, Wetstein, and the rest, on whose work Gibbon had relied. Instead, Travis quickly fired off two more letters to the *Gentleman's Magazine*, where he tried to assemble all the positive evidence he could find in favor of the comma, beginning with the testimonies of individual authors through the centuries.[21] Curiously, he works backward from the time of Erasmus almost to the apostle himself, from Lorenzo Valla and Nicholas Lyra back through the earliest church fathers, rehearsing every quotation of the text that he can find. He thus provides a long consensus over the centuries in order to lend authority to the passage. He does not see that it was precisely Gibbon's contention that *after* the invention of the comma, it had naturally passed for genuine, and that no later testimony could possibly prove its authenticity. It is therefore only in the last part of his letter, when Travis comes to the earliest testimony, that his quotations begin to tell. Did not Tertullian quote the text—the same Tertullian who had been born early enough to have conversed with Christians "who had actually sat under St. John's ministration of the Gospel"? And what of Augustine, whose reiterated references to the Trinity seemed to Travis to be obviously derived from this verse? And Jerome, who after all had translated it directly from the Greek for the Vulgate?[22]

Even more persuasive to Travis, however, was the long continuity that the decrees of councils and the liturgies of the church provided as testimony for the suspicious passage. Once again, he takes them up in reverse chronological order, beginning with the Lateran Council of 1215. The fact that this was the largest assembly of its kind, and that it had been attended by many Greek bishops, gave it special authority. The comma was also confirmed under Charlemagne and (still retreating) by the orthodox bishops under Hunneric at the Council of Carthage (486 A.D.). Curiously, Travis, like Gibbon, found the circumstances of that meeting decisive, but in the opposite direction. The avowal of the trinitarian passage, he agreed, had

21. *Gentleman's Magazine*, 52, June–July, 1782, pp. 278–79, 330–32. These are combined into one in the *Letters*, pp. 17–57. Travis does add two further testimonies to his rebuttal in the first letter. The first is drawn from the Louvain New Testament of 1574, which also preserved the comma, on the authority of "many Latin copies, and also by two Greek copies produced by Erasmus, one in England, the other in Spain." Travis suggests that Erasmus must have suppressed the latter, since he never mentions it. (In fact, Erasmus noticed that the Spanish editors were never able to produce their manuscript.) Travis quotes further from the Louvain editors, "We have ourselves seen several others like these." The second authority is Amelotte's French New Testament, where, according to Travis, Amelotte says that he himself has seen the comma in the most ancient Vatican manuscript. Travis later withdrew this statement from his published book without explanation, but presumably because Amelotte's integrity had been severely questioned.

22. Travis, *Letters*, pp. 34–38.

been made there in public—only three centuries after the death of St. John. But he denies that it could have been forged at that time, since all the bishops in Africa would have objected, and had it been in the least doubtful, all the Arians would have immediately protested. The fact is that the quotation by the orthodox bishops was received in a silence which could only have meant consent. The comma must have preexisted the council. To this Travis adds the testimony of the ancient service books. The verse had been read in the Roman church from an early time, in the Greek church as well, and continuously ever since throughout Christendom. The existence of such creeds and confessions going back at least to the fourth and fifth centuries seemed to Travis proof that they must have been "coeval with Christianity itself."[23]

Travis concludes this third letter with a quick review of the evidence of the early versions of Scripture itself. Once again he finds the suspicious verse already in the fifth century, this time in an old Armenian translation and in a Byzantine collection of Epistles. But the best evidence, he believed, for the existence of the verse was its appearance in that most ancient of all versions of the New Testament, the "Old Italic" Latin translation made in the first century while St. John was still alive. "And thus the origin of the Verse in question, is, at length, carried up, not by inferences, or implications, alone, however fair and obvious, but by PLAIN, AND POSITIVE, EVIDENCE, to the age of St. John himself."[24]

To the ordinary reader, certainly to the religiously disposed, Travis's reply may well have seemed conclusive. Gibbon had argued that the absence of evidence in the early manuscripts and in the church fathers was sufficient to condemn the suspected passage. Travis replied to the contrary that there was more than enough solid evidence for its authenticity going right back almost to the apostle himself. If the question could be reduced to a matter of fact, Travis felt that he had presented more than enough facts to make his case. Yet Travis was dissatisfied. He realized that he still had not properly attended to all the objections that had been raised to the text. He promised the readers of the *Gentleman's Magazine* to return to the subject. For the moment the letters were well received and Travis was emboldened to bring out a whole book on the subject.

2

Travis was in an awkward position. Since Gibbon had not stated the grounds of his argument—content only to cite his sources—it was hard to

23. Ibid., p. 52.
24. Ibid., p. 55. Unfortunately, the Old Italic version had not survived.

see how to refute him except by calling on others who had elaborated his position. But the argument had been going on for so long a time it was hard to know just how to focus it and whom to rebut. Travis decided to concentrate on some of the more recent English critics of the comma, deliberately overlooking such earlier opponents as Sandius, Simon, and Emlyn, in order to deal with Dr. George Benson and Sir Isaac Newton. If he had wished simply to rebut Gibbon, he might better have attended directly to the evidence in Mill and Wetstein and to the arguments of De Missy; but he was concerned now to tackle the most recent arguments against the comma. Benson's work had appeared in 1748; Newton's posthumously in 1754, and both had tried to review everything before them. By taking them each in turn and adding a few remarks on some others, Travis hoped to cover the whole field and answer all objections. So he starts with a long new letter on Benson.[25]

Apparently, Benson had started life in a dissenting English household, where we are assured, he could read through the Greek New Testament by the age of eleven.[26] He had strengthened his Calvinist education at the University of Edinburgh, and then settled at Abingdon near London, where he took up the ministry. Somehow he picked up Arminian views and was forced to give up his congregation, although he soon found another in London. If Benson started life as a Calvinist, he ended it as a Socinian, and one of his last works caused a scandal by defending Servetus against the persecution of Calvin. In 1731, he began to write a paraphrase and notes to each of the books of the New Testament. When at last he got to the Catholic Epistles and the letters of John, he had necessarily to face the problem of the Johannine comma. He decided to treat it in a separate dissertation, which he appended to his book.[27] His chief source of inspiration, he says, was the work of Thomas Emlyn, who removed whatever scruples he may have had and "set the matter in a clear light." But he also knew the work of Mill, Simon, and Wetstein and quite a few others, each of whom had written earlier on the subject. He tries to summarize the arguments on both sides of the question, reviewing closely the testimony of the fathers, the manuscripts, and the early versions, before finding, as he does, against the passage. Benson's erudition was unmistakable and he appears to have

25. This appears as the third letter in the book, *Letters*, pp. 59–221.

26. There is a life of Benson prefixed to his posthumous *History of the Life of Christ* (1764), and a funeral sermon by Edward Pickard; both summarized in the *Biographia Britannica*, 2d ed., ed. Andrew Kippis, 2 (London, 1780), pp. 201–8.

27. *The Paraphrase and Notes on the Seven (commonly called) Catholic Epistles . . . to which are annexed several Critical Dissertations*, 2d ed. (London, 1756), pp. 631–46. The advertisement insists that there were no changes from the original edition of 1748.

been highly regarded on the Continent.[28] It seemed necessary to Travis to answer him point by point.

Benson appears to have been won over to his antitrinitarian views by Emlyn; and though Travis does not say so, he found much of *his* answer to Benson in the work of Emlyn's old opponent, a French Protestant clergyman named David Martin. Travis vs. Benson is thus pretty much a recapitulation of Martin vs. Emlyn. It was their exchange at the turn of the eighteenth century that brought the question to a head in England and influenced all later writers. Emlyn had anticipated Benson by moving from Protestant dissent to an overt Unitarianism; but it had cost him dear, since he was successfully prosecuted for blasphemy in 1703 and forced to spend some time in prison. This lesson was not lost on either Locke or Newton, among others, whose discretion, even more than Erasmus's, was obviously meant to be (as Gibbon puts it) "prudent."[29]

Emlyn says he was moved to his heretical views by seeing the disagreement among Protestants over the meaning of the Trinity in the boisterous disputes of the 1690s.[30] In his retirement, Emlyn resumed his study of the trinitarian problem by consulting his Bible and suspecting the Johannine comma. In 1715, in a somewhat easier climate, he published *A Full Inquiry into the Original Authority of that Text 1 John v. 7*, which he addressed to Convocation. It is a systematic work that relied however for most of its information on the great folio volume of John Mill which luckily appeared in 1707, just when Emlyn was giving the matter serious thought. Mill's work, we have seen, had been read by Gibbon and was an obvious source for anyone interested in the text of the New Testament. He had spent thirty years canvassing the evidence and collating the manuscripts with an energy and rigor that had never been attempted before. The great preface (168 folio pages alone) considered the problems of the canon and the transmission of the text and described some thirty-two printed editions and eighty-seven manuscripts, as well as a host of patristic citations. To describe his colla-

---

28. For praises by Baumgarten and Michaelis, who started to translate his commentaries into Latin, see the *Biographia Britannica*, p. 205n. According to the *DNB*, even his opponent, Masch, called him *meritissimus*. Kippis admits that he was not a man of great originality, but was rather learned and industrious.

29. For Emlyn, see the life by his son prefixed to the fourth edition of his *Works*, 3 vols. (London, 1746); his own account of the trial in *A True Narrative of the Proceeding of the Dissenting Ministers of Dublin against Mr. Thomas Emlyn and of his Persecutions*, reprinted in *A Collection of Tracts*, 2 vols., 2d ed. (London, 1731). See also the life in Robert Wallace, *Antitrinitarian Biography*, 3 vols. (London, 1850), 3:503–38.

30. He refers in particular to the storm over Sherlock's works; in 1707 he published his own belated reply, *The Supreme Deity of God the Father Delineated in Answer to Dr. Sherlock's Arguments*. According to Kippis, Emlyn was a "high Arian," that is, he believed that Christ was the first created being and an object of worship; see *Biographia Britannica*, 5 (1790), p. 597.

tions, Mill provided some 21,000 notes and was said to have offered some 30,000 variant readings, more than enough to alarm the conservative world, though not enough to shake the faith of a true believer. (When the deist, Anthony Collins, seized on the variants to try to discredit Christianity, Mill's protégé, Richard Bentley, showed how, on the contrary, they could actually be treated as copious and persuasive evidence for an original text.)[31] Mill had appended to his massive work a whole dissertation on the comma (pp. 739–49), which decided in its favor, even in the face of much contrary evidence. Gibbon condemned this lame conclusion as an indication that Mill, unlike the Catholic Simon, had wanted to be a "slave," although it would have been more charitable to say that he had wanted badly to remain a loyal Anglican. In any case, Mill supplied enough evidence from the fathers and the manuscripts for Emlyn and Benson and Gibbon each to mount a formidable attack against the comma.

To meet the argument from silence from such an imposing source required great ingenuity, and this was what had been supplied by Emlyn's opponent, David Martin. From 1715 to 1722, the two men exchanged a half dozen tracts arguing the case and subjecting the evidence once again to renewed scrutiny.[32] Emlyn used the labors of Mill and Simon and Louis Ellies Du Pin, who had written recently on the canon, to show that there was really nothing in the manuscripts, the early versions, or the fathers to indicate the existence of the comma.[33] The argument from silence (which had already been used by Erasmus) always depended on the range and depth of the scholarship employed, and the great labor of recent erudition made the claims of Emlyn much more plausible than they had been earlier. It was now possible to speak of hundreds of manuscripts in Greek and Latin, of a vast body of patristic writing, some of it just then receiving critical attention, and of many versions in the ancient languages, Syriac, Ethiopian, Coptic, and so on. To say now that none of it revealed the existence of the comma, not even where one might most expect to find it in the documents of the original Arian controversy, was a powerful argument indeed. And it was easy from this perspective to see how the first editors might have erred. After all, Stephens and Beza had written their annotations "at a Time and

---

31. *Remarks upon a Late Discourse of Free-Thinking* by Phileleutherus Lipsiensis [Bentley] (London, 1713); in answer to Anthony Collins, *Discourse of Free-Thinking* (London, 1713). See Fox, *Mill and Bentley,* chap. 8, pp. 105–15.

32. The three tracts by Emlyn may be read in the second volume of the *Collection* and in the *Works.* They include besides the *Full Inquiry, An Answer to Mr. Martin's Critical Dissertation on 1 John 5. 7* (1718), and *A Reply to Mr. Martin's Examination of the Answer to his Dissertation* (1720).

33. Louis Ellies Dupin, *A Compleat History of the Canon and Writers of the Old and New Testaments,* translated from the French (London, 1699–1700).

Place flaming with bitter zeal and Prejudice against all Antitrinitarians, where Servetus had been cruely burnt at the stake but three years before"—and with Beza's hearty approval. "Is it any great Wonder then if they durst not, or would not cast out such a text."[34] As for the Dublin manuscript, Mill had described it as written "in a modern and careless Hand," which Emlyn was able to see for himself on a visit to Dublin in 1725. Later, Benson was able to get an exact copy of the disputed text from a friend, and also found that it agreed almost exactly with the British manuscript of Erasmus.[35]

It was up to Martin to try to penetrate this apparent silence and see if there was not some evidence to the contrary in the fathers and the manuscripts—enough at least to save the comma.[36] It meant somehow discovering early quotations and manuscripts, despite the obvious learning of such as Simon and Mill. And it meant upholding somehow the printed versions of Erasmus, Stephens, and the Complutensian editors. In the polemical exchange that followed, not many of the arguments were new, but the issues were sharpened. Since neither man was able to review the bulk of the evidence firsthand, much of their energy was expended on trying to determine through others the reliability of the manuscript evidence in Dublin, Paris, Rome, and Berlin.[37] Martin was forced to agree that only two Greek manuscripts had survived with the comma: those in Dublin and Berlin. Emlyn was able, through correspondents on the spot, to suggest that both were late and unreliable witnesses to the early text. In Berlin, the library-keeper, La Croze, wrote decisively to deny the antiquity of the manuscript, which he believed was only a copy of the Complutensian text—even to repeating its errors. Its modern parchment and ink gave it away immediately as a fraud. La Croze was eager to offer his opinion despite the fact that he

---

34. *Reply to Martin, Collection*, 2, p. 143.

35. Ibid., p. 163. Apparently Benson's copy went first to the eminent textual critic Joseph Wasse, who ascribed it to the thirteenth century or later; see Benson, *Paraphrase*, p. 640n. For the identity of the Dublin with the Erasmian manuscript, Benson cites the author of the life of Daniel Waterland (p. 79), and David Casley, a student of Richard Bentley's, who compiled *A Catalogue of the Manuscripts of the King's Library* (London, 1734), with a plate and a long note on the comma; pp. xxi–xxiii. Casley believed that the comma was a gloss that had gotten incorporated into the text, rather than a willful forgery.

36. David Martin, *A Critical Dissertation upon the Seventh Verse of the Fifth Chapter of St. John's First Epistle*, translated from the French (London, 1719); *The Genuineness of the First Epistle of Saint John, Ch V. v 7*, translated from the French (London, 1722).

Contemporary notices of Martin (1639–1721) in Nicéron, Chaufepié, and Marchand are summarized in the *Bibliographie universelle*, vol. 27.

37. So for the Armenian version, Emlyn relies on Christopher Sandius to deny the comma, who said he inspected it with the Armenian bishop of Amsterdam, *Inquiry*, p. 2. He has other sources to undermine the authority of the Complutensian manuscripts, ibid., p. 26.

was a firm believer in the Nicene Creed, which he would not defend, he says, with a fake.[38] Martin naturally preferred the evidence of the Latin manuscripts, which were relatively numerous but inconclusive, since the oldest also seemed to lack the comma. Indeed it seemed best to deny the possibility of dating any of the old codices securely, though this was becoming hard to do in the age of Mabillon and Montfaucon.[39] Even more difficult was the evidence from the fathers, where Martin, like Travis afterward, was able to find what seemed to be some early quotations of the comma, but all of which Emlyn denied.

When at last the dust settled and the exchange was concluded, it was still a little hard to say who had gotten the best of it.[40] The only thing that seemed clear was that the problem of the authenticity of the verse had come to depend more than ever on a review of the evidence—just as in the case of any secular author—and that it was at least as potentially solvable, if one could ever assemble all the relevant testimony and evaluate it critically. So Emlyn had asked rhetorically, "whether any Evidence, as is brought against this Verse before us, wou'd not be judged by you sufficient against any Passage in any Classick Author whatever?" And neither Martin nor Travis, who were as eager, it seems, as Emlyn to collect the evidence that they were sure would bear them out, were willing afterward to deny the premise. Apparently, neither side was content any longer simply to invoke the authority of the church or the notion of plenary inspiration, but both were eager now to establish the historical facts, as Emlyn claimed, "by ocular inspection." "We settle a Matter of Fact on positive Testimonies of Witnesses," Martin agreed.[41] But even so, the biblical project had only recently begun, and even the great Bentley, who had just then embarked on the task, faltered, unable to complete his work, although it was (rightly) clear to Emlyn that Bentley's projected edition of Jerome's New Testament would certainly have eliminated the comma.[42]

38. La Croze's letter (June 1720) is quoted by Emlyn in *A Reply to Martin, Collection,* 2, pp. 119–22.

39. According to Martin, the age of the Berlin manuscript was "a Point to be discussed by those learned Men, whose particular study has been about the Ink, the Parchment, and the form of the Characters, and other such Matters, whereby they judge almost exactly of the time a Manuscript was wrote in; and yet they are often mistaken." Quoted in Emlyn, *A Reply, Collection,* 2, p. 118.

40. At least one Unitarian, Newton's protégé at the Mint, Hopton Haynes, thought that Emlyn had completely vanquished Martin; see his *Causa Dei contra Novatores: Or the Religion of the Bible and the Religion of the Pulpit Compared* (London, 1747), p. 31. Haynes translated Newton's tract on the comma into Latin; see Wallace, *Antitrinitarian Biography,* 3: 455–58.

41. Emlyn, *Inquiry,* p. 44; *Answer to Martin, Collection,* 2, 101–2, 109.

42. *An Answer to Martin's Criticism,* in *a Collection,* 2, pp. 77–78. Emlyn quotes from *Two Letters to the Learned Dr. Bentley concerning His Intended Edition of the Greek Testament* (London, 1717),

It would be tedious to try to follow Travis step by step through all his argument. Suffice it to say that Travis thought he could refute Benson, and through him Simon, Emlyn, and the rest, by showing that they were wrong about each of the three main bodies of evidence. To begin with, he was confident that there *were* many church fathers, both early and late, Latin and Greek, who had quoted the verse, and he cites them verbatim and at length. Later he tries to explain away the absence of quotation in the rest—the peculiar silence of many of the antitrinitarian fathers that seemed to suggest that the comma had not been there to help them in their disputes with the Arians. He suggests that many of the church fathers must have read the comma to mean a unity of witness, not of being, and so not as a trinitarian text, in which case they would not have thought to quote it against the Arians.[43] He then rehearses all the objections that had been made to the early printed versions, reaffirming the value of their testimony about the manuscripts. Here Travis was forced to navigate some treacherous waters because a number of scholars since Martin (like Gibbon's favorite, De Missy) had further succeeded in identifying and examining many of the manuscripts which Erasmus, Stephens, and the Complutensian editors had all agreed contained the comma—only to dispute their testimony. What was the "British" manuscript that had convinced Erasmus to restore the comma? Was it the one now in Dublin? Travis denied it. Was it old enough to be helpful? Travis was sure that it was.[44] And what about the fifteen manuscripts that Stephens had claimed to consult in the Royal Library in Paris? Were they not still there, ready to testify either for or against the comma? And where were the manuscripts in the Vatican that the Complutensian editors had used? As we have seen, by Benson's day a number of scholars on the spot had contributed their firsthand testimony—almost all negative, and all summarized by De Missy. To Benson, like Emlyn before him, it seemed perfectly clear that no Greek manuscript

---

where Bentley promised to settle the question as a matter of fact (pp. 23–25). Emlyn in his *Reply to Mr. Martin's Examination*, ibid., p. 154, refers to a recent public lecture by Bentley at Cambridge on the text, where "he has been far from defending it." Apparently, Emlyn had to rely on hearsay for the praelection, and so must we, since it has quite disappeared, and with it all of Bentley's arguments. But there is no doubt that by then he had come out quite definitely against the comma; see James Henry Monk, *The Life of Richard Bentley*, 2d ed., 2 vols. (London, 1833), 2: 16–19.

43. This was a dangerous argument to make since it was normally used by the Unitarians to undercut the idea of the Trinity. Travis sides with the fathers who held the contrary view, hoping to show here only how this text might have been overlooked by some of the old patristic writers; *Letters*, pp. 317–19.

44. *Letters to Gibbon*, pp. 149. He uses here an account of the manuscript by Dr. Wilson of the University of Dublin, against the biographer of Dr. Waterland, Casley, and Benson; pp. 150–53.

existed early enough to substantiate the claims of the early editors to the validity of the comma. But since it still remained difficult, or in the case of the Vatican, impossible to consult the manuscripts directly, this lack of ready access made confirmation awkward, and Travis, like Martin before him, was eager to exploit the confusion.[45]

Finally, there was the matter of the other old versions of the New Testament in different languages: Old Latin, Syriac, Armenian, Coptic, and so on, which Benson had cited on the authority of Mill, to show the absence of the comma. Even here Travis failed to give in, arguing that the verse had indeed appeared in some of those manuscripts. And if it was not in the ancient Syriac or Coptic versions, that proved nothing, since many other undoubted passages were also missing from those defective works.[46] Once again, ignorance of the languages forced both parties to rely on the efforts of others. In the end, Travis was pleased to think that for each particular argument, he had been able to find an alternative, and that he had therefore been able to show Benson's dissertation to be without equal, "for intrepidity of assertion, disingenuousness of quotation, and defectiveness of conclusion."[47]

3

It took a very long essay to dispatch Benson; Travis made shorter work of Newton, although his argument still required much detail and some repetition.[48] But what was it that had drawn the great scientist to the comma anyway?

It has become apparent only lately, thanks to the study of Newton's private papers, that he was obsessed with theological and biblical questions throughout his long and busy life, and that he left a great pile of manuscripts on the subject—at least a million words.[49] And we also know now

45. Thus he suggests that neither Mill nor Casley ever saw the Dublin manuscript directly, whereas Martin's informant had; and that it was the prejudice, not the proximity, of La Croze to the Berlin manuscript that had turned him against it; *Letters to Gibbon*, pp. 155–71. He returns to the subject still later in his book to refute J. J. Griesbach's personal inspection of the manuscript with the testimony of J. F. Zoellner, who wrote to Travis to deny that the Berlin manuscript was just a transcript of the Complutensian, ibid., pp. 302–6; and app. xxiii, pp. 51–60, where the whole letter is given.

46. Ibid., pp. 188–96.

47. Ibid., p. 221

48. Letter no. 4, *Letters to Gibbon*, pp. 223–94.

49. Gale E. Christianson, *In the Presence of the Creator: Isaac Newton and His Times* (New York, 1984), p. 250. The bulk of the material remains unedited in Jersalem; see Richard H. Popkin, "Newton as a Biblical Scholar," *Essays on the Context, Nature, and Influence of Isaac Newton's Theology*, ed. James E. Force and Richard H. Popkin (Dordrecht, 1990), p. 115n.8. There is a brief

that he was a secret antitrinitarian. It was natural for him, therefore, to take
an interest in the question of the comma, which, as we have seen, was hotly
contested in his time, both in the great public disputes between Anglicans
and Socinians, and among the Anglicans themselves, about the nature of
the Trinity. Newton formulated his own ideas in two carefully composed
letters that he addressed to his philosophical friend and kindred Unitarian
spirit, John Locke, in 1690.[50] Locke nearly had them published anony-
mously in Holland through his old associate Jean Le Clerc, but took them
back just in time when Newton got cold feet. The letters languished for a
long time in manuscript, until retrieved and published in 1754.[51] Eventually, they were reprinted in a more complete and accurate form by John
Horsley in the fifth volume of Newton's works in 1775, just on the eve of the
Decline and Fall.[52]

Apparently, Newton had been worrying about the Trinity for a long
time. He too, well before Emlyn and Benson, had grown away from a youthful Calvinism toward an unorthodox Christianity. According to his latest
biographers, he was an Arian by 1673, and remained so to the end of his
long life, though only a few ever suspected it.[53] By then, he was already cer-

---

selection in *Sir Isaac Newton's Theological Manuscripts*, ed. H. McLachlan (Liverpool, 1950).
The best study remains Frank E. Manuel, *The Religion of Isaac Newton* (Oxford, 1974).

50. Newton sent the papers to Locke at his request, November 14, 1690. He refers in the letter to earlier work on the subject, which he has now enlarged; see *The Correspondence of Isaac
Newton*, ed. H. W. Turnbull (Cambridge, 1961), 3:82. The two letters follow under the title "An
historical account of two notable corruptions of Scripture, in a Letter to Friend," November
14, 1690, pp. 83–129; it was followed by a third, written soon afterward but only now published, pp. 129–44.

51. Le Clerc had early tangled with Simon; Locke was soon being publicly (and correctly)
accused of Socinianism, though he remained perfectly circumspect to the end of his life. For
Locke's deep interest in Simon, Le Clerc, and the problems of biblical criticism, his corre-
spondence with Limborch is especially helpful. See also H. McLachlan, *The Religious Opinions
of Milton, Locke and Newton* (Manchester, 1941); Gretchen G. Pahl, "John Locke as Literary
Critic and Biblical Interpreter," *Essays Critical and Historical Dedicated to Lily B. Campbell* (Los
Angeles, 1950), pp. 137–57; Massimo Firpo, "John Locke e il Socinianismo," *Revista storica
Italiana*, 92 (1980), pp. 35–124; Mario Montuori, *John Locke On Toleration and the Unity of God*
(Amsterdam, 1983), and especially now John Marshall, *John Locke Resistance, Religion and Responsibility* (Cambridge, 1994). Locke's concern about persecution is reflected in the several
long accounts he gave to Limborch in 1699 of the prosecution of some Socinian heretics under Queen Elizabeth; *The Correspondence of John Locke*, ed. E. S. De Beer (Oxford, 1979), 6:638–
42, 695–99, 763–65.

52. For the circumstances, see David Brewster, *Memoirs of the Life, Writings and Discoveries of
Isaac Newton*, 2 vols. (Edinburgh, 1855), 2:323–27; Newton, *Correspondence*, 3:123–24.

53. "He identified himself with Arius both intellectually and emotionally." Richard S. West-
fall, *Never at Rest: A Biography of Isaac Newton* (Cambridge, 1980), p. 318. See also Christianson,
Newton, pp. 250–54. Nevertheless, Manuel quotes from a manuscript where Newton con-
demns Arius along with Athanasius for introducing metaphysical concepts "not warranted by
Scripture." Manuel, *Religion of Newton*, p. 58. Newton's Christology, like everything else in his

tain that the scriptural texts had been deliberately altered to support the
trinitarian idea and needed correction. He naturally fastened on the
comma as well as another long-suspected passage, 1 Tim. 3:16, and he
plunged characteristically into the subject, not content with secondary
works but reading the fathers and the Scriptures for himself, so that Locke
could say that he had never met anyone better versed in the text.[54] (Newton, however, seems not to have bothered much with manuscripts, except
for the book of Revelation, in which he took a special interest.) Through
Le Clerc, who had previously tangled with Simon, he discovered the works
of that famous French biblicist and made some additions to his letters.[55]
Eventually, he met John Mill and sent him some information about the
Apocalypse, but by then he had long made up his own mind about the
comma.[56]

Newton's first letter is a generous tract filled largely with arguments that
we have met already, about the lack of evidence in the fathers, the manuscripts, and the printed editions. But he furnished his own explanation for
the corruption of the text. In the first place, he suggests, some of the early
Latin Christians interpreted the eighth verse, about the unity of the spirit,
blood, and water, allegorically, to mean the Father, Son, and Holy Ghost.
"Then Jerome for the same end inserted the Trinity in express words into
his Version." That was how the seventh verse first got into the text of the
Bible. Sixty-four years after Jerome's death, the Africans quoted it at the
Council of Constantinople against the heretic Vandals under Hunneric.
Later still the Latins began to place Jerome's variations in the margins of
their Bibles, from whence it began to creep into their texts, until in the
twelfth century it entrenched itself for the rest of the Middle Ages. "And
when printing came up it crept out of the Latine into the printed Greek
against the authority of all the greek MSS and ancient Versions."[57] In tracing further "the footsteps of the insertion"—in effect writing the history of
the comma—Newton reviews the patristic evidence also to make his point,
beginning with the montanist Tertullian, and his follower, Cyprian, who
were among the first to force the allegorical interpretation which led even-

---

thought, had been earned by himself, and should probably not be classified too easily. It is
enough for us that he was always and consistently antitrinitarian.

54. Lord Peter King, *The Life and Letters of John Locke* (London, 1858), p. 263.

55. See Le Clerc to Locke, 10/20 January 1692, *Correspondence of Locke*, 3:353–55; Newton,
Correspondence, 3:123n. Newton owned English editions of Simon's *Critical Histories* of the Old
and New Testaments, and his *Critical Inquiries into the Various Editions of the Bible*; see John Har-
rison, *The Library of Isaac Newton* (Cambridge, 1978), p. 239.

56. See the exchange, January 29–February 21, in which Mill thanks Newton for his lec-
tions and promises to print them in his New Testament; *Correspondence*, 3:303–07.

57. Newton, *Correspondence*, 3:83–84.

tually to the fraudulent comma. He pins the fraud directly on Jerome by referring to the preface which usually preceded the canonical epistles in the New Testament, where it is expressly defended, though it was not in the previous old Latin translation. He then arrays against Jerome the evidence of all the other early translations, especially the Old Latin, Syriac, and Ethiopic; the many writers just preceding and following him; and the scribes who copied the Greek texts in after-ages. Later, he reviews the Latin manuscripts to show that the oldest of those, too, lacked the comma. From all this it seemed to him conclusive that the suspicious passage had been lacking in all the Greek manuscripts from which Jerome—or the author of the preface that was attributed to him—pretended to have borrowed it. Newton does not forget to examine and dismiss each of the printed editions in turn, from Erasmus to "the imaginary books of the dreaming Beza."[58] And he concludes by arguing that the comma spoils the internal coherence of the Epistle, which reads much better and more smoothly without it.

Of course, Travis would have none of it, and had already anticipated most of these arguments in dealing with Benson. He had tried to show there that the comma certainly preceded the Vulgate, and he accepted the testimony of Jerome's preface which he insisted was genuine against the growing doubts of modern scholars, including Emlyn and Benson. He could only show again that there was some early evidence for the existence of the verse just where Newton, like Benson, had been unable to find it: in some of the other ancient translations of Scripture, in many writers just before and after Jerome's time, and in a few of the Greek manuscripts in all ages. Needless to say, this required much attention to detail and some painful reiteration.

For the sake of completeness, Travis ends his letter with a few further remarks that were provoked by the two latest editions of the Greek text, by William Bowyer and Johann Jacob Griesbach. Bowyer was a scholar-printer whose father had learned the trade assisting with Walton's *Polyglot*. In 1763, he published a Greek New Testament in which he tried to take advantage of the suggestions that had been made by Wetstein and others. Among the many changes he offered, was to drop several famous passages from the text as lacking manuscript support, including the Lord's Prayer (Matt. 6:13), the pericope of the woman in adultery (John 7:53–8:11), and the Johannine comma, as well as many sentences and single words. Nor was he satisfied to make his suggestions in the footnotes, but placed them boldly in the text, marking them off with brackets. In addition, he offered many conjectural emendations, all in English, which his friend Jeremiah Mark-

58. Ibid., 3:106.

land thought accounted for their popularity, but which seem to have anticipated much later scholarship.[59] The notes grew in subsequent editions
and were separately printed. Bowyer dismissed the comma with the familiar arguments of Newton and Wetstein.[60]

Griesbach was a much greater scholar, who had learned his trade in Germany from the textual critic Johann Salomo Semler. "Hermeneutic skill,"
Semler had argued, echoing Erasmus, "depends most of all upon the certain and exact knowledge of the linguistic usage of the Bible, and also the
capacity to discern the historical circumstances of the biblical discourse."[61] Like his master, Griesbach insisted on the "historico-grammati-
cal interpretation" of Scripture, and he expressly denied the plenary
inspiration of the text, even to pointing out (as Erasmus had long ago) that
the apostles were capable of making mistakes.[62] He had traveled widely in
Europe in quest of manuscripts, spending long hours in the university libraries in England and the British Museum, as well as the Royal Library in
Paris and elsewhere, and he put his researches to work in an edition of the
Greek Bible (1775) and a series of exegetical works.[63] He too dismissed the
comma on the usual grounds, but he is remembered today more especially
for his contributions to the classification of manuscripts and to the synoptic problem. Travis was not impressed by any of the Germans, although it is
clear that they had already assumed the mantle of modern biblical scholarship and were introducing new methods of coping with the sources and
new conclusions about the text that were transforming the subject. Here

59. See Bruce A. Metzger, "William Bowyer's Contribution to New Testament Criticism,"
Chapters in the History of New Testament Textual Criticism (Grand Rapids, 1963), pp. 155–60.
Bowyer's *Novum Testamentum Graecum* (London, 1763) received a second edition in 1783.

60. *Critical Conjectures and Observations on the New Testament*, 3d ed. (London, 1782), pp. 472–
75. It was both praised and criticized in its time and translated into German; Metzger thinks it
much underestimated and offers examples of Bowyer's prescience. Bowyer, it should be said,
also redited Bentley's *Dissertation on the Epistles of Phalaris*, with some additional remarks
(1777). See John Nichols, *Biographical and Literary Anecdotes of William Bowyer* (1782; reprinted, New York, 1974), pp. 344–45, 477.

61. Semler, *Vorbereitung zur Theologischen Hermeneutik*, (Halle, 1760), 1:160; quoted in Ger-
hard Delling, "Johann Jacob Griesbach: His Life, Work and Times," in *J. J. Griesbach: Synoptic
and Text-Critical Studies 1776–1976*, ed. Bernard Orchard and Thomas Longstaff (Cambridge, 1978), p. 184n.41.

62. Delling cites Griesbach's *Vorlesungen uber die Hermeneutik* (1815) for the best statement
of his method, *Griesbach*, p. 10. It was Erasmus who originally pointed out Matthew's lapse of
memory in quoting Jeremiah.

63. *Libri Historicis Novi Testamenti Graece* (Halle, 1775); 2d enlarged edition, *Novum Testamentum Graece*, 2 vols. Halle, 1786–1806). Griesbach used many early manuscripts in the text
as well as the notes and sets out the synoptic problem in a *Commentatio* which is edited and
translated in the commemorative volume above. Delling gives a list of Griesbach's published
works, *Griesbach*, pp. 16–21.

he only touches on a few specific points, overlooking the main thrust of their arguments; it was Travis' chief strategy to try to poke holes in the enemy's armor in order to discredit a position which he thought depended on a perfect accommodation of the texts. This often left him overlooking the forest for the trees.

It was time to conclude his work, and in a final letter, Travis tried to tidy up the whole tangled question of the comma by suggesting that it could be reduced to three main allegations: the absence of the comma in many Greek and a few Latin fathers; its absence in all the extant Greek manuscripts; and finally, its inconsistency with the rest of John's epistle, or as Travis puts it, "the supposed injury done to the context of the Apostle." Did the verse fit? Or would its removal help? Travis was willing to allow a mysterious hiatus in the transmission of the comma between the death of John, which he set down precisely in 101 A.D. and the Council of Constantinople in 384 A.D., allowing that it might have been *partially* lost then. Whether this was by accident or fraud, he would not say, since he believed that either was possible. An early scribe might have missed the boat and led the rest astray, or the Arians might well have excised it from the text in their period of ascendancy. As for the internal matter about the consistency of the text with the rest of the epistle, it will be no surprise to discover that Travis found against the antitrinitarians that it was not only consistent but absolutely crucial to the purpose of the apostle.[64] In short, he concludes, "The Verse in question, seems, beyond all degree of serious doubt, to have stood in this Epistle, when it originally proceded from the pen of St. John." He had collected all the evidence before the fifth century and afterward, and had shown conclusively that there was not a single negation or positive contradiction, not "the smallest direct impeachment of the authenticity of the verse, throughout all the annals of all antiquity." It might seem strange that some of the fathers had overlooked the passage, and that the Greek manuscripts (though not the Latin) should have somehow disappeared, but these were mere "presumptions," no more than negative evidence, which Travis believed he had "compleatly and satisfactorily explained, and avoided—or accounted for, and defeated."[65] Finally, Travis could not help reproving Gibbon for his continual sniping at Christianity, especially by insinuation, and his shameless scurrility. He closes by challenging Gibbon either to resist or submit.

---

64. Emlyn had pointed out long ago that "'tis so easy by one fetch or other, according to Mens various Fancies, to wind almost anything into an obscure Context, when once it is resolved it *must* be in." *An Answer to Martin's Dissertation*, in *Collection*, p. 69.

65. *Letters to Gibbon*, p. 347.

Of course, Gibbon did neither. He was profoundly offended both by the tone and the content of the work, and perfectly sure that it was all obfuscation. "The brutal insolence of Mr. Travis's challenge," he wrote in his autobiography, "can only be excused by the absence of learning, judgment and humanity." Next to Travis, even Davis looked like a respectable enemy![66] But it was not easy to imagine a reply. Fortunately for Gibbon, another young scholar with an uncertain future but a keen philological training was also provoked and decided to take up the cudgels—not for Gibbon, who was a stranger to him—but for the truth of the matter and the honor of the discipline. Richard Porson was a disciple of Richard Bentley, and he hoped to win the same kind of fame for himself that Bentley had obtained nearly a century before when he had exposed that other great fraud, the *Epistles of Phalaris*, in a model of philological criticism and sarcastic vituperation. Porson was not far off; his *Letters to Archdeacon Travis* has claims to be the second greatest piece of philological criticism in the English language, and it won him a lasting reputation. It also proved to be a thorough defense and justification of Gibbon's critical judgment.

66. *Autobiography*, p. 210.

CHAPTER NINE

Porson versus Travis

1

Richard Porson was just twenty-five years old when he read Travis's letters in the *Gentleman's Magazine*. He had come from an obscure East Anglian family, but was luckily discovered by a nearby country gentleman and educated first locally, then at Eton and Cambridge. From the beginning, he was famous for his wonderful memory. In school, he avoided a practical joke when a classmate substituted a different text for the Horace he was supposed to be reading aloud, by reciting the verses by heart and without hesitation. Later, at Cambridge, a friend called on Porson to ask about the meaning of a word in Thucydides. On hearing the word, Porson immediately repeated the passage. How did he know which one? "Because," he said, "the word occurs only twice in Thucydides, once on the right hand and once on the left. I observed on which side you looked, and therefore knew the passage to which you referred."[1] He himself preferred to think his powers were the result of application, not genius. In order to remember a text, he said, "I have read it a dozen times, and transcribed it six." His friends thought otherwise, and it is true that he could remember as much English literature as anything in the classics, apparently without much trouble. Dr. John Johnstone recalled some winter evenings with Porson in 1790–91. "Many a midnight hour did I spend with him, listening with delight while he poured out torrents of various literature, the best sentences

1. E. H. Barker, *Literary Anecdotes and Reminiscences,* 2 vols. (London, 1852), 2:23. Cf. *A Short Account of the Late Mr. Porson . . . by an Admirer of his Genius* (London, 1808), p. 9. No one can swear to the reliability of the many anecdotes told about Porson, but at least they describe the impression he left on contemporaries, and allowing for exaggeration, something about the man.

of the best writers, and sometimes the ludicrous beyond the gay; pages of Barrow, whole letters of Richardson, whole scenes of Foote, favorite pieces from the periodical press."[2]

At Cambridge, Porson settled on Greek but loved to read English on the side, especially Swift and Pope. In a way he tried to straddle both sides in the Battle of the Books, mastering the great modern works of erudition and taking as his own particular model Richard Bentley. On the other hand, he loved some of the very works that had made fun of the scholars, and occasionally imitated them too. Just before he began his reply to Travis, he dashed off three letters to the *Gentleman's Magazine*, parodying Hawkins' pompous *Life of Johnson*, with great skill and good humor. He was passionately fond of Swift's *Tale of a Tub*, we are told, and whenever he saw a copy of it in a stall, he would buy it.[3] He had no literary pretensions himself, and wrote very little, not even letters. When asked why, he said that he doubted that he could produce anything that posterity would admire. Bentley had said the same. Porson claimed that he would be satisfied with a simple epitaph: "One Porson lived toward the close of the eighteenth century, who did a good deal for the text of Euripides." And indeed, he is still remembered largely for his notes—and his brilliant, if erratic conversation.[4]

At Cambridge he declined orders because he would not subscribe to the Thirty-nine Articles. This frustrated his academic career for a time, though some admirers helped him out eventually with a pension that provided a modest income and left him free to pursue his classical researches. Later, he was elected Regius Professor of Greek (1792), although he never did subscribe to the Articles. His religion remains a little obscure. He seems to have stayed an Anglican and never publicly opposed the church. He may well have inclined to Socinianism, as did even many clergymen in his time, but he did not show much interest in theology. He told his friend William Maltby that it would require fifty years of hard reading before he could be satisfied on all controversial points. And he thought that the learned Bishop Pearson might have outdone Bentley, if he had not "muddled his head with theology." Another anecdote tells of Porson walking one day

2. Samuel Rogers, *Recollections of the Table Talk . . . to which is added Porsoniana* (New York, 1856), p. 305. Johnstone is quoted in the *DNB*.

3. Ibid., p. 327. He loved Pope's Homer and (so we are told) could recite the whole of Smollett's *Roderick Random* from beginning to end; ibid., pp. 306n. 327. And he enjoyed writing doggerel, an example of which is given in M. L. Clarke, *Richard Porson: A Biographical Essay* (Cambridge, 1937), p. 16.

4. Rogers, *Recollections*, pp. 330–31. For a recent appreciation, see, besides Clarke, Denys Page, *Richard Porson (1759–1808)* (reprinted from the Proceedings of the British Academy, London, 1960).

with a trinitarian friend, speaking about the Trinity. Along came a buggy with three men in it. "There," said the trinitarian, "is an illustration of the Trinity." "No," said Porson, "you must show me one man in three buggies, if you can."[5]

Porson's first serious efforts were some short notices that he contributed to P. H. Maty's *New Review* (1783–84) of a number of scholarly editions of Greek classics: on Schutz's Aeschylus and Brunck's Aristophanes, and on the fragments of the Greek poet Hermesianax. At twenty-three he was corresponding with the famous scholar David Ruhnken about Aeschylus, and he began to think of editing the text. But his proposal to go to Florence to collate the Laurentian manuscript was rejected by the Cambridge Press and the project fell through. Even while his reply to Travis was in progress, he wrote an article for the *Monthly Review* defending the genuineness of the *Parian Chronicle* against its latest critic. And in 1790, there appeared the notes and preface that Porson had written earlier to a new edition of Toup's *Emendationes in Suidam*. Porson was still very young, but he had already made a considerable reputation among scholars when he addressed himself to the letters of the Archdeacon Travis.[6]

Porson, like most eighteenth-century philologists, had a keen eye for forgery. In the parody of Hawkins he interpolated a spoof, which he borrowed from the critics of Bentley, denying that one whole section of the work could possibly be by the author. "The Knight's style is clear and elegant," he suggested ironically, "this account is cloudy, inconsistent, and embarrassed." He was fortunate to live in an age, Porson boasted, which was "so sharp-sighted in detecting forgery."[7] As a result, he was not taken in for a moment by the Shakespearian frauds of the two Irelands. When he was prevailed upon to visit the father and look at the manuscripts, he said nothing at first. Ireland insisted that he put his name down among those who believed in their genuineness. Porson excused himself diplomatically on the grounds that he was no English antiquary; but being pressed, he said, "Mr. Ireland, I detest from the bottom of my heart subscriptions of all kinds, but especially such inscriptions to articles of faith." On the other hand, Porson did not accept Robertson's arguments against the authenticity of the *Parian Chronicle*, nor had he any use for the scholar-skeptic, the fa-

5. Barker, *Anecdotes*, 2:2, 23.

6. Most of these early works may be consulted in Porson's *Tracts and Miscellaneous Criticisms*, ed. Thomas Kidd (London, 1815).

7. Richard Porson, *The Correspondence*, ed. Henry Richards Luard, Cambridge Bibliographical Society Publications, octavo ser., 8 (1867), p. 13. He adds a reference to the *Dunciad*, p. 17. The satirical device is anticipated by William King, who used it against Bentley; see Levine, *The Battle of the Books*, p. 63.

mous Père Hardouin, who had argued that most of the ancient authors were medieval forgeries. He found the work of Thomas Payne Knight on the Greek alphabet (1791), too much given "to conjecture and imagination." He preferred the best methods of modern philology and antiquities, of Bentley and Scipione Maffei, whose work he recommended against Hardouin. He was certainly no pyrrhonist; he hoped to reconstruct, not deconstruct, the original texts, and most of his own energy was devoted to restoring the Greek poets.[8]

2

Porson was exasperated into action by a note in the *Gentleman's Magazine* (August 1788), extravagantly praising the letters of Travis. According to the author, who signed himself Eblanensis, Gibbon's strictures against the Johannine comma had been effectively squelched by Travis.[9] Gibbon, he continued, might well have thought it worthwhile to digress against the comma with the weight of scholarly opinion behind him, but Travis had shown how his whole argument could be completely demolished. The treatise against Gibbon, Eblanensis insisted, could hardly be matched in any age "for fidelity in stating objections, and sagacity in removing them, for the tokens which it gives of industry in research, and soundness of judgement." Travis had spoken "with that intrepid plainness, which, while it surprises the mind, persuades it." The only question left was whether the enemies of the comma had made their case: Newton, La Croze, Le Long, Michaelis, Benson, Emlyn, Griesbach—and now the Unitarian who called himself "Sosipater"—or whether it must fall before the objections of Travis. Eblanensis was sure it must, and repeated Travis's charge that silence by Gibbon could only mean defeat.[10]

This was too much to bear, and Porson quickly replied with a letter of his own to the *Gentleman's Magazine*. He was willing to allow with Eblanensis

8. For Ireland and the Parian Chronicle, and the review of Knight's *Analytical Essay on the Greek Alphabet*, see Porson, *Tracts*, pp. xviii–xix, 81–82, 150. For the dispute between the historical pyrrhonists and the philologists and antiquaries, see Joseph Levine, *Dr. Woodward's Shield: History, Science and Satire in Augustan England* (Berkeley, 1977), pp. 157–58; Arnaldo Momigliano, "Ancient History and the Antiquarian," *Studies in Historiography* (New York, 1966), pp. 1–39.

9. *Gentleman's Magazine*, 58, pt. 2, August, 1788, pp. 700–702. Porson enumerates a number of previous articles by "Vindex" applauding Travis in ibid., 1784, p. 565; September, 1785, pp. 686–87; and March, 1787, p. 211. But it was the challenge laid down by Eblanensis to which he responded. Vindex came back in March, 1789, p. 225.

10. *Gentleman's Magazine*, 58, pt. 2, August, 1788, pp. 700–702. "Sosipater" was Theophilus Lindsey, who had written against the comma in the *Gentleman's Magazine*, 56, pt. 1, May, 1786, pp. 394–95; in "A Gleaning of Remarks on Mr. Travis's Attempt to Revive the exploded Text, 1 John v. 7," in *Commentaries and Essays*, published by the Society for Promoting Knowledge of the Scriptures, 1 (1785), and "even to nauseousness" in his *Vindiciae Priestleianae*. His career is

that Travis's book was "scarcely to be paralleled in any age"—but for very different reasons. "For intrepidity of assertion, disingenuousness of quotation, and defectiveness of conclusion," Porson countered, "it has no equal, [and] stands aloof beyond all parallel, as far as my reading extends, either in ancient or modern times!"[11] It was hard to say which offended him more: Travis's ignorance, or his insolent manner. Here he confines himself to a few brief remarks on Travis's unfair and hypocritical attack on Erasmus, and on the graceless retractions of fact that Travis had been forced to make in the second edition of his book. But he quickly followed the letter with a half dozen more (1788–89), and soon afterward with a large book in which they were brought together, enlarged, and revised. Porson had spent nearly two years on it, he remembered, and received thirty pounds for it, although the publisher lost money and it was not reprinted.[12] Nevertheless, it made his public reputation.

Porson set out to defend Gibbon's work, but he mixed his praise of the *Decline and Fall*, as Gibbon noticed a little ruefully, with a pinch of salt. In his preface, Porson took some trouble to explain that his defense of Gibbon and his attack on the comma were not meant to undermine either orthodoxy or the Trinity. He intended only to impugn that kind of orthodoxy that rigidly used every argument, whether fair or unfair, true or false, in its own defense, "that spurious orthodoxy, which is the overflowing of zeal without knowledge." Porson had no doubt that he "does best service to truth, who hinders it from being supported by falsehood."[13] Even the infidel (Gibbon, therefore) deserved a hearing, though to be sure Porson meant first of all to befriend those honest *Christians*: Erasmus, Newton, La Croze, Griesbach, and the rest. And, if an impartial judge could be found, Porson had no doubt that he would declare Gibbon's history, "one of the ablest performances of its kind that has ever appeared." His industry, accuracy, and reading were extraordinary; his attention, memory, and style were admirable. "His reflections were often just and profound; he pleads eloquently for the rights of mankind, and the duties of toleration; nor does his humanity ever slumber, unless where women are ravished, or the Christians persecuted."[14]

As for Gibbon's dislike of Christianity, Porson was willing to allow a pure and virtuous motive. "We can only blame him for carrying on the attack in

---

described by his follower, Thomas Belsham, *Memoirs of the Late Reverend Theophilus Lindsey* (London, 1812); see esp. p. 178.

11. *Gentleman's Magazine,* 58, pt. 2, October, 1788, pp. 875–77.

12. Rogers, *Porsoniana*, p. 302.

13. *Letters to Travis*, p. xxv.

14. *Letters to Travis* (London, 1790), pp. xxvi–xxviii. Porson cites chap. 57, note 54, for the first; and the whole of chap. 16 for the second.

an insidious manner, and with improper weapons. He often makes, when he cannot readily find, an occasion to insult our religion; which he hates so cordially, that he might seem to revenge some personal injury." He had even stooped to puns and twists of language to turn Scripture into ribaldry and Jesus into an impostor.[15] Nor, as we have seen, was Porson completely happy with Gibbon's style. At times, Gibbon's attempts at elegance led him to lose sight of English, and even of sense. Worst of all, Porson was annoyed at Gibbon's "rage for indecency" which pervaded the whole work. Nevertheless, he would not allow these faults to lower his esteem for the great work, which he continued to admire as a whole. If only Gibbon had been willing to acknowledge an occasional mistake, like the one about Gennadius, which was pointed out to him in the *Gentleman's Magazine*, but which he continued to ignore.

Porson's preface was written last, but he drafted it to set his argument with Travis in the framework of the whole controversy to date. He was confident that the great weight of scholarly opinion was on his—and Gibbon's—side, and would immediately reveal Travis's ignorance.[16] He begins therefore with a brief account of those first printed editions, from Erasmus to Beza, that had originated the problem of the Johannine comma. He then surveys the question as it arose in more recent times, from the formidable attack by the Arian Sandius, and the still more formidable criticism by the Catholic Simon, to the long rely of the German Kettner, which together had already assembled nearly everything that could be said on either side.[17] He has some fun with Kettner's many reasons for why the fathers might be impeded from citing the comma: 27 for the second century, 29 for the third, and 42 for the fourth! (Thus the twenty-fourth reason of the third set was that the infant Constantine should not be offended!)[18] But the arguments against the text were accumulating in Newton and especially in Mill, who (just as Gibbon had said) had assembled all the evidence against, only to decide "unaccountably" in favor. Even the abbé L.

15. Ibid., pp. xxviii–xxix. Once again Porson cites chapter and verse (chap. 59, note 32; chap. 11, note 63).

16. He lists all he can find to support the comma: Bishops Horsley and Seabury; the Bamptonian lecturers, Dr. Croft and Mr. Hawkins; and most recently, the Reverend Mr. Coulthurst, who preached a sermon at Cambridge, November 30, 1788. In a note he adds the famous Dr. Waterland, who had given equivocal support to the comma in 1723 and afterward; *Letters to Travis*, pp. 20–21 and note. It was, all told, not a very impressive array.

17. There were two Christopher Sands, father and son, who settled in Holland. The latter (1644–80), who studied for a time at Oxford (1664), was well known as a font of Arian opinion throughout Europe. For a brief account of his career and publications, see Robert Wallace, *Anti-Trinitarian Biography*, 3 vols. (London, 1850), 3:318–28.

18. *Letters to Travis*, p. iii.

Roger of Bourges, a defender of the text, had admitted (in 1715) that the brackets in Stephens' edition had been misplaced. Martin had tried to support the argument against Emlyn to no avail, and an anonymous English editor of the Greek New Testament had thrown the comma out of his text in 1729 with a long and able explanatory note.[19] The attempt by Leonard Twells to reply could only repeat lamely what Martin had already said.[20]

Porson ends his survey with that thorough German scholar Johann Albrecht Bengel, who had also wished desperately to believe, but only succeeded in amassing the arguments against the comma, much as Mill before him. In a long note to his 1734 edition of the text, Bengel allowed that it was in no genuine manuscript; that the Complutensian version was interpolated from the Latin; that the Codex Britannicus was worthless; that Stephens' bracket was misplaced; that the comma was never cited by a Greek father and was omitted by many Latins; and that it had not been erased by the Arians. Surely then the verse was spurious? "No; this learned man finds a way of escape; the passage was of so sublime and mysterious nature, that the secret discipline of the church withdrew it from the public books, till it was gradually lost." Porson was incredulous. "Under what a want of evidence must a critic labour, who resorts to such an argument!"[21]

19. The anonymous editor was Daniel Mace, a Presbyterian minister, *The New Testament in Greek and English Containing the Original Text . . . and a New Version*, 2 vols. (London, 1729). His long note (pp. 921–35) relies on Mill and Simon, among others, and is a very able discussion of the various kinds of evidence against the comma. He is particularly thorough in deciding against Jerome's preface. There is a modern appreciation in H. McLachlan, "An Almost Forgotten Pioneer in New Testament Criticism," *Hibbert Journal*, 37 (1938–39), pp. 617–25; cf. Bruce M. Metzger, *The Text of the New Testament: Its Transmission, Corruption, and Restoration*, 2d ed. (Oxford, 1968), pp. 110–11.

20. Leonard Twells, *A Critical Examination of the New Text and Version of the New Testament* (London, 1731). Twells disparaged Mace's translation generally, and fastens on the comma at pp. 123–54. He amasses all the evidence he can from Martin and others to show that there *were* Greek manuscripts, old versions, and church fathers to attest to the comma. In this he anticipates almost everything in Travis. In passing, Porson also mentions the brief tract on the comma by Bishop Smalbroke, published originally in 1722, addressed to Bentley, and reprinted in Somers, *Tracts*, 1:458–72. Smalbrooke favored the comma but thought that Martin's defense was inadequate.

21. *Letters to Travis*, pp. 7–8. Porson is here following Wetstein; see C. L. Hulbert-Powell, *John James Wettstein, 1693–1754* (London, 1937), p. 249. Bengel provided a Greek text with notes and three long excursuses in which he set out his principles of textual criticism as well as collations drawn from Mill and his own collections. In his *Gnomon of the New Testament*, he repeated his observations on the comma. There is a translation of the second edition (1759) by William Fletcher (Edinburgh, 1866), pp. 135–46. See also the *Memoir of the Life and Writings of John Albert Bengel* by J. C. F. Burk, trans. Robert F. Walker (London, 1837), which describes his editorial labors and the fierce criticisms they provoked, among them Wetstein's. There is a modern study by G. Mulzel, *J. A. Bengel: Leben und Werk* (Stuttgart, 1970). For an appreciation of his scholarship, which includes the first theory of the classification of manuscripts into fam-

Fortunately, the next generation of continentals, including Wetstein and Griesbach, left no doubt about their censures of the comma, although the concise nature of their commentaries left some of the argument still to be elaborated.

Such anyway was the state of the controversy when Gibbon "expressed the general opinion with great exactness and impartiality in a passage in the third volume of his History." Perhaps it was only someone with Porson's learning who could see how brilliantly Gibbon had been able to summarize the long and complicated argument in so small a space. It may be, Porson speculates, that Gibbon though this passage would be overlooked in the tumult caused by so many other parts of his work; or perhaps he thought that the scholarly consensus behind him was enough. If so, he must have been disappointed by the appearance of Travis's letters. Porson says that he himself had closely read through Mill, Wetstein, and Newton, and was already persuaded by their arguments against the comma when Travis's work appeared and he was compelled to rethink the matter. For this he might have been grateful, except that on reading the *Letters to Gibbon,* he discovered "such astonishing instances of error, such intrepid assertions contrary to fact, that I almost doubted whether I was awake when I read them." It did not take long to discover that Travis was a stranger to all criticism, that he had read nothing much beyond Martin's old works, and that he was, as J. D. Michaelis said rightly, "Half a century behind-hand in his criticism."[22] Porson then adds at some length a review of the reception of Travis's work by a slew of Continental critics, beginning with Michaelis, all of whom agreed on its futility. He quotes with particular relish from the *Annales literarii* (Helmstadt, 1786), whose authors were astonished to find that Travis had been provoked by Gibbon—as though the dispute were still undecided. Travis was so vexed, they found, that he had "brought forth this child of his diligence, or rather this abortion, with a vast body, but no brain." Porson found their particular objections to Travis so agreeable that he says that had he found their review sooner, he would have printed it entire.[23]

---

ilies or recensions, later developed so fruitfully by Semler and Griesbach, see Frederick Henry Scrivener, *A Plain Introduction to the Criticism of the New Testament* (Cambridge, 1874), pp. 404–5; F. G. Kenyon, *The Text of the Greek Bible,* 3d ed. A. W. Adams (London, 1975), pp. 176–77; Metzger, *The New Testament,* pp. 112–13.

22. He was reasonably sure that Travis had not read, and certainly not used, Newton, De Missy, and Griesbach, when he wrote his first letters, and very rarely consulted Emlyn, Bengal, and Wetstein. The case of De Missy was particularly egregious, since Gibbon had expressly relied on him; see *Letters to Travis,* pp. 12–13.

23. *Letters to Travis,* p. xv–xvi and note.

3

So much for the preliminaries. Porson does not pretend to many new arguments in the letters that follow. He was content on the whole to arrange and sift and summarize the evidence as lucidly and comprehensively as he could.[24] And here he had the advantage of a clear mind and a superb philological training, including a direct acquaintance with the problems of editing and authenticating Latin and Greek manuscripts, as well as a complete knowledge of the latest literature on the subject in several languages. Philology had pronounced itself a progressive discipline in the eighteenth century and the moderns had hailed its cumulative character. As it continued its slow advance in method and substance, the torch passed gradually from England to Germany, and it began to turn into the professional university discipline that we know from the nineteenth and twentieth centuries.[25] Porson did much by his example to bring the new critical standards into the English universities, though many Englishmen, including Travis, remained ignorant of the Continental achievement. Porson's knowledge was thus superior even to Bentley's in some matters, although it was more circumscribed. Increasing specialization seems to be one of the costs of modern progress. Bentley's *Dissertation* was a model for Porson, but Porson took the exposure of the Johannine comma more narrowly that Bentley had the *Epistles of Phalaris*. Bentley had tried to recreate almost the whole world of the early Greek tyrant in order to show the anachronistic character of the fraudulent letters. Porson might have done the same thing for the comma; but he chose instead to concentrate on the more specifically textual problems and errors in the arguments of its proponents, taking them one by one. This was very effective, but it did less to describe the original situation—to construct a history—than it did to explode the mistaken theories of its proponents.

When Porson discovered that Bentley had once lectured on the comma, he was naturally eager to discover what the great man had said. Bentley had hoped to edit the New Testament as it appeared in Jerome's time, confident that he could exactly restore the original from the Greek and Latin

24. "It will be enough for me, if I can collect what is scattered through many works; dispose in a better order, or set in a clearer light, what others have written; for those who want leisure or courage to wade through the whole controversy . . . , " *Letters to Travis*, p. 16.

25. For the history of biblical interpretation in the period, see the contemporary work of Gottlob Wilhelm Meyer, *Geschichte der Schrifterklarung seit der Wiedererstellung der Wissenschaften*, 5 vols. (1802–9); and W. G. Kummel, *Das Neue Testament: Geschichte der Erforschung seiner Probleme* (Friedburg, 1958). Sebastiano Timpanaro shows how all the ingredients of nineteenth-century textual criticism were anticipated earlier; see his *La genesi del metodo del Lachmann*, 2d ed. (Paris, 1981), chap. 2.

manuscripts. He announced his scheme, and was forced to defend it against the criticism of young Conyers Middleton, but he was never able to complete it. He got some help from abroad in collating manuscripts, including the famous Vatican codex that had been so elusive, but increasing age and the magnitude of the project seems to have put him off. Nevertheless, everyone wanted to know his opinion of the comma, and it appears that he finally delivered it in a public lecture in 1717, which has since disappeared; Porson looked for it to no avail. According to a contemporary, who had actually seen it, it was, "a regular and historical narrative of the manner in which the context in this part of St. John was cited by different authors from the earliest date down to Erasmus, and a decided rejection of 1 John v. 7." Bentley was a staunch trinitarian but did not see that the doctrine needed any false support.[26] Reading Bentley's lecture might perhaps have discouraged Porson from proceeding, though it is not likely, since so much new matter had been unearthed by such as Wetstein and Griesbach. In any case, the modern reader must still be impressed by the mastery of Christian literature that the young Porson possessed, and the keenness of the intellect that could put it all together so lucidly.

The first letter, we have seen, began with Erasmus. The next several consider the other early versions of the New Testament from Lorenzo Valla and the Complutensian Polyglot to the evidence of the manuscripts in all the different ancient languages, and then to the Greek and Latin church fathers. This, of course, had been the structure of the argument from Erasmus to Gibbon, but it was often obscured by the intricate controversies surrounding each possible witness, and it is one of Porson's merits to have restored it to clarity, even while keeping all the necessary detail. "Since the external authority of any text of Scripture is founded on the concurrence of ancient MSS and ancient versions, and citations of ancient writers, it will readily be granted, that wherever any of these pillars of evidence be withdrawn or weakened, the superstructure which they were intended to support, must totter of course; and that if all three be unsound, it must be in great danger of falling."[27] It takes the rest of a long work to show how all the efforts of Travis to reinforce the three pillars had failed, and that the su-

---

26. See the letter of Dean Vincent to Charles Burney, September 3, 1806, describing the lecture he had read some twenty-five years before. James Henry Monk, *The Life of Richard Bentley,* 2d ed., 2 vols. (London, 1833), 1:16–19. In a note to his preface, Porson refers to the lecture as "still extant," though it had disappeared by the time Monk wrote Bentley's biography. See Porson, *Letters to Travis,* p. viiin.; Porson to John Hailestone, February 10, 1790, Porson, *Correspondence,* pp. 33–34. Conyers Middleton, writing much earlier, also reports that Bentley condemned the comma. Why? "Because some manuscripts and some Fathers have omitted it." Middleton, *Works,* 2:373 (Monk, p. 19).

27. *Letters to Travis,* pp. 21–22.

perstructure must come down. Like his master, Bentley, Porson tried to leaven the tedium of the long argument with his wit and invective and by writing it all out in English, so that it could be accessible to a wide if local audience.

Once again, it may not be necessary to track Porson in detail, although much of his genius lay precisely in his patient attention to details. Suffice it to say that in each area of testimony, he remorselessly reviewed the evidence proposed by Travis to disclose its weakness. Thus Travis had been able, by drawing on Valla and the early printed versions, to enumerate some thirty-one Greek manuscripts that he believed contained the comma. How did it happen then, Porson asks, that none of these manuscripts now survived, excepting only the one at Dublin, which Wetstein assigned to the sixteenth century, and the other at Berlin, which La Croze and Griesbach had similarly discarded? The answer was easy. Either they had been eaten by worms, or rotted away, or they had been destroyed by those pestilent Arians, which would not have been difficult: for all they had to do was to get their hands on every manuscript of the New Testament that then existed and mutilate or destroy all those which contained what Martin had called one of the most beautiful passages in the Bible. "My blood boils," Porson added later, "whenever I think of those sacrilegious Arians, sometimes forging and sometimes erasing Scripture. . . . Yet some part of my indignation is involuntarily diverted to the holy fathers of the church, who seem to have been in a sleep approaching to a lethargy, while the enemy came and followed the tares."[28] Finally, if all those possibilities failed, it must have been the devil's work. "For it is a fact which Beza *positively* assures us, that the devil has tampered with the text, 1 Tim. III. 16; and that Erasmus lent him a helping hand."[29]

Porson then goes on to dispute the existence of each of the manuscripts alleged to contain the comma, beginning with Valla's work. Was Valla's silence about the comma proof that he had found it in his manuscripts? Of course not. Porson saw that the methods used in the fifteenth century to collate manuscripts were a far cry from those that had developed since. And he shows exactly how Valla was likely to procede and why it was more probable that he did not find the comma than that he did.[30] In successive letters he must do the same for the claims of the Complutensian editors, Stephens and Beza. It was not hard to show that Travis's brave effort to re-

28. Ibid., pp. 155–56.
29. Beza reassures us that Erasmus's aid to the devil was unwitting; but what, asks Porson, shall we do with Wetstein, Griesbach, and the rest, who *knew* what they were doing? Ibid., pp. 23–24.
30. Ibid., pp. 24–25.

store the comma to the manuscripts that Stephens had used, against the criticism of Le Long, who had actually sought them out, was equally improbable.[31] Wetstein too had gone to Paris and seen with his own eyes five of the seven manuscripts that Stephens had employed, and every one of them had omitted the comma. But apparently Travis had not read Wetstein, or else had chosen to ignore him.[32]

As for the Dublin manuscript that had assumed so much prominence in the dispute, Porson's arguments were again familiar. Travis (following Martin) had tried to deny that it was the same one that Erasmus had called the *Codex Britannicus,* because it contained some differences in language. But the differences were just the sort that Erasmus in a hurry was likely to have made. Had not Travis made precisely the same kind of errors in his own transcription of the note about the comma in the Complutensian edition? "Might we not argue from these variations, that Mr. Travis did not copy that part of his appendix from the Complutensian edition, or that he used a copy differing from all the others?" The only difference was that Erasmus admitted haste, but Travis must plead guilty to ignorance![33] Whatever Erasmus had meant when he told Lee that he would reinstate the comma if it turned up in a manuscript, the words were an invitation to discover a copy. How opportune that it should have immediately turned up![34] The argument from silence could either be reinforced, or imperiled, by the accumulation of new evidence. But the hope that further investigation would turn up the comma was fading fast, and Porson makes the most of it. New manuscripts of the Bible in Greek and Latin and all the ancient languages were still coming to light, but most still strangely lacked the comma, while nothing whatever had turned up to confirm those early sightings in the printed editions. That left only the Vulgate. But it was plain that not even there did the manuscripts actually support the suspicious passage. Porson himself had collated some fifty Latin manuscripts and he reports

31. Le Long reported his findings in a letter to Martin, which was printed in the *Journal des savants,* June 20, 1720, pp. 643ff. It was rebutted by Martin in his *Vérité du texte* with arguments that Travis now repeats.

32. *Letters to Travis,* pp. 76–78. Porson goes on to show the general inaccuracy of Stephens' text and in a long postscript corrects some misapprehensions even among better critics, as Simon and De Missy; pp. 87–100. "It seems to be the fate of this *marvellous text* [Martin], to lead both friends and foes astray," pp. 96–97.

33. *Letters to Travis,* pp. 110–11. Porson has much more to say to confirm the identity of the two codices.

34. For the history of the British manuscript, the so-called *Codex Montfortianus,* after Erasmus, see James Rendel Harris, *The Origins of The Leicester Codex* (London, 1887). Harris guessed that it was forged by a Franciscan monk named Roy, who once owned the manuscript, pp. 46–53.

the results. He shows that the great variety of readings that he found for 1 John v. 7 sometimes added and sometimes subtracted particular words; sometimes preceded and sometimes followed the unsuspected verses; sometimes appeared in the margin in a different hand; and "in short, changed shapes faster than Proteus or Empusa." Was this not grounds enough to suspect corruption? Porson, it is true, was willing to argue against belief in the comma, *even* if all the Latin manuscripts agreed against the unanimous consent of the Greeks. And so he was hardly likely to give consent to a passage which, "by having been more frequently copied, has also been more frequently interpolated than any other." But he could show also that the twenty-nine oldest, fairest, and most correct of the Vulgate manuscripts (he adds a few to Wetstein's list) did not even contain the verse. Should we give greater weight to age or numbers? He shows the reader, by directly examining some early Latin versions in the Harleian collection, just how the clause might have been transferred from the margin into the text—how it was no more than a late interpolation.

We have reached now what was the seventh letter, about halfway through the book. Porson continues his assault on the evidence of the archdeacon by disposing first of the old versions in Syriac and Coptic, then (in the eighth letter) in the Armenian and other oriental languages. "You will perhaps, Sir, interrupt this railery by asking me, whether I understand the Armenian language? Truly, Sir, no better than yourself." Here, no doubt, was a disadvantage for both the combatants, but here again, Porson's superior knowledge of the secondary literature, his careful reading of the experts, allows him to undermine Travis's positive assertions and tip the balance. No ancient version, he concludes positively, contained the comma. By the time he turns his attention to the church fathers and early creeds, the several pillars that had supported the comma were tottering indeed. One by one, Porson examines each doubtful quotation in Greek and Latin to dispute its authority or relevance, until only Cyprian is left. Even then, he argues on the testimony of the later writer, Facundus, that Cyprian was not *quoting* anything, but simply interpreting the eighth verse mystically, and thus setting the stage for the later interpolations. Porson gives Augustine and Jerome much of a whole letter (the eleventh), with particular attention to Jerome's spurious preface to the Catholic Epistles. But long before the end, the tottering edifice was falling to the ground. After four hundred pages of withering criticism, it was hard to evade Porson's conclusion. If the Johannine comma had been known from the beginning, the ancients would have seized upon it for their creeds, quoted it against the heretics, and trumpeted it in every book that they wrote upon the Trinity.

In short, if this verse be really genuine, notwithstanding its absence from
all the visible Greek MSS except two; one of which [the Dublin MS] awk-
wardly translates the verse from the Latin, and the other [the Berlin MS]
transcribes it from a printed book; notwithstanding its absence from all
the versions except the Vulgate; and even from many of the best and oldest MSS. of the Vulgate; notwithstanding the deep and dead silence of
all the Greek writers down to the thirteenth and most of the Latins down
to the middle of the eighth century; if in spite of all these objections, it
be still genuine, no part of scripture whatsoever can be proved either spurious or genuine; and Satan has been permitted, for many centuries,
miraculously to banish the finest passage in the N.T. from the eyes and
memories of almost all the Christian authors, translators, and transcribers.[35]

4

Needless to say, Gibbon was delighted. Travis had somehow tried to hold
him personally responsible for condemning the text; the bigots at Oxford,
Gibbon found, were no better than the bigots at Rome. But now, he wrote
in his autobiography, the "wretched Travis howls under the lash of the mer-
ciless Porson." In a note, Gibbon paid tribute to his defender. "I consider
Mr. Porson's answer to Archdeacon Travis as the most acute and accurate
piece of criticism which has appeared since the days of Bentley. His strictures are founded in argument, enriched with learning, and enlivened
with wit, and his adversary neither deserves nor finds any quarter at his
hands." Gibbon could well believe that the heavenly witnesses would no
longer be accepted by any court. But he was not so optimistic to think that
the offending phrase would actually be removed from the Bible, since
"prejudice is blind, and authority deaf." Yet even so, he imagined that the
more learned clergy would be won over and "have the secret satisfaction of
reprobating in the Closet what they read in the Church."[36]

It was natural that Gibbon should want to meet his young benefactor,
and he swiftly invited him to his home. It is hard to imagine two more oddly
matched personalities: Gibbon, short and stout and oddly deformed by his
prominent goiter, but immensely polished and sociable; Porson, tall and
lean, but a little uncouth, not very ambitious, and certainly unsociable.
Nevertheless, Porson appeared and was treated with great kindness and respect. While they were getting acquainted, Gibbon suddenly said, "Mr. Porson, I feel truly indebted to you for the Letters to Travis, though I must
think that occasionally, while you were praising me, you have mingled a lit-

---

35. *Letters to Travis,* pp. 402–3.
36. Gibbon, *Autobiography* (Murray), p. 323 and note.

tle acid with the sweet." Still, if Porson were ever to look at the *Decline and Fall* again, Gibbon would like his comments. Porson was very flattered. He thought Gibbon's history without doubt the greatest work of the eighteenth century and was in the habit of repeating long passages from it. Yet (so we are told) he continued to believe that there was no better exercise for a schoolmaster than to turn a page of it into English.[37]

To many it looked as though Porson had won the day and finally ended the long controversy. But one of his benefactors, Mrs. Turner, "a lady of very pious disposition," was so distressed that she immediately cut him out of her will, leaving him only a paltry legacy.[38] And Travis was altogether unbowed. It seems to be true in the history of forgery that a definitive victory is hard to achieve. One problem is that the argument from silence can nearly always be circumvented by the hope, if not the fact, of new evidence. Suppose an old manuscript should suddenly appear with the missing comma? This had been the fervent wish of the orthodox for two centuries. Even so, it was hard to see how that could be sufficient in the face of so much contrary evidence and the strange silence of so many different documents. It seemed far-fetched to suggest that the ancient Arians must have gone about snipping the offending passage out of most of the ancient Bibles and successfully concealed the deed, until the comma could be rescued somehow in the fullness of time. (Why God, not to say the orthodox bishops, should have allowed this, was never very clear.) Porson was not the only one to find the possibility inconceivable. It was much easier to imagine the trinitarians putting the comma in than the Arians taking it out, and there was good concrete evidence for that in the margins of some of the manuscripts. Nevertheless, it remained the fervent hope of the orthodox that they might still discover a new manuscript or two, or at least puncture the negative arguments against the old ones and thus retrieve some positive evidence for their side.

Of course, the orthodox did not *want* to see that the inconvenient hypothesis of the enemy could actually accommodate all the facts more completely, simply, and exactly than their own. They did not want to see it, because it took away one of the best props for their trinitarian convictions, and also because it seemed to shake altogether the authority of the Bible in these matters. "They take every detached sentence," Porson complained, "for a distinct assertion or apothegm, and apply it according to its apparent

37. Rogers, *Porsoniana*, pp. 202–3.

38. [Thomas Turton] *A Vindication of the Literary Character of the Late Richard Porson* (Cambridge, 1827), p. 152n.; John Selby Watson, *The Life of Richard Porson* (London, 1861), pp. 81–82.

meaning, after they have forcibly torn it from its context."[39] If Gibbon and
Porson were right on this particular occasion, it was hard to avoid the im-
plication that the whole body of Christian conviction might also have developed over time perhaps as much by human as divine inspiration, and
that all this was not immediately obvious in the pages of Scripture. In accepting the recourse to history and the methods of modern philology to
determine his cause, Travis sensed that he might lose much more than the
comma—though that may be more obvious to us than it was to his contemporaries. And it may help to account for his stubborn resistance and his
bad temper.

So Travis and his friends continued to resist, although their position was
increasingly awkward. Toward the end of 1789, there was a new flurry when
someone named "Kuster" again took up Travis's part in the *Gentleman's
Magazine* about the early printed versions. If Porson's arguments were allowed, Kuster protested, it would only prove that Stephens was a cheat,
Beza no better, the Berlin MS a forgery, and so also the *Codex Britannicus* of
Erasmus.[40] This called forth a particularly sharp response from Porson ("A
Reproof Valiant to Mr. Travis's Reply Churlish"), who began to realize that
the other side was not listening. Porson had never accused Stephens of
fraud; on the contrary, he had taken great trouble to show how he had only
made a careless and innocent mistake in punctuation. Once again he
shows how the manuscripts that Stephens was alleged to have used in the
Royal Library in Paris had been correctly identified by Le Long, Wetstein,
and Griesbach—even though they disagreed on some small matters—and
not one of them contained the comma.[41]

In 1791, Travis took a trip to Paris to look for himself at the manuscripts
there. He then added what he discovered, a little tardily, to a new, third edition of the *Letters to Gibbon* that appeared in 1794. Apparently, Travis could
not find much more to say in reply to Porson, so he was content to deny the
heretic's victory and simply add a bit more to what he had already written.
It remained only too clear to him that Gibbon and Benson had "sacrificed
the faithfulness of facts to their own predilections."[42] Personal inspection
merely confirmed what he knew already, that the manuscripts still extant
were not those that Stephens had used. Once again he insisted on the variants that they showed from the printed text, overlooking Porson's observation that such variants were exactly what were to be expected from the
printing and editing methods of the time. (It would really have been more

39. *Letters to Travis*, p. 371.
40. *Gentleman's Magazine*, 59, pt. 2, November, 1789, p. 972.
41. Ibid., 60 (1790), pp. 128–33.
42. Travis, *Letters to Gibbon*, 3d ed. (London, 1794), pref.

suspicious had they had no variants at all!) Nor does Travis offer any explanation for what happened to the missing originals. As for those that did appear in the Royal Library with Stephen's marks but without the comma, it seemed to the archdeacon that they must simply be counterfeits, "on whose unresisting pages some busy and dishonest librarian, or some other person equally forward and dishonest, has inscribed forged and false marks of R. Stephens from some undue and improper motive, most probably to advance their reputation by the credit of his illustrious name." At a stroke, Travis was thus able to restore both Stephens' reputation and the Johannine comma!

In much the same way, Travis tried to rescue the Dublin manuscript with the additional testimony of friends on the spot, Dr. Richard Nun, a paper manufacturer in Dublin, and Dean Ycard, an experienced paleographer, who tried to date the manuscript from its external characteristics. The result showed that Porson and his allies had clearly placed the manuscript much too late and that it was more likely to be from the fourteenth than from the sixteenth century. If that was still a bit late for Travis's purpose, what did it matter? It was after all only a copy of an earlier version, and *that* could well have been older than anything now known.[43] With a similar argument, Travis tried to rescue the Berlin manuscript too, and he prints the suspicious passages in facsimile for the reader to judge. He adds a few other remarks but otherwise leaves the original argument pretty much intact and unaltered.

Porson did not reply. With such a weak retort, he may have felt that it was unnecessary. "Such replies," he had anticipated, "will carry their own refutation with them to all readers who are not eaten up with prejudice."[44] And indeed to many observers it appeared that Porson had made his point beyond refutation. Porson returned instead to the Greek poets, never again to write a book. A natural lethargy and too much drink brought his scholarship to a sad and premature conclusion. If, in the end, we remember him more for what he did for Euripides and some other ancient poets, for his brilliant conversation and his largely unfulfilled promise, we can still read the *Letters to Travis* with admiration both for its argument and its style. It is not often that one can derive much amusement from a philological lesson, but Porson saw that there was something to be gained from both the ancients and the moderns, from mixing wit and erudition, and the *Letters to Travis* may still be read in a way that almost everything else on the subject may not, as a classic of close reasoning and philological argument.

43. Ibid., pp. 277–85.
44. Porson, *Letters to Travis*, p. 405.

5

Yet even while Porson was declining further battle, another young Cambridge don—ambitious, combative, and very learned—was about to enter the lists. Herbert Marsh had gone abroad to travel, but wound up studying theology with Michaelis at Leipzig and corresponding with Griesbach on the text of the New Testament. Altogether he spent about a dozen years in Germany becoming perfectly proficient in the language and up to date in the new philology. Michaelis was now an old man (he died in 1792), laden with honor. His father had been a biblical scholar before him, and in his youth he set off to England to read manuscripts in the Bodleian Library. He kept up with English biblical scholars afterward, like the Hebraist, Bishop Lowth, whose influential work on Hebrew poetry he edited and annotated. (Lowth, it should be said, once wrote a letter to Michaelis resolutely denying the comma.)[45] The young German scholar began to translate some of the English biblical commentaries of his day, including the works of George Benson.[46] He was particularly renowned for his knowledge of Hebrew and the Eastern languages, for which he wrote several useful introductions and grammars. Eventually, he became professor of philosophy at Gottingen in 1747, where he remained until his death forty-five years later; his obituary in the *Gentleman's Magazine* listed some seventy-eight publications, and he left others in manuscript.[47] For thirty years or so he edited and contributed to the *Orientalische und exegetische bibliothek* and its sequel, one of the many new learned journals that were helping then to redefine the philological discipline.

Among his many works was a famous handbook, an introduction to the New Testament which he published first in 1750 and then in enlarged editions for the rest of his life. It was turned into English in 1761, and then again—from the fourth edition, but now six times the size of the original—by young Marsh. The Englishman had set out first to amuse himself

45. "We have some wranglers in theology, sworn to follow their master, who are prepared to defend anything, however absurd, should there be occasion. But I believe there is no one among us in the least degree conversant with sacred criticism, and having the use of his understanding, who would be willing to contend for the genuineness of the verse." Lowth to Michaelis, in Michaelis, *Literarischer Briefwechsel,* 2:428, translated by Ezra Abbot in his appendix to William Orme, *Memoir of the Controversy Respecting the Heavenly Witnesses* (New York, 1866), p. 184. Lowth's work (1758–61) was reprinted with Michaelis' notes at Oxford, in 1763: *Roberti Lowth de Sacra Poesi Hebraeorum Praelectiones, cum Notis et Epimetris.*

46. Among other English influences on him was the work of Kennicott on the Old Testament. See the memoir by J. G. Eichhorn, *An Account of the Life and Writings of John David Michaelis,* trans. Patton, in the Student's Cabinet Library of Useful Tracts, 2 (Edinburgh, 1835), pp. 26, 35. Michaelis seems also be have translated the first four books of *Clarissa!*

47. *Gentleman's Magazine,* 62, March, 1792, pp. 202–4.

while ill in Germany, but he soon saw that he might do a useful service by making the great work conveniently available to his countrymen and by bringing it up to date with some notes and essays of his own. He began to publish the *Introduction* in 1793 under the auspices and at the expense of Cambridge University, but it was only completed after Marsh's final return to England in 1801.[48]

While Marsh was still at his translation, he received a letter from Michaelis. The old man pointed out that things had been very different four decades ago when he first published his *Introduction*. "I feel a satisfaction, and even a degree of astonishment, at the progress of learning in the present age." He was particularly pleased with the rapid advance of scholarship in the last ten years. "The republic of letters is at present in possession of knowledge, of which it had no idea in the middle of the century." It was as maturity to infancy.[49] Marsh agreed, German scholarship now led the world; yet even so, he saw that he would have to add several thousand new references as well as a number of essays to bring the work of Michaelis freshly up to date.[50] Nor did he hesitate to correct, as well as improve his master, where he could.[51]

Michaelis was not a clergyman, and he protested his impartiality throughout his work. His only ambition, he insisted, was to establish a correct text through the necessary employment of all the relevant ancient languages. "It is the business of a critic to inquire, not which is the best, but which is the genuine reading, or that which proceeded from the writer himself; the style and character of the authors must be examined." His express model was the philology that had been devoted to the pagan classics. "Every commentator on the Bible should first exercise his talents in the Greek and Latin classics, or at least be well acquainted with the critical researches of other literati, without which he is exposed to the danger of committing

48. John David Michaelis, *Introduction to the New Testament*, trans. Herbert Marsh, vols. 1–2 (London, 1793). Marsh explains the delay over the rest in the preface to the next two volumes (1801). Marsh's commentary was eventually translated into German (1795–1803); and the whole work into French at Geneva (1822). See J. E. B. Mayor, in Thomas Baker, *History of the College of St. John, Cambridge*, 2 vols. (Cambridge, 1869), 2:744. Mayor includes much information and long extracts from Marsh's works, pp. 735–898.

49. "The system of biblical criticism has been placed in a new light, and reduced to a state of greater certainty." *Introduction*, 1:i–ii. For this, Eichhorn gives Michaelis himself the chief credit, *Life*, p. 31.

50. For a summary of the work of Bengel, Semler, Woide, Michaelis, Matthaei, Alter, Birch, and Griesbach—all known to Marsh and used by him—see Scrivener, *Introduction*, pp. 402–17.

51. Marsh's work was much appreciated in Germany, where his notes were translated into German (by Rosenmuller) and widely praised and reviewed. There is a summary in Baker, *History*, p. 755.

glaring mistakes." The best work on the New Testament had always been
done by the best scholars of Greek literature.[52] March agreed again, and
like Michaelis, he argued that the philological facts were independent of
religious preconceptions and could stand on their own. "Accuracy and impartiality," he insisted, in words that both Gibbon and Porson would have
approved, "are the two great virtues of a critic."[53] Porson, it should be said,
knew the work of Michaelis, and March the work of Porson.[54]

For Marsh and Michaelis, as for Porson and Gibbon, the idea that an impartial perspective could be made to yield an objective truth was ax-
iomatic. Nor, in principle, did Travis disagree. For Marsh, the question of
the comma could thus be detached from religious conviction and determined by a neutral philology and history:

> Polemical divinity must be totally separated from sacred criticism, for a
> reading is not rendered spurious by its opposition to an established
> creed, nor genuine by their agreement. The text of the New Testament
> must be determined, before articles can be formed from it, and we argue
> in a circle, if we condemn a text because it contradicts a theological sys-
> tem, when that very system depends on the authenticity of the text. The
> only business of a critic is impartially to weigh the evidence which may be
> brought for or against a reading, and to determine on that side on which
> the scale preponderates.[55]

The Johannine comma, like the rest of Scripture, was therefore a matter of
fact to be settled in accordance with the evidence.

Michaelis' *Introduction* was an attempt to collect all the relevant facts that
were needed to establish a correct and reliable text for the New Testament.
The two volumes that Marsh translated in 1793 (the first of the original two
quartos), addressed the problems of authenticity, inspiration, and language for the whole work, and then each kind of evidence needed to establish its diverse readings. Like Bentley earlier, Michaelis welcomed the
thousands of variants that criticism had exposed as positive evidence for
the original text.[56] And like most of the enlightened critics of his time, he
saw no danger to religion in the disinterested pursuit of philological and
historical truth. In a section on "inspiration," Michaelis argued that the
question of whether the New Testament was *genuine* was more important
than whether it was *inspired*. "Had the Deity inspired not a single book of

---

52. *Introduction*, 1:269, 312.

53. Marsh note, *Introduction*, p. 526. It is likely that Travis would also have approved the
idea, though less obviously the practice.

54. See, for example, Marsh's introduction to vol. 2, pt. 2.

55. *Introduction*, Marsh note, vol. 2, pt. 2, p. 754.

56. Ibid., pp. 182–83, 265. Marsh recommends Bentley in his note, pp. 497.

the New Testament, but left the Apostles and Evangelists without any other aid, than that of natural abilities to commit what they knew to writing, admitting their works to be authentic, and possessed of a sufficient degree of credibility, the Christian religion would be the true one." It was possible to doubt, and even deny, the inspiration of the New Testament, and yet be fully persuaded of its truth. There was even some advantage in denying inspiration to the historical books, since some inconsistencies and errors in them could not then be used to undermine the truth of the religion.[57] In the next two volumes (the second quarto of which Marsh translated in 1801) Michaelis took up the problem of the Canon, and then each individual book of the New Testament, including the epistles of John.

At that point it was only natural for Michaelis to want to examine the comma for himself. In the first editions of the *Introduction* he still wavered on the matter, but now he was ready to dismiss it decisively as a forgery. In the first volume, he raised the question briefly in considering the only two manuscripts that still contained it: the *Codex Britannicus* and the *Codex Ravianus* at Berlin. He repeats the arguments against them by his predecessors: Wetstein, La Croze, and De Missy, and especially now by G. G. Pappelbaum, whose inquiry into the Berlin manuscript was published in that city in 1785. (Marsh adds some further support in two long notes of his own.)[58] It is true that Travis had recently tried to defend the Berlin MS, using Pappelbaum, "but he is a most partial advocate, having never seen the manuscript himself, and having no further knowledge of the subject than the intelligence, which he received from Berlin, of which he printed only as much as suited his purpose."[59] Later, Michaelis found even more decisively against the comma that it should be absent from the early fathers. If it had turned up in a third-century writer, he says, he would have found that stronger proof of its authenticity than any of the existing manuscripts. But he would not accept the ascription to Cyprian or any other.[60] Elsewhere,

---

57. In a note of his own, Marsh added that the truth of Christianity was independent of the biblical testimony. "For the value of a diamond depends not on the genuineness of the gold in which it is set, nor is truth affected by the instability of the vehicle in which it is conveyed. It did not follow that if the Bible was a forgery, that Christianity must be a forgery too. If the New Testament was destroyed, who would say that our religion would cease to be true? *Introduction*, pp. 72, 378.

58. Ibid., p. 297; and for Marsh, pp. 755–57, 770–72. Michaelis had reviewed Travis in the *Neue orientalische und exegetische bibliothek*, 2:152–56.

59. Ibid., p. 297. Here Michaelis cites his own review of Travis in the *Neue Orientalische Bibliothek*, 2:152–56. Travis summarizes Pappelbaum in an appendix.

60. Ibid., pp. 368–69; 2, pp. 422–25. The passage from Cyprian in the third century, *De unitate ecclesiae*, reads thus: "Dicit dominus, Ego et pater unum sumus: et iterum de patre et filio, et spiritu sancto, *scritum est: et tres unum sunt.*" Michaelis points out that the underlined words could refer equally well to the eighth verse, and that was how they were understood by Facun-

he devotes a long section of his book to a discussion of the Stephens manuscripts, before accepting a typographical error as the best explanation. Michaelis had a friend in Paris do a fresh and conclusive examination for himself as early as 1764.[61]

It was in the second quarto volume, however, that Michaelis turned his full attention to the comma. Neither he nor his translator saw any use to a pious fraud. "The hope of acquiring an additional proof of some established doctrine, or of depriving an adversary of some argument in its favor, may seduce even a true believer to the commission of a pious fraud. Blinded by prejudice, and bound by the fetter of a theological system he finds his favorite doctrine in every line." In 1750, Michaelis points out, when he first printed his introduction, the notion that the comma was spurious was not so obvious as now, and his criticism had provoked much opposition and cries of heresy—even though he never questioned the trinitarian doctrine. He reviews the various attempts since, both to defend and attack it, from J. S. Semler, whom he thought the best, to Travis, whose work "betrayed the utmost partiality."[62] To the usual arguments, Michaelis added one of his own and also the special authority that he could bring as a master of the oriental languages. His new argument was that the second-century sect of the Alogi, who were antitrinitarians, accepted the epistle of John, though they rejected some other parts of the New Testament where they were inconvenient, so that the New Testament could not have contained the comma then.[63] He was also confident that the comma was not in the Syriac, Arabic, Coptic, Armenian, Ethiopic, and Slavonian versions either.

Michaelis anticipates Porson's surprise that in the face of the almost universal silence of antiquity, a Protestant could still accept the passage as gen-

---

dus, a sixth-century Carthaginian commentator, who believed that Cyprian was simply expounding on that verse. In any case he asks "whether a passage found in no Greek manuscript, quoted by no Greek father, and contained in no other version than the Latin, is therefore to be pronounced genuine, merely because one single Latin father of the first three centuries, who was a bishop of Carthage, where the Latin version only was used, and where Greek was unknown, has quoted it?"

61. Ibid., pp. 316–29. Michaelis quotes from a letter by one Fleischer, December 16, 1764, p. 321. He excuses his long disquisition on the grounds that Stephens' text of 1550 was scarce and Martin's objections had never been fully refuted.

62. *Introduction*, 2d ed. (1802), 4:413–14. Marsh was particularly fond of "the immortal Semler," who he thought, "was a great critic and divine," and an independent thinker; see ibid., vol. 2, pt. 1, p. 641. He is usually thought to be the most learned biblical critic of the eighteenth century; see Hans W. Frei, *The Eclipse of Biblical Narrative: A Study in Eighteenth and Nineteenth Century Hermeneutics* (New Haven, 1974), pp. 109–13. Semler first tackled the comma in his *Historische und critische Sammlungen über die genannten Beweisstellen in der Dogmatik*, 2 vols. (Halle, 1764), pt. 1.

63. Chap. 31, sec. 4, IV, pp. 428–31. The evidence is all from Epiphanius.

uine. But Bengel, we have seen, had found a way to avoid the conclusion. Among other suggestions, he had explained its peculiar absence from the early documents in this way: since both the seventh and eighth verses began with the very same words, he proposed that a scribe could easily have overlooked the seventh accidentally while copying it. (His eye might slip from one to the other without knowing it, an error well known to palaeographers as *homoioteleuton*.)[64] But Michaelis did not see how this could account for its nearly *universal* absence. Moreover it was absurd to explain an omission of a passage in St. John, before it was shown that it ever contained it. Suppose I demanded some money in court and the magistrate asked me for a contract to support the demand. I answer that I haven't got one, but that it easily might have been lost in the late war. The example of the comma was even worse, since the loss of a single document had to be matched in that case by the disappearance of more than eighty manuscripts. Michaelis goes on to show how the original must rather have been invented in the margins of the Latin Bible and interpolated eventually into the Latin and Greek texts.

Marsh never got around to annotating this last volume of Michaelis, but he did get into the quarrel on his own as a result of a note that he had attached to the first part of the *Introduction*.[65] He wrote there to describe a discovery he had made for himself sometime before 1793, just when the quarrel between Porson and Travis was at its height. It seems that one day he walked over to the Cambridge University Library to look at the Greek manuscripts, which he had earlier catalogued, to see what he could find to the point. He was particularly intrigued by an old codex whose readings seemed very different from those in the *textus receptus*. Turning it over, he discovered the name "Vetablus" on the inside cover, and recollecting that one Vetablus was a Hebrew professor at the University of Paris in the mid-sixteenth century, it occurred to him that this might be one of the missing manuscripts that had been employed by Robert Stephens—"because," he explained, "Vetablus was one of Stephens' intimate friends, and was likewise connected with him in his literary disputes." Collation confirmed his suspicion, and Marsh appended a note to Michaelis claiming additional support for the old notion that many of Stephens' manuscripts could be identified now and were clear proof against the comma.[66]

As usual, Travis would not concede. In his new *Letters to Porson* (1794), he replied to "the learned translator of Michaelis." Marsh had argued

---

64. This old argument was already being made by Henry Hammond in his commentary on the New Testament (1653).

65. *Introduction*, 2–2, p. 795.

66. Marsh, *Letters to Archdeacon Travis* (Leipzig, 1795), pp. 3–6, *Introduction*, 2:795.

in his note, on the basis of his collation of the Cambridge manuscript with Stephens' printed text, that they were identical; they shared too many unique readings for it to be a coincidence. Travis replied by questioning the number of unique readings and turning up many discrepancies that Marsh had overlooked. The manuscript could not be the one that Stephens had used, any more than any of the others that had been alleged, and Stephens' crotchets had been placed where they were meant to go .[67] Marsh now replied in his own turn with some *Letters to Archdeacon Travis* (1795) in which he vindicated his note and reaffirmed the identity of the Cambridge manuscript with the one of Stephens. The crotchets had been misplaced and it was easy to see how this could have happened. "In the year 1792," Marsh wrote, "I published at Cambridge a short essay in defense of the authenticity of the Pentateuch; in this essay p. 13 are three marginal notes, marked with what printers call a star, a dagger, and a double dagger. In the text the star was placed right: but after the word where the dagger should have been placed, the compositor set no mark at all, but set the dagger, which belonged to "Egyptian words," line 4. after "Hebrew," line 9: and totally omitted the dagger." This, Marsh insisted, was a greater error than Stephens', for it was a much larger mark and was set at a much greater distance from its proper place. "Yet this glaring mistake I did not detect, though I read the several proofsheets at least ten times, before the Essay was printed off." They had also been read by friends, the university printer, and a literary reviewer—all mistakenly.[68] How much easier was it to imagine such an error in the sixteenth century when the methods of editing and printing were so much more careless.

The new *Letters to Travis* employed some other arguments against Travis,[69] and some more about the Stephens' manuscripts, which only stirred a fresh controversy, this time with Isaac Milner. On the whole, Marsh was content to restate and reinforce the views of Porson, now professor of Greek. Milner, however, remained unconvinced by the Vetablus argument and claimed to have asked Porson's opinion on the matter, only to discover that the great scholar had not yet made up his mind about the identity of the Cambridge manuscripts, and that he thought Marsh's cer-

---

67. *Letters to Porson* (1794), pp. 410–14.

68. *Letters to Archdeacon Travis*, pp. 130n.

69. One in particular was urged at great length. Marsh showed (supporting Wetstein) how the manuscripts printed by the Marquis of Velez, in the sixteenth century, and which contained the comma, were no more than Stephens' readings from the Latin; see the third letter and long appendix, pp. 40–69, 253–93. Marsh also furnished another appendix (pp. 241–52) with fuller extracts from Pappelbaum to show how "partial and inaccurate" had been Travis's account of the Berlin manuscript in his appendix (Travis [1794], pp. 74–80).

tainty, which the young clergyman had likened to a mathematical theo-
rem, was unwarranted. Marsh immediately questioned Milner's account,
claiming to have positive proof that in July 1794 Porson *had* examined the
matter for himself and decided in his favor. Indeed, so important had the
question then appeared—the whole fate of the comma seeming to rest
upon it—that the University Senate passed a grace giving leave to Porson
to borrow the manuscript in order to inspect it. Meanwhile, Marsh, who
was back in Leipzig, had some friends look at it independently and collate
it further for him. When Travis's book appeared in May or June, Porson
came down to Cambridge to look into the matter more carefully. A friend,
Thomas Jones, immediately sent Marsh an account of what happened and
was able to assure him categorically that Porson had "established your
opinion as to the identity of the two manuscripts beyond a doubt."[70]

Gibbon missed this last flurry; he died in 1794. Travis died also, still
young, a couple of years later, perhaps chagrined by this latest indignity.[71]
Marsh went on vigorously to a long and successful career in scholarship
and the church, not forgetting to keep up his battle against the comma and
many other targets, though to be sure he remained an unwavering trinitarian throughout.[72] Opinion was swinging unmistakably to Gibbon's side
now, within the church as without; but still the battle was not over.

6

Just one old manuscript or patristic citation and it might still be possible to
refute the skeptics! The valiant labor of Archdeacon Travis to sustain tradition was taken up in the next generation by several stalwart Anglican clergyman, most notably by Thomas Burgess, bishop of Salisbury. Although he
was once a friend and companion of Porson's and a man of considerable
Greek learning, he set himself in later life to undoing Porson's pernicious
work and defending the comma. Once he caught wind of a manuscript at
Lincoln College in Oxford that might contain the disputed passage. He in-
quired immediately and received a letter from the very learned rector
there. "Porson's book never shook my conviction of the authenticity of that
important verse," the rector wrote, "which has so long and laudably en-

70. Isaac Milner, *Strictures*, p. 252; Marsh, *Reply to the Strictures*, app. sec. 1, pp. 19–20. The
letter was from Thomas Jones to Marsh, July 24, 1794. See also the letter of H. C. A. Eichstadt
to Porson proclaiming his friendship with Marsh, March 1, 1801, Porson, *Correspondence*,
pp. 67–68 (Baker, *History*, pp. 758–59). Marsh wrote a short memoir of Jones in 1808.

71. He died "not without a suspicion that the controversy severely affected his health, and
contributed to shorten his days," Orme, *Memoir*, pp. 93–94.

72. See Marsh, *A Course of Lectures containing a Description and a Systematic Arrangement of the
Several Branches of Divinity* (Cambridge, 1810–22), 4:13–27; *Lectures on the Authenticity and*

gaged your present study. The artful and superficial way in which he treated the interesting subject, and his unmannerly behaviour to Mr. Travis, brought me some years ago into St. Mary's pulpit, with a sermon upon the disputed text." Unfortunately, the good rector could not find the manuscript—nor could he find what he had said about it in the sermon, which he insisted had contained the verse. He had looked at the manuscript originally, he assured Burgess, in the presence of Dr. Parsons, the late bishop of Peterborough, but it had already disappeared when he delivered the sermon and could not now be found. And thus, writes Porson's defender, "and thus did the Lincoln College MS., like other MSS already mentioned, shrink from too close an inspection."[73]

While a student, Burgess was known as the best Greek scholar at Cambridge. He seems to have met Porson about the time that the *Letters to Gibbon* were appearing (1785), and frequently turned up in his rooms in London and at the house of their mutual friend, Charles Burney. His biographer tells us that he always spoke with respect about the acuteness and learning of his new friend.[74] One day, Samuel Parr suggested to him that it would be a good idea to persuade Porson "to collate and fairly state the evidence pro and con" about the Johannine comma and the other disputed text in Timothy, "and in a luminous way to subjoin his own opinions." He thought the learned world would be very grateful to have the tangled matter sorted out.[75] What Burgess thought about it then we do not know, although he was already an adamant trinitarian.[76] The young scholar went on to learn Hebrew, write on Homer, and correspond with the best Continental scholars of his time. In 1814, he argued with Herbert Marsh about

---

Credibility of the new Testament (1840). For his trinitarian orthodoxy, which seems to have been modeled on Michaelis, see *A Letter to the Conductor of the Critical Review on the Subject of Religious Toleration: With Occasional Remarks on the Doctrines of the Trinity and the Atonement* (London, 1810), pp. 26–27; Baker, *History of St. John*, pp. 802–3. Between 1801 and 1804, Marsh engaged in a fierce controversy over the composition of the Gospels; in 1807 he was elected Lady Margaret Professor of Divinity at Cambridge. His whole career would seem to deserve further study.

73. Crito Cantabrigiensis [Thomas Turton], *A Vindication of the Literary Character of the Late Prof. Porson* (Cambridge, 1827), pp. 333–34. Burgess refers to the manuscript in his *Letter to the Clergy of St. David's*, p. 85.

74. John S. Harford, *Life of Thomas Burgess* (London, 1840), pp. 161–62.

75. Ibid., pp. 149–50.

76. According to Harford, he contributed a letter to the *Monthly Review* in 1790 defending the ante-Nicene fathers against the charge of unorthodoxy on the Trinity; and his first published sermon in the same year was on "the Divinity of Christ, proved from his own Declarations." In 1791, he wrote against the Unitarian Priestley. See Harford, *Life of Burgess*, pp. 137–41.

the Aeolic digamma, and a few years later took on Payne Knight on the same subject. About the same time, he became increasingly preoccupied with the Unitarians, and when the manuscript of the *De Doctrina Christiana* turned up a little later, he resolutely denied that it could be by Milton because of its unorthodox view of the Trinity.[77]

When Burgess finally got around to considering the comma, he was a bishop, and he spent more than a decade trying to refute his old friend Porson in a series of publications upholding Travis.[78] Unfortunately, there was nothing more to be said that had not been said already, and more than once. Burgess could only look to the Latin manuscripts, resurrect some of the older scholars to match against the new, insist on the testimony of Cyprian, and argue for the internal fit of the verse into its context. Even his biographer, who was persuaded by him, saw that he had to give up much crucial ground.[79] Burgess found some allies among the clergy, much as Gibbon had predicted, in such bishops as Horsley and Middleton. But he also found much opposition among the clergy, which might have surprised Gibbon. Burgess was answered in a devastating tract by the bishop of Ely, Thomas Turton (under a pseudonym, Crito Cantabrigiensis, but not disguising his clerical status): *A Vindication of the Literary Character of the Late Prof. Porson from the Animadversions of the Right Reverend Thomas Burgess* (Cambridge, 1827). Turton set about rescuing Porson's integrity as a scholar, ostensibly avoiding the substantive question of the comma, but the conclusion was inescapable. Porson had been right in detail and on the main question, and no new evidence had turned up to unsettle the matter.[80]

Still the old hunt continued, and a few years later a German scholar did discover a couple of new manuscripts that contained the missing comma. At once, Burgess rushed into print again, though he was literally at death's door. He had finally found the needed proof, although the discoverer, Dr. Scholz, had dated the new manuscripts too late to offset the authority and

---

77. Milton's work was first published in 1825; Burgess fought the attribution first in the Royal Society of Literature, which he had founded, and then in a treatise, *Milton Contrasted with Milton and the Scriptures* (1829); see Harford, *Life of Burgess*, pp. 345–47. In 1820, he brought together his various trinitarian defenses in a single book: *Tracts on the Divinity of Christ* (London, 1820).

78. For bibliography, see Orme, *Memoir*, pp. 130–36: Harford, *Life of Burgess*, p. 404n.

79. For example, the Greek manuscripts, St. Augustine, etc.; see ibid., pp. 423–27. There was an immediate reply in the *Quarterly Review*, 26 (1822) and a response to the reply by "Ben David," *Three Letters to the Editor of the Quarterly Review* (1825), and a further reply in the *Quarterly Review*, December, 1825. See Orme, *Memoir*, pp. 136–43, 150–51, 153–56.

80. Porson was supported by a writer in the high-church *British Critic*, reviewing Turton, 4 July, 1828, pp. 1–32.

antiquity of the vast number of manuscripts that omitted it.[81] After a life-time of conviction, it was impossible to persuade the dying bishop, but by then, it appears, he had lost most of his following.

Meanwhile, there had been several other skirmishes at the beginning of the new century to keep the issue alive, although they did not much advance the argument. In 1815, an obscure but very learned Presbyterian clergyman named Frederick Nolan, brought out a large book defending the Greek Testament in general and the comma in particular. He seems to have been provoked by J. J. Griesbach's latest effort to arrange the Greek manuscripts into families, but he did not forget Porson either.[82] Most of his labor was expended on trying to rescue a Latin tradition, separate from the Greek, and anterior to it, which would support the early existence of the comma. "If in fact, the positive testimony of the Latin Version, could be sufficiently confirmed by the testimony of the Latin Fathers; and if the negative testimony of the Greek Text could be satisfactorily accounted for, and an adequate cause assigned for the silence of the Greek Fathers: no plea could be advanced of sufficient weight to warrant a prescription of the Heavenly Witnesses, or justify their exclusion from the Canonical Scriptures."[83] Nolan tried with great ingenuity to place the discussion in its exact historical context, beginning with John's epistle itself, which he read as a reply to a number of contemporary heresies. And he tried to show that the later controversies with Arians and Sabellians were not really trinitarian disputes, since they involved only two of the three persons, so that the comma was no use then to the orthodox—which they naturally did not quote. (So much for its absence among the early church fathers.)[84] But de-

81. J. M. A. Scholz was a Catholic professor of theology at Bonn; after traveling the world, he drew up a comprehensive list of Greek manuscripts, adding 616 hitherto unknown. He had already rejected the comma in his German translation of the New Testament in 1830. In 1836, he rejected it again in his edition of the Greek text. See Bruce M. Metzger, *The Text of the New Testament: Its Transmission, Corruption and Restoration*, 2d ed. (Oxford, 1968), pp. 123–24. Burgess responded in *Three Letters to the Rev. Dr. Scholz* (Southampton, 1837). See Orme, *Memoir*, p. 197.

82. There was a British edition of Griesbach's New Testament in 1810 with an appendix on the comma. Marsh recommends Griesbach's theory of recensions replacing individual manuscripts in his *Course of Lectures*, 2:35–45; and the impartiality of his readings in a letter of 1825, where he talks about their "constant correspondence on subjects of critical theology," quoted in Baker, *History of St. John*, p. 740.

83. *Two Letters on the Text of the Heavenly Witnesses* (London, 1822), appended to *An Inquiry into the Integrity of the Greek Vulgate or Received Text of the New Testament* (London, 1815), p. 157.

84. Ibid., pp. 525–26, 531–43. He has to supply two versions for Jerome, one in which the disputed verse was suppressed, the other where it was retained for the learned, ibid., pp. 562–63.

spite his undeniable learning, there were too many ifs to his argument, and the biting criticism of another obscure clergyman, John Oxlee, seems to have won the day, although only after several further exchanges.[85]

A still more problematical effort to rescue the comma appeared in 1822 as *Palaeoromaica: Or Historical and Philological Disquisitions*. The anonymous writer seems to have been a Scottish clergyman named John Black, who was the author of a life and translation of Tasso. He revived the paradox of Hardouin that Latin was the original language of Christ and the Apostles, and that the Greek New Testament was a translation from the Latin—though not as Hardouin had thought, of the Vulgate. He tried to show that the *textus receptus* was clearly a retranslation from the Latin by listing a series of words and phrases in twelve different classes to prove that what was called Hellenistic style had been formed not by Hebrew but by Latin and Greek. This had the advantage of explaining why some of the early editors had wanted to affirm the authority of the Latin manuscripts over the Greek, while others had complained of Latinizing in the oldest Greek manuscripts. For the comma, it meant that the Latinized elements that had been discovered in the *Codex Britannicus* and the Complutensian versions of 1 John v. 7, and that had been used to prove its falsity, were a result of a re-translation from a genuine original, and that the comma was therefore authentic! Grant the premise about the Latinate character of the New Testament world and the rest followed; but a host of writers found the argument untenable, and although the author replied to his critics, he failed to convince anyone. Even Burgess was dissatisfied.[86]

Perhaps the best evidence that the controversy was winding down was that it finally received a history in 1830. Many of the authors involved in the quarrel had introduced their works with retrospective surveys of the argument, and Burgess had republished two collections of extracts from earlier authors. But it was the Reverend William Orme, writing under the pseudonym Criticus, who devoted a whole book to the subject, which was later continued for another generation by the American Ezra Abbot.[87] Orme's

---

85. *Three Letters to the Rev. Frederick Nolan* (York, 1825). Oxlee also answered Burgess in *Two Letters to the Bishop of Salisbury* (1828). There is a brief notice on Oxlee (1779–1854) in the *DNB*. He claimed to know 120 languages and dialects and was deeply versed in Hebrew and Talmudical lore.

86. The controversy is summarized in Orme, (*Memoir*), pp. 124–30. Burgess replied in a postscript to his *Vindication*, and in *The Greek Original of the New Testament asserted in Answer to a recent Publication entitled Palaeormaica* (1823).

87. *Memoir of the Controversy respecting the Three Heavenly Witnesses 1 John v. 7*, ed. Ezra Abbot (New York, 1866). Burgess edited *Adnotationes Millii* (Camaerthen, 1822), with Latin pieces by

work extended from Eramus to Travis and Porson, Burgess and Oxlee, and finally to his contemporary Thomas Hartwell Horne, who had just brought his authoritative biblical handbook up to date by coming out decisively against the comma.[88] Horne had remained doubtful until the sixth edition of his book (1828), when at last he drew up a masterful account of the arguments on both sides and decided against the passage. His conclusion, he hastened to add, should have no effect on the doctrine of the Trinity, which had other support.[89] Orme's account consisted largely of extracts drawn from his sources, with occasional comments; it was meant to be dispassionate, but he left no doubt that he too sided with the critics. He praises Gibbon, but especially Porson and Marsh.[90] By the time that Abbot came to reprint the work in 1866, it seemed to him that the whole question was now obsolete and the spuriousness of the comma had been conceded by all "fair-minded scholars."[91] Gibbon's new editor, H. H. Milman, who by no means shared Gibbon's Christian antipathies, could report in 1838 that "the controversy has continued to be agitated, but with declining interest

---

Wetstein, Bengal, Bentley, Selden, and some others, and *A Selection of Tracts on 1 John v. 7* by Barlow, Smalbrooke, Hammond, etc. (London, 1824).

88. Orme also mentions and extracts from several other writers on both sides of the question, including Dr. Adam Clarke, *The Succession of Sacred Literature* (1807); Joseph Jowett in the *Christian Observer* (1807); Charles Butler, in *Horae Biblicae*, in the *Philological and Biographical Works*, 2 (1817); Bishop Middleton on the Greek article (1808); J. P. Smith and J. Pharez in the *Eclectic Review* (1809–10). Dr. Hales of Dublin wrote first against the comma in his *New Analysis of Chronology* (1811), and then reversed himself at length in his *Faith in the Holy Trinity* (1818). Another exchange occurred when the German, F. A. Knittel, was translated from a work written on the subject in 1785 by William Alleyn Evanson (London, 1829), only to be answered by "Clemens Anglicanus" (1829); see Orme, *Memoir*, pp. 170–72, 178–80. Abbot adds several American tracts on the subject, including one by the Rev. Henry Ware, *Two Letters to the Rev. Alexander McLeod containing Remarks upon the Texts from which he preached April 30 and May 7* (New York, 1820). McLeod's first text was the comma, which he defended and Ware opposed.

89. Henry Hartwell Horne, *An Introduction to the Critical Study and Knowledge of the Holy Scriptures,* 4 vols., 6th ed. (London, 1828), 4:462–87. The first edition had appeared in three volumes in London, 1818, "the result of seventeen years' prayerful, solitary, unassisted, and not unfrequently midnight labour." Horne had learned from Porson, Marsh, and most recently from Turton, each of whom is cited. He also credits the *Christian Observer* (1807) for a neat summary of all the places in the church fathers where one might have expected to find the absent passage. Only one new Greek manuscript had turned up recently with the comma, the *Codex Ottobonianus* in the Vatican, which Horne dismisses as fifteenth century. There were many later and larger editions of the *Introduction* in both England and America, where for a long time it held the field as a standard text.

90. He sees "how clearly Gibbon had looked over the matter, while the choice of his epithets at once illustrates his knowledge of the subject, and the delight he took in reproaching the professors of Christianity." Orme, *Memoir*, p. 48.

91. Abbot (1819–84) was the outstanding New Testament critic in America and a prime contributor to the American Revised Version. He early accepted the opinions of his teacher,

even in the more religious part of the community; and may be considered to have terminated in an almost general acquiescence of the learned in the conclusion of Porson."[92] A few years later it was quietly dropped from the Revised Standard Version of the text after 250 years in place. It took longer for the Roman Catholic Church to acquiesce, but it too finally acceded to scholarly opinion and dropped its defense of the disputed passage.[93] Interest in the Johannine comma was no longer polemical, but only curious now, and historical.

7

In a recent commentary on John's epistles by Raymond Brown (1982), there is an inevitable excursus on the Johannine comma. Gibbon, who is not mentioned, is thoroughly vindicated. The editor, who is a clergyman, accepts the unanimous verdict of contemporary scholarship that the comma arose well after apostolic times, "as a trinitarian reflection on the original text of 1 John, and was added to the Biblical MSS. hundreds of years after John was written."[94] Brown agrees with Isaac Newton that the meaning of the phrase in context is obscure and that the internal evidence for its authenticity is lacking. A hundred years is a long time in the annals of modern scholarship, and Brown must take account of a massive accumulation of new evidence. He claims now that the comma appears in only eight

---

Andrews Norton, who published a *Statement of Reasons for not believing the Doctrines of Trinitarians concerning the Nature of God and the Passion of Christ* (1833). Abbot was able to benefit from the accomplishments of a whole new generation of scholars who vastly enlarged the boundaries of New Testament study, including Tischendorf and Tragelles. See the article in the *Dictionary of American Biography*, based on the memorial volume of essays, *Ezra Abbot*, by J. H. Thayer et al. Even so, one Charles Foster was still making a last-ditch effort for the comma in 1867; see his *New Plea for the Authenticity of the Text of the Three Heavenly Witnesses, or Porson's Letters to Travis Critically Examined* (Cambridge, 1867). A contemporary attempt to defend the comma is by Edward F. Hills, *The King James Version Defended! A Christian View of the New Testament Manuscripts* (Des Moines, 1956); see Metzger, *The New Testament*, p. 136n.

92. *Decline and Fall of the Roman Empire*, 6 vols. (Boston, 1860), 3:556n. Yet in 1862 a majority of the English clergy were still proclaiming their complete conviction in the "plenary Inspiration and Authority of the whole Canonical Scriptures as the Word of God," Josef L. Althoz, "The Mind of Victorian Orthodoxy: Anglican Responses to *Essays and Reviews*," *Church History*, p. 191n.

93. See Hugh Pope, *The Catholic Student's "Aids" to the Study of the Bible* (London, 1926), 1:108–9.

94. *The Epistles of John*, trans. Raymond E. Brown (New York, 1982), app. 4, pp. 775–87. Cf. John R. W. Stott, *The Letters of John: An Introduction and Commentary*, 2d ed. (Leicester, 1988), pp. 182–83, who provides a good list of English-language commentaries. For the modern period, a good summary is Stephen Neill, *The Interpretation of the New Testament 1861–1961* (Oxford, 1966). See also Rudolf Bultmann, *The Johannine Epistles: A Commentary*, trans. R. P. O'Hara et al. (Philadelphia,), pp. 2–3, 81, with a full bibliography.

of about five thousand Greek manuscripts and lectionaries, and in four of
these in the margins only.[95] None of the eight can be dated before 1400
when Manuel Kalekas is known to have translated the comma into Greek
from the Latin Vulgate. The earliest mention by a Greek author is 1215 A.D.
The comma is also absent from the versions in every other language before
1500 except for the Latin. Its first appearance in a Latin Testament was after 600; in the Vulgate after 750. Its earliest clear appearance was in the *Li-
bor Apologeticus* of Priscillian, who died in 385, after which it turns up with
some frequency in the antitrinitarian controversies of later times. Neither
Terrullian, Cyprian, or Augustine knew it. (Jerome's *Prologue* is assigned to
the fifth or sixth century.) The comma probably appeared first in Spain or
North Africa on behalf of the beleaguered trinitarians, after which it began
its modern career.

No doubt, there will be more evidence eventually about the invention
and career of the comma, but no one can hope any longer to restore it to its
former place in Scripture. We know too much about it and the world in
which it was made. Travis was right about one thing: Gibbon had used his
animus against Christianity to deny the comma. But he drew the wrong
conclusion. It was not Gibbon who had made the comma a late interpolation and a pious fraud, but some unknown scribe many centuries before.
Gibbon only discovered that this was so through the critical historiography
he borrowed from his predecessors and that he employed in his work—
maliciously no doubt, but correctly—as even the orthodox began grudg-
ingly to see. He had claimed a philological method that was beyond ideol-
ogy, and his successors within the church and outside were increasingly
wiling to subscribe to that principle, even while they wavered over the practice.

No one insisted on this more than Herbert Marsh. In his *Course of Lectures,* he described the whole series of editors who had labored over the
Bible since the days of Erasmus, and when he got to Wetstein, he considered the charges that had been made against him, that he had allowed his
religious bias (his alleged Arianism) to affect his judgment. It was true,
Marsh allowed, that "men of *every* religious profession are exposed to the
temptation of adopting what they *wish* to adopt, and of rejecting what they
wish to reject, without sufficient regard to the evidence *against* the one, and
in favour of the other." But it was not necessary, since bias could be re-
strained. Wetstein had always supported his conclusions with good evidence and better authority. "He alone contributed more to advance the

95. Abbot could only find two out of several hundred; p. 204.

Criticism of the Greek Testament than all who had gone before him."[96] Moreover the conflict of opinion could sometimes lead to a good result. Prejudices could cancel each other out, as Gibbon saw, and leave a residue of truth. If a perfect text of the New Testament could never be attained, Marsh conceded, it could at least always be improved and brought closer to the original.[97]

So it appears that in the early modern period everyone, of whatever persuasion, increasingly sought the neutral ground of matter of fact. Everyone, from the radical Unitarians to the most orthodox trinitarians, from "Sosipater" to George Travis and Thomas Burgess, and Cardinal Wiseman in Rome, appealed to the philological evidence to make their case and persuade the world.[98] But as the facts accumulated across the centuries, it became ever more clear that there was no good evidence for the comma. More insidiously and decisively, as each jot and tittle of Scripture was placed under the scrutiny of a relentless philology, the whole history of Christian doctrine was gradually transformed and historicized, so that the ideas of the early church, even including the idea of the Trinity, were each placed in their original context and shown to change and evolve.[99] If therefore, it can be said that there was any one victor in the long quarrel over the comma, it was, I think, not so much unorthodox religion as the claims to autonomy of philology and history. By the end of the nineteenth century and the beginning of our own, nearly every Christian denomination, including the church of Rome, and almost everyone else, had come to accept the fact—often against their wills and certainly not because of their

96. Herbert Marsh, *A Course of Lectures containing a Description and a Systematic Arrangement of the Several Branches of Divinity,* pt. 2 (Cambridge, 1813), pp. 21–23.

97. Marsh, *Course,* pt. 4 (1822), p. 8.

98. Cardinal Wiseman, *Two Letters on Some Parts of the Controversy concerning the Genuineness of 1 John v. 7* (Rome, 1835), reprinted in *Essays on Various Subjects,* 1 (London, 1853). Wiseman tried to establish the priority of the Latin Italic version in North Africa, preceding the Vulgate and the Greek. He was answered by, among others, William Wright in his translation of Seiler's authoritative *Biblical Hermeneutics* (1835), app. pp. 613–52. (See Abbot, *Memoir,* pp. 186–92.)

99. On Semler's "historical method," see Albert Schweitzer, *Paul and His Interpreters,* trans. W. Montgomery (1912; reprinted New York, 1964), pp. 4–7; Frei, *Eclipse of Biblical Narrative,* pp. 109–13; and especially, G. Hornig, *Die Anfange der historisch-kritischen Theologie* (Gottingen, 1961), chap. 8. As Schweitzer puts it, "He demands that the New Testament be regarded as a temporally conditioned expression of Christian thought . . . that many conceptions and arguments, not only of the Old Testament but the New, have not the same significance for us as they had for the early days of Christianity." This was, of course, precisely the conclusion that the "moderns" had discovered about Homer and the classics. See J. G. Eichhorn, quoted in Victor P. Furnish, "The Historical Criticism of the New Testament: A Survey of Origins," *Bulletin of the John Rylands Library,* 56 (1973–74), pp. 360–65.

wishes—that the Johannine comma was not in the original epistles of the apostle and, that as a consequence, it must be dropped from Scripture.[100] But by then, it seems, a new goddess had been enthroned, and Clio was ready to win more votaries to her cause than all three persons in the Trinity. In four sentences and six footnotes, Gibbon had anticipated that result and done his own small piece to hasten that end.

100. In 1897, the Holy Office was still worried about the danger of questioning the comma; in 1927, it allowed scholars to pursue the matter and even to hold contrary opinions, provided that they submit to the judgment of the church. See Pope, *Catholic Student,* 1, pp. 108–10; "Johannine Comma," in the *New Catholic Encyclopedia.*

Index